Journey to Heartbreak

THE CRUCIBLE YEARS OF
BERNARD SHAW 1914-1918

STANLEY WEINTRAUB

WEYBRIGHT AND TALLEY
New Yorl

JOURNEY TO HEARTBREAK

Published by:
Weybright and Talley
750 Third Ave.
New York, N.Y. 10017

LIBRARY OF CONGRESS CATALOG CARD NUMBER: 76–149002
MANUFACTURED IN THE UNITED STATES OF AMERICA
VAN REES PRESS, NEW YORK

FIRST PRINTING, AUGUST 1971
SECOND PRINTING, OCTOBER 1971

FOR MY MOTHER

Preface

Writers in wartime have been on the intellectual barricades as long as there have been writers and wars. World War I was, for literary London, no exception, but few writers of such high literary estate in their time have been so embattled as was Bernard Shaw from 1914 through 1918. From the activities of G.B.S. and his contemporaries, a case study emerges of the embattled intellectual in wartime—through Shaw's effect upon his times and their impact upon him as a creative person. Few writers have responded so creatively and on such a scale as Shaw to the sense of heartbreak he felt for a world he might have considered well lost.

This is the third of a series in which I have attempted to explore biographically the interaction of literature and political events in twentieth-century England. This book is in some ways a prelude to the earlier ones. *Private Shaw and Public Shaw* (1963) focused upon the Lawrence of Arabia-Bernard Shaw relationship and concerned the interwar years 1922 to 1935. *The Last Great Cause* (1968) examined writers and politics during the Spanish Civil War period, 1936 to 1939.

Without the support and encouragement of the Guggenheim Foundation and the Institute for the Arts and Humanistic Studies and the Central Fund for Research of the Pennsylvania State University, this book could not have been researched and written. I am indebted, too, to many helpful men and women on both sides of the Atlantic, particularly Professor Sidney P. Albert, Professor Arthur Athanason, Miss Elizabeth Barber, O.B.E., Professor Quentin Bell, LaFayette Butler and Charles T. Butler, William Clark, Professor Ralph Waterbury Condee, Professor Louis Crompton, Shirley Drew, Professor Harry L. Geduld, Professor Stephen Grecco, the late Sir Basil Liddell Hart, Serrell Hillman, Mary Hirth, Susan Hughes, Mary Hyde, Lady Jones (Enid Bagnold), Lord Kennet, Professor Dan H. Laurence, Charles W. Mann, Professor Frederick P. W. McDowell, Professor Arthur H. Nethercot, Professor Warren Roberts, H. L. Rubinstein, Frank Swinnerton, Dame Rebecca West, and the late Leonard Woolf.

Many libraries and archives assisted in making this biographical study possible, especially the Berg Collection, New York Public Library; the British Museum; the Burgunder Collection, Cornell University Library; the Goldsmith's Library, London University; the Historical Manuscripts Commission, London; the Houghton Library at Harvard; the Humanities Research Center, University of Texas; the Huntingdon Library; the Johns Hopkins University Library; the Library of the London School of Economics and Political Science; the Pattee Library of the Pennsylvania State University; the Sterling and Beinecke Libraries at Yale; and the Van Pelt Library of the University of Pennsylvania.

For permission to publish copyright material I am indebted to Professor Quentin Bell (for the Virginia Woolf estate), to the executors of the estate of Mrs. Patrick Campbell (for extracts from Shaw's letters to her and her replies), to Lord Kennet (for extracts from his mother's unpublished diaries), to the London School of Economics (for extracts from Beatrice Webb's unpublished diaries), to the proprietors of *Punch*, and to the Society of Authors and the Shaw Trustees (as specified on the copyright page).

My editor as always has been my wife, Rodelle, but slips and slipshodness can only be attributed to those occasions when she was overruled.

Stanley Weintraub

University Park, Pennsylvania
August 4, 1970

Contents

His favorite saying is that he measures the executions he has done by the shrieks of the wounded. . . . The most striking instance of this is the war of 1914–1918. It is an established tradition . . . that Shaw was a pro-German, a Pacifist, a Defeatist, a Conscientious Objector, & everything that an enemy of his country could be without being actually shot as a traitor. Nothing could be more absolutely wide of the truth. . . .

—Bernard Shaw on himself thirteen years after.

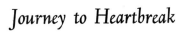

Journey to Heartbreak

1

Before the Deluge

HIS MAJESTY'S THEATRE, just above the great intersection where the Haymarket empties into broad, teeming Pall Mall, had reigned by 1914 as London's leading playhouse for seventeen years. Built by actor-manager Herbert Beerbohm Tree out of prudent borrowings from the Prince of Wales's wealthiest financier-friends and the five-figure profits from his immensely successful dramatization of *Trilby*, it had been at first, in the aged Victoria's honor, Her Majesty's, a palatial structure of red granite and indeterminate limestone which looked as if it had been designed for Louis XV. When it opened in 1897, even the most abrasive dramatic critic in London, who signed himself "G.B.S.," had been impressed. "You feel," he wrote, "that you are in a place where high scenes are to be enacted and dignified things to be done." In the larger of the two commodious rooms in the dome of His Majesty's which had been fashioned into a town residence, Tree gave elaborate after-theatre supper parties, especially after the first night of a play, often hosting them without changing from the costume in which he—inevitably, at his own production—had starred.

Scheduled for opening at His Majesty's on April 11, 1914, was the newest play by the writer who still sometimes signed himself "G.B.S.," and by dint of assiduous self-advertisement and the most literate comedies since Shakespeare's day, had become the best known personality in England. His wife, Charlotte, abroad on a holiday, Shaw left their flat on the upper level of a once stately Georgian house at No. 10 Adelphi Terrace for the twenty-minute walk, alone, to the theatre, up the Strand and around Trafalgar Square, crowded with Saturday sightseers and loungers, into Pall Mall. It was perfect spring weather for walking; the word "halcyon," in fact, seems almost to have been invented to describe the English spring of 1914. Almost everything seemed good, and what did not as yet seem good appeared certain to get better. Science and education seemed to offer the utopian promise that not only was the world capable of infinite improvement, but so were its inhabitants, especially those so fortunate as to live in England. Although this was more illusion than reality, nowhere would that optimism be better symbolized than onstage at His Majesty's. The play, already a box office success in Berlin and Vienna, was a twentieth-century story of a young Cockney guttersnipe who, through a sturdy will and the instruction of a professor of speech, is able to pass for a duchess at a fashionable garden party.

Outside the theatre Bernard Shaw preached the gospel to which he gave life onstage—the need to will one's self-improvement, to redistribute the world's wealth and equalize human opportunity, the abolition of class privilege, and the brotherhood of man. There was little outward reason to expect anything else to happen, in God's good time, and newspapers being hawked on the corners of streets that fed into Trafalgar Square were already giving more attention to Shaw's play than they were to uneasy stirrings from the Continent, foreshadowings of events that would turn Trafalgar Square, before the end of summer, into a vast, tasteless recruiting platform for the Army. Rumblings of approaching European war were dismissed in most capitals as bluster. The English government believed that the glaring horror of the possibility would in itself be a deterrent—that the war could be so catastrophic to all sides was so obvious that all the

Great Powers would shrink from it. The German government believed that the English government believed it.

Backstage at His Majesty's, a war of a different kind had been in progress almost up to the parting of the first curtain. The lack of harmony between the leading actors and the playwright had been in flagrant contradiction to Shaw's past working relationships with his casts, as well as to the comedy's optimistic themes, although in part the stormy mentor-pupil relationship in the play produced onstage sparks akin to those Shaw's direction of the leading lady had been causing in rehearsal. Mrs. Stella Patrick Campbell, in her forty-ninth year and a grandmother, had been the tempestuous beauty of the London theatre since her Mrs. Tanqueray more than twenty years earlier, and only a few months before she had encouraged, then spurned, Shaw's most ardent extramarital advances since his marriage, at forty-two, in 1898. Now, although as unresponsive to Shaw's coaching as she had been to his courting, somehow in performance she had to succeed in shedding her years as the eighteen-year-old Eliza Doolittle. The *Daily Express* was thoroughly ungentlemanly about it on the morning of the opening. "Where is youth these days?" it inquired. "Far from being at the helm it is lucky to be allowed to scrub the decks. A new play is to be performed tonight at His Majesty's. The combined ages of its author, its leading lady and its manager is 166. Sir Herbert is 60, Mr. Shaw is 57 and Mrs. Patrick Campbell, who plays a flower-girl of 18 is 49."

Sir Herbert Beerbohm Tree, the play's Professor Higgins and last of the great Victorian actor-managers, was idiosyncratic, unmethodical, and fawned upon by a claque of satellites who praised, and meddled in, everything he did. Shaw, who produced his own plays, tried to direct the pair of balky prima donnas in how to play *his* roles, but the outcome was unlike anything in his experience. Tree's problem, Shaw said afterwards, was that "he had to impersonate a sort of man he had never met and of whom he had no conception. He tried hard . . . and when he resigned himself to his unnatural task, he set to work to make this disagreeable and incredible person sympathetic in the character of a lover, for which I had left so little room that he was quite baffled. . . ."[1] In the circumstances even the irrepressible Shavian wit found difficulty in emerging, but when Henry Higgins waxed too sentimental over Eliza, Shaw pleaded, "I say, Tree, must you be so treacly?" Tree was not amused, although the remark convulsed everyone else in the theatre, including Henry Dana, Tree's manager, who told him, "You know, Guv'nor, if you put a cat, a dog and a monkey into a sack together, what can you expect but ructions?"

Stella Campbell, certainly the cat of Dana's fable, found Eliza's inelegant diction impossible, but Shaw persisted, once telling her sharply when she tried to conceal her inadequacies in enunciation with irrelevant stage business, "Good God! You are forty years too old for Eliza; sit still and it is not so noticeable."[2] He wrote his comments for specific players on separate sheets, to be distributed after rehearsals, and Mrs. Campbell, with lavatory wit, on one occasion accepted hers with "Thank you, Mr. Shaw, I can always find a good use for a piece of paper!"[3] But when Shaw interrupted a speech to plead that she coarsen her refined stage manner, she refused to continue rehearsals until Shaw left the theatre, and sent word that he was to communicate further instructions only through Stanley Bell, the assistant stage manager. Twice Shaw gathered up his papers and left on his own, once when Mrs. Campbell so badly mangled the accents Shaw had taught her that he abandoned his usual rehearsal location in the center of the dress circle in such haste that he forgot his notes. Returning for them, he heard his Eliza still declaiming her maimed lines and shouted down to her, "Accursed woman, can't you wait till I am out of earshot!"[4]

When out of range, Shaw managed to direct the pair through detailed letters. The immense and caustic pre-opening letter to Tree, Shaw told Mrs. Campbell, "will pull him together if it does not kill him."[5] It did neither. Tree reflected in his notebook instead, "I will not go so far as to say that all people who write letters of more than eight pages are mad, but it is a curious fact that all madmen write letters of more than eight pages."[6] Shaw's last instructions to his Eliza had been entitled "FINAL ORDERS," and in them the playwright returned to a favorite source of metaphor—war. Much would depend, he wrote, "on whether you are inspired at the last moment. You are not, like me, a great general. You leave everything to chance, whereas Napoleon and Caesar left nothing to chance except the last inch that is in the hands of destiny. I could have planned the past so that nine tenths of it would have gone mechanically even if your genius had deserted you, leaving only one tenth to the Gods. Even as it is, I have forced half the battle on you. . . ." Stella responded with a conciliatory note: "I'll obey orders faithfully."[7] She did, and the play was a sensation. Although Shaw's name had long been a household word, after twenty years of playwriting it was his first substantial West End success.

In spite of his rehearsal tribulations, he had assumed the success of the production. *Pygmalion* possessed the leading actress and leading actor-manager in London in starring roles at the most fashionable theatre in London. Further, as he confidently told a reporter from the *Observer*, "It has already been translated into German and Swedish and Polish and Hungarian and it has been performed with monotonous and unbroken success in Germany, Vienna, Stockholm, Prague, Warsaw, Budapest, and the German section of New York." But he ironically confessed his misgivings. "There must be something radically wrong with it if it pleases everybody, but at the moment I cannot find what it is."

For the public the evening of April 11, 1914 was most memorable for Eliza's "Not bloody likely!" The first-night audience gasped with shock, then laughed with such abandon that it threatened the continuity of the play while assuring its success. As the performance continued, Shaw was torn between delight at Mrs. Campbell's ravishment of her audience and rage at Sir Herbert's carefree misunderstanding of his role. To Shaw the conclusion of the play was the most relentless travesty of his dramatic intentions he had ever witnessed, although the stallholders, unaware of those intentions, left the house in a happy glow. The last Shaw saw of the performance as he hurried out of the theatre before the curtain was "Higgins shoving his mother rudely out of the way and wooing Eliza . . . like a bereaved Romeo."[8] It was exactly what he had painstakingly coached Tree not to do, for G.B.S. felt that only to those incapable of rising above sentimentality did

the relationship between Shaw's Galatea and his Pygmalion appear to
have the makings of a marriage. Furious, he refused supper, visits
backstage, the privilege of kissing the leading lady, and interviews
with the press. Instead he went home alone and soothed his anger by
reading Shakespeare for an hour in bed before going to sleep.

The next morning Shaw had settled down sufficiently to invite
Stella and her new husband (she had married George Cornwallis-West
the week before) to Ayot St. Lawrence for Sunday lunch and tea.
Shaw motored up ahead, and they came with Beppo, West's huge
black retriever, who distinguished himself by removing people's hats
on command and playing hide and seek. Then there were the Sunday
papers to discuss, one of which reported some booing when the curtain fell, probably leveled by the righteous at the author whose sanguinary word had created such a sensation. Stella brightly suggested
that it was directed at Tree by Shavians in the audience infuriated by
his acting.

While he remained amused by the furor over his six-letter word,
Shaw also remained furious about Tree's travesty of the last scene,
written to turn romance upside down: Cinderella and the Fairy
Prince were supposed to conclude ironically on a note of mutual respect—and dislike—for one another, however much the audience hoped
for matrimony. The scene as played caused the *Illustrated London
News* to congratulate G.B.S. on his "happy ending, which, when you
think of it, you will discover Bernard Shaw is hardly less addicted to
than the most confirmed of stage sentimentalists." The bundle of
press clippings Shaw sent Charlotte several days after the opening
indicated general approval of the play; still, Shaw found it curious
that Eliza's expletive remained, even more than the news pages, the
chief interest of the press and the public, and popular indignation kept
the theatre box office busy. The London newspapers, with two ex-
ceptions, found themselves unable to put the terrible word into type,
using instead suggestive letters and asterisks. The *Evening Standard*
reproached Shaw for an unpardonable breach of good manners, while
the *Morning Post* worried that other playwrights, following Shaw's
example, would begin sprinkling their works with the lurid language
of the street corner. (The *Sketch*, unable to wait for the opening, had

published a Saturday editorial begging Shaw to withdraw the naughty word or at least substitute the word "ruddy," and Tree had sent for the author that afternoon to show him a copy and indicate his concern.) "Greatly daring, Mr. Shaw," the *Times* chided on Monday, "you will be able to boast that you are the first modern dramatist to use this word on the stage; but really, was it worth while? There is a whole range of forbidden words in the English language. A little more of your courage, and we suppose they will be heard too; and then good-bye to the delights of really intimate conversation."

A few days later a dispatch indicated that Shaw had removed some of the offense before it became necessary to answer irate bishops in the letters columns of the *Times*. The Cockney guttersnipe, it was said, continued to use the unprintable word, but it was no longer repeated by a young society girl parroting it because she thought it the latest thing in the slang talk of the smart set. The announcement was premature, but Shaw did ready himself for the bishops before the play had completed its first week by explaining sweetly in an interview in the *Daily News*, "As I happen to find the word detestable when used by a smart, or would-be smart, lady as piece of smartness, and as it was evident that without a strong antidote Mrs. Campbell's irresistible utterance of it would set all smart London bloodying all through the season, I carefully made another lady follow up Mrs. Campbell by repeating that word as a fashionable affectation, with an effect which will, I hope, effectually prevent any occurrence of that folly in real life." Tree tried a different gambit, defending "bloody" to reporters as neither blasphemous nor indecent and hallowed in literary usage from the revered Shakespeare to the moderns. He told reporters the week after the opening,

Mrs. Patrick Campbell uttered the Word at today's matinee, and nobody was shocked. The only thing which has made the press criticisms so vehement is the flatness of the political situation. The Word was passed by the Lord Chamberlain and there my responsibility ends. There is nothing blasphemous or obscene in the Word. It may be found in the works of Rudyard Kipling. It may not be good taste for ladies of gentility to wear gaudy feathers in their hat, but they are not obliged to follow Eliza's taste and example either in this or in the use of the Word. Besides

I would like to state that a word which is generally applied to Queen Mary Tudor should not be censored in a flower-girl.

Unsatisfied, hack playwright Sydney Grundy later in the *Daily Mail* offered the opinion that although there was no harm in Shaw's "incarnadine adverb" when informed by genius, "on his pen it is poison."*

The *Daily Express* had shrewdly invited an authentic flower girl to the opening for the purpose of an exclusive interview with her afterward. She was another Eliza—Eliza Keefe of Tottenham Court Road —but apparently better reared than Shaw's Eliza Doolittle, for Mrs. Keefe also objected to the language. "There was one word in particular," she told the *Express*, "which Mrs. Patricia Campbell said when she was supposed to be a lady. The editor says I must not repeat it, but it begins with a B and ends with a Y. *Well!!!* No self-respecting flower girl would say such a word, when she was on her best behaviour, specially when she was supposed to be educated and speaking in a drawing-room."[9]

Letters to the editor on the subject entertained readers of the London dailies for weeks afterward, one in the *Morning Post* summing up how middle-class Englishmen felt, although it was itself very likely tongue-in-cheek and worthy of G.B.S. himself. "The other day," it went, "I was driving down the Haymarket and my taxi happened to collide with another in front. 'Take care, you bloody fool!' shouted my driver. I was about to speak to him most severely when I looked up and there I saw His Majesty's Theatre right in front of me. What Bernard Shaw writes you can hardly blame a cabman for saying."[10]

Triviality manifested itself inside the theatre as well. Tree complained that the play was too long and Mrs. Campbell's costume changes overly prolonged. Mrs. Campbell objected that Tree took thirty-second pauses between each word, and five minutes be-

---

* In the 1890s Shaw, then a drama critic, had labeled Grundy's work for the theatre as flabby adaptations of the "mechanical rabbit" French drama of the 1840s, and Grundy in return had cryptically called Shaw "the crankiest of the stove-pipe fanatics."

tween each bite of the apple he munched in the fourth act. Still, Tree, happy with a hit grossing more than £2000 a week, suggested hopefully to Shaw that the success had established modern drama at His Majesty's, but rather than the smiles and positive assurances he expected, Tree received curt advice to stop playing for laughs and to never again play Higgins once the current run ended. Fiscally, however, all was optimism. Shaw received £237.9.4 in royalties for the first seven performances, and the play looked as if it could run for years.

To recuperate from the agonies of launching *Pygmalion*, Shaw went off on a six-day walking and motoring holiday into Yorkshire, wandering over the moors and by the rugged seacoast with Beatrice and Sidney Webb. A walking tour for Shaw was a curious affair. When it involved lodging somewhere other than at a friend's country house, he would telephone or telegraph ahead to book rooms, then tell his chauffeur, "Go to that hotel and wait for me." When he arrived his luggage would have arrived ahead of him, and he would have had his exercise.

Shaw regularly welcomed the opportunity for a walking holiday with the Webbs, for he could switch to nontheatrical matters, the Webbs having few cultural interests and little small talk, seldom deviating from the sociopolitical obsessions that had drawn them together and directed their lives. With the help of the Shaws' money they had founded the *New Statesman* the year before, and Beatrice's reaction to Shaw's success with *Pygmalion* (to her diary) was, "He is making piles of money—which is fortunate for the *New Statesman*—and he seems most friendly in his intentions toward Fabianism and all its works."[11] Shaw had more than good intentions toward Fabianism. He had been among its stalwarts for thirty years, but was not so narrowly committed in his interests as the Webbs and lived among other worlds and other works.

On the twentieth Shaw drove the Webbs to York to catch the London train, then set off for home at a more leisurely pace. He was in no hurry to return, for entreaties to revisit *Pygmalion* were constant.

"Come soon," Stella had warned him, "—or you'll not recognize your play."[12] Shaw feared it was true. Instead he planned a second walking tour with Granville-Barker for early May, ignoring Stella's next warning that Tree's performance was now "a most original and entertaining affair and most popular with his friends and admirers."[13] Enjoying his success, Tree added a needling postscript to Shaw in a telegram: "Business magnificent in spite of Higgins."

Charlotte had arrived in the United States with actress Lena Ashwell at the moment American newspapers were reporting the *succès de scandale* of her husband's play, and reporters sought her out for comment. She had none. Finally, in Boston two weeks later, she agreed to an interview. "You Americans have strange opinions of my husband. . . . Well, few persons do understand Mr. Shaw. He is a great man, a dreamer of wonderful dreams, an idealist and an individualist. . . . He is a bashful and retiring man by nature but he never leaves unanswered those who attack him." What Charlotte was referring to had nothing to do with outrage over *Pygmalion*, for Shaw, once the dreamer of utopian dreams about the betterment of man, had been having apocalyptic nightmares about the imminence of war and had been writing articles and letters to newspapers suggesting how England could avert the disaster. Early in 1912 he had proposed an agreement between Britain, France, Germany, and the United States that any country which made war on a neighbor without first submitting its grievance to the judgment of the signatory powers would find itself at war with the four. On the first of January, 1914, he had repeated in the London *Daily News* his claim that European peace could be safeguarded by an English pledge to defend France if attacked by Germany, or Germany if attacked by France. "Like all sensible proposals," he wrote, "this would be received at first blush as revolting and impracticable . . . [but] I like courage (like most constitutionally timid civilians) and the active use of strength for the salvation of the world." Public reaction was negative. England was preoccupied with turmoil in Ireland, division within the old Tory and Liberal parties, and an increasingly guerrilla-minded suffragette movement. Besides, any indiscreet talk about war "might fire the magazine."

On May 8 the secretary of the Theatrical Managers Association wrote to inform Tree, then president of the association, that one of its members had objected to Eliza's notorious expletive, which he requested be omitted from further performances since it lowered the standard of the profession and might result in revocation of licenses for theatres staging the play. Tree declined, yet his backing of Shaw earned him no credits with the playwright, who steadfastly refused, then reluctantly agreed, to witness the one hundredth performance, in confidence, he told Tree, that there would be none. It had been a boom year for Shaw, and he had no eagerness to milk additional royalties from a play that, however much applauded by substantial audiences, filled him with loathing for its distortion in performance. His previous year's royalties from Brentano's for American sales of his books came due at the end of March, and just after the opening of *Pygmalion*, he received his check from them—$3581.80. A similar accounting from Constable & Co. in London was recorded two days later, and it was for three times the American sum—nearly £2100. Royalties for German and Austrian publications and performances in Siegfried Trebitsch's translations brought him an additional £500, while performances of *Fanny's First Play* in Boston, *Caesar and Cleopatra* in Toronto, *Man and Superman* in Glasgow and Copenhagen, *The Doctor's Dilemma* in Holland and New Zealand, and dozens of other performances of his plays around the world that spring brought him substantial sums. Early in May he sold the first American serial rights to *Pygmalion* (along with *Great Catherine* and *Androcles and the Lion*) to *Everybody's Magazine* for an additional £738. And Tree kept furnishing Shaw with ten percent of weekly house grosses regularly exceeding £2000.[14]

As soon as she returned to England in May, Charlotte went to see *Pygmalion*, with G.B.S. Their marriage, strained six months before by the Mrs. Pat affair, "resumed the familiar social pattern. Mrs. Annie Besant [on a visit from India] came to lunch, they visited the Webbs and the Granville-Barkers; met the philosopher Henri Bergson at one luncheon party and the composer Richard Strauss at another. Writers, musicians, politicians, visiting diplomats, notabilities of all kinds came to Adelphi Terrace. G.B.S. and Charlotte were asked out everywhere."[15] No. 10 Adelphi Terrace was itself an unprepossessing house; it was once the location of the Webb-founded London School of Economics, which Charlotte helped support by leasing the two top floors as her residence at £300 a year. When the school had grown too large for its quarters, it, rather than the Shaws, moved out, the lower part of the old Adam building then being occupied by the staff of H. W. Massingham's weekly the *Nation*.

Among the people who lunched with Shaw at Adelphi Terrace before the deluge was Prince Lichnowsky, the German ambassador, who was asked what he thought of the published Shavian proposals to inhibit the threat of war. As far as the Ambassador was concerned, problems of war and peace were best left to the diplomats and the politicians and were not to be meddled in by amateurs. "He evidently did not consider that sort of thing my business," Shaw later wrote, "and dismissed it by telling me that Sir Edward Grey, our Foreign Secretary, was the best friend Germany had in the world, and that he would not be a party to any action that implied the slightest mistrust of him."[16] What Lichnowsky, too passionate an Anglophile to notice, failed to understand in his conversations with Grey is that after eight years as Foreign Secretary "Grey had perfected a manner of speaking designed to convey as little meaning as possible. . . ."[17]

Elsewhere there were words in the press connecting Shaw with Germany in a way which, however innocent, would soon be turned against him. Disembarking from the *Vaterland* in New York, Berlin critic Alfred Kerr, casting about in an interview for something of current interest to say, poured out his praise for Shaw, "who was very much pleased with the reception of his plays in Germany," he confided to a reporter. (*Pygmalion*, he had no need to say, had opened, in German, in Vienna and Berlin before its appearance in London in its original language.) "And he told me," Kerr added, "that the Germans were the only people who appreciated his dramas. The English did not understand him and the French did not want any play unless it was written about the Seventh Commandment."

More connected with Shaw, then as before, was the Fifth Commandment, for late in May G.B.S. published a volume containing several plays he had produced prior to *Pygmalion* and prefaced by a nearly book-length treatise, "On Parents and Children." Observing that the plays had been criticized fully when they first appeared, notably *Misalliance*, the play about parents and children, the *Times* lavished most of its long review upon the treatise, except for ironic concluding lines noting that the separate preface to *The Dark Lady of the Sonnets* was "one of the best things ever written about Shakespeare, about as good when it seems wrong as when it is certainly right." Shaw, the *Times* observed, was as much interested in morality "as an early Christian in religion," but it was not the usual morality. "We are all experiments, Mr. Shaw insists, and we should hope that our children may be more successful experiments than ourselves; therefore it is better to let your child see what an unsuccessful experiment you are than to attempt to convince him that you are an experiment perfectly successful." Using a term rarely associated with Shaw by the respectable press before, the *Times* concluded that most of what he had to say was "what we should call common sense if it were not so uncommon. . . ." Certainly Shaw read the review, and almost as certainly he liked being credited at long last with common sense. The accolade would not last out the year.

Shaw's opinions, although often dismissed with skepticism, were just as often sought. In his fifty-eighth year, white-bearded, and with only his mustache and eyebrows still showing russet traces, he had become the closest thing England had to a popular philosopher on unpopular issues. A self-made sage, he had first offered his opinions gratuitously and found them treated contemptuously. After three decades of politics, polemics, and playwrighting, however, G.B.S. owned the best-known initials in England. When it wanted a comment on an issue that would be certain to be read, the press asked Shaw. When it wanted insurance against embarrassing empty seats at an annual meeting, an organization asked Shaw to speak. When a do-gooding group wanted formidable names on its letterhead, it asked—among others—Shaw (and often got more than it bargained for). Yet Shaw somehow found time for all of these, and more, and he kept up demanding professional and social schedules as well, with long weekends at his home at Ayot St. Lawrence, a Hertfordshire village two hours' drive north of London.

The weeks between Derby Day in late May and Cup Day at Ascot in mid-June were the height of the spring social season, although not Shaw's kind of society. (Small luncheons and large public meetings were more to his taste.) The State Ball at Buckingham Palace was held on schedule, although with some inconveniences for guests resulting from an increase in suffragette agitation. An army of police stood by to prevent disruption of the festivities, while on the same day, in the Birmingham Art Gallery, a militant suffragette drew attention by hacking with a butcher's cleaver at George Romney's famous painting, *Portrait of a Boy*. In London most galleries and museums operated under severe restrictions, for Sargent's new portrait of Henry James, commissioned in honor of the novelist's seventieth birthday, had already been slashed, and a bomb detonated in Westminster Abbey, damaging the Coronation Chair. Prison, hunger strikes, and forcible feeding notwithstanding, the irresistible force had met the immovable object of Prime Minister Asquith's Liberal government at its most illiberal. To a symposium on the subject in the *Evening Standard* on June 9, Shaw observed with his usual unflattering bluntness, "As we have neither conviction enough to dare to starve the militants to death nor common sense enough to pledge ourselves to the inevitable reform, there is nothing to be done but wait until the women provoke a mob to lynch them and the Government hangs a satisfactory number of the mob in expiation. Then the women will get their votes after the last inch of mischief and suffering has been squeezed out of a situation which several reasonable and civilized countries already have disposed of without the slightest trouble. That is England all over."

The next day Mrs. Pankhurst, exhausted and ill from prison ill-treatment and rearrests, was carried in a procession to Downing Street to demand an interview with Asquith. She was refused.

Unpopular causes continued to cut into Shaw's creative time, but he was having difficulty getting going on a new play anyway. He had an atmosphere, a symbolic character, and a sense of foreboding about the future of Europe which he wanted to put into it. It was not taking shape satisfactorily in his mind, but neither could he get it out of his mind. Still it appeared on the surface as if his play production were undiminished, for he had a popular play running in London and had just published an earlier one, *Misalliance*, with its lengthy preface that ran to more pages than the substantial play itself. Shaw was always providing his readers with value for their shillings.

Both preface and play made Shaw a logical choice to address a London meeting on an uncomfortable subject, and in mid-June at the "Next Steps in Education" Congress at the Imperial Institute, three speakers discussed sex education: a physician, an educator, and G.B.S. Dr. Letitia Fairfield of the London County Council stressed teaching the teachers so that they would be better informed. Mr. Paton, High Master of the Manchester Grammar School, insisted that sex instruction was the parents' duty, but was unfortunately pushed upon the parson and the schoolmaster. Further, "the best antidote to impure pleasure is the pure pleasure of English sports. To keep fit is to keep good."

Shaw spoke last, saying that he believed with all his soul that schoolmasters who urged the importance of offering boys a surfeit of athletics as a cure for sex fixations were frightfully wrong. It would be better, he urged, to teach children the facts of life, beginning before puberty, even though they could not then fully understand. The problem was not how to suppress, but how to satisfy, the sexual impulses of young people. One could not, as in some countries, head off the problem by marrying off the children. It was better, he thought, to tide over the years between puberty and maturity by developing a real interest in art, in music, in literature, therefore keeping the imagination rather than more physical passions at work.

A few days later he appeared in his sage role again, this time by invitation of the *Times*, which carried a story on how English tax laws then penalized marriage by forcing husbands and wives to file joint returns and thus putting them in a category where a higher percentage of tax was collected, or in a category where two incomes too low for taxation together became taxable. Since Shaw had written to the *Times* on the subject four years earlier, a reporter went to Adelphi Terrace to elicit his further comments. It was humiliating to wives who controlled their own incomes, Shaw observed, and prophesied that if the law went unchanged it would squeeze the middle class out of existence. He had argued with the commissioners earlier when they demanded that he should include Charlotte's income with his own for computation of tax. Now he and his wife on principle filed separately, although they knew that the government would combine the two and charge them additional taxes. It was a bill he had no choice but to pay, he said, for a law on the books since Dickens's day provided for imprisonment for life for nonpayment of taxes.

Always at war with conformity, Shaw, answering his mail the next day, returned a request for his autograph together with five shillings that the petitioner had included for Shaw's favorite charity. It was a curious device to tempt a response, and Shaw responded by explaining to his correspondent that anyone who furnished his own autograph forged his own name. Back went the five shillings to New Zealand, with advice to spend the money sensibly, burn the autograph collection, and find some way instead of giving value to his own name.[18]

The autograph collector would have had a field day at a supper party Shaw attended at the Savoy the following week, for over to Shaw's table came a man with a biograph apparatus who took motion pictures of the group, getting into his lens James Barrie, Shaw, W. B. Yeats, G. K. Chesterton, Granville-Barker, Mr. Asquith, Mrs. Campbell, Charles Ricketts, Edward Marsh, Marie Tempest, Rupert Brooke— just back from the South Seas—and Gerald du Maurier. The banquet was not at the Savoy Hotel; rather it was Barrie's "Cinema Supper" at the Savoy Theatre. Invitations had been issued to more than one hundred guests, mostly from the theatre, but with a sprinkling from society. They were to participate in what Barrie had planned as Act I of a revue-like entertainment, with other sketches to follow, almost all of them by the host: Marie Löhr and Dion Boucicault in *Why? A Conundrum*; Lillah McCarthy (Mrs. Granville-Barker) and Henry Ainley in *One Night*; Jean Aylwin, Edmund Gwenn, and Henry Vibart in *When the Kye Came Hame*; Irene Vanbrugh and Godfrey Tearle in *Taming a Tiger*; Gerald du Maurier and Granville-Barker in *The Bulldog Breed*; and Marie Tempest, O. P. Heggie, and Graham Browne in *The Adored One*. In separate sketches using their own material were music hall comedian Frank Tinney and actress Ina Claire.

It was the most luxurious, snobbish social affair of an already luxurious season, and certainly most of the guests had never banqueted before where men with movie cameras filmed their arrival and followed everything they ate or drank. It was all part of Barrie's un-Lucullan intention to splice together shots from the Cinema Supper as an introduction to the filmed scenes in his revue. Some of the guests knew what Barrie was up to. Many found out only afterward, one of them protesting from 10 Downing Street that the Prime Minister had attended what he thought was a private party. Only a few Barrie intimates ever saw the processed film.

The next day Shaw was back before the cameras, rehearsing another sketch by his Adelphi Terrace neighbor. (Public highjinks were new to the pair, although privately Barrie and Shaw had indulged themselves by throwing wads of bread at each other's flat windows.) Barrie's codirector was Granville-Barker, and the shooting location was a site in Hertfordshire not far from Shaw's home. For the film, Shaw, G. K. Chesterton, William Archer, and Lord Howard de Walden entertained onlookers on the set by donning cowboy costumes, riding bicycles seemingly over precipices, climbing down ropes into abysses, rolling down hills in barrels, wading through streams, and otherwise acting in an undignified manner for the still silent screen. The "perilous cliff" from which Shaw had to lower himself by rope was only about ten feet high, but after looking down he decided to remain where he was, waving his arms and declaiming into the rain. "You can't be heard on this movie camera," Lady Howard de Walden shouted back, "so save your breath, G.B.S., and for goodness sake come down, and don't waste so much film." Chesterton, his immense girth swathed in cowboy garb, was supposed to cross a "roaring river" in a canoe, but swamped it and fell out into the shallow stream, all of him except his head very visible. When he lay there very still, the others rushed in to help him wade ashore.

More rain halted the frolic; however, the next day they returned to Holland Hibbert's farm for more shooting, were rained out the following day, and enthusiastically returned for more a day later, the conclusion of the scenario to be Lady Howard de Walden's capturing of Shaw in a butterfly net.[19]

Then the spell wore off, at least as far as G.B.S. was concerned. He discovered that it was not private fun for select viewers, but was meant to be shown in public and for a fee and that it was part of a proposed full-length film burlesque in which each actor would impersonate himself. He typed out an irritated note to Barrie, and the rest of the expensive joke collapsed, with Shaw's attitude made very clear in a fragment he called "still another version" of Barrie's *The Adored One.** In it he rewrote the ending, concluding with a role for himself:

> MR. SHAW (*rising in the stalls*). Wait a bit, wait a bit. If there's to be any shooting I should like to be in it myself. I scorn to shoot a woman. The person I want to shoot is Barrie. Barker and Miss [Lillah] McCarthy I understand—but what is Barrie up to? A Scotchman doesn't give a supper for nothing. What's his game? Why has there been so much flashing of lights—and a man turning a handle? I believe Barrie has done us. I want his blood. Let's make safe and shoot him. All those follow me who etc. etc.

That the Cinema Supper and attendant film frivolities, complete in guest list to the Prime Minister, took place five days after an ominous political assassination at Sarajevo in Bosnia was indicative of the English state of mind. Two weeks later Lloyd George was still telling a group of bankers in London, "In the matter of external affairs, the sky has never been more perfectly blue." Yet Shaw's old Fabian friend, historian Graham Wallas, had written in *The Great Society,* published less than a month earlier, "Let a European War break out— the war, perhaps between the Triple Alliance and the Triple Entente, which so many journalists and politicians in England and Germany contemplate with criminal levity. If the combatants prove to be equally balanced, it may, after the first battles, smoulder on for thirty years. What will be the population of London, or Manchester, or Chemnitz, or Bremen, or Milan, at the end of it?"

Parliament, and most Englishmen, professed little interest in Europe,

---

* Since only the typescript fragment exists in the British Museum Shaw Archive, it is not certain that it is by Shaw and could possibly be by Barrie himself.

for one problem outside England eclipsed everything else. Ireland—
particularly the Protestant northeastern six counties—seemed on the
verge of civil war, the Ulster loyalists wanting no part of home rule
for the entire island, since it very likely meant the end of the Protestant ascendancy. To Shaw "the arming and drilling and singing of ter-
rifying hymns" and the chalking up of "No Surrender!" and "To Hell
with the Pope!" on the walls of Derry would end differently if Ulster-
men would only realize that the fanatics were thus shutting six counties out of Ireland's destiny. But Sir Edward Carson, the Unionist
"uncrowned king of Ulster," had been demanding the exclusion of
Ulster from even the most watered-down Home Rule legislation. An
amending bill hung fire, and the Cabinet as well as both houses of
Parliament feared violence. "Give us a clean cut for Ulster or come and
fight us," Carson threatened in a speech on July 13, at the 224th anniversary celebration of the English victory at the Boyne, and seventy
thousand partition-bent volunteers, many of them illegally armed,
roared approval. No wonder then, when another of the fruitless Royal
conferences to break the deadlock over Ireland ended a fortnight
later, English concern over war turned west instead of east.

For the most part, except for keeping fences with European Socialist groups in repair, the Fabians were uninterested in the world
outside England. Although it paralleled British working-class interests,
the attitude was primarily a result of the Webbs' remorselessly inward
approach, which focused upon how to remedy the condition of England. In spite of Shaw and Wallas, Sidney Webb, as late as late July, refused to believe in the possibility of war among the great European
powers because, logically, "it would be too insane." The new Fabian
Research Department, launched by Beatrice Webb the year before
and chaired by Shaw, looked almost exclusively into domestic problems, although it was planned in 1915 to publish studies of trade un-
ionism in Germany, France, and Belgium. Up to that point, the department had proven most useful in preparing special analytical sup-
plements for the *New Statesman*, from one on the theatre to others
on rural economic problems, public and private electricity supply,
and national insurance. Shaw presided over its second annual conference at Barrow House in the Lake Country that July, and signed

its report, a manifesto that confessed, "Socialism suffered first from clever solutions of those problems which were not adopted, and not re-examined with a view to finding out whether their unpopularity was not due to a misfit, psychological or political. The Department keeps our ideas under continuous reconsideration."[20]

There were also the spartan lunches at Webbs' home in Grosvenor Road to discuss *New Statesman* policy, which, carefully reflecting Fabian interests, remained detached from Europe. As early as its first number in 1913, the *New Statesman* admitted that Fabians shared the British public's "abysmal ignorance" of foreign affairs, and it still had only one regular foreign correspondent, in Berlin, but he wrote on German labor and industrial issues, not on German militarism. The *Statesman* had many growing pains, from the independence of its editor, Clifford Sharp, to the refusal of Shaw to sign his articles and editorials or to permit his pieces to be subject to the editor's pencil. To the careful, unemotional Webbs, publishing a Shavian polemic as if it were the considered opinion of the *NS* editorial board was threatening the weekly's continued existence. To her diary Beatrice Webb noted that Shaw, whatever his kindness and loyalty, "had in fact injured the N.S. by his connection with it: we have had the disadvantage of his eccentric and iconoclastic stuff without the advantage of his name. . . . Persons who subscribed for their weekly portion of Shaw are angry and say they were got to subscribe under false pretences. The N.S. is, in fact, the only weekly in which Shaw's name never appears and it is his name that draws, not his mind." Sharp wrote to her similarly aggrieved. "His personal attitude refuses one not merely the liberty of criticism but the right to possess any view of one's own at all. I believe you and Mr. Webb are probably the only people in the world towards whom this indifference is modified by, as it were, a long inbred habit of affection and respect."[21] Like Pygmalion-Higgins, Shaw remained insistent on being mentor to whatever segments of humanity that would listen. And if none listened? A hero of a later play of his would say that all he knew was "that I must find the way of life, for myself and all of us, or we shall surely perish. And meanwhile my gift has possession of me: I must preach and preach and preach no matter how late the hour and how short the day. . . ."[22]

Pygmalion continued its eight performances a week, but with slightly diminishing grosses, as the weather drove potential stallholders out of London for the summer. Still, despite the end of the season, the fashionable and the blue of blood continued to frequent His Majesty's, including Their Majesties Queen Alexandra (widow of Edward) and Empress Alexandra Feodorovna of Russia, who, Mrs. Campbell wrote G.B.S., "clapped and nodded with joy." Earlier she had written that Tree had "only one ambition in the world," that Shaw "should be pleased with his Higgins."[23] Shaw knew that although the hundredth performance was approaching, those chances were nonexistent. Tree, who had played a lifetime of romantic endings, had figured out how to turn Shaw's conclusion his way without altering a word: in the brief interval between the last lines of the play and the lowering of the curtain, he would throw flowers to Eliza, providing a broad hint that matrimony was in store for the professor and his pupil. On Wednesday, July 8, G.B.S. made good his promise and found not only the flagrantly false ending, but even earlier in the play, that Tree had "contributed to my second act a stroke of comic business so outrageously irrelevant that I solemnly cursed the whole enterprise. . . ."[24] What Shaw had seen was Mrs. Campbell pretending to walk through a wall. "Don't go in there," said Tree, "that's my bedroom." In the audience there was some faint laughter and a good deal of shocked silence.[25]

Shaw would not see Tree afterward, but instead wrote him what he thought of the performance. "My ending makes money; you ought to be grateful," Tree answered. Shaw fired back, "Your ending is damnable: you ought to be shot."[26]

Although *Pygmalion* was still making money, houses as summer came had been often only little better than half-full, and Tree, bored with playing the disagreeable Higgins (he had unsuccessfully urged Shaw to let him play the comic dustman Alfred Doolittle), posted closing notices. After a late-July end to the run, he would go to Marienbad, his favorite German spa. Mrs. Campbell was furious. When the notice had gone up on June 28, she had written to Shaw (exaggerating the take) that it was absurd that such an announcement should be made at the end of a £2000 week and that he should do something about it, but Shaw had no interest in prolonging the run.

A month later Shaw recorded the royalties forwarded by His Majesty's for the final seven performances— £149.16.8. By then Tree was off on his holiday, intending to drive through France and Luxembourg to Marienbad. The French, he found, were agitated by the likelihood of war. By the time he arrived in Luxembourg, everyone he met thought that war was imminent, but Tree insisted that the present state of civilization made that impossible and described the situation as only "a political game." The next day he drove on to Frankfurt, with thoughts of *Pygmalion* far behind him.

As one controversy trailed off to an end, Shaw was beginning another. In the *Nation* Ernest Newman, who had succeeded Shaw as the most impudent, and most interesting, music critic in London, had reviewed a performance of ballet music by Richard Strauss, concluding, "It is pitiable to think that all that is left of the man who wrote *Don Quixote* is the platitudinarian and futilitarian who had written *The Legend of Joseph.*" In the July 1 issue, G.B.S. rushed to the defense, as he had earlier defended Wagner from Newman's pen. Newman had attacked Strauss's *Elektra*, too, Shaw recalled, and now conceded that it contained "quarters of an hour of dazzling genius." Thus a suggestion occurred to the retired musical critic.

Since *The Times* set the example, paragraphs of the news of a hundred years ago have become familiar in our older newspapers. If the *Nation* could devise some means of printing the opinions which Mr. Newman will have some years hence, instead of his first impressions, your readers would be spared the irritation of being told, at the moment when a masterpiece is being performed, that it is not worth hearing, and learning after the performances are over that it contained quarters-of-an-hour-of dazzling genius. —Yours, etc.,

It should have been of some concern to Shaw that Newman opened his rejoinder with the line, "It was a voluptuous joy to me to find I

had drawn Mr. Shaw again. . . ," and of even more concern that
Newman denied, on the basis of the composer's latest work, that
Strauss was a distinguished musician at all: "He is simply a distinguished financier who deals in music." Newman was clearly at the
top of his form, while G.B.S. seemed to be searching for a way to forget those concerns, foreign and domestic, that kept surfacing and im-
peding his work. Unwisely, he sent off his own rejoinder, which was
printed in the *Nation* on July 14 and described by Newman as "damp
fireworks," and, with regard to the alleged history of Newman's attacks on Wagner, blatant libel. "Will Mr. Shaw climb down, or must
I bring him down?" Shaw suggested dropping a matter that he insisted had been misinterpreted. "If he will cease asking me for the
name of that imaginary editor who did not dismiss him, I, on my
side, will not press him for the names of the hundred composers
who could easily have composed *Joseph* and refrained. . . . And so I
leave the last word with Mr. Newman."

Newman thanked Shaw for leaving him with a last word that, as
house critic, he would have taken anyway, and used it for a confession.

Mr. Shaw rightly opines that I gave him "expressive provocation" to
begin this controversy. I did indeed, and of malice aforethought. For three
years I have been trying to decoy Mr. Shaw into another argument. After
each article I have written on Strauss I have said to myself: "This will
draw him"; but Mr. Shaw has refused to be drawn. When *Joseph* came
along I saw a special opportunity and made a special effort. I knew this
was the poorest long work that Strauss has ever written. I know I had
only to say so in picturesque language to goad Mr. Shaw into committing
himself irrevocably to the opinion that it is a masterpiece; but to make
quite sure I baited the trap with an almost too obvious hint to Mr. Shaw
that it was his bounded duty to contradict me. The bait took: the unwary
Mr. Shaw rushed into the trap: and here we are.

There was more in Newman's reply calculated to draw Shaw's
blood, but the letter was dated August 3, 1914, and a different kind of
bloodletting would fade such continued controversies into insignificance.

On placards mounted on hoardings and tacked up on the backs of London omnibuses, Horatio Bottomley's journal *John Bull* that weekend advertised the slogan "TO HELL WITH SERVIA." Less sanguine than the author of the headline, Shaw realized that events in Servia were only a convenient coincidence: the dynamite charge that was Europe had many fuses. To his German translator and friend, the Viennese Siegfried Trebitsch, Shaw telegraphed, "Into what a repulsive situation has civilization brought itself. It rends itself instead of standing firmly against the one common enemy in the East.* Imagine you and me at war with one another! Can there be anything more senseless? Under all the circumstances you have my most friendly wishes."[27] It would be months before Trebitsch received the message, for it had crossed to the Continent by way of Ostend, in Belgium.

* Czarist Russia.

2

The View from Torquay

ALL THE LARGER nations except England had made their decisions by August 1, each finding in the Russian-Austrian quarrel about Serbia its own pretext for initiating a remaking of European boundaries and balance of power. Although in England that weekend Asquith and Grey appeared to hold back, throwing France into temporary consternation, Grey had made the inevitable clear to the Cabinet: "If Germany dominated the Continent it would be disagreeable to us as well as to others, for we should be isolated." But the peace bloc was strong and united, and it was obvious to him that only the violation of Belgian neutrality would crack the considerable opposition to war. Still, Grey let it be known on August 2, even before the German twelve-hour ultimatum to Belgium, that—if necessary—Britain would defend the Channel and the North Sea coasts of France.

From the moment Belgium rejected German demands to permit occupation and passage of troops through to France, no newspaper reader in England doubted what would happen next. Shaw noted afterward about the weekend, "1 Aug to Torquay via Dorchester and Salcombe. . . ," an itinerary better explained in a memorandum of

Charlotte's: "Arranged to go to Germany and on to the International Socialist Congress at Vienna, but had to give it up because of war news. Went to Devonshire (Salcombe) instead. England declared war on the 4th Aug. We went to Hydro Hotel, Torquay that day."[1] "At the outbreak of the war," Shaw wrote later, "I was at a hotel in Devon; and the first I heard of it when I came down in the morning was from a very ordinary and typical Englishman on the elderly side of forty, who, after a fairly successful attempt to say unconcernedly 'I suppose we shall have to fight them' suddenly became spitefully hysterical and changed 'them' into 'those swine' twice in every sentence."[2] The news had turned around the most sacred vacation period in the English calendar—Bank Holiday weekend. Carefree throngs were still pouring through London railway stations heading for the beaches while other vacationers, rushing home in anxiety, emptied out of returning trains. In their midst, waving their own small flags, were knots of civilian-clad French and German reservists, eager to return home before it was too late to get home.

On Bank Holiday Monday, *after* the German invasion had begun, the British government irresolutely telegraphed to Germany demands for a "satisfactory reply" to its request to uphold the neutrality of Belgium. It was too late to expect the Germans to meekly return to their own frontiers, and no one expected the ultimatum to do more than expire at midnight Berlin time and leave England at war. At last Englishmen would be asked to fight and sacrifice not for imperial aggrandizement but out of altruism; not for material gain, it seemed clear, but for justice and freedom. In a confusion of generous feelings, Rupert Brooke quickly summed up the mood in a sonnet beginning, "Now, God be thanked, Who has matched us with His Hour." Nagging doubts about the pointlessness of the war now cast aside, most Englishmen felt restored, rejuvenated—"like a swimmer into cleanness leaping," in another romantic phrase of the one-time young Fabian from Cambridge.

Belgium had wrought the change. The English perspective was exemplified in a *Punch* cartoon labeled "No Thoroughfare!" Brave little Belgium (no one thought of Serbia in such terms) was the stern, small boy in wooden shoes barring the way to the German trespasser, a greedy, corpulent figure with a string of sausages hanging out of his pocket. Being against defending Belgium was arraying one's self on the side of Sin, although by the time the government in Whitehall stirred, Belgium was as good as lost.

G.B.S. kept his head—"relatively," he hedged—because his patriotism, as an Irishman, was not involved. He was on the English side, he said, "as a matter of policy and of neighborliness," the way Serbia felt toward Turkey, or Belgium toward Germany. He could not see the war as "a simple piece of knighterrantry," with England "as Lancelot-Galahad, and Germany as the wicked Giant, and Belgium as the beautiful maiden we had to deliver."[3] Yet perhaps it was Quixote-like for G.B.S. to believe that he was so much a master of the arts of persuasion that he could turn public opinion around and break "the spell of silent cowardice" that committed half a world to bloodshed because it had stumbled backward into war.

For the rest of the summer and into the fall, Shaw lived in self-styled religious retreat in Torquay, at the Hydro Hotel. He wanted to be able to think about the situation while free from the pressures of war-mad London and produce a reasoned appraisal. It was difficult, for the daily press badgered him, ravenous for "name" opinion. By Wednesday he had drafted an initial personal statement, in which he confessed exasperation with patriotism, yet agreed that England had no choice, given the situation in which she had placed herself, but to go to war on the side of France; however, if the outcome were to redound to the benefit of the Czar and his medieval empire, both warring parties would have committed a crime against civilization. Talk of "smashing" Germany was only "schoolboy brag" he warned; the real danger could be the emergence of "inexhaustible Russia" over a prostrate Europe. The warring nations had to look beyond "killing by machinery" and immediately begin drafting the "inevitable Treaty of Peace which we must all sign when we have had our bellyful of murder and destruction."

Here, at least, Shaw had some impact upon the *NS*, an unsigned paragraph of his pointing out how untrustworthy and uncivilized Russia was in comparison to Germany, how it was the civilization of the West that mattered, and that eventually had to realize its interlocking responsibilities in peace. An *NS* editorial made it clear who the real enemy was:

We all know, and it is of crucial importance that we should never for a moment forget it, that in the present war the three most enlightened and illustrious communities in the Old World are tearing at each other's throats under the eyes of a vast Power, medieval in thought though modern in its appliances of war, that might, should they exhaust each other, threaten them all, the ideals they stand for and the culture that through painful centuries of development they have evolved.

The first Sunday of the war provided Shaw with a new focus for exasperation, as pulpits echoed with patriotic slogans. It was hypocrisy, he wrote to the *New Statesman*, to suggest, by pugnacious prayer to a God Englishmen possessed in common with their enemies, that Christ was really Mars. He had a suggestion, whimsical and of unlikely appeal to both sides: that churches all over Europe close their doors until the war stopped, to remind the belligerents "that though the glory of war may be a great and ancient glory it is not the final glory of God." The idea failed even to appeal to the *New Statesman*.* The militancy of the clergy disgusted him, and the only passivity he observed among churchmen of the more popular denominations was their failure to protest the closing of a church at Forest Hill "in which God was worshipped in the German language. One would have supposed that this grotesque outrage on the commonest decencies of religion would have provoked a remonstrance. . . . But no: apparently it seemed to the bishops as natural that the House of God should be looted when He allowed German to be spoken in it as that a baker's shop with a German name over the door should be pillaged. Their verdict was, in effect, 'Serve God right, for creating the Germans.' " Having just completed a long preface to his religious stage parable, *Androcles and the Lion*, he set about putting his war afterthoughts into an afterword and included the incident at Forest Hill.

To place some personal statement in print he succumbed to a com-

---

* But Shaw afterward did work what he had written to *NS* into his war pamphlet, *Common Sense about the War*.

mission from the London *Daily News and Leader,* which published his first signed article on the war on Monday, August 11. It was typically businesslike, on the order of a Shaw preface. "Now that we are at war," he began, "it is as well that we should know what that war is about." As for what it was *really* about, Shaw dismissed all the patriotic and pugnacious slogans: "Our national trick of virtuous indignation is tiresome enough in peaceful party strife at home. At war it is ungallant and unpardonable. Let us take our pugnacity to the field and leave our hypocrisy and bad blood at home. . . . This war is a Balance of Power war and nothing else. . . ." England's first business was nevertheless to fight that war, he went on, for its power at the eventual peace table depended upon its part in the conflict. Yet he insisted that there was still an opportunity to develop an "intelligent and patriotic foreign policy—patriotic in the European as well as the insular sense. . . . History will not excuse us because, after making war inevitable, we run round at the last moment begging everyone not to make a disturbance, but to come to London and be talked to kindly but firmly by Sir Edward Grey. . . ."

Almost at once came an idealistic reply from his contentious old friend Wells.

I find myself enthusiastic for this war against Prussian militarism. We are, I believe, assisting at the end of a vast intolerable oppression upon civilisation. We are fighting to release Germany and all the world from the superstition that brutality and cynicism are the methods of success, that Imperialism is better than free citizenship, and conscripts better soldiers than free men. This war is not going to end in diplomacy, it is going to end diplomacy. At the end there will be no Conference of Europe on the old lines, but a Conference of the World.

With the war barely a week old, and Belgium and France rapidly being overrun, Englishmen in the first throes of mobilization and indignation could have hardly found Shaw's suggestion of shared war guilt palatable, however much they agreed with him that it was now necessary to fight. Also among those who did not share his views were the Webbs, who pulled whatever wires were left unmanned at the

New Statesman by Clifford Sharp. From Torquay Shaw appealed to them for understanding. It was no use his trying to write for the *Statesman*, he declared to Beatrice the day after his *Daily News* article appeared: "It will talk very judiciously and sensibly and safely all round the war; but it wont strike at the vital parts." It was "pure luck" he wrote perversely, that the invasion of Belgium gave England an excuse, for it was Grey's type and class that made wars inevitable, and it was necessary to see to it that Grey was not apotheosized as an angel of peace, with the Kaiser as "Pantomime Demon." The *New Statesman*, Shaw suggested to Beatrice, had to be wary of being caught editorially napping, for there would be a reaction against Asquith and Grey once the disillusionment of war exhaustion occurred. The Webbs were unpersuaded, Beatrice sure that Shaw's personal dislike for Grey had affected his politics.* She was curiously certain, too, that his dislike for Asquith was based upon a nonpolitical grievance, that he had "offended G.B.S. by treating him as a ladies' man and not as a serious political thinker," and that Shaw had an "Irish objection to British policy."[4] There were grounds for the latter.

From the roof of the Hydro Hotel where Shaw sunned himself on clear days and had already begun drafting a lengthy manifesto on the war, no traces of the war were yet to be seen, but he felt—as an Irish outsider—as if he were "witnessing an engagement between two pirate fleets, with, however, the very important qualification that as I and my family and friends were on board the British ships I did not intend the British section to be defeated if I could help it. All the ensigns were Jolly Rogers; but mine was clearly the one with the Union Jack in the corner." Ripples from the war came quickly in Shaw's direction, however. The German hotel porter handed Shaw his *News and Leader* with the assurance that he felt the same way as Shaw did in his article. Later in the day, although he had registered as an "enemy alien" immediately on issuance of such instructions, the porter was arrested, handcuffed, and deported inland to Exeter, apparently so that he would not signal messages to German submarines. (Eventu-

* Shaw had never forgiven Grey for his "thinking Imperially" in condoning the 1906 "Denshawai horror" in Egypt, when villagers who attacked English officers shooting pigeons in their villages were executed for their crime.

ally he resumed his occupation, but as a Swiss.) That evening, when Shaw and the visiting Granville-Barker went for a walk along the beach before going to bed, a panicky coast guard threatened to fire on them if they approached any closer to him. He was fifty yards away. Shaw afterward wrote his German translator that the evening promenade concerts in London "were announced in a patriotic manner, with the announcement that no German musician would be represented on the program. Everybody applauded the announcement, but nobody attended the concerts. A week later a program of Beethoven, Wagner, and Richard Strauss was announced. Everybody was indignant, and everybody went to hear it. It was a complete and decisive German victory, without a single man being killed."[5]

Before long a friend who had become an enemy alien appealed to Shaw for help. A harmless teacher of his own language in a respected school, he had been not only dismissed summarily by the headmaster, but assaulted in the process. G.B.S. inquired whether there was anything against him except his nationality, and was told that there was absolutely nothing (although every German was assumed to be a spy), but that the German language would never again be permitted to pollute the curriculum of an English school. In London the *Daily Mirror* exulted in the hunting down of alien meat-cutters seeking fresh supplies in Smithfield. " 'Strafe him, boys!' " the *Mirror* reported one patriotic laborer shouting "as another German was chased across Farringdon Street into Holborn by some 300 people. He attained a marvellous speed and the men perched on the vans and wagons shouted sporting phrases at him." In London, too, Shaw's sister Lucy, ill for years and with a German nurse companion (like everything else, paid for by Shaw), was in danger of losing Eva Schneider to deportation or protective custody, as she had been classified as an "alien enemy." Although Dr. Des Voeus (who had been engaged by G.B.S. to look after Lucy) went to the Home Office to vouch for her and to request exemption for her from deportation, the Home Office would only grant permits for a month at a time. It would mean going through the agony of repeated supplication right up to the end of the war. In such fashion, although remote from London and with his immediate source of current information the *Torquay Times*, Shaw could not remain immune from events. Besides, forwarded relentlessly from his secretary Ann Elder at Adelphi Terrace and from Ayot St. Lawrence as well were bundles and boxes of mail and newspapers.

As much as possible, Shaw tried to follow a normal routine, although what he was writing had little to do with his normal pursuits. He would go to the roof garden to work until noon, leave to go for a swim before lunch, then work in the sitting room of his suite through the afternoon, usually oblivious to the chatter of Charlotte and her guests. Sometimes he would break into the afternoon regimen with an automobile ride; often in the quiet evenings he would have dinner— which had to include a spartan vegetarian menu for him—with friends. One evening he promised that after dinner he would entertain his host and other guests with a reading of something he had just completed, but just as he began to read he halted and confessed, "I shall have to go back to the hotel for a moment—I've left part of my teeth behind."

Shaw disliked looking forward to September. There was a touring company of *Pygmalion* in the works, but he hoped he would not have to return to London to rehearse it and that all tours would be abandoned for the duration. The war might be good for some things, he thought—a boost for the suffragettes, for Irish freedom, for domestic socialism. But it was almost his total professional preoccupation. He hardly dared think of the work he was not getting done, he confided to Beatrice Webb. It was not merely a temporary delay, he was sure, for he suddenly felt how very old he was getting to be. Still, he sought the Webbs' support for his war articles, carefully downplaying his interest in having the *NS* print some of them by pointing out that it was only "a mere waste paper basket" for him compared to the mass circulation London daily papers. (Since the *NS* only had a three thousand weekly audience, he knew it was a telling point.) Besides, he confided, he had no desire to set off fireworks in church, a curious metaphor for a journal otherwise thought radical, although he thought the *NS* was likely to have its pro-Grey policies backfire in time. One of the chief points he would make in his manifesto-in-progress was that the war would be fought in vain if Junkerism were not discredited by it and that the smug and selfish squirearchy represented by Grey was a British equivalent to Junkerism that the *NS* would do well to expose for what it was. He tried the idea on Beatrice, although he knew she was in no mood to support it. You think that the whole world is a fool, and only you are right, she had already told him.

The cleavage between the Webbs and Shaw on the war was indicative of the disarray on the left. With the Conservatives unwilling to attack the Liberal government, there was no parliamentary opposition unless the Labourites, who opposed the policies that had produced the war, continued to oppose. Ramsay MacDonald, then, but not always, a hero to Shaw, had resigned his leadership of the Labour Party on August 5 when his party executive committee was equivocal; he had then branded Grey as "a menace to the peace of Europe for the last eight years." It was not a belief shared by many of the Fabians among the Labourites, among them the Webbs, to whom Shaw explained vainly his ideas about "Weltpolitik" and "Realpolitik."

At Ayot St. Lawrence Shaw's servants found a strange gentleman at the door looking for Shaw. Firmly they refused to furnish Shaw's forwarding address, but he insisted that his mission was a matter of life and death for thousands of people and that he had known Shaw for many years. Finally he pocketed Shaw's Hydro address and left. It was Ebenezer Howard, pioneer of the garden city urban planning movement, who wrote to Shaw on August 15.

A few days ago I suddenly awoke with a thought of Peace Propaganda working by entirely new means—that of aeroplanes. I calculate that from an aeroplane capable of carrying three men besides the aviator, but only carrying one, there might be taken 3 cwt of printed matter, and as every pound might easily represent four thousand messages, there will be a total of one million two hundred thousand messages. These would spread themselves over a very wide area whose length might be hundreds of miles and my present idea would be to travel southward from some point, say in Belgium, till one reached Switzerland, travelling of course at a very great height, and again at night I woke up with the thought that I must myself go up in such an aeroplane and deliver a special message carefully prepared. Such a message I now enclose, but it does not satisfy me, and the less because I have been reading your articles in the "Daily News," and I feel that the Russian side of the problem, which Germans must feel very acutely, is too absolutely ignored.

Will you help me (1). By saying what you think about the idea generally. Some say it is premature at this stage and would not have any influence. On the other hand, the sooner the thing is done if it is in any measure effective the more lives may be saved. But here obviously, one must be very careful that the message should not produce the opposite effect of that which is sought.

(2). By revising or entirely re-writing the message. I am presently going to the "Daily News" to see whether they would finance such a scheme. It is obvious that a similar method of propaganda may be adopted at a later stage in dealing with the Russian problem.

He was well aware of the difficulties involved in the mission, Howard added, but he was certain that if the attempt were worth making a way out of the difficulties could be found. Thus his proposed message to Germany was enclosed for Shaw's study.

A Friendly Message to the German People

This message descends to you from the Heavens. You are a brave, intelligent, highly educated and fair-minded people, against whom the British nation has never before fought. You are of kindred blood, and of similar religion.

Yet you and we are at war with one another. Why is this? It is because your despotic rulers have attacked the territory of Belgium, a friendly neighbour, whose lives and liberties are as dear to them as yours are to you. By this outrageous and cowardly conduct your rulers have aroused deep indignation in England, and not only in England, but throughout the world. . . .

Are not your rulers your enemies as well as ours? It is by their conduct and that of other rulers of Europe that this war, so full of cruel suffering to millions, has been brought about. You—soldiers and sailors in arms— you civilians—you women—have it in your power to stop this war . . . thus saving hundreds of thousands of lives and vast treasure.

You can do this by at once demanding an Armistice; in order that you may frame a free Constitution such as that now enjoyed by the people of France, Great Britain, its Colonies and the United States of America; and in order that then you, as a great and free Nation, may obtain such fair and honourable terms as you, as a brave and enlightened people, will deserve; and then we and you, joining hands with all other Nations, will form a Great Peace Army and create a new social order.

Eventually—in a later war—Howard's idea would be used wholesale, but on a postcard Shaw punctured the naivete of civilian interference:

Hydro Hotel, Torquay.   16/8/14

A gorgeous notion, but utterly impracticable for a thousand reasons. The Nations involved need no message; they are just as horrified and peace-desirous as you are, but none the less they must fight it out now.

You can do nothing but sit quietly at home and go on with your peaceful work.

G.B.S.[6]

Intervention on Shaw's own part was another matter. He saw himself as one of the rare outside observers who was both articulate and informed, and to whom, because of the magic of his name, people would listen. H. G. Wells was another, he thought, and he praised Wells's *Daily Chronicle* piece that declared that England would have been an unfit place for a man of honor to live had the government, once the Germans moved, backed down on its promises to Belgium and France. Nevertheless, Shaw regretted the promises and determined that if no one else were willing to say uncomfortable truths in print, he would have to go it alone, even at the risk of a break with his oldest and closest friends, the Webbs, whom he had met when they were all nobodies in their twenties, caught up in the radical ferment of late-Victorian London. Her political perspectives were becoming warped by admiration of "ambitious and successful plutocrats," he told Beatrice, and it was, he added, the reason why she, so indifferent to literature, had increasing respect for the writer side of G.B.S.—he had been making money out of "potboilers" like *Pygmalion* (the play was unmentioned, but he refused to take its success with Tree seriously). "Are you not ashamed of yourself?" he asked her.[7]

G.B.S. had been having sent to him at Torquay all the newspapers and magazines he usually read, and more, and in addition the official

assemblages of documents made by the various foreign offices. These
had appeared quickly after the outbreak of war to justify each nation's
position; the German *White Book* was rushed out on August 4 and
responded to by an English *White Book* and a French *Yellow Book*,
among others.* While Shaw mulled over the documents, for the most
part holding his fire, what would be his position was already in print
in the August 15 *Nation* in a letter to the editor from Bertrand Russell, a forty-three-year-old fellow in mathematical logic at Trinity College, Cambridge. Russell, after examining the *White Books*, concluded
that the government might have dissuaded Germany from invading
Belgium had it made clear that this would have meant war with
Britain, and that all he could draw from the Government's failure to do
so was that saving Belgium had always been less important than using
Belgium.

It thus appears that the neutrality of Belgium, the integrity of France
and her colonies, and the naval defence of the northern and western
coasts of France, were all mere pretexts. . . .

I cannot resist the conclusion that the Government has failed in its
duty to the nation by not revealing long-standing arrangements with the
French, until, at the last moment, it made them the basis of an appeal to
honor; that it has failed in its duty to Europe by not declaring its attitude
at the beginning of the crisis; and that it has failed in its duty to humanity
by not informing Germany of conditions which would insure its non-par-
ticipation in a war which, whatever its outcome, must cause untold hardship and the loss of many thousands of our bravest and noblest citizens.

Like others in England who saw the war as a monstrous and unnecessary horror, Russell found his patriotism in conflict with his pacifism,
desiring the defeat of Germany "as ardently as any retired colonel," yet
sickened by what "the national propaganda of all the belligerent nations" had done. In London and Cambridge, he saw close professional
and personal friendships shattered by sudden explosions of warlike

---

* There were also other diplomatic self-exculpating books: the Austro-Hun-
garian *Red*, Belgian *Gray*, British *Blue I* and *Blue II*, Italian *Green*, Russian
Orange I and *Orange II*, and Serbian *Blue*.

feelings from reasonable men motivated by unsuspected reservoirs of hate and violence, by sentimental appeals to patriotism and honor. Even more than the daily newspaper accounts of defeats and retreats across the Channel, it brought the war home.

The war was coming home, even to Torquay, as the first month of fighting came to an inconclusive close. Four divisions of the British Expeditionary Force had landed in France between August 9 and August 17 and were engaged almost at once, for the German enveloping movement had swept through much of Belgium and had then divided, extending tentacles toward the Channel as well as toward Paris. By the end of August, the wounded began crowding hospitals and commandeered resort hotels; sometimes when he descended from the Hydro roof to listen to Basil Cameron's symphony concerts at the pavilion, the front rows were occupied by convalescent wounded Belgians, for whom Shaw sometimes helped set chairs. "The band played Tipperary for these warriors," he noted, "who, instead of rising on their crutches and bursting into enthusiastic cheers, made it only too clear by their dazed demeanour that they were listening to this tune for the first time in their lives." One day in Torquay when Basil Cameron lunched with the Shaws, someone at the table reported that the flourishing Anti-German League had succeeded in having another church closed because the service was conducted in German by an elderly clergyman who had worshiped in that language all his life. "It's like passing a vote of censure on God for creating Germans," Shaw observed. But the English mood then would have been for such censure, and that mood was being carefully cultivated.

When a meeting was called for September 3 by C. F. G. Masterman, then the Cabinet's propaganda chief, to ask eminent literary men who commanded confidence abroad "to take steps to place the strength of the British case and the principles for which the British troops and their allies are fighting before the populations of neutral countries," Shaw remained at the Hydro, intent upon his war treatise. Masterman, officially chancellor of the Duchy of Lancaster, mobilized his troops around a large, sunlit blue table at Wellington House, Buckingham Gate, to press them to intensified patriotic utterances, and most supplied what was asked for with enthusiasm. Barrie and Hardy were there, and Galsworthy, Wells, Bennett, Chesterton, Granville-Barker, Gilbert Murray, Ford Madox Hueffer (afterward *Ford*), Kipling, and lesser (but often more popular) names such as Anthony Hope Hawkins, H. Rider Haggard, A. E. W. Mason, and Arthur Conan Doyle. The writers were a *Who's Who* of the English literary firmament, names guaranteed to inspire confidence abroad; thus Masterman was eager to have them all put their names to a patriotic declaration, convinced of the overwhelming logic of numbers. "Many of us feel," it stated, "that, even if Belgium had not been involved, it would have been impossible for Great Britain to stand aside while France was dragged into war and destroyed." It supported "the free and law-abiding ideals of Western Europe" over "the iron military bureaucracy of Prussia." Fifty-three signed, including all of Shaw's closest writer friends, from William Archer to Israel Zangwill; on September 17 the statement was released above their signatures.

Before the month was out, most of the Wellington House group had begun doing their duty. Rudyard Kipling addressed a mass meeting at Brighton on September 8, declaring, "Our petty social divisions and barriers have been swept away at the outset of our mighty struggle. All the interests of our life of six weeks ago are dead. We have but one interest now. . . ." Galsworthy produced a "Credo" that stressed "national honor." Alfred Noyes produced an imaginative pamphlet accusing Germany of sending to England "packets of bacteria" manufactured in Berlin, and E. F. Benson punned on German influence in Turkey in *Deutschland über Allah*. Jerome K. Jerome, invoking, ironically, a quotation from *Man and Superman*, pointed out in the *Daily News* that it was time to turn talking into action. Hardy published a poem, "Men Who March Away," in the *Times* and won enormous popularity with it.

> What of the faith and fire within us
> Men who march away
> Ere the barn-cocks say
> Night is growing grey,

Leaving all that here can win us;
What of the faith and fire within us
Men who march away?

Most of the others who had been at the conference turned out propaganda that looked less like literature. Anthony Hope rushed out *The New (German) Testament*, a pamphlet that restored to prominence a 1911 book by General von Bernhardi, and *Germany and the Next War*, in which he turned the general's words against him—an easy task, since von Bernhardi had such things to say as "Aspirations for peace . . . seem to dominate our age, and threaten to poison the soul of the German people. . . . War is not merely a necessary element in the life of nations, but an indispensable factor of culture, in which a truly civilized nation finds the highest expression of strength and vitality." Ford Madox Hueffer put aside his manuscript of "The Saddest Story" to write for his friend Masterman a Belgian refugee poem, "Antwerp," and two volumes of war propaganda, *When Blood Is Their Argument: An Analysis of Prussian Culture* and *Between St. Denis and St. George: A Sketch of Three Civilisations*. After submitting the delayed "Story" to John Lane, who published the unmilitary novel as *The Good Soldier*, he joined the Army in August 1915 as a private, less convinced by his own propaganda than by the financial and marital problems he faced at home.

Mason and Barrie found the prospect of pamphlet writing unsatisfactory and together decided to personally propagandize America. The authorities quickly approved, and they embarked secretly from Liverpool on the *Lusitania* on September 12. Before they even arrived the Embassy in Washington had to cable "that in the present state of American neutrality any idea of a mission must be abandoned at once. It could only embarrass the authorities, would be bound to provoke counter-demonstrations, and had indeed already been the subject of attacks in the pro-German Press." The secret orders had remained so confidential that reporters were at the dock in New York to interview them, and the two writers sheepishly turned their propaganda mission into a private visit. When he sailed home, Mason lied twelve years off his forty-nine and joined the Army.

Somerset Maugham, whose first play was initially produced in German (and in Germany) and whose happy memories of student life in Heidelberg were fictionalized in one of the rare moments in *Of Human Bondage* where the pervasive grimness lifts, spent the autumn of 1914 utilizing his medical training with a Red Cross ambulance unit near Ypres, correcting his proofs of that novel there by the light of a candle and with a background of booming artillery. He had not been at Wellington House and had no desire to write anti-German propaganda, but when he was relieved and went back to England, he was recruited for the Secret Service, his "cover" as a writer enabling him to travel abroad inconspicuously.

What the writers' role was to be in the war had occupied the *NS* the week before the Wellington House meeting, when it had editorialized that "almost without exception during the last fortnight our eminent novelists have rushed into print as authorities on all matters of foreign policy and military strategy." Shaw, like Clemenceau a believer that war was too serious a matter to be left to the generals, was privately annoyed and took the *NS* position, but Arnold Bennett wrote to Sharp, "As war is preeminently an affair of human nature, a triumph of instinct over reason, it seems to me not improper that serious novelists (who are supposed to know a little about human nature and to be able to observe accurately and to write) should be prepared to express themselves concerning the phenomena of a nation at war without being insulted."[8]

Bennett and others had pecuniary as well as patriotic motives, for in the first weeks of the war, normal writing income had dried up, and he and other writers were looking for other sources of revenue. Authors, Shaw observed, were "almost as hopeless at economics as they are at mathematics. When war descends on them they do not sit down to a calculation of how it will affect their business: they feel romantic impulses to sacrifice and service which do credit to their feelings, but which end in their being ridiculously gulled by people who do not share their feelings but who are sharp enough to see their chance and take it."[9] Wells and others, agent J. B. Pinker was soon complaining, quickly had begun to write war articles for little or nothing, often out of misguided patriotism, while in America their pieces were pirated before they could be copyrighted.* Shaw estimated that he had had £500 a year cut off from Germany alone, while a slump in the theatres was already hurting him at home, reducing his August and September professional income to practically nothing. For a while London theatres admitted soldiers and sailors in uniform free, and several managements quickly produced hastily written patriotic plays about the war which no one, especially soldiers and sailors, wanted to see. Most theatres merely kept open. Shaw, at least, had *Pygmalion* to market, not war propaganda but a play about the war between men and women.

One of the first things to have occurred in the theatre world after August 4 was that actors had been asked to "do their bit" for the war effort by accepting half-salaries, and many of them, "in an ecstasy of patriotism," Shaw said afterward, "did so, to the handsome profit of their exploiters. It was such a paying game that the said exploiters presently approached me with the proposal that 'of course' I would halve my fees for the duration." Shaw's answer was that he would have to double his fees, for not only was the war certain to increase his taxes, but inflation and the rise in the cost of living would require a corresponding increase in his income. In finally consenting to make no change upward, he wryly "claimed credit for an heroic sacrifice, only possible for an author with some settled property at the back of his royalties. The exploiters were deeply shocked by my lack of public spirit and set me down as an arrant pro-German." The real gainer, eventually, was the theatre landlord, Shaw concluded. Crowding the dimmed streets of London's entertainment district every night on leave were eighty thousand troops seeking something to do, and West End theatre rents kept rising. "The fortunate lessee who had a theatre for £100 a week, was offered £200 for it; and the new lessee was offered £300 before he turned the corner.... The difference was profiteering: war profiteering."[10]

---

* On October 10 *The New York Times* reprinted "When the Truce Comes," one of Bennett's *Daily News* series, of October 1, without permission. Other American papers were doing the same thing with articles that bore no copyright notice. H. G. Wells had been encouraging the practice by giving his articles to the American press.

Both the road company and the American company rehearsed *Pygmalion* in London in early September, Shaw at first keeping his hand in by mail. To Dorothy Dix, trying out for the touring cast, he recommended delivering Eliza's lines as if she were reciting Shakespeare for a prize in fine diction, and he enclosed a handwritten chart of Cockney sounds to help her get the "true guttersnipe bleat."[11] On the twenty-second, Shaw finally came to London for rehearsals and to prepare for a series of six Fabian lectures he had agreed to give before the outbreak of war. By that time Mrs. Campbell and company were ready to leave for New York, with Stella trying every stratagem to evade serious rehearsals for Shaw. Eventually he saw her—and Wu Pu, her Pekinese—off on the *Lusitania* boat train on Saturday morning October 3, and he returned to Torquay to write.

Although he was holding his heavy guns for the *NS* piece, Shaw had not wanted to be publicly silent; he had, however, encountered heavy resistance to some of the things he wanted to say on subjects ranging from Belgium to widows' pensions. C. P. Scott of the *Manchester Guardian* had, in fact, refused a Shaw letter to the editor, apologizing diplomatically that although he agreed personally with G.B.S., he supposed one's duty now was "to encourage and unite people and not to exercise and divide." The result was that while he was in London briefly in late September, he gave in to a determined Irish-American lady journalist from New York, Mary Boyle O'Reilly, and tried out some of the material from his manifesto, unbending for an interview after she told him that she had just come from David Lloyd George, who had confided to her that "The cleverest man in England is an Irishman." (Since Lloyd George, the Chancellor of the Exchequer, was a Welshman, it was a moment of rare modesty.) A fragment of the interview turned up in the *New York Times* in mid-October, when a friend to whom Miss O'Reilly had written released her letter (mailed from Bordeaux) to the press, but it was not until long extracts from the interview were published early in November that it created a sensation. In his pamphlet G.B.S. planned to equate the English officer caste with Prussian Junkerdom and suggest that if they had any brains soldiers would shoot their officers and go home to attend their own affairs. To Miss O'Reilly he explained what he meant, emphasizing (if the capitals in the published interview are any clue), "In both armies THE SOLDIERS SHOULD SHOOT THEIR OFFI-CERS AND GO HOME, the agriculturalist to his land and the townsman to his painting and glazing." The interview was full of infuriatingly Shavian paradoxes.

We always learn in war that we never learn from war. I am pleased with the spirit of those who advise war for its own sake as a tonic. . . . I have no objection to the modern nostrum of hygienic war. Let those who believe in it resort to one of the wild spaces of the earth and blaze away at one another until the survivors (if any) feel they can return to civilian life purified by artillery fire. War of this kind must be commercially and politically disinterested; it must not be forced on foreigners or made an obstacle to the business of the world.

England alone of European nations has a hired army. As a Socialist I am strongly in favor of compulsory conscription. There you catch the capitalist and his son, and his son's son.

The real objection to military service is that we are all afraid of being killed. All armies consist mostly of cowards; this is what makes war so thrilling.

While we so waste and degrade human life that the residuum of unemployables runs into millions, the less said about the horrors of making a man a soldier the better.

There was much more, all of it deliberately ironic and provocative. In a sense it was wasted—thrown away upon an unknown newspaperwoman—for more than a month passed before it made headlines, thus depriving Shaw of the reactions by which he may have hoped to test his pamphlet in advance. But one of the headlines it did make, half a world away, would haunt G.B.S. for the rest of the war. In the San Francisco *Bulletin* for November 2, the page two lead oversimplified, " 'Shoot Your Officers and Go Home!' Says Shaw."

While he supplied so liberally from his partially finished piece to Miss O'Reilly, he was refusing requests to put his thoughts down for a price. One English editor requested an article from Shaw on the war, asking him to name his fee. Shaw declined, pointing out that he was "very nearly" done with one already committed: "It is 35,000 words long; and its present destination is a special war supplement of The New Statesman. It would be cheap at £1500; but your windows would cost something to mend." Also waiting for him at Adelphi Terrace was a request from Charles Sarolea, war correspondent and former Belgian consul in Scotland, to contribute to a magazine's special Belgian relief number. Shaw supplied a letter for publication that stated that England did "not only fail to save the neutral soil of Belgium from violation in the worst form by rapine, fire, and sword," by concealing its intentions until it was too late, but also that England had gone on to abandon Belgian refugees "to the impulse of private charity as we abandon beggars."[12] (The Belgians—more than a hundred thousand of them—had been made wards of the Metropolitan Asylums Board and given bleak billets in which to sit out the war.)

In Torquay Shaw tinkered further with his manifesto, describing it to his sister in a vein that caused Lucy to write wryly to Ann Elder, "I heard from the 'Super-One' a couple of days ago: he seems to be throwing himself, to the extinction of everything else, into a war article. I trust, it may not get us all arrested and shot for High Treason."[13] Clifford Sharp, who was as horrified by it as he expected to be, and may have had more realistic nightmares about firing squads, appealed to the Webbs for help when it arrived. As Miss O'Reilly had already learned, Sharp discovered that Shaw intended to equate Sir Edward Grey's caste with the Junkers in Germany, a metaphor that Shaw justified to Sharp by references to German-English dictionaries and that the editor was convinced would send the NS into libel litigation, if not into bankruptcy. Sharp shuddered further at G.B.S.'s pointing to British secret diplomacy as one of the causes of the German invasion of Belgium and his perpetrating other allegations that at the least were unpatriotic and at the worst might be treasonable. There was only one solution for Sharp—he had to proofread Shaw's copy himself. Shaw resisted. He always dealt directly with the printer, he insisted, and intended to do so again to safeguard his text. Sharp appealed directly to Shaw that there were indeed technical points which needed correction: Shaw had written "hydrogen" instead of "nitrogen," had misspelled certain proper names, had gone on too long for the projected size of the supplement, and worst of all, had written something that would be greeted with jeers in England and cheers in Germany. Shaw admitted that his piece would make some Englishmen howl and that he *did* want it read in Germany. If his view were logical, he was confident that it would eventually impose itself. In the meantime the long effort had left him too exhausted to argue about it.

Word of the abuse he was taking in the *NS* offices from Sharp and his assistant editor, J. C. Squire, came to Shaw in Torquay, who took it calmly. In London H. W. Massingham of the *Nation* had heard of the matter and of Shaw's reaction and remarked to Frank Swinnerton, "That's the worst of Shaw: he can't get angry."[14]

Shaw's outspokenness about the degrading pensions for service widows had been written into his text as well, but before it had gone to press it became the subject for two Cabinet meetings, the King having written to Asquith to recommend greater generosity and bolstering his point by quoting Shaw on the subject. Nothing was settled at the first meeting, but at the second, on October 13, the Prime Minister called for a vote. Some members asked for a secret ballot, but Asquith overruled that and asked how many present were in favor of a weekly widows' benefit as high as seven shillings and sixpence. Only Churchill responded. Asquith and nine others voted for six shillings and sixpence, while Lloyd George and eight others held out for five shillings.[15] Had Shaw known he might have revised his polemic, or put the incident into the play in which he later satirized both Asquith and Lloyd George.

On October 12 at the Park Theatre in New York, the American production of *Pygmalion* had opened before an audience of happy ticket buyers and hostile critics. Shaw had warned George Tyler, the producer, not about the economic hazards inherent in the playwright's politics, but about the leading lady's whims. Give her what she wants, he wrote, short of shortening the play. Most important, he had warned, was to give Stella—or build for her if none existed—a dressing room on stage level, "for Mrs. Campbell wants to cut the play, partly because its length hurries her dressing and interferes with the delightful levees she holds in her dressing room. . . ." On the opening night, there *was* such a levee after the third act, when for the benefit of reporters and well-wishers Stella delayed the fourth act curtain long enough to write and gravely dispatch a cablegram to G.B.S.: "From all appearances your play a great success. You are a made man." Critics agreed that whatever the merits of the play, it was going to be a hit, and the *Nation*'s reviewer added sarcastically, "With strange foresight Bernard Shaw caused his 'Pygmalion' to be brought out first in Germany and so made hay before the advent of the war-cloud. After profitable runs in that country and in London, it comes to New York at a time when his nonsense offers welcome relief. In business sagacity Mr. Shaw is as forward as in all other matters."[16] In a sense he was right; G.B.S. had foreseen the war, although he had hardly arranged the various premieres of his play around it.

The opening kept Shaw in the news, even from his unpublic hideaway remote from London. Reporters inquired whether he had received Mrs. Pat's cablegram and whether he would capitalize on his success to visit America. It would be unfair to the press, he said. "For twenty years they have always filled up any spare space in their columns by announcing that I was on my way to America, and thereby kept the United States under a strain of expectation, which they have got used to. If I were to disappoint everybody by actually coming at last, I should create a good deal of ill-feeling."

The next day the *New York Times* front-paged an interview with Shaw under the title, "Shaw Sees America Leader of Tomorrow. Dramatist Pictures Peace Conference With Wilson Presiding After Europe is Ruined." (G.B.S. meant it, had planted the interview, and was concerned about getting his ideas through to Wilson.) A day later the *Times* took two columns to report an item that made Shaw seem less pro-Berlin than his detractors had suggested he was: "German Dramatist Answers G. B. Shaw. [Herbert] Eulenberg Says Militarism is Forced Upon His Country." The German Press Bureau had released an open letter to Shaw that, among other things, chided,

You raised your voice a little, Bernard Shaw! But what did you propose to us: "Refrain from your militarism, my dear Germans, and become again the congenial, complacent poets and thinkers, the people of Goethe and Beethoven, whom no one hated! Then we will surely help you against the bad Russians!"

Is not this proposal a bit too naïve for you Bernard Shaw? We are situated in the midst of Russians and Frenchmen, who have formed an open alliance against us for more then twenty years. . . . When such enemies surround us, does not your friendly counsel, Bernard Shaw, seem as if you said to us: "Just let yourself be massacred, Germans! Afterward your British cousins will vouchsafe you their protection."

Do you think that we would carry on our militarism and our expensive drilling if we lived on an island as you do? . . . We call to you, Bernard Shaw, in the name of Europe, and ask you for your voice in the struggle.

It is a splendid thing that this serious time has also aroused the poets, the thinkers and artists as political and diplomatic advisers, and we should not let ourselves be crowded out of this profession, for which, thanks to our minds, we are not less fitted than the high-brow Lords and Counts. Men of our guild from Thucydides and Herodotus to Petrarch and Rubens, and our Humboldt and your Beaconsfield have ever shown themselves to be good intermediaries and peace advocates. And that, believe me, Bernard Shaw, is of more importance to our people, as well as to our Kaiser, who for over twenty-five years has avoided war like a poison, than all other bloody laurels. . . .

Invocation of the Kaiser's peace-loving qualities drained all the subtlety from the appeal, but it did have the effect of making Shaw appear—from the German point of view, at least—as an adherent of the other side.

At home, however, Shaw was still busy defending himself and his manifesto to Sharp as not being pro-German. It was a "superb performance" and would reflect "eternal glory" on his editorship, he told Sharp on October 21, but confessed agreement that whether the paper would survive it was "another matter." But there he had an opportunity to head off ultrapatriotic opprobrium, he explained. He had written, at the urging of popular novelist Hall Caine, a piece about Belgium sure to be well received when it appeared in the *Daily Telegraph*'s fund-raising and celebrity-laden *King Albert's Book*. If it got into print first, as Shaw hoped it would, it would prevent NS readers from beginning the supplement "under the hostile impression that I am a Back Down and Stop the War Man."[17]

Even as he wrote to Sharp, however, Shaw knew that this possibility was suddenly in grave doubt. On the sixteenth Caine had confessed his concern about Shaw's contribution. "Our friends at the *Daily Telegraph* tell me," Caine wrote, "that you are against the war." There was no way to satisfy his detractors, Shaw thought, not even rewriting his piece, which he refused to do, telling Caine to advise his *Telegraph* friends to "boil their heads." There the matter rested, Shaw still hoping that the charity book would appear before his manifesto.

Near the end of his stay at Torquay, Shaw watched with dismay as the date of his first Fabian lecture of the season approached. He had no hope of having six fully prepared lectures ready, he confessed to Beatrice. Researching and writing the war supplement had occupied most of his time, and while he could not cancel the series, he disliked the idea of perpetrating a fraud. Even so, he thought afterward that he had held back his fire too long for optimum effect. "But there were difficulties," he explained to playwright Alfred Sutro. "I did not dare to write red hot. I had to slave for months getting the evidence; and I had to revise and revise, and give the stuff to people to read, and ask them whether it was unfair, was I hitting below the belt, was I off the evidence and so forth. . . . It makes me sick to recollect the drudgery of it all!"[18]

Finally, work on the supplement nearly done, Shaw satisfied himself about the London lectures by preparing an announcement for them (still to be given under the pre-war and no longer timely title of "Redistribution of Income") which included a prospectus he had written that he felt was honest to the situation.

It is not possible to furnish a complete syllabus of Mr. Shaw's lectures; as he has been compelled to turn aside from their preparation to the more pressing subject of the war. In any case Mr. Shaw's platform practice is to speak extemporaneously and to be guided by the context of current events in choosing his illustrations and determining the order in which he will take the various sections of his subject; and therefore, though the propositions he will advance have been carefully chosen and matured, being the conclusions to which he has been led during more than thirty

years' experience as a lecturer on Socialism, the Fabian Society could not
offer a formal syllabus with any certainty. . . .

The subject cannot be exhausted in six lectures but it can be covered
fully enough. . . . Mr. Shaw's power of making economic subjects attractive will not be unduly taxed on this occasion, as he will have to deal with
some unexpected aspects of his theme. For instance, one of his lectures
will be on Idolatry. He will have a good deal to say on Character and
Talent, on Art and Religion, on War and Democracy, and on Morals and
Manners; and he will deal with incomes and canons of taxation not as
textbook abstractions but dramatically, as human affairs. . . .

Back in London G.B.S. lunched with his old friend William Archer,
and their talk gravitated quickly from theatre to war, Archer displaying
fiercely patriotic views about the performance of the Army and the
Navy. The Army, of which no one had expected much, Shaw told
him, had done splendidly, while the Navy, of which everything had
been expected, had done nothing. Archer went away peeved. "It was a
purely *a priori* theory," he thought, springing from Shaw's "passion
for seeing, and believing, the opposite of what other people saw and
believed." It was Shaw the jester "wearing the cap and bells in and out
of season."

Shaw had no intention of wearing cap and bells for his lecture
series, although promise of that kind of performance might have filled
additional seats. As a fund-raising effort for the Fabians, the Kingsway Hall lectures got off to a slow start on October 28, the war creating immense disinterest in economics, but after some effort at giving
away free tickets, the Society succeeded in making the house look
full, a task that had been complicated by the existence not only of
five-shilling seats but others that went for 10/6 and a guinea.

Belying his concern about having to speak extemporaneously, Shaw
came prepared with a text, one that used examples from war and war
taxation as examples of redistribution of income. War proved the
Fabian point, he declared, "as we have recently seen how ruthlessly
war exposes the pretences of private capitalism and forces a nation to
prompt recourse to socialistic measures. Thus we find General Bernhardi, the evangelist of Prussian militarism, suddenly realizing at the

end of his gospel that the civil measures he has been postulating as necessary to the national safety are all nakedly socialistic. . . ." It was unfortunate that G.B.S. had not known of Sir Edward Grey's grim prediction on the eve of war. The consequences of the war would be terrible, he declared impulsively. "It is the greatest step towards Socialism that could have been made. We shall have Labour Governments in every country after this."

The second lecture, on November 4, was an improvement over the first, Shaw wrote Mrs. Campbell in America, for "smart persons of a soulful type—Lady Diana [Manners], for example, began to appear among the dowdy real people whom you call, generically, suffragettes."[19] Disabled by the severe headaches that had plagued him intermittently since his youth, Shaw put extra effort into his talk to compensate, and it came off well, although the press for the most part snubbed it. His increasing notoriety, however, would make it more and more difficult for the press to ignore him, as his war article, to be printed under his signature in the NS (the only way Sharp would have him), was in the press, and Shaw was badgering Sharp to prevent it from being held up. A bullet through the Kaiser would make it obsolete, he pointed out, and to make the urgency of its immediate release clear he noted that he had been offered, and had rejected, £700 for American publication if it could be held from release in England until Christmas.*

Shaw had yet another firecracker to ignite in Sharp's sanctuary, but Sharp would not accept it, even as a letter to the editor; Shaw called it his "move on the American President." There was a real danger, given the power of German-American opinion in the United States and anger at English searches of American vessels for contraband, Shaw thought, of Wilson "coming down on the wrong side." On Saturday, November 7, his "Open Letter to the President of the United States of America" appeared in Massingham's *Nation*.

Publication of Shaw's letter was a courageous move on Massingham's part; however, even he could not print it without an editor's prefatory comment that while the *Nation* agreed with Shaw that

---

* Instead Shaw received, after deduction of agent's fees, £368.17 from *The New York Times* for American and Canadian rights to *Common Sense*.

America's influence would be decisive upon the peace if not upon the war, "His Irish mind puts the case with an indifference to which we cannot pretend. We have got to save Western Europe from a victory of Prussian militarism, as well as to avenge Belgium and set her on her feet again." It was not that Shaw was indifferent, but that he felt objectivity to be more persuasive than emotionalism in appealing to a powerful neutral. Objectivity, or the appearance of it, was hardly separable from hostility in the wartime climate of moral blacks and whites, and, as Shaw observed afterward without modesty, "I was apparently the only publicly articulate person in London who could conceive that the Belgians had any case distinct from the British case."

In the open letter, Shaw asked Wilson to use his impartial good offices to ask all belligerents to get out of Belgium, "for the effect of our shells on Belgium is precisely the same as that of the German shells, and by fighting on Belgian soil we are doing her exactly the same injury that we should have done her if the violation of her neutrality had been initiated by us instead of by Germany. . . ." In spite of "the panics of our papers, with their endless scares and silly inventions," Shaw went on, people were already tired of war, and the West had to realize that it had no future without friendship. "In London and Paris and Berlin," he told Wilson, "nobody at present dares say 'Sirs: ye are brethren: why do ye wrong to one another?'; for the slightest disposition toward a Christian view of things is regarded as a shooting matter in these capitals; but Washington is still privileged to talk common humanity to the nations."

The open letter made headlines around the world, and in Washington, Wilson could not help but have seen it. In Chicago and New York at the same time Forbes Robertson was filling the Blackstone Theatre with *Caesar and Cleopatra*, while Mrs. Campbell and Philip Merivale were drawing enthusiastic houses at the Park for *Pygmalion*; other Shaw performances were going on in Minneapolis, Edinburgh, Milan, Aarhus, Amsterdam, and Dublin. The "great war article" (Shaw's own term) would appear a week later and was certain to gyrate editorial seismographs on both sides of the Atlantic. It might be assumed, then, that G.B.S. had every reason to feel some elation over the waves he was making, but, he wrote Stella, "London is darker than ever. They are trying to frighten the men into enlisting. I am telling them not to enlist until their wives are properly provided for. At present they get sixteen shillings a week until the man is shot, when they get five."[20] There was good reason. The insane war, he thought, was producing "no result except kill, kill, kill. The Kaiser asks from time to time for another million men to be killed; and Kitchener asks for another million to kill them. And now . . . they have settled the fact that their stupid fighting can't settle anything, and produces nothing but a perpetual Waterloo that nobody wins. . . ."[21]

3

The Storm over *Common Sense*

IN THE AUTUMN of 1914, the impulse to "do one's bit"—or at least to be observed doing it—had reached such proportions in London that young women, Shaw recalled, "had only to dress themselves presentably and parade the streets waving collecting boxes and paper flags at the passers by to have pennies showered on them. The police had to interfere finally, as the public would not discriminate between authorized collectors and enterprising cadgers. Giving away money was an easy outlet for the sacrificial impulse. . . ." Similarly, patriotic females plunged through London crowds to pick out able-bodied young men not in uniform and impale them with embarrassingly symbolic—and often thoroughly unjustified—white feathers, singing, "Oh! we don't want to lose you; but we think you ought to go,"* that Shaw recalled, "had a specially irritating effect in its cock-

* The song itself went on with
>   For your King and your Country
>   Both need you so.
>   We shall love you and miss you
>   But with all our might and main
>   We shall cheer you, thank you, kiss you
>   When you come home again!

ney form of 'Ow wee downt wornt—te le-oose yew—bat we thinkew orter gow.' I remember making a private note that only the most perfect speakers should be allowed to sing war songs." Too hoary-bearded to be a target for the passionate feather wielders, Shaw was afterward pleased that he came through the war years "without letting a single siren get a penny out of me for a flower or a flag."[1]

The song had come from a recruiting play called *England Expects*, produced by arch-jingo Horatio Bottomley at the London Opera House. Phyllis Dare, who sang the famous number, generally received such ovations that she had to repeat it several times during the performance. Demagogues like Bottomley, who had quickly changed the "To Hell with Servia" tune he had played in his magazine *John Bull* the weekend before the war began, took quickly to the road to whip up war hysteria. It was a year later that Shaw finally experienced a Bottomley performance, but the formula was in all respects unchanged by its success. When the notices went up that he would address two meetings in Torquay, Shaw had told Cyril Scott, the composer, that he would go to one of them. Knowing Shaw's private opinions, Scott registered surprise. "Oh, just curiosity," Shaw explained.

Bottomley, unprepossessingly short and paunchy, but with an electric platform manner, assured his audience that it would be a short war and predicted the exhaustion and defeat of the German armies flooding through France and Belgium. He had private knowledge, too, he confided, that Archduke Ferdinand had been assassinated on orders from the Kaiser. "Bear in mind," he would say confidently, "I speak of that which I know. Tomorrow it will be officially denied, but take it from me that if Bottomley says so it is so!!" Finally came the peroration, before a large recruiting table flanked by a Union Jack,

If the British Empire resolves to fight this battle cleanly, to look upon it as something more than an ordinary war, we shall one day realize that it has not been in vain, and we, the British Empire, as the chosen leaders of the world, shall travel along the road of human destiny and progress, at the end of which we shall see the patient figure of the Prince of Peace, pointing to the Star of Bethlehem that leads us on to God.

Expecting "a fire-eater," Shaw found instead that enemy tear-gas shells could not have been more effective. The throng "rose solemnly, and in a broken-hearted manner sang God Save the King. . . ."*[2]

Returning to his hotel, Shaw reported to Scott, "It's exactly what I expected: the man gets his popularity by telling people with sufficient bombast just what they think themselves and therefore want to hear."[3] Shaw had no intention of telling people what they wanted to hear, only what, in his opinion, they needed to hear. It entailed certain risks.

Writing to Stella, he wondered, in effect, why women did not replay *Lysistrata* to protest the slaughter in France and declare, "We have the trouble of making these men; and if you dont stop killing them we shall refuse to make any more."[4] The stupidities of petty patriotism infuriated him, the newest and most senseless the report in the *Times* that the Lambeth Guardians had decided to discontinue the tradition of giving the workhouse children an egg on Christmas morning in order to make them aware that their country was at war and that some form of self-denial was appropriate under such conditions. "And yet no thunder falls from heaven," he wondered to Stella. "Do we two belong to this race of cretins?"[5] He could not have made any deliberate mental note of the lines, but somehow they remained with him and emerged, somewhat altered, in the prophetic play he had had in mind before events had outdistanced prophecy.

On November 14, 1914, when *Common Sense about the War* appeared as an eighty-page supplement to the regular Saturday issue of the *New Statesman*, the British 1st and 7th Divisions were practically annihilated as they struggled to hold on to a sliver of Belgian territory in the vicinity of Ypres. Prussian troops pouring through the gap were met at close range by the Royal Field Artillery and a scratch force of cooks, tailors, transportmen, and clerks, led by a new lieutenant from Sandhurst who did not survive the day. When heavy rain fell, the Prussians hesitated in the quagmire and dug in, extending

---

* Bottomley was paid £25 per weekly meeting (£17.10 per meeting if he addressed more than one meeting the same day), plus between 65 and 85 percent of the gross admission fees.

trench warfare along the whole Allied line. British casualties through November would number 89,954, and although they would increase sharply from this time until March 1917, the front lines would not shift as much as ten miles in either direction. In shop windows in London there were placards reading "Business as Usual," to which some shopkeepers had added "Though There's a War On."

From the moment *Common Sense about the War* appeared, Robert Lynd said afterward, "the war was spoken of and written about as a war between the Allies on the one hand, and, on the other, Germany, Austria, Turkey, and Bernard Shaw."[6] That *Common Sense* was not written out of a desire for self-advertisement and personal gain is made clear from the circumstances: G.B.S. abandoned all remunerative professional work for nearly three months to write it, strove— but for an abortive letter to the editor and the apparently unpremeditated interview with Mary Boyle O'Reilly—to keep out of the public eye (and press) for the entire time, and asked no fee from the *New Statesman* when it was published, although ever since the war began he could have named his price for pieces on the war.* He disliked war not only for its dangers and inconveniences, but—as one who looked forward to a better world—"because of the loss of so many young men, any of whom may be a Newton or an Einstein, a Beethoven, a Michael Angelo, a Shakespear, or even a Shaw. Or he may be what is of much more immediate importance, a good baker or a good weaver or builder." It was a sheer waste of life out of which he received no emotional satisfaction, "the young Germans who lay slain and mutilated in No Man's Land" being no different than "the British lad who lay beside them...."[7]

Common Sense was quickly condemned as perverse frivolity. The seeds of the indictment were in the preoccupations dear to Shaw but peripheral to his argument and in the paradoxes sown not out of caprice or the desire to create didactic comedy out of a universal tragedy, but planted to shock readers out of what Shaw saw as their

---

* When he did jump the gun on the supplement by a week with his long open letter to President Wilson, it was only out of a sense of urgency, and for it he received a token fee of six guineas from the *Nation*.

inertia and blindness. Thus his suggestions that soldiers on both sides shoot their officers and go home and that ordinary citizens refuse to pay for diplomatic wars in which their nations indulged. Further, he found no more justification for Grey's unacknowledged foreign policy of containing Germany than for Von Bernhardi's declared foreign policy of breaking that encirclement. "If we send the Kaiser to St. Helena . . . ," he observed, "we must send Sir Edward Grey there too." He saw Belgium as the inevitable and pathetic buffer-state victim of big-power rivalry and ally Russia as less civilized than admittedly militarist Germany. He carped at exploitation of labor by war industries, inoculation of soldiers against their will, and religious hypocrisy on both sides. All these lesser issues obscured the serious aims that may justify *Common Sense*'s having been called a generation later "one of the sanest documents that came out of the war."[8]

The chief target of the pamphlet was the self-righteous patriotism that stood in the way of a negotiated peace, and to the shocked country it appeared as a "surrender of the whole moral basis of our position as a peaceful and almost pastoral people surprised by a raid of Huns." It was a balance-of-power war, he contended, and had to be fought, won, and a settlement made with a minimum of sentimentality, moral superiority, and illusion. It was also not enough for England and France to win; it was important, too, that the Junker classes in each country be stripped of their powers as a result of the war, for they represented to Shaw the reactionary bias of landed wealth toward militarism, discipline, and autocracy. It was necessary for reforms in the military to make men more willing to serve and for economic and social reforms at home to make the peace worth having. It was necessary to have a peace without reparations (which he saw both as blackmail and as the likely cause of a colossal depression if exacted), and it was necessary to make that peace as soon as possible. "This war will stop," he predicted, "when Germany throws up the sponge, which will happen long before she is utterly exhausted, but not before we ourselves shall be glad enough of a rest. Nations are like bees: they cannot kill except at the cost of their own lives."

"What have we done for Belgium?" he asked. "Have we saved her soil from invasion? Were we at her side with a half a million men when the avalanche fell on her? Or were we safe in our own country praising her heroism in paragraphs which all contrived to convey the idea that the Belgian soldier is about four feet high, but immensely plucky for his size?" It was now England's duty to drive the Germans out of Belgium, he acknowledged, while insisting nevertheless that it was England's fault, in part, that the job had to be done. It was also England's duty to provide public funds to care for her refugees and employment to take them off the dole, although many Englishmen remained out of work, and the Belgians competed with them for what jobs there were. "Hence we arrive at the remarkable situation," Shaw observed with a wryness his countrymen found difficult to accept, "of starving Britons and Belgians looking hungrily through barbed wire fences at flourishing communities of jolly and well fed German prisoners of war (whose friendly hat wavings to me and my fellow passengers as I rush through Newbury Racecourse Station in the Great Western Express I hereby acknowledge with all possible good feeling). I therefore for the present strongly recommend to all Belgians who have made up their minds to flee to England to pick up German uniforms . . . and surrender to the British. . . ."

Looking ahead, he foresaw the need to study "how so to redraw the map of Europe and reform its political constitutions that this abominable crime and atrocious nuisance . . . shall not occur again," and to do so only with the consent of the peoples concerned. That settlement had to be safeguarded, too, by a "League of Peace" with real power to keep the peace "by a combination of armed and fanatical pacifists of all nations," rather than by an unworkable and unrealizable disarmament and "a crowd of non-combatants wielding deprecation, remonstrances and Christmas cards." Marxism could not be left out of the settlement either, for he considered "the bond of international Socialism . . . the only bond upon which the identity of interest between all workers never becomes obscured." Concluding, Shaw dismissed the breast-beating over the destruction of Louvain and the shelling of Rheims Cathedral as "a strong hint from Providence that though we can have glorious war or glorious cathedrals we cannot have both."* A world that found war glorious, he warned, made it undeniably possible that a diabolical rhythm may be set up in which civilization will rise periodically to the point at which explosives powerful enough to destroy it are discovered, and will then be shattered and thrown back to a fresh start with a few starving and ruined survivors." His last paragraph foreshadowed a more immediate prospect, the Orwellian shifting of power combinations that would occur throughout the rest of the century: "If this war does not make an end of war in the west, our allies of today may be our enemies of tomorrow as they are of yesterday, and our enemies of today our allies of tomorrow as they are of yesterday; so that if we aim merely at a fresh balance of military power, we are as likely as not to negotiate our own destruction."

The reaction to *Common Sense* was predictable. For all its prescience and statesmanship, there was also something in it to outrage almost everyone. As one wag put it in verse,

> . . . Shaw's *Common Sense* is quite immense;
> I liked it—damn his eyes!
> He may be right, but all the same,
> Why can't the blighter play the game?[9]

In America the pamphlet appeared a day later in the *New York Times* of Sunday, November 15, and the results were similar. If any-

---

* When publisher William Heinemann forwarded to Shaw for his signature a petition from Romain Rolland that protested the bombardment of the cathedral at Rheims, Shaw returned it with a note:

My dear Heinemann, Rolland ought to know better than to repeat all this halfpenny newspaper rubbish about Rheims. I am one of the two or three people in Europe who really care about Rheims; but if I were a military officer defending Rheims I should have to put an observation post on the cathedral roof; and if I were his opponent I should have to fire on it, in both cases on pain of being court-martialled and perhaps shot. If this war goes long enough there will not be a cathedral left in Europe; and serve Europe right too! The way to save the cathedrals is to stop fighting, and not to use them as stones to throw at the Germans. I won't sign.—Yours ever. . . .

thing, they were even more vehement, the journalistic ineptitude of the *Times* abetting the furor, for the *Times* divided the manifesto into three parts spread over three Sundays, thus exacerbating the outrage by separating facts from comment, and comment from conclusions. Further, it led off the first installment with a large portrait photograph of G.B.S. wreathed in a contented smile, as if he were surveying happily the carnage of Europe about which he had written. It was all self-advertisement, said an Englishman at the Biltmore (who claimed to be a friend of Shaw's) to a *Times* reporter. "Shaw would write an advertisement on the grave of his own mother." The *New York World* agreed, summing up its interpretation of Shaw's thesis in a five-part paradox:

1. Great Britain was abundantly justified in making war with Germany.
2. The explanation given by the British Government for making war against Germany was stupid, hypocritical, mendacious, and disgraceful.
3. Shaw alone is capable of interpreting the moral purpose of the British people in undertaking this necessary work of civilization.
4. The reason the British government's justification of the war is so inadequate is because no British government is ever so clever as Bernard Shaw.
5. Even in the midst of the most horrible calamity known to human history, it pays to advertise.

Various patriots have various ways of serving their country. Some go to the firing line to be shot and others stay at home to be a source of innocent merriment to the survivors.

In London crotchety playwright Henry Arthur Jones told Shaw that England was his mother and that Shaw had kicked her deathbed, and went on to publish an open letter to G.B.S. that alleged new parentage for Shaw:

The Hag Sedition was your mother and Perversity begot you. Mischief was your midwife and Misrule your nurse, and Unreason brought you up at her feet—no other ancestry and rearing had you, you freakish homunculus, germinated outside of lawful procreation.[10]

The Prime Minister said privately that Shaw should be shot, J. C. Squire more publicly recommended that he be tarred and feathered,* and a cartoon appeared showing Shaw as a mixed breed of Irish terrier and a German dachshund, decorated with an Iron Cross. R. B. Cunninghame Graham, a friend who had fought with the police in Trafalgar Square on "Bloody Sunday" in 1887 while Shaw prudently exited, declared in the *Daily News* that Shaw's indictment of "his hereditary enemy, England" would all be in vain, but warned, "Those who fire paper bullets aim at the annihilation of the soul. . . . Literature is a nice thing in its way. It both passes and gives us many weary hours. It has its place. But I submit that at present it is mere dancing on a tight rope. Whether the war could have been avoided or not is without interest today." Yet he confessed, "We, perhaps by accident, have been forced into the right course. . . ."

The criticism Shaw most respected came from Arnold Bennett a few days after the supplement appeared, yet he erred by treating it with a disdainful flippancy it did not deserve at a time when he should have welcomed the reason and restraint he claimed his *Common Sense* sought. Privately, Bennett explained his reactions to his agent, J. B. Pinker:

I shall be sending you tomorrow a copy of an article dealing drastically with the bad parts of Shaw's manifesto on the war, published yesterday. About two-thirds of Shaw's statement is strictly first-class, and indeed quite unequalled. Most of the rest is absurd, and may do some harm. I should therefore particularly like my article to appear in some newspaper in the United States, preferably New York, whether I am paid for it or not. It will appear in the *Daily News* on Thursday. If the *New York Times* can cable over other things of mine, I do not see why their London representative should not cable this article, especially as Shaw's article appeared in the *New York Times*.[11]

* Not-so-publicly, Squire agreed with much of what Shaw said, especially about wartime religious hypocrisy, about which he composed an irreverent quatrain:

God heard the embattled nations shout,
Gott straffe England and God save the king,
God this, God that, and God the other thing,
Good God, said God, I've got my work cut out.

Pinker arranged for Bennett's article to appear in the *New York Times* on the eighteenth.

One of *Common Sense*'s greatest values, Bennett wrote, "is courage, for in it Mr. Shaw says things that no one else has been able to say . . . [and] perhaps inaugurates a new and healthier period of discussion. . . . On such subjects as recruiting, the treatment of soldiers' and sailors' dependents, secret diplomacy, militarism, Junkerism, the Church, Russia, peace terms and disarmament it contains the most magnificent, brilliant, and convincing commonsense that could possibly be uttered." Had Bennett stopped there the outcome would have been different, but he went on to observe that G.B.S. on the causes of the war, on Grey, and on Belgium was flippant and perverse as well as historically inexact—so much so "as to amount to a scandal. . . . The present is no hour for . . . disingenuous, dialectical bravura. . . ." Shaw, he concluded, should rewrite the weak sections and thus strengthen his argument. Responding to Bennett the next day in a letter to the editor, Shaw wrote that it was "just like an Englishman" to uphold Asquith and Grey, and defending himself against charges that he accused the government of diplomatic sharp practice, he insisted that there was "more muddle than Machiavelli" in British prewar policy, and that Bennett, by accepting the official position, was actually stating the German case effectively enough to win an Iron Cross. Not he, but Bennett, was contradictory and muddleheaded in calling Germany a burglar when the need was "to bring a whole continent of war-struck lunatics to reason." But he saw no chance of doing so unless such reasonable men as Arnold Bennett "reserve his fine old Staffordshire loathing for my intellectual nimbleness until the war is over." But Shaw in some cases *had* substituted intellectual nimbleness for facts, not having all the resources for research he needed in the relative isolation he had sought in Torquay.*

---

* Despite Bennett's reservations, he was apparently pleased to receive a suggestion from international law expert Mark Judge (and endorsed "by G.B.S. himself," Bennett noted in his *Journals*) that he edit Shaw's manifesto for volume publication. Nothing came of the proposal, but Shaw did authorize an *NS* reprinting early in 1915.

Writing back to Bennett, Pinker noted that he had run into Henry James and had asked him whether he had read Shaw's manifesto. Like Shaw an alien long resident in England, James was unlike the Irishman in his increasing passion for the adopted country, a devotion easier to come by since the United States, unlike Ireland, was not still occupied by English troops, and James in 1915 (with Pinker as one of his sponsors and Asquith as another) would seal his sympathies in the war with England by becoming a British citizen. In addition James had just been talking with someone recently returned from Belgium with graphic descriptions of the devastation, and his emotions were at a high pitch. "I have it here," he cried to Pinker, shaking a copy of *Common Sense*, "and have made several attempts, but his horrible flippancy revolts me. To think of a man deliberately descending into the arena at the present crisis and playing the clown!"[12]

Reaction to *Common Sense* ranged from "the most honest, wittiest, and most serious pronouncement on the war yet made by anyone of distinction" to "a striking illustration of the extent to which a usually clear-headed man's judgment may be warped by prejudice." Most succinct was the *Westminster Gazette*, which editorialized vehemently about "Bernhardi Shaw." In the *Weekly Dispatch*, Robert Blatchford was more vituperative, asking why the censors "didn't stop Shaw," who was "a bumptious Merry-Andrew, hungry for more notoriety," and demanding that Parliament take up the matter. A few days later, Rowland Hunt, an M.P. from Ludlow in Shropshire, asked the Solicitor-General in Commons whether Shaw's pamphlet had been passed by the censor, and if so, why had the censor permitted it to be published in its present form. The official confessed to not having seen it or read it and pointed out that it had not been submitted to the censor. "Is the honorable gentleman aware," Hunt went on, "that the statements in this pamphlet are not only false, but very injurious to this country? [Cheers] Are we to understand that those of the Bernard Shaw type can publish anything they like, however detrimental to this country?" The Speaker intervened at that point, but the question was indicative of how beleaguered Shaw had already become within a fortnight of publication of *Common Sense*. Others, like

Bertrand Russell, had been saying much the same thing, but none were, like Shaw, a household word, a name whose every utterance commanded scarce newsprint.

Whether or not the matter of G.B.S. was responsible, a week after the question in Commons the government under its wartime powers issued an Order in Council:

No person shall by word of mouth or in writing, or in any newspaper, periodical, book, circular or other printed publication, spread false reports or make false statements or reports or statements likely to cause disaffection to his Majesty or to interfere with the success of his Majesty's forces by land or sea, or prejudice his Majesty's relations with foreign powers, or spread reports or make statements likely to prejudice the recruiting, training, discipline or administration of his Majesty's forces.

On its front page the *Daily Express* printed the new regulation under the heading, "Will Mr. Keir Hardie Please Note, Also Mr. Bernard Shaw." Hardie* (1856–1915), a veteran Labour M.P. from a Welsh mining constituency and one of the few who outspokenly opposed the war, had written to Shaw after the publication of *Common Sense* in terms, Shaw said afterward, "that, in their generosity, cordiality, and intimacy, went so far beyond anything that had occurred in our previous relations (always quite friendly) that I put off answering his letter until I could find time to do so adequately. He died before I carried out my intention."[13]

While Blatchford had been demanding a Parliamentary inquiry into Shaw's unpatriotic position, minor author George Sturt confided a more thoughtful but no less negative view to his diary:

22 November. . . . Shaw's pamphlet, "Common Sense about the War" ultimately unpalatable. The manner adopted by the author is offensive and the opinions expressed are not the result of any new perceptions. . . .

* To an English friend former President Theodore Roosevelt wrote sympathetically, "Of course you have some creatures who represent types with which we over here are only too familiar—the unhung traitor Keir Hardie, the blue-rumped ape Bernard Shaw, and the assemblage of clever and venomous but essentially foolish and physically timid creatures of the type of the editors of the *Nation*" (September 4, 1914, in *Letters*, vol. 8).

He has made up his mind long ago what he would think, and no change of circumstance is permitted any longer to alter his fixed view. He has taken an attitude, once for all. He has to live up to his past, though the sky fall. And thus, though his opinions are so egregious, he is a pedant, narrow-minded and incorrigible as the worst. In making up his mind what to say, not whether it is true is the chief consideration, but whether it is appropriate to the part of G.B.S.

And so he stands conspicuous as an example of what I take the Germans to mean by "Kultur". As in that nation of pedants, so with Shaw: the spontaneous movements of the individual life are subdued to a rule. He lives by a ready-made principle. Nothing can touch him, through his armour of morality. He is "Kultured"—to a system of his own perhaps, but still to a system. It is the vice of the Pharisees: and that is what Shaw must be reckoned spite of all his disguises: a Pharisee, a Pedant. Pretending to care for freedom of thought, he will not allow thought to stray aside from the narrow track he laid down for it five and twenty years ago. It must not explore any new fields of emotion, nor may any new experiences of the man's own inner nature be subjected to its analysis: but everything must be made to yield the old results. . . . The "New Statesman" claims forbearance towards the pamphlet because Shaw is an "artist": but this is precisely what he is not in this case. The true essayists give us "the life that glowed in their own perceptions": but Shaw does not do this. His understanding of the English woefully inadequate, too. . . .[14]

Although private confidences added little to the harassment of Shaw, those attacks that dismissed him as a publicity seeking clown hurt the most, for what he wanted most was to be taken seriously, and terms like "transparent buffoonery" applied to him by the London *Outlook* contributed to the damage. *Punch*, with an anonymous set of verses, was even more devastating, but at least one could reflect that the magazine's specialty was satire:

> To Mr. Bernard Jaw.
> ILLUSTRIOUS Jester, who in happier days
> Amused us with your Prefaces and Plays,
> Acquiring a precarious renown
> By turning laws and morals upside down,

Sticking perpetual pins in Mrs. Grundy,
Railing at marriage or the British Sunday,
And lavishing your acid ridicule
On the foundations of imperial rule;—
'Twas well enough in normal times to sit
And watch the workings of your wayward wit,
But in these bitter days of storm and stress,
When souls are shown in all their nakedness,
Your devastating egotism stands out
Denuded of the last remaining clout.
You own our cause is just, yet can't refrain
From libelling those who made its justice plain;
You chide the Prussian Junkers, yet proclaim
Our statesmen beat them at their own vile game.
Thus, bent on getting back at any cost
Into the limelight you have lately lost,
And, high above war's trumpets loudly blown
On land and sea, eager to sound your own,
We find you faithful to your ancient plan
Of disagreeing with the average man,
And all because you think yourself undone
Unless in a minority of one.
Vain to the core, thus in the nation's need
You carp and cavil while your brothers bleed,
And while on England vitriol you bestow
You offer balsam to her deadliest foe.[15]

By this time the proprietors of the *Daily Telegraph* had had enough and sent for Hall Caine on the evening of the twenty-seventh to inform him that Shaw's *Common Sense* was "shocking," "disgraceful," and "a pack of damnable falsehoods," and that they could not permit a contribution by G.B.S. to go into their *King Albert's Book*. If he insisted on keeping it, Caine was told, the book would never appear. "Always chivalrous in his sense of personal obligation," Shaw wrote of Caine, "[he] declared that he owed it to me to resign the editorship; but I dissuaded him, pointing out that nothing mattered at the moment but getting the money for the Belgians. . . ." Even here, however, Shaw privately had mixed feelings, especially about the Belgian refugees in England, for "those of us who kept our heads saw that the support of the refugees could not be left to private hospitality; and a prodigious begging on their behalf [had] set in, stimulated by the stories of the atrocities which the refugees brought, and which they soon had to supplement liberally from their own imagination, so great was the demand for them." Near Shaw's home in Hertfordshire, a young Belgian soldier convalescing from a wound described graphically "how a beautiful woman, with her hands chopped off at the wrists, had held up the bleeding stumps and said 'Avenge me, brother.' He assumed the rank of Count, and was made much of at shooting parties in the country before returning to his native land to resume his normal career as a tailor's cutter."* As a result Shaw's rhetoric in Belgium's cause remained free from sentimentality; nevertheless, Caine, whose point of view was a good deal closer to the *Daily Telegraph*'s than to Shaw's, believed that there was always room for serious and sincere criticism, even in wartime, and he knew the *Telegraph* had no quarrel with Shaw's *King Albert's Book* contribution but rather with Shaw's conspicuous "Now step I forth to whip hypocrisy" stance. Caine stayed with the charity book and saw it through, Shaw taking comfort in his realization that "The Daily Telegraph of that day, being under its old traditional management as a bourgeois paper, [was] obliged, as such, to keep twenty years behind the times in domestic politics whilst being otherwise breezily up to date. . . ."

For Caine the war remained a professional catastrophe for which the *King Albert's Book* frustrations were only a preliminary. Throughout the war he worked on other volunteer projects, writing Shaw two years later, "I have earned practically nothing since the beginning of the war (having given my services to the country) but I have just paid £3000 Income Tax on lump sums received for cinema rights in works done long ago."[16]

The last laugh in the *Telegraph* matter was Shaw's, for a few weeks afterward he received a letter from the Commission for Relief in Belgium:

* In peacetime he may have been a tailor's cutter, but in actuality the Belgian in question was ordered back to the front in early December 1914.

The Belgian Minister in London, Count de Lalaing, has specially authorised me to write and ask if you could find it in your heart to help the Commission for Relief in Belgium by means of your powerful pen? Seven million Belgians, still in their own country, must be fed, and some £800,000 to £1,000,000 per month will be required to do this. Most of the food and much of the money must come from America, as no more foodstuffs will be allowed to be exported from England. His Excellency the Belgian Minister, and those other Excellencies who constitute this neutral Commission are of opinion that no lever of help could be more powerful than an article signed by you setting out the predicament and the claims upon humanity of unfortunate Belgium. They quite realise that they are asking you to contribute in kind more than many have given in substance.

The suggested article would be distributed free and broadcast through the Press of America and other countries. If you require data I should be glad to send particulars of the famine which now threatens Belgium, or, as the Commission have entrusted me with this important request, to call and see you at your convenience to supply any available facts emphasizing the duty of neutral and other nations towards the afflicted people in Belgium.

The Commission ask me to say that they earnestly hope you will help them.[17]

Shaw assumed that the reason he had been approached was the wide press coverage of his open letter to President Wilson about Belgium, which apparently made the Belgians happy not only by the large stir it created around the world, but because Shaw separated Belgium's case—that of a forcibly and reluctantly involved neutral—from that of the Allies. There seemed to be no question but that Wilson had seen it as well as the much more detailed *Common Sense*, which made some parallel points. Other than the immense publicity it received, another reason was Wilson's brother-in-law, Stockton Axson, a professor of English at Rice Institute, who shortly afterward gave a lecture on Shaw in Philadelphia. He had stopped there overnight en route to Washington with Henry Van Dyke, U.S. Minister to the Netherlands, who was en route to confer with Wilson on the situation abroad. Shaw was too much the dramatist to be partisan, said Axson, praising his coolness. "Some of my German friends were very happy when the first [*New York Times*] article appeared . . . I haven't seen any of them since the publication of the third, but if they got any joy out of that, they find their happiness in an odd way." The playwright was neither pro-German nor anti-English, he explained: "Shaw is often ten minutes ahead of the truth, which is almost as fatal as being behind time." It was a perspective that had its drawback. The *New York Sun* editorialized:

> Mr. Shaw's position is not admirable when he chooses their days of tribulation for sticking pins into his own people, even though some of the things he says may be unpleasantly true. But it cannot be denied that he has some sane views on the situation. The pity is that he must always impair the force of the useful things he has to say by flippancies, impertinences, and out-of-place girdings at those whose courage he should help to maintain. He reminds one of a man who insists on wrangling over the mistaken construction of a chimney while the house is burning down.

By the end of November, Shaw saw himself embattled on all fronts, not only by his usual adversaries, but by people whose causes he had made his own for years. Seeing the war as an avenue to place women in tasks closed to them in peace, with the vote a logical outcome, suffragette leaders had quickly decided to support the government. Emerging from hiding, Christabel Pankhurst came back to London to address a public meeting on the "German Peril," and used the opportunity to turn on G.B.S. for "perversity and contrariety" and for "jests empty of the kernel of good sense." Her mother, Mrs. Emmeline Pankhurst, the stubborn old vixen of suffragism, added her appeals to young men to join the army in spite of Bernard Shaw and insinuated that Shaw was a Nero fiddling while his Rome burned. Skeptics wondered whether the Pankhursts were more interested in defense of King and Country or in killing off a substantial segment of the male population in England, but G.B.S. kept his silence.

Smarting under the attacks that he was pro-German, but unwilling to declare himself as pro-Asquith and Lloyd George, Shaw tried to clarify his position by way of Ireland. Telegraphing to George Russell (the poet "AE") in Dublin, he inquired what the best Irish publication would be to print a letter of his urging Irish support of France and decrying the "silly pro-German slosh" by which some Irish papers were mischievously getting back at England. Russell suggested the *Freeman's Journal*, the organ of the Irish Nationalist Party, and within five days a letter from Shaw appeared there that denounced pro-Germanism as a betrayal of Ireland's "old comrades, the French, for the sake of Prussia." (Pointedly Shaw excluded England.) An editor's note following the letter took the steam out of Shaw's message by insisting that all it demonstrated was an astonishing ignorance of the real state of things in Ireland, that pro-German sentiment was puny and not indicative of the swelling pro-Allied mood in Ireland.[18]

Before his piece had appeared, Shaw received from County Kerry a letter from Mabel McConnell, a former secretary of his now married to a young Irish revolutionary, Desmond Fitzgerald. His *Common Sense* pamphlet was a fine piece of work, she began, but its main impact upon her was that it made her "wish more than ever that you would stop bothering about such a childish and vacuous people as the English and come right over here to work . . . as Roger Casement is doing to make Ireland a Nation before Europe." Since Sir Roger had been attempting to get Germany and her allies to recognize Ireland, this was a subject Shaw had to handle gingerly. He had been "on the point of mentioning" publicly, he answered, that Casement "was perfectly in order in exercising our inalienable right as a nation to consult any other nation as to our future or present or past relations; but I didn't quite know what his credentials were; and in this war emergency I did not want to start more hares than I could help." As for devoting himself to his native land, Shaw was skeptical that it would appreciate his services. "The place is too small for me. The earth and all the fullness thereof are good enough for me. . . . Ireland must have an ambassador in the great world; so I am better as I am. You may possibly remember also that I am an elderly gentleman of 58½, and that my bolt is shot."[19]

Far from accepting Shaw's shrinking from revolutionary responsibilities as final, Mabel insisted that the *Freeman* failed to represent the true feeling of the country, which was pro-German, that Sir Roger was a true Irish knight "of the old times," and that she fully intended to subvert Shaw's allegiance. In vain Shaw insisted that it was in Ireland's best interests not to become another Belgium for Germany, much less an invited one, and that Ireland would cut her own throat by succumbing in war to her hatred of England. "I want to rub your eyes for you and waken you up," he told her with friendly bluntness. "The day of small nations is past. . . . Only as a member of a great commonwealth is there any future for us. We are a wretched little clod, broken off a bigger clod, broken off the west end of Europe. . . ." Ireland had to be, he thought, "a very highly civilized people or nothing," and that meant making the most of its ties with larger countries and the language that put them into communication with a fifth of the human race. If nationalism and freedom meant shrinking Ireland into "a little village community" with a language "that nobody in the world speaks," he wanted no part of it.[20]

That Shaw may have been right on Ireland and the war, and both the *Freeman* and Mabel Fitzgerald in their contrary ways pious but wrong made no difference: privately as well as publicly, his attempts to find ground on which supporters of his point of view could stand had again failed.

Trying again, Shaw produced a highly ironic piece of rhetoric in which he only *appeared* to Clifford Sharp to have shifted his position; actually he remained consistent with *Common Sense*. It was "a model," Shaw said, "of the way to rally Old England in the interests of New England: a model which delighted the Jingo in him, though he could not work up to it. . . ." The article was "The Last Spring of the Old Lion," that appeared, signed, in the *NS* on December 12. It was a stirring tale of the old British lion who for centuries "held to his one idea, that none shall be greater than England on the land, and none as great on the sea," but who in recent generations only "lay and basked and smelt no foe that a pat of his paw could not dispose of." But the distant strains of *"Deutschland, Deutschland über Alles"* stirred him in time to respond, "Never that whilst I live," and when the lion's sovereignty of the sea seemed about to be challenged, "That was the end. From that moment it was only a question of when to spring. For a lion with that one idea at heart, with that necessity deep in his very bowels, must be crafty: must win at all hazards, no matter how long he crouches before that right moment comes." But each German provocation is somehow balked and Germany vaguely humiliated, and the lion decides that Germany will not make the overt move necessary to initiate its own final frustration unless it can be persuaded "that the lion is sentimentally attached to her, and thus becoming a bit of a Pacifist and will not fight."

The formula works. "And the lion crouched. Almost before he was ready, the devil's own luck struck down the Archduke by the hand of an assassin, and Austria saw Servia in her grasp at last. She flew at Servia; Russia flew at Austria; Germany flew at France; and the lion, with a mighty roar, sprang at last, and, in a flash, had his teeth and claws in the rival of England, and will now not let her go for all the Pacifists or Socialists in the world until he is either killed or back on his Waterloo pedestal again." Thus the roar of the lion was not "the bleat of a peaceful sheep attacked by a wicked wolf," and

all sorts of chords in me echo the demand that the lion's last fight shall be the best fight of all, and Germany the last foe overcome. But I am a Socialist, and know well that the lion's day is gone by, and that the bravest lion gets shot in the long run. I foresee that his victory will not, like the old victories, lead to a century of security: I know that it will create a situation more dangerous than the situation of six months ago, and that only by each western nation giving up every dream of supremacy can that situation be mastered. A lion within frontiers is, after all, a lion in a cage; and the future has no use for caged lions fighting to defend their own chains. In future we must fight, not alone for England, but for the welfare of the world. But for all that, the lion is a noble old beast; and his past is a splendid past and his breed more valiant than ever: too valiant nowadays, indeed, to be merely English *contra mundum*. I take off my hat to him as he makes his last spring, and shall not cease to wave it because of the squealing of the terrified chickens.

Shaw was wrong: the dream of supremacy still flickered; however, there was more muddle than craft in the tiring beast. Shaw was recording what would prove to be only the next-to-last spring of the old lion.

While the war against Bernard Shaw raged in England, Shaw went on delivering his half-dozen Wednesday evening Fabian lectures. The crowds were large and the press coverage small, but a young woman journalist who wrote under the Ibsenite name of Rebecca West was at the fifth lecture. Wryly she noted that the audience had been a typical theatre audience, not the cheerless few who made a habit of attending dry lectures on economics. There were young people, and gay dresses, and dating couples, and the explanation lay in the lecturer, for "one of the most hopeful and moving things about modern life is the way that, once the public has been fascinated by the imaginative work of a writer, it immediately consults him concerning the saving of its soul and the State." It had disastrous consequences upon the writer, tempting him (as it had in peacetime, she thought, with John Galsworthy) to desert his real medium for a transient utility; for this reason she observed the cluster of prominent Fabians on the platform with hostility, for whatever their "cheerful worthiness" they were guilty of diverting G.B.S. from his true work, "for genius is not an essence to be used to flavor the common stuff, but a brew of humanity whose virtue lies in its strength and disappears with dilution."

When Shaw came onto the platform she

perceived more plainly than ever before that his genius is peculiarly unfitted to support the companionship of the lesser. The passing of middle age has wiped the aggressive strangeness from his face, by mitigating with silver the redness of his hair and the pirate twist of his eyebrows, and has revealed a predominant quality of noble and unhysteric sensitiveness. In the public life there is not time for such sensitiveness . . . and hence we have had those endless dogmatisings on science and politics which tumble out of his mind like a cartload of bricks in response to questions which he should never have been asked, and which he should have been too busy with his own work to answer. And when he began to speak, and the Irish accent shivered over his musical voice like the wind over a lake, one perceived another reason why he should not enter into politics.

The other reason to Miss West was not Shaw's Irish wit but the Swiftian mockery that had led him into such habits of controversy that he questioned the war rather than inspired its prosecution "like a Shelley." It was this that had drawn Shaw, she thought, into public affairs. Shaw, however, was extending further the ideas that had inspired his plays and their prefaces, as in the interjection that later drew the largest applause of the evening: "What I mean by a gentleman is a man who leaves his country in his debt when he dies."[21]

Although Shaw resisted turning away from his announced subjects to make the series a forum on the war, he was willing to go off on other tangents, as when young playwright St. John Ervine introduced him at that fifth lecture by confiding that he sometimes passed on to G.B.S. ideas for plays that he was unable to write himself, one of them a play about God. "The suggestion that I write a play about God," Shaw responded as he began, "is one that I rather resent, because I have never written a play on any other subject; and as a matter of fact that is the subject of these lectures, as you will find when I get to the end of them."

Why he had left the theatre for the lecture hall was too complex a question for the London stage in wartime to answer, and Rebecca West, for all her lack of sympathy with the G.B.S. stand on the war, understood. "Pure art, soaring out of space and time, is the divinest thing that man can make, but unfortunately in these days of clashing events it can only be carried on by the deaf. And the artist who, like Mr. Shaw, abandons it, at least shows that he has good hearing and is listening to the world."*[22]

On December 2 the series came to an end with Beatrice Webb in the chair to introduce G.B.S., in place of another young Fabian economist, G. D. H. Cole, who was unable to attend. It was the opportunity for a gracious bow in Beatrice's direction.

---

* G. K. Chesterton understood the humane vision that articulated what Shaw wrote and did, writing several years before the war added another dimension to Shaw's activities: "Here was a man who could have enjoyed art among the artists, who could have been the wittiest of the flaneurs; who could have made epigrams like diamonds and drunk music like wine. He has instead labored in a mill of statistics and crammed his mind with all the most dreary and the most filthy details, so that he can argue on the spur of the moment about sewing-machines or sewage, about typhus fever or twopenny tubes. . . ."

I should imagine that if you were to go into the society of the rich, into the society, in fact, into which Mrs. Webb was born, and if you were to ask the ladies who there pass what I suppose they find a pleasant existence discussing with the gilded youth of this country, and with the most distinguished politicians, pleasant affairs in pleasant rooms in a pleasant manner—the sort of fate to which Mrs. Webb was condemned by birth, by the way—if you were to ask them what was the most intolerable, most horribly repulsive, most uninviting sort of fate to which a human being could be condemned, I suppose they would say: Discussing with a number of old-fashioned trade-union secretaries, each of them smoking and most of them drinking, the history of sordid trades and sordid conditions, or going into a sweater's den in the East End and, in order to investigate the conditions there, practically accepting the position of a sweated woman and struggling for a livelihood in that way. Well, curiously enough, Mrs. Webb took to investigation as other women take to drink. It was Mrs. Webb's vocation: she has a genius for it, which certainly within my knowledge is not paralleled in the case of any other individual. And having entered on that career, Mrs. Webb, who was then Miss Potter, did a very sensible thing—she looked round for a husband who had the sort of genius that she wanted, and, discovering that in Mr. Sidney Webb, she married him. I have always felt a little sore because Beatrice Webb passed me over on that occasion: I believe I should have done it just as well as my friend Webb. But ever since it has been my business to get up on platforms and display an enormous mass of information and a command of facts which I owe altogether to Mrs. Webb, but which my audience has generally imagined to have proceeded from my own profound study.[23]

Through the happenstance of an absent chairman, Shaw had extemporized the germ of what would be his play *The Millionairess*, although it would be some time* until he would actually begin work on it. Like Beatrice, the Epifania Ognisanti di Parerga of his play is a "born boss," a wealthy woman who leaves her money behind her and finds a job in an East End sweater's den, but, hard-driving and talented, soon acquires control of the business and reorganizes it. Like Beatrice, she looks round for a husband who has the sort of genius she wants and marries him.

* The play was not begun until 1931. It was produced in 1935 and has since had its greatest success with Katherine Hepburn in the title role.

The incentive to work, or lack of it, profoundly disturbed Shaw, who saw in its weakening in England the seeds of self-destruction. "I believe there will always be people who will humbug you, who have a natural aptitude for being beggars," he told his concluding Kingsway audience. "But there is always the remedy at hand. . . . You know my old proposal. Every citizen should come up before a board of citizens, some tribunal, and be requested to justify his existence, say, for the last two years, and if he cannot justify it put him in a lethal chamber. I think if something of the kind were done, even if the penalty were not carried out, it would create a sense of responsibility which is altogether absent in our existing society."* Ironically the welfare state Shaw sought to bring into existence was only multiplying the problem by further diminishing incentives to work, and Shaw's drastic solution was only a dramatic way of calling attention to it—a twentieth-century restatement of Aristotle's aphorism about the unexamined life not being worth living.

The suggestion, when taken literally by his audience, proved outrageous, but just about everything Shaw said or did in the waning weeks of 1914 was interpreted with horror, and Shaw sometimes reacted by flinging out even more outrageous ideas, such as defending Germany's treaty-breaking seizure of Belgium as an understandable attempt to break from an encirclement that could have been suicidal. Nevertheless, confusing both his friends and his enemies, he also attacked Prussian militarism and advanced it as sufficient cause for working toward Germany's defeat. H. G. Wells responded by calling him muddleheaded, and Shaw objected in a mock-facetious letter in the *Daily Chronicle* that, despite its tone, exposed how embattled he felt: "There is a point at which Mr. Wells' mind gives way," he wrote.

---

* Again this provides the germ of a later play, *The Simpleton of the Unexpected Isles* (1934), in which an angel appears in the Unexpected Isles to announce the Day of Judgment. "The lives which have no use, no meaning, no purpose, will fade out," he declares. "You will have to justify your existence or perish." Every day, Shaw says in his preface to the play, "is a day of judgment; and its recognition as such is not the end of all things but the beginning of a real civilization." It was the message, Shaw pointed out, of Ibsen's Button Moulder, who asks Peer Gynt, "What does it matter if you disappear?"

"There are two symptoms. One of them is the now familiar and apparently inevitable English symptom of this kind of breakdown; a sudden and unprovoked attack on me. Mr. Wells, without a word of warning, calls me muddle-headed. Muddle-headed! Me! Bernard Shaw! the man whose clarity England can often hardly bear! I ask you—! Well no matter. . . ."[24]

Too exasperated to let Shaw have the last word, Wells fired off a rejoinder to the *Chronicle* that summed up a decade of ill-concealed ill feeling on his side of the stormy friendship:

Mr. Shaw objects to my calling him muddleheaded. But I have always considered him muddleheaded. If I have not called him that in public before, it is simply because I thought the thing too obvious to need pointing out.

If we see a man making an ass of himself, we indolent English accept him rather than face the boring task of pursuing him into the recesses of his unsoundness. We hump our backs. If we believe a man is systematically propagating some specific error we may take the trouble to study and combat him, but if we perceive that he is flinging himself about in a paroxysm of merely personal activity we leave him alone, or if we notice him, we notice him as we fling a hairbrush at a nocturnal cat, because the irritation has become intolerable.

And that is how things stand between Mr. Shaw and myself. I have been quite exceptionally disposed to take him seriously, and find out what he amounts to, and this is what I find he amounts to. He is an activity, a restless passion for attention. Behind that is a kind of jackdaw's hoard of other people's notions; much from Samuel Butler, scraps of pseudo-philosophical phraseology such as that "Life Force" phrase he got from Dr. Guest, old Hammersmith economics, worn fragments of Herbert Spencer, some Nietzsche, conveyed no doubt from the convenient handbook of Mr. Orage, shreds of theosophy, current superstitions, as for example his idea that fear "poisons" meat, or that wool is a more "natural" and hygienic clothing than cotton, sweepings of all sorts of "advanced" rubbish, but nothing anywhere of which one can say "Here is the thought of a man." And it is just this incoherent emptiness, combined with an amazing knack of fluent inexactitude which gives him his advantage in irresponsible attack, and which from his early repute as the Terror of the Fabian

Society has spread his vague and unsubstantial fame about the globe far beyond the range to which even his confusedly entertaining intellectual forces would have taken it.

Mr. Shaw is one of those perpetual children who live in a dream of make-believe, and the make-believe of Mr. Shaw is that he is a person of incredible wisdom and subtlety running the world. He is an elderly adolescent still at play. To understand that is to have the clue to all Shavianism.

It is almost as if there was nothing happening in Flanders. It is almost as if there was no pain in all the world. It is under the inspiration of such delightful dreams that Mr. Shaw now flings himself upon his typewriter and rattles out his broadsides. And nothing will stop him. All through the war we shall have this Shavian accompaniment going on, like an idiot child screaming in a hospital, distorting, discrediting, confusing. . . . He is at present . . . an almost unendurable nuisance.[25]

This was Wells at the height of his pro-war fervor attacking Shaw at the extremity of his antiwar feeling. Theirs was always a wary friendship, but one of the ironies of the months to come would be their drawing close together. Shaw made it easier, as on this occasion, recalling, "He filled a couple of columns of the *Daily Chronicle* . . . with abuse of me in terms that would have justified me in punching his head: but when we met [the] next day at a subcommittee of the Society of Authors our intercourse was as cordial as before: it never occurred to me that it could be otherwise, though he entered with obvious misgivings as to his reception, which at once gave way to our normally jolly friendliness."

As powerful and widely read as it was, Wells's attack was less damaging to Shaw than the half-truth being spread about London that German propagandists were happily distributing Shaw's war manifesto in neutral capitals. (Appropriately truncated versions of *Common Sense* could look pro-German, just as other selections could look pro-English.) The result was that Shaw was not free from attack even in the usually friendly Labour press, and almost every time he wrote a letter to an editor in his own defense, whether to a London or a provincial paper, it was published side by side with an editorial denouncing him. It took barely two weeks after *Common Sense* was released, in fact, for Shaw to feel compelled to write to the *Daily Citizen*, a Labour paper, about the large volume of his mail on the war, particularly some of the anonymous letters. "May I appeal to their authors," he asked, "to bear in mind in future that young ladies are now very largely employed as secretaries to public men, and that letters that are not suitable for their perusal should be marked 'Obscene' on the envelopes." One abusive letter accusing him of pro-Germanism amused him because it began with an illiterately Germanic misspelling: "You son of a bitsch. . . ." Almost alone among the faithful was Ellen Terry, who began a letter from America, "Dearest G.B.S. (who is splendid about the war). . . ."[26]

Shaw's correspondence reached such proportions by early December that he felt compelled to have a postcard printed to respond to at least one kind of mail he was getting, the kind supporting his position:

I have received so many letters upon Common Sense About the War that I have had to give up all hope of dealing with them separately. Even the very kind and entirely reassuring letters elicited by my protest in The Daily Citizen must go unanswered. Many branches of the Independent Labor Party and other Liberal and Socialist organizations have passed resolutions which have been of the timeliest service to me publicly, and which have given me sincere personal gratification. In the hope of being able to write a separate letter in every case I have deferred my acknowledgements until it has become plain that I must make them in this fashion or not at all. It is the best I can do; and I rely on the same kindness that prompted the letters and resolutions to accept my thanks in this indiscriminate but very earnest form.

G. Bernard Shaw

Also in Shaw's mail was news that brought the war closer to him than the skirmishes in the press. Although he and Charlotte were childless, actor Robert Loraine—a veteran of Shavian leading roles since his John Tanner in *Man and Superman*—had asked G.B.S. for permission to list the Shaws as next of kin when he joined the Royal Flying Corps. When he left for France, Charlotte, as befit a next of kin, made inquiries at London shops as to what was appropriate to send to officers in the field; salesmen suggested to her silver-mounted dressing cases, dispatch boxes, portable baths, roasting jacks, and armchairs. Then she asked men who had come home from the front, and they suggested bromo paper* instead, urging her to wrap it in a way that would disguise what it was so that it would not be stolen. To Shaw it was another nail in the coffin of war as romance.

Before long the Shaws were informed that Lieutenant Loraine, while an artillery observer, had been severely wounded by antiaircraft fire and was in a hospital in Lilliers. Once he was evacuated to England on December 11, Charlotte was dispatched by G.B.S. to the War Office (a short walk from Adelphi Terrace) to find out where he was. A sympathetic Horseguards colonel located his hospital, at 26 Park Lane, and the Shaws set out to see Loraine, but were informed that he was not well enough to see anybody. The only way G.B.S. could then fulfill his next-of-kin function was to write a spuriously cheery letter, which he did that weekend, confessing that he had been alarmed on hearing that Loraine had lost a lung "because one of my uncles lost a lung, and though he recovered all his previous robustness of habit, yet he died of it after lingering in this state for forty-seven years." What happened to Loraine, as Shaw described it to Stella after he had seen him, was that he had been shot "in the small of his back, the bullet coming out of his collar bone after going through his lung and knocking his heart into his left elbow."

Was there, Shaw asked, "anything you want that we can get you or send you, or anything that we can do that you want done [?]" Paradoxically he continued, "I hope, anyhow, that you are bad enough not to be allowed out again; for really you have done enough for honour, and there are plenty of fellows who will stop shrapnel quite as effectively as you and who are not useful to their country in other respects as you are." As for his own heroism, Shaw reported, "For my own part, I have been giving exhibitions of moral courage far surpassing anything achieved in the field; but so far I have not yet received the V.C.; in fact sarcastic suggestions that I should receive the iron one

* A fast-printing photographic paper, also called "bromide paper."

are not lacking. However, you will find the papers rather less sanctimonious than they were before I gave their show away. . . ."

Toward the end of the month, Loraine was allowed visitors, all of whom were warned to evidence no astonishment at seeing the once handsome leading man now shrunken to a white-bearded stranger in a wheelchair, down to eighty-nine pounds from his former one hundred eighty-two. On Christmas Day he was permitted a bath, and while being wheeled down a hallway for the great event caught sight of another patient in a similar conveyance, a shockingly gaunt specter. Turning to greet him, Loraine suddenly realized that for the first time since he had been wounded he was staring into a mirror. Quickly realizing what had happened, the nurse offered some consolation. "You'll be all right," she reminded him, "you've pulled through."[27]

At Christmas London shops were full, and Christmas trees were plentiful at Covent Garden. Stocks of food were high, and rationing not even in the planning stages. French wines still were being shipped across the Channel, and an advertisement appeared in the daily papers that "Thanks to the iron grip of the British and French Fleets on the High Seas, Perrier water is being shipped safely via Marseilles as usual. Beware of German waters—Apollinaris, Johannis, Canbrunnen and the like. . . ." At the Duke of York's, *Peter Pan* was in its eleventh year, and at the Hippodrome, *Hullo Tango!* was still running. Mark Sheridan's chorus opened, and one of its songs would become famous:

Here we are, here we are, here we are again!
There's Pat and Mac and Tommy and Jack and Joe.
When there's trouble brewing, when there's something doing
Are we downhearted? No!

In the West End, Shaw saw a revival of *The Flag Lieutenant* (a bad play of 1908 resuscitated because its title sounded box office), buying a ticket—he wrote Stella—because, "having a headache coming on, and feeling that I must sit down somewhere, I went into the Haymarket Theatre, where there happened to be a matinee."[28] On the streets people sang and whistled "Sister Susie's sewing shirts for soldiers," and at the Royalty Theatre, *The Man Who Stayed Home* (to run 584 performances) demonstrated to the girls who still distributed white feathers that beneath the tweed coat of a civilian there might possibly beat the gallant heart of a secret-service agent. To Robert Loraine, for whom a future in the theatre now seemed bleak, Shaw wrote that the London stage was in worse condition than Loraine, "but the profession keeps alive by giving performances for the relief of the Belgians; also by reciting patriotic odes at the [music] halls, the interest being kept up by announcements that the reciter is on 96 hours' leave from the trenches. By this means he often secures an engagement for a whole fortnight."[29] He remained unbowed, still offering to all comers the same brand of seemingly detached common sense, and it still sounded alarmingly like treason.

4

Shaw Embattled

"Do YOU never ask yourself what has become of my sonnets?" Shaw's query to Stella early in 1915[1] could have referred to the easy amorousness of their earlier correspondence, now turned (in his description) to "a scrap of newspaper." A darker significance lay in what the line suggested about Shaw's creative life. He had seldom been more active, or less involved as a playwright. *Common Sense* was being translated into Dutch, Spanish, and French, and although many news agents patriotically refused to carry it, sales of the supplement as a back number climbed toward seventy-five thousand. As heated as had been his exchanges with the Webbs over *Common Sense*, Shaw nevertheless had gone off over the New Year holiday for his traditional and recuperative ten days' walking and motoring with the Webbs. The predictable result, Beatrice noted in her diary, was ten days of "tempestuous and heated argument" over Shaw's ideas for settling the war and for bringing about equality in peace. "He has been firing off brilliant but ill-digested stuff at the newspapers and in lectures," she wrote. "Yet his aims are straight. . . . And his protest against the self-righteousness of British public opinion about the causes of the war is, in my humble opinion, justified. We were all three of us gloomy as to the results on the Socialist and Labour Movement. It rids us of the Rebels, Feminist and Guild Socialist. The danger is that the country may slip into a subtle form of reaction—lose faith in democracy and gain enjoyment from the mere display of Power. . . ."[2]

The holiday over, the Fabian Research Department, a committee beginning a study aimed at formulating Fabian policy on peace and the prevention of war, continued under Shaw's chairmanship as if he had no disagreements with the rest of the Fabian hierarchy. The idea had evolved from a gift of £100 to the society from Joseph Rowntree. A Fabian Executive Committee meeting on January 15 discussed how the money was to be spent, Beatrice Webb (to whom the check had been given) suggesting that a young member of the Research Department, who was a writer and former civil servant and interested in legal questions, be employed as secretary of a subcommittee to study the question and develop proposals. Shaw had no objection to that, and Leonard Woolf, who needed the money, took on the part-time job. (His wife, Virginia, had finished a novel before the war that was still unpublished, and under the nervous strain of the times her health had again broken down.)

A week later Shaw and the Webbs were at another meeting, this time a session of the *New Statesman* board, to hear Sharp predict a net loss for 1915 of about £1800, although *Common Sense* had caused sales to rise about a thousand copies a week. Pessimistically he predicted that he would keep only about £200 as a net gain, but after discussion the board agreed to carry on in the red for another year. Shaw put up an additional £500, Manchester businessman Ernest Simon £600, and the frugal Webbs £200, leaving Sharp to find the remaining £600 from the fifteen other (and smaller) shareholders in the company, or somehow manage to lose less money.

It was no strain for Shaw to help prop up the *Statesman*. He was writing nothing new for the theatre, but his box office receipts had never been higher than during the first year of *Pygmalion*. It seemed to be appearing on stages everywhere—in Swansea, Southampton, Reading, Norwich, and other provincial cities via Charles Macdona's company; Philadelphia, Pittsburgh, Cincinnati, Louisville, Indianapolis,

St. Louis, and Chicago via Mrs. Campbell's company; and on the Continent in Christiania (Oslo), Stockholm, Trondheim, Amsterdam, Copenhagen, Bologna, and Moscow. There were reports, which Shaw denied, that he was coming to America to oversee Granville-Barker's production of *Androcles and the Lion* in New York, and in New York the American Commission for Relief in Belgium reported receipt of a check from G.B.S. for $260, accompanied by a letter in which he observed that he could not decently ask people around the world to contribute to Belgian relief without setting an example himself.

Praise and blame were coming from strange quarters. Cecil Chesterton, who like his brother G.K. had hawkish views on the war, observed while in the United States that he agreed with Shaw that Britain would have come into the war on France's side whether or not there had been the provocation of Belgium; and on a personal note he confided the paradox that it was Shaw who had brought him to the Catholic Church in the 1890s: "He shook me up when I was a solid little Freethinker." Shaw also found himself lauded in the Berlin *Vorvarts*, which retracted its earlier attacks on him made when "he was suspected of being an English patriot." Now it understood from his criticism of England that he was "a man without a Fatherland," and to further prove the *Vorvarts'* point, it printed the text of the telegram Shaw had sent his German translator on the day the war began.* Belatedly it had just arrived in Vienna, where Siegfried Trebitsch had given it to the *Neue Freie Presse*. Ironically on the same day the Berlin editorial had appeared, Shaw had written another letter to Trebitsch, to be delivered circuitously via Switzerland. He was not pro-German, whatever the rumors were, Shaw said, and did not think the Germans would have any respect for him "if I did not play for my side now." Neither was he anti-German, he insisted: there were no nationalities anymore, only "men in a certain uniform who are trying to kill you."[3]

In London the first resignation from the Society of Authors in patriotic protest against member G.B.S.'s statements on the war brought appeals from the Society's executive committee that Shaw

* See p. 24.

coax the defecting member back into the fold lest he set a precedent for others. Shaw thereupon wrote to J. F. Muirhead, but in a less conciliatory tone than he might have had he not run into H. G. Wells, who—having private second thoughts about the war which were much more mixed than his public ones—immediately reestablished their old friendship, offered Shaw his "highest testimonials" about his courage, and promised to visit. To Muirhead Shaw deflated the knight errantry into which the English role in the war had been patriotically oversimplified. England, he observed, was no Lancelot-Galahad, nor was Germany the Wicked Giant holding the Beautiful Maiden (Belgium) in thrall. Shaw could hardly have more irritated the loyal Muirhead, who in a rebuttal referred politely to "the myopia of genius" that was capable of "the most extraordinary microscopic and telescopic powers" yet was at times "unable to see clearly the simple contours visible to every man of normal vision."[4]

As indelicate as he could be with individuals for whom he felt little more than scorn, Shaw could be the epitome of tact and consideration with others. His affection for Robert Loraine, as with Granville-Barker, was that of childless father for surrogate son, and with Loraine lying critically wounded in a hospital nearby, he hardly knew what he could do to help, even committing the ultimate sacrifice—for him— of listening without objection to Loraine's vivid and proud description of "how he dropped four monster bombs on a little town, two in the market place and one at each end of the main street."*

At the end of January, when Loraine was placed on rehabilitation leave with the recommendation that sea air would be good for his mending lung, he had a deck cabin booked for him on a ship sailing

---

* Shaw apparently turned this kind of perverse pride upside down in *Too True to Be Good* (1931), where Aubrey Bagot, a wartime pilot turned (in a postwar lapse into irrational behavior) into a burglar, recalls the first time he "dropped a bomb on a sleeping village. I cried all night after doing that. Later on I swooped into a street and sent machine gun bullets into a crowd of civilians: women, children and all. I was past crying by that time." Later he is awarded "a very poorly designed medal" for his exploits. (Other traits in Aubrey's background and character suggest that T. E. Lawrence, whom Shaw first met in 1922, may have also been involved in the characterization.)

for Buenos Aires. As soon as G.B.S. heard of it, he posted a note to Loraine: "Charlotte talks of your sea voyage as quite close at hand— a week or so hence. Have you any money? If not, can I be of any use?" A postscript followed: "I always make it a rule to inquire into a man's private affairs with extreme delicacy; but I think my meaning is clear."

Loraine needed comfort more than funds, in particular, some assurance that he would be able to return to useful service and that his time in the interim would not be wasted in lonely boredom. First he thought of studying Morse code so that he could be useful in air communications, for he worried that he would never again be able to pilot a plane. Then he thought of doing a book on military flying and asked Shaw for advice. Pages of it arrived, almost a treatise on how to write a book on a technical subject for the lay reader, and—for one who had never flown—a demonstration of remarkable intuition into the nuances of Loraine's Royal Flying Corps experience. "All this will be very interesting," he added, encouragingly, "and exactly what the public wants to know. It will also be technical in the way the reader likes things to be technical: that is, intelligibly technical. Technical terms madden people when they dont understand them; but when the meaning is clear they like them, because they can repeat them in private conversation with an air of knowing all about it." In addition to strategy and tactics, Shaw had other ideas, among them the including of "any theorising and generalising" that seemed safe to Loraine. For example, Shaw suggested, "Everybody wants to know whether we shall have in future to live under bomb-proof shelters by electric light and never see the sun, or else to give up war."

Shaw's detailed prospectus either frightened Loraine into abandoning the project or proved a substitute for it, for Loraine sunned himself on the *Alcantara*'s deck, fed himself back to near normal weight, cultivated a buoyant moustache to replace his beard, and practiced Morse code on both outward and return trips by relieving the wireless operator, on one occasion intercepting a cryptic message that led to the tracking down and sinking of a German submarine. By April he was fit to return to the front, and in the crowd of friends seeing him off at the railroad station the evening he left was Ellen Terry's younger brother Fred, who dashed up from the Strand Theatre, where he was playing Charles II, in his wig and costume, to shake Bob's hand and wish him God speed.[5] "There was never anyone, in my time," a young actress then remembered, "who could wear a square-cut coat and lace ruffles, a white wig and a rapier as could Fred Terry, with such grace and dash and virile magnificence. It was as if these were indeed the garments he put on every morning when he got out of bed; as if they were not costumes but clothes."[6] G.B.S., whose long memory stored up impressions for plays he would finally set down on paper a decade or even a generation later, may have remembered the scene when he wrote *In Good King Charles's Golden Days*, on the eve of yet another world war.

Before Loraine had left on his Atlantic crossing, Shaw had received a transatlantic cable from Max Eastman, editor of the radical *Masses*:

WILL YOU TAKE OVER APRIL OR MAY NUMBER OF THE MASSES MAGAZINE FILL ALL SPACE AS YOU WILL WITH STORIES EDITORIALS VERSE ARTICLES SUGGEST CARTOONS ANYTHING YOU CHOOSE UNCONDITIONAL FREEDOM OF EXPRESSION WILL ADVERTISE YOU AS EDITOR OF THAT ISSUE PROBABLE CIRCULATION TWO OR THREE HUNDRED THOUSAND FROM ATLANTIC TO PACIFIC COAST. . . .

Shaw answered that it was too large a task for him to undertake at the time, but Eastman, eager to catch G.B.S. as a guest editor at what appeared to be the peak of his notoriety* wrote again even before Shaw's answer arrived, repeating the earlier cable and adding

---

* For similar reasons Shaw was offered at the same time his choice of American lecture engagements, one agent offering £2000 for five lectures and £200 for each additional one, plus an additional third of the tour profits. Another offered fifteen lectures within twenty-five days at $1000 each, all expenses paid. There had been other proposals ever since *Common Sense* had appeared, but Shaw turned them all down.

IT WOULD BE THE MAKING OF OUR MAGAZINE IN THIS
COUNTRY AND SO DO A GREAT SERVICE TO SOCIALISM
AS WELL AS TO US ON THE OTHER HAND WE BELIEVE
IN YOUR POINT OF VIEW AND WE WANT TO PROPA-
GATE IT.[7]

Shaw remained unmoved. He was not interested in creating further divisions and contributed to the popular view of himself primarily through a *New Statesman* piece satirizing the superpatriotic
anti-Germanism of Cecil and Gilbert Chesterton, whose fury at the
enemy expressed itself "mostly in splendidly readable pen-pictures of
an absurdly fictitious conflict of Prussian paganism with a profound
and elementary Christianity and sanity in the French peasantry."
Since the historian Michelet had written of the "holy bayonet" and
the poet Peguy of the glory of war, since the London *Daily Mail*
had written in 1911, "Patriotism and militarism remain the dominant
characteristics of the French people," and Maurice Barrès observed
on the day the war began, "Finally the happy day is here," it was
only reasonable for Shaw to conclude that France, revenge-bent since
its defeat by Prussia in 1870, had not viewed the prospect of war with
alarm.

Whatever their disagreements on religion, economics, or war, Shaw
enjoyed living in the same world with the Chestertons and did not
find it inconsistent that while he attacked a Cecil Chesterton polemic on Prussianism in the *New Statesman*, he could at the same time
write a preface for the American edition of the book, praising the
"British shrewdness and humour [which] enable him to use his intellectual ingenuity to play the very exciting game of making the most
imposing cases of all sorts of quite desperate causes. . . ." For a time
Cecil had to preach for both brothers, for G.K. became seriously ill
in the summer of 1914, his bed eventually breaking down under
the constant strain of his leviathan bulk. Shaw offered financial help,
knowing how unbusinesslike both Chestertons were. "You won't hurt
me," he had written during the *Pygmalion* run, "as I have just now
an unnecessarily large . . . balance."[8] G.K.C. had to stop writing
altogether that November, and in January 1915, when he was so ill

that he ceased to recognize his wife, Frances, Shaw renewed his offer to help and kept his friend's name before the public in such pieces as "Chestertonism and the War."

Paradoxically, by Chestertonian standards, Shaw was equivalent to being an enemy alien, his views about his native Ireland and about the war with Germany making him an unrecognized symbol of sanity in a pair of islands dominated by extremists. On the other island at the same time, Mabel and Desmond Fitzgerald were still promoting pro-Germanism and Irish insurrection, and Shaw still tried vainly to turn them toward moderation. Before long they were expelled from Kerry by the British authorities and removed eastward to Wicklow. The unhappy revolutionaries appealed to Shaw, who wrote back unsympathetically that he wondered what else the Fitzgeralds expected the authorities to do, when in the midst of an appalling war they made it obvious, and from a western Irish coastal town, that they sought England's defeat and Germany's victory: "Surely not to leave you in the western coastguard station with all its possibilities of signalling to your friend the enemy?" Most of Ireland, he insisted, knew that there was no choice but "to see the English and French through this fight with Prussia . . . I had much rather you rallied to my banner. . . ."[9]

People in London, if one judged by what appeared in the press, had a different idea as to what Shaw's banner really represented, a situation emphasized by the revival at the Kingsway Theatre on February 13 of his satire *Fanny's First Play*. G.B.S. took great pains with it, supervising the casting and sitting in his usual spot in the dress circle at rehearsals to note where enunciation was imprecise, to sharpen stage business, and to check that props and costumes helped create the atmosphere he wanted. Although a minor work, *Fanny* held the record for longest run by a Shaw play (622 performances); but the new run was imperiled by veiled warnings in London papers that a true Britisher would neither produce, act in, nor go to a play by the author of *Common Sense about the War*. The *Times* headlined its review by Shaw's old friend and critic, A. B. Walkley, "Untimely Shaw Revival at the Kingsway," and Walkley began his notice with the observation, "It may seem to the judicious that the moment is not happily chosen for resuming the old Shavian capers, which were among the strangest by-products of the long peace. Fun of travestied facts and lopsided judgments then agreeably stimulated a languid world." Further, he noted, the play, especially the "irrelevant Induction" which prefaced it, was "intolerably tedious."

Walkley had been parodied (as Trotter) in the Induction to the play, which gave him another, and unspoken, reason to appeal to playgoers' sense of patriotism in staying away. Controversy, however, was often a sound business tactic, and the brief furor only helped the play do well initially at the box office. St. John Ervine fueled the issue too, answering a *Westminster Gazette* attack on G.B.S. by suggesting that Shaw's writings on the war were responsible replies to the emotional *Evening Tremblers* and *Morning Shudderers*. Interviewed on the matter, Shaw said that he had had the friendliest first-night audience he could recall and that "the reporters who were sent to see me torn limb from limb withdrew copyless." Tours of his plays in the provinces, meanwhile, were doing excellent business, Shaw drawing the moral from them that the British Empire had not reached the condition that would cause its collapse "at the first word of truth and common sense uttered within its frontiers. We are really not all fools, hypocrites and vituperative cads. . . ."

Across the Atlantic a George M. Cohan-Willie Collier revue, *Hello Broadway!*, in burlesquing the plays of the year, had lighthearted words for both *Pygmalion* and *Mrs. Warren's Profession*, belying the real mood of that part of the country. Patsy Pygmalion, the revue's flower girl, begged everyone to buy a rose from her because she needed the money badly: "I'm paying royalties to Bernard Shaw." Testing the undercurrents, however, Barker wrote to Shaw while playing with his wife Lillah in *Androcles* at Wallack's Theatre, that G.B.S. was no longer as loved as he had been. The old enemies were more vindictive than ever, and old friends had turned sour, even Elinor Robson Belmont, for whom Shaw had written *Major Barbara*. News from Germany, published both in London and New York, had not been helpful, for in mid-February "A Neutral Observer" reported from Berlin:

The Royal Theatre is continuing its Shakespearean productions, although most Germans seem to think that Mr. Bernard Shaw has succeeded in creating a far more satisfactory and truer portrait of the modern Englishman. Mr. Shaw's essay, published last November, was handed to me for perusal, and I learned later that it had been widely circulated by Germans as propaganda literature, for the purpose of bringing to the attention of neutrals, a "truthful and unbiased survey of England and the English."

Elsewhere it was reported that Shaw's plays, particularly *Candida* and *Pygmalion*, remained in Austrian and German repertoires, but these, and others with unflattering portraits of Englishmen, vanished once Shaw was belatedly declared an enemy alien.

Qualms about Shaw's loyalties even reached his tiny Hertfordshire village, many in Ayot St. Lawrence becoming convinced that he really was a German sympathizer because he kept a night light on in an upstairs window, the way someone known to be of German ancestry did in the neighboring village of Codicote. It was, neighbors thought, to light the way for German aircraft. Only after a sudden heavy snowfall in late January had Shaw shown himself with regularity in Ayot, working with other men in the village to saw up and remove trees downed by the storm and blocking the narrow roads. The activity—Shaw loved sawing wood as exercise, and did so into his nineties—brought him closer to the village folk and allayed their suspicions about his activities.

D. H. Lawrence's neighbors were even more suspicious of him, especially in Cornwall, where he had moved in despair after the prosecution and suppression of his novel *The Rainbow* later that year, ostensibly because it was obscene, but in large measure because it denounced the war, while critics generally as sane as the *NS*'s J. C. Squire suggested with the sincerity of the war-mad that Lawrence must have been "under the spell of German psychologists." If, from their tiny cottage at Tregethern (which might have been construed by the hysterical as overlooking the Atlantic shipping routes), Frieda hung out the washing or D. H. tarred the leaky chimney, suspicion strengthened that they were signaling German submarines. After all, why else would the aristocratic former Frieda von Richtofen—cousin to the enemy flying ace—be living in a five-pounds-a-year, two-room cottage, remote from London, with a red-bearded and penniless writer of questionable morals who talked and wrote openly against the war?

Nothing effective had been done to save *The Rainbow*, and the Lawrences themselves were saved from beggary only by such gifts as thirty pounds from Ottoline and Philip Morrell, twenty from Edward Marsh, and five from Bernard Shaw (who did not know him). Between attempts at a successor novel to the suppressed one, Lawrence busied himself with an unpublishable polemic he called *The Reality of Peace* and wrote despairingly to a friend in London, "When I see people in the distance . . . I want to crouch in the bushes and shoot them with invisible arrows of death. I think truly the only righteousness is the destruction of mankind, as in Sodom. Fire & brimstone should fall down."

In London journalists appeared to be working overtime to emphasize the need for concern about G.B.S.—the most visible public symbol of skepticism about the war—one writer producing a lamely humorous pamphlet titled *Commonsense about the Shaw*, dedicated

To
the memory of
the heroic dead
who have fought and died for us
whilst fools at home contend.

Using Shaw's words against him, Harold Owen quoted him to the effect that Belgian neutrality had become a figment when England had made secret arrangements for sending troops to her defense years before. It *was* sophistry on Shaw's part, even though the Germans found sufficient documentary evidence in government files when they took Brussels to claim, cynically, *ex post facto* justification for their invasion. How indefensible this reasoning was, Owen demonstrated by a description of a cartoon which had appeared in January in the New York *Herald*. It has represented "a burglar (with a *Kaiserliche* moustache) standing over the body of his victim as it lay on a bed decorated at its head with the Belgian crown. And the 'caption' of the cartoon ran: 'Under the pillow of the victim was found a weapon to be used for defence, thus absolving the burglar from all blame.'" Shaw's claim to objectivity on grounds that he was an Irishman and thus could have the outlook of an alien, "only takes the words out of our mouth," said Owen. "Of course he is: he would be an alien anywhere." G.B.S.'s friend Arnold Daly said much the same thing although with different intentions in mind when, during a before-the-curtain speech at his New York revival of Shaw's *You Never Can Tell*, he asserted that the playwright "hadn't an enemy in the world, though none of his friends liked him." Oscar Wilde had said it of Shaw twenty years earlier, although the *New York Times*'s editorial writer did not know it, suggesting that Shaw must have first said it himself of himself. "As words are commonly used," the editorial went on, "if nobody likes Mr. Shaw, he has no friends and innumerable enemies. His writings, at least, have many admirers as well as many severe critics, and not one of the latter can deny to them the enormous merit of interest. He cannot be ignored, no matter on what subject he speaks, and . . . he loves to live in constant storms of his own creation. . . ."

Notoriety alone could not sustain the box office, and in London the revival of *Fanny's First Play* began faltering badly after a month. Whether or not it was the result of the press campaign against Shaw finally taking effect, the play closed after a six-week run, Shaw's only consolation being that the Kingsway management had lost no more than if the theatre had been closed and that there were "large khaki audiences on Saturdays. . . ." The revival had not been one Shaw wanted in any case, but worthwhile playwrights were not risking their new plays, if they were writing them at all, under conditions of the West End's first experience of war, and theatres hungered for material. Since March 31 was the end of the fiscal year for purposes of G.B.S.'s income tax return, *Fanny*'s failure concluded the year on a sour note, but the year had also included *Pygmalion* and a gross professional income of £16,595, the largest in his life. Ironically, because of increased war taxes, it meant that he had become a substantial supporter of the war he continued to denounce, writing Siegfried Trebitsch in Vienna that April that the surtax alone he had just paid had amounted to more than £1000, which he would rather have used "to buy in

Vienna some good picture for our National Gallery. . . ." Trebitsch had informed him sadly that Shavian plays were no longer being produced in German-speaking Europe, and Shaw answered that should England win he would ask Sir Edward Grey "to add to the treaty of peace a clause in which Berlin and Vienna shall be obliged each year to produce at least 100 performances of my plays for the next twenty-five years." More interesting than the letter was that Shaw's irreverent remarks to Trebitsch were being quoted regularly and at length in the enemy press, in this case the *Münchener Neueste Nachrichten* and the *Frankfurter Zeitung*.

During Easter 1915, Shaw was in Ireland, a guest for a fortnight of Sir Horace Plunkett, Home Ruler, agricultural reformer, and founder of the Irish cooperative movement. After that he went on to Coole to stay with Lady Gregory, where another guest, Augustus John, kept Shaw busy sitting for his portrait, painting six variations in eight days. "Unfortunately," G.B.S. wrote Mrs. Campbell, "as he kept painting them on top of one another until our protests became overwhelming, only three portraits have survived. . . ."[10] Shaw thought they were splendid, which indeed they were. One went on display that spring at the New English Art Club, John not concerned about press reaction that might confuse subject and execution.

G.B.S. and Charlotte returned from Ireland in mid-May on a ship crowded with survivors of the *Lusitania* sinking, all of them fearful that the waters between two islands were infested with U-boats. Although he had lost friends among those who had sailed on the *Lusitania*, Shaw lost a great many more of them by scoffing at the tears and outrage lavished on the nearly twelve hundred "innocent victims" when innocent hundreds of thousands of equally human beings, he said, were being sent to their deaths on the Western Front and at Gallipoli, the only difference being that they had been misled into khaki.

The G.B.S. view, for all the opprobrium heaped on him, was not nearly as extreme as the statement issued by the Pope, which condemned equally German submarine warfare and the English blockade of German ports. "I know of no more frightful crime," said Pope Benedict XV of the *Lusitania* sinking. "How distressing to see a gen-

eration prey to such horrors! I have a father's heart, and my heart is
torn; but do you think the blockade which hems two Empires and
condemns millions of innocents to famine is prompted by very humane sentiments?" A press agency asked Shaw whether he thought
the Pope's statement "commends itself to the ethical ideas of the
masses," and Shaw was quick to answer that it was not the business
of the Pope to commend himself to the ethical ideas of the masses,
but rather to furnish ethical ideas to the masses. "And certainly," Shaw
added, "the 'ethical' outlook that finds romantic excitement in the
slaughter of thousands of young soldiers at Neuve Chapelle and Aubers
[Festubert] by the most infernally cruel methods and then bursts
into screams of horror and vindictive fury because a shipful of civilians
have been surprised by an easy death seems badly in need of the
sternest Papal rebuke for its callous selfishness. The Pope can hardly
be expected to represent God as sharing the general American & British
belief that saloon passengers have more valuable souls than common
soldiers because they have heavier bank balances."[11] The comment
fanned renewed popular outrage against Shaw, yet his views on the
war were throughout strikingly parallel to those of the priest-diplomat
who had become Pope the year before.

Soon after disembarking in England, Shaw traveled to the Lake
Country, where on the shores of Lake Derwentwater the Fabian Research Department was meeting. Barrow House, Derwentwater, leased
to the Fabians in 1912, had grounds sloping down to the lake, its own
boating pier, and a beach for swimming. As in previous years, women
were quartered in the house and a tent camp set up for sixty men.
These were hardly luxurious facilities, but they were compensated
for by the camaraderie, intellectual stimulation, and the lake setting.
There a non-Fabian group headed by an elder statesman of international diplomacy, Lord Bryce, and including Lowes Dickinson,
joined the Fabians as consulting members to consider the work that
had been done by Leonard Woolf and his subcommittee of the Research Department on a League of Nations for the prevention of war.

All the outsiders had been working independently on the same
subject and had had a chance to read the Woolf report before the

meeting. It made for relative harmony.* "A point was there reached," Shaw said, "at which it was apparent that the sounding of the report by skilled discussion and criticism had been carried to exhaustion."[12] As "International Government," it was published as an *NS* supplement on July 10, 1915, and then, under the same title but with added material, prepared for book publication the next year. According to historian Sir Robert Ensor, it was "seminal" to the League of Nations and was on President Wilson's desk at the end of the war.

For the book version, G.B.S., in his capacity as chairman of the Research Department, wrote a substantial, rather than a perfunctory, preface, concluding that world peace was very likely no longer practicable "without new super-national machinery of a much more definite and permanent kind than the old Concert of Europe which . . . was so hard to keep in tune. . . ."[13] But Leonard Woolf, who had drafted the final text and did much of the preliminary work, insisted that the book be published in England without the Shavian preface, not because he was wary of Shaw's notoriety on war questions, but "on that ground that, as a young man and writer, I wanted my book to be judged on its merits and defects; it should stand solely on its own legs, and not on those of a great man's preface." Shaw agreed, and the preface appeared only in the later American and French editions. "Most great men," Woolf afterwards thought, "would have felt some slight resentment or hurt at this treatment of what was a kind and generous act on his part. Many years later I found that the opposite was true for Shaw, for Sir Frederic Osborn showed me a letter written to him in 1917 by Shaw explaining why he would not write a preface to some book and Shaw added, 'I think you will see, on consideration, that Woolf, the author of the Fabian Research Department's book on Supernational Organisation, to which I, as chairman of the Department, had to supply a preface, was quite right in insisting that the English editions should appear in the first instance without my preface.' "[14]

After the Fabian conference, Shaw set off on his favorite kind of holiday, "a week of walking over mountains." He stayed often, when

* Except that a young man named Walter Lippmann, according to Leonard Woolf, received a "dressing-down" from G.B.S.

in a walking mood, with a relative of Beatrice Webb near Presteigne, on the eastern edge of Radnorshire. During the war years, he became a familiar sight in the town and spent hours in the quiet of Radnor Forest and the neighboring hills, once, while looking out at the hills that encircled Presteigne, remarking to the Webbs with arms outstretched, "No man ought to be in the government of this land who does not spend three months every year in the country—and in such country as this." He was careful with his royalties and author's fees in London, but that reputation was belied in Radnorshire, where on one occasion in paying a tailor for repairs he put down twice the sum he had been asked for. When the tailor pointed out the error Shaw told him, "I earn my money more easily than you."[15]

Back in London, G.B.S. returned to work he had begun in Ireland, a sequel to his war supplement that he planned to call *More Common Sense about the War*. It threatened to make good what a Viennese paper gravely reported early in June, that he had shut himself up in his house, put sentries at the doors, and feared to show himself in public out of concern that he would be assassinated by a patriotic London mob.

There was no sign of such hostility when *Man and Superman* opened in Edinburgh on June 11 at the Lyceum Theatre. It was the first time the play was done in its entirety, complete with Hell scene, and when Esme Percy had requested permission for his company to do it, Shaw answered that he had never conceived the possibility of its being done in full at one sitting, that Percy had no more sense than a dormouse to propose performing such a marathon, that no one would come to see it, and if any did, they would not be able to endure it. "However—Carry on!" Percy did, and even commissioned a local poet, Donald Mackenzie, to write a lengthy prologue to the third act —as if the five-hour play were not long enough.[16] It was a gala evening. The Scottish newspapers did not even allude in advance to Shaw's notorious war reputation, perhaps feeling that it would only augment the box office.

The box office needed no help. "A less modest man than Mr. Shaw," the Edinburgh *Evening Dispatch* reported the next day, "might find the popularity he has achieved in Edinburgh quite overpowering. To witness what play has the Lyceum Theatre been so packed before on a lovely evening in mid-June? There was not a vacant seat, and some who were anxious to assist at this very special occasion could not obtain admission. It was a great tribute to Mr. Shaw the super-advertiser. To analyze too precisely the motives which caused this remarkable audience to assemble might be invidious." Was the *Dispatch* thinking about Shaw's current notoriety? A few lines later its peculiarly Scots reasoning became clear, as it explained why an Edinburgh audience which would stay away in great numbers if Hamlet were played in full crowded the Lyceum for five hours of Shaw: "We are afraid the conclusion can hardly be avoided—because the third act of 'Man and Superman' is laid partly in Hell. The audience expected something just a little bit naughty. Instead, even a Watch Committee of Free Kirk elders would not have been so very much scandalised."

The *Dispatch* found nothing to shock in the Hell scene, which at best was "clever conjuring with words and ideas," and at worst "philosophy gibbering on the brink of lunacy." The play, it concluded, was "better without it." As for the peculiar prologue to that act, harangued at the audience from the orchestra pit by an actor garbed as the ghost of Shakespeare, it "contained some witty lines, which were recited in unctuous manner by Mr. William J. Rea, but it seemed rather supererogatory," and "it was good to get out again into the cool air of the evening." Had the *Dispatch*'s critic been listening during the Hell scene, he might have found some shockable lines, particularly those lines of the Devil's that seemed more pertinent in 1915 than they had been when written in 1903, and would increase in pertinence as man moved into the nuclear age:

Have you walked up and down upon the earth lately? I have; and I have examined Man's wonderful inventions. And I tell you that in the arts of life man invents nothing; but in the arts of death he outdoes Nature herself, and produces by chemistry and machinery all the slaughter of plague, pestilence and famine. The peasant I tempt to-day eats and drinks what was eaten and drunk by the peasants of ten thousand years ago; and the house he lives in has not altered as much in a thousand centuries as the fashion of a lady's bonnet in a score of weeks. But when he goes out to slay, he carries a marvel of mechanism that lets loose at the touch of his finger all the hidden molecular energies, and leaves the javelin, the arrow, the blowpipe of his fathers far behind. In the arts of peace Man is a bungler. I have seen his cotton factories and . . . machinery . . . they are toys compared to the Maxim gun, the submarine torpedo boat. There is nothing in Man's industrial machinery but his greed and sloth: his heart is in his weapons. This marvellous force of Life of which you boast is a force of Death: Man measures his strength by his destructiveness. What is his religion? An excuse for hating me. What is his law? An excuse for hanging you. What is his morality? Gentility! an excuse for consuming without producing. What is his art? An excuse for gloating over pictures of slaughter. . . . Their imagination glows, their energies rise up at the idea of death, these people: they love it; and the more horrible it is the more they enjoy it. . . .

Over such battles the people run about the streets yelling with delight, and egg their Governments on to spend hundreds of millions of money in the slaughter, whilst the strongest Ministers dare not spend an extra penny in the pound against the poverty and pestilence through which they themselves daily walk. I could give you a thousand instances; but they all come to the same thing: the power that governs the earth is not the power of Life but of Death; and the inner need that has nerved Life to the effort of organizing itself into the human being is not the need for higher life but for a more efficient engine of destruction. The plague, the famine, the earthquake, the tempest were too spasmodic in their action; the tiger and crocodile were too easily satiated and not cruel enough: something more constantly, more ruthlessly, more ingeniously destructive was needed; and that something was Man, the inventor of the rack, the stake, the gallows, and the electrocutor; of the sword and gun; above all, of justice, duty, patriotism and all the other isms by which even those who are clever enough to be humanely disposed are persuaded to become the most destructive of all the destroyers.

Above the *Dispatch*'s review, in the same column, was another view of Hell, from a letter home written by a lance corporal in the London Rifle Brigade and picked up by the *Dispatch* from the *Daily Telegraph*. "The charge was given," he wrote, "and I guarantee the whole brigade left those trenches like one man. . . . The enemy's fire was absolutely withering, and line after line of our brave men went down.

One was certain that nothing could live under such a fire, but our men got there, and the German cowards turned and ran when our bayonets were ten yards away from them." The letter continued in the same spirit. "The experience was wonderful and terrible. I want to tell you that among so many brave men it would have been an honour to die. I also want to tell you that during the charge my thoughts were with home and mother. . . . The brigade came out of the trenches at 6.30 a.m. on Saturday, and marched to a field some distance away from the fighting line to have a muster roll-call. There are some things one never forgets, and that is one of them for me. I can imagine no sight more pathetic than that parade. . . . Brothers were looking for one another, friends were seeking friends. We were all tired and hungry, but elated with victory. . . ."

From Ireland G.B.S. had written to Gilbert Chesterton again inquiring about his health, and Chesterton responded on June 12, apparently recovered, for he described himself as "only in a very comparative sense a skeleton," and announced, predictably, "I do not agree with you about the war. . . . If it were an easy war to end it would have been a wicked war to begin. . . . I have always thought that there was in Prussia an evil will. . . ." Ten days later Shaw replied with equal friendship and candor.

I am delighted to learn under your own hand that you have recovered all your health and powers with unimpaired figure. . . .

It is perfectly useless for you to try to differ with me about the war. *Nobody* can differ with me about the war: you might as well differ from the Almighty about the orbit of the sun. I have got the war right; and to that complexion you too must come at last, your nature not being a fundamentally erroneous one.

At the same time, it is a great pity you were not born in Ireland. You would have had the advantage of hearing the burning patriotism of your native land expressing itself by saying exactly the same things about England that English patriotism now says about Prussia, and of recognizing that though they were entirely true, they were also a very great nuisance, as they prevented people from building the future by conscientious thought. . . .

Shaw concluded with references to the new pamphlet he was working on, which, until he discovered that the title had already been used, was to be called *Uncommon Sense about the War*. Horrified, G.K.C. wrote a frank, friendly letter explaining why he thought Shaw's position was stubbornly unrealistic: "You are wrestling with something too romantic for you to realize. It is the real thing. . . . Your weakness touching what you call 'the nonsense about Belgium,' after all is simply that it is not nonsense. . . . You are out of your depth my dear Shaw; for you jumped into this deep river to prove that it was shallow. . . ." Shaw had again viciously attacked Sir Edward Grey, which seemed not only cruel but unnecessary, since Grey, his eyesight failing, was incapacitated for long periods of time, not in control of his ministry, and widely and erroneously reported to be ready to retire. People like himself, Chesterton said, were supporting Grey's war not because they were dupes of, or supporters of, Sir Edward, but because it was the most reasonable response in the situation they faced. "But you cannot bear to be on the democratic side, even by accident," Chesterton observed, "so you would rather twist out some extraordinary tale of the Kaiser being taken at disadvantage by the hellish cunning of English country gentlemen. . . ." With the respect and affection each felt for the other, their friendship would have survived the gentle G.K.C.'s shrewd admonitions, although they very likely would not have changed a word of Shaw's polemic. With that, perhaps, in mind, Chesterton put the letter in his desk, unposted. It was never mailed.[17]

On July 3 Shaw mailed a copy of the sequel to Beatrice Webb, asking for her impressions. It was clear that he expected it to appear in the same way that *Common Sense* had been published, as a *New Statesman* supplement; again he worried that it would appear too belatedly to have any useful impact. Beatrice frankly reported that it was ill-tempered and illogical, and Shaw answered that he could easily make it agreeable, but risked then making it ineffective, for if he made people angry they would pay attention to what he said. *More Common Sense* was already making people angry, as word of its alleged contents drifted around, for among the few thinkers he singled out for praise in it was the notorious Houston Stewart Chamberlain, English son-in-law of Richard Wagner. His portentous work, *Die Grundlagen des neunzehnten Jahrhunderts,* had been translated into English as *The Foundations of the Nineteenth Century.* "An interesting book," Shaw asserted as late as 1936, "which at the time of its appearance I recommended everybody to read."[18] In it Chamberlain attractively (to some readers) warped genetics, politics, and logic to establish the Aryan myth later adopted by Adolf Hitler, and won the thanks of the Kaiser, who told him, "It was God who sent your book to the German people and to me." (A year later he would become a naturalized German and receive the Iron Cross.)

Although he hedged his praise, Shaw placed Chamberlain in "the great tradition of Kant and Goethe, Schopenhauer and Richard Wagner," carefully adding that he was "interesting only to readers of genius, or of the high intelligence to which genius appeals. . . ." Chamberlain looked to the Protestant North of Europe "as the instrument of evolution in modern civilization," a grandiose racial concept about which Shaw was skeptical, equating it with the Ulster-Ireland problem, yet tolerant, because he detested czarist Russia and feared a future Yellow Peril. Shaw had already shocked Rebecca West by giving her a copy of *Foundations,* assuring her that it was a marvelous book. Her misgivings increased when she took J. M. Kennedy, then an assistant to the foreign editor of the *Daily Telegraph,* to meet Shaw at his Adelphi Terrace flat; Kennedy came away murmuring that all he could find to admire in G.B.S. was his courage in pontificating on foreign affairs when he knew he had no knowledge of history, geography, and foreign languages.*[19] H. G. Wells chaffed Shaw unmercifully about Chamberlain, and Shaw's public attitude toward the pre-Fascist philosopher gradually became more cautiously ambivalent; but to have publicly advocated him in any form and at any time was an explosive matter.

Most of *More Common Sense* was taken up by Shaw's explaining and updating his controversial positions in the earlier pamphlet, but

---

* A much publicized Shaw blunder was his letter to the editor on the Monroe Doctrine that assumed that Russia still owned Alaska.

one page went on to explain why he thought that writers and intellectuals in general should involve themselves in public events and
policy-making:

The truth is that the work of Government, even when delegation of
routine is carried on to the utmost practicable extent, involves drudgery
of the most soul-destroying and staling sort: so much so indeed, that people who have no souls and who are born stale, can attain the highest positions in the kingdom if only they add to these qualifications toughness
enough to work twelve hours a day for forty years. Yet in the face of this
we still maintain for the most difficult public work the arrangements that
served when few statesmen could read or write; when news from France
often took weeks to arrive and even at that might arrive before news from
York. . . . The result is that there is no high political thinking done in an
emergency, or indeed out of it, by practical statesmen. A sort of irresponsible Council has to be conducted in "featured" articles in the London
and New York papers, by clever people like Mr. H. G. Wells, Mr. Arnold
Bennett, Mr. Jerome K. Jerome, Mr. A. G. Gardiner, Mr. George Trevel-
yan, Mr. Lowes Dickinson, Mr. Sidney Webb and myself, with personal
interludes of the sort which Bunyan labelled as "Christian snibbeth his
fellow," and no mandate or authority beyond what we can extort by the
terror or persuasiveness of our pens.[20]

Nothing came of the immense labor Shaw had put into his new
manifesto, for Clifford Sharp refused to print it under any conditions, and it never appeared elsewhere, but Shaw salvaged parts of it,
which appeared in somewhat different form in journals over the next
year. Among them was his "Coalition of Intellectuals" piece, but
even sooner than its publication he had an opportunity to fire again
at Grey—a sop offered by the uncontrite Sharp in the form of a review of a book by Gilbert Murray on the superhuman virtue of Grey's
foreign policy. As an additional sop, Sharp lifted some of the safer
segments for the anonymous New Statesman column, "Notes of the
Week," while Shaw rationalized his rebuff in a letter in the Nation
on another subject, all the while inferring that the threat of censorship (rather than Sharp) kept him from saying more than he did.
"[If] I cannot offer a study of diplomacy with every page half-

blacked out . . ." he wrote, "had not I better keep my clarification safe in my desk, as I am, in fact, doing?"

Other activities kept G.B.S. from worrying overmuch about the still-birth of *More Common Sense*. He attended myriad meetings, from political ones to sessions on vegetarianism (he was for it), vaccination (he was against it), and psychical research (he was skeptical). He had new worries about Harley Granville-Barker, who had—he wrote Murray—"chucked the theatre." The season at Wallack's in New York had been a financial disaster, for rather than exploiting *Androcles*, Barker had played a group of plays in repertory (an idealistic but un-commercial decision) and had come back to London £5000 in debt. Barker owed £2000 to Shaw, who promptly wrote the debt off, but Shaw could not so easily write off Barker's having been stolen from his wife in New York by Helen Huntington, an heiress a dozen years older than the thirty-seven-year-old Barker. When he and Lillah returned from America in June 1915, he assured her that everything was over between Helen and him, but they never returned to their rooms at 5 Adelphi Terrace, near the Shaws, and Barker, depressed by debts, despondent about his marital situation, and certain that the war had ended any reasons to take the theatre seriously, joined a Red Cross unit and went to France, from there keeping in touch with Helen Huntington. G.B.S. and Charlotte looked after Lillah.

Androcles was published that summer, with a long reappraisal of the Gospels as a preface* and a topical afterword in which Shaw pointed out the relevance of the play in a world where even among

---

* Most commentators view the preface as yet another survey of the recognized inconsistencies among the four versions of the Christ story, but revulsion at pulpit patriotism apparently caused Shaw to reread the Gospels with great seri-ousness, giving him cause to blame Peter for labeling Jesus as "Christ, the son of the living God!" and thus precipitating the obsession of Jesus with the divinity of his mission, and pointing to Paul as the villain of the piece, an "anti-Christian" who made of his own pathological fears of sin and of death a reli-gion of redemption from Original Sin through vicarious atonement, thus turning healthy Christianity into the unhealthy travesty of "Crosstianity," with the move-ment started by Jesus as the nucleus of his new church. " 'I come as an infallible patent medicine for bad consciences' is not one of the sayings in the gospels," Shaw observes.

men who make a profession of religion, the majority are as warlike as the majority of their congregations.

We were at peace when I pointed out, by the mouth of Ferrovius, the path of an honest man who finds out, when the trumpet sounds, that he cannot follow Jesus. Many years earlier, in The Devil's Disciple, I touched the same theme even more definitely, and shewed the minister throwing off his black coat for ever when he discovered, amid the thunder of the captains and the shouting, that he was a born fighter. Great numbers of our clergy have found themselves of late in the position of Ferrovius and Anthony Anderson. They have discovered that they hate not only their enemies but everyone who does not share their hatred, and that they want to fight and to force other people to fight. They have turned their churches into recruiting stations and their vestries into munition workshops. But it has never occurred to them to take off their black coats and say quite simply, "I find in the hour of trial that the Sermon on the Mount is tosh, and that I am not a Christian. I apologize for all the unpatriotic nonsense I have been preaching all these years. Have the goodness to give me a revolver and a commission in a regiment which has for its chaplain a priest of the god Mars: *my* God." Not a bit of it. They have stuck to their livings and served Mars in the name of Christ.

It had taken some courage to put his war afterthoughts into the play volume, for Shaw knew that public reception of the book could focus on afterword rather than play. Yet he felt it was a risk worth taking.

At least one copy of *Androcles* had quickly found its way to France. James Barrie, an Adelphi Terrace neighbor of Shaw's, had received an inscribed copy from the author and after reading it through wrote Shaw that he was sending the book to one of his godsons at the front. It was one of the last pieces of mail George Llewelyn Davies received. A grandson of George du Maurier, he was at twenty-one the oldest of five sons of Arthur and Sylvia Llewelyn Davies. The childless and wifeless* Barrie had informally adopted them all when

---

* Mary Barrie, long frustrated by Barrie's inability to consummate their marriage, had run off with the much younger writer, Gilbert Cannan. Although blessed—predictably—by H. G. Wells, the new conjugal relationship eventually failed.

he began a platonic love affair with Sylvia Davies, who had died in 1910, three years after her husband. It had been as passionate as Barrie could ever get, and when George stopped a bullet while on night patrol near Ypres, Barrie mourned for him as for an authentic son. Dwelling too close to Shaw to exchange letters, he nevertheless could not bear to break the news in person, writing a short note ending, "I know you will be very sorry for us."

Other soldiers had been reading Shaw then, and not only in the trenches. G.B.S. got one letter from a Royal Flying Corps lieutenant in a prison camp at Karlsruhe, asking for copies of his books for the camp library—but nothing published since the start of the war, since prisoners of war were forbidden such material. Would G.B.S. also pass on similar requests to Galsworthy, Chesterton, Wells, Belloc, Hardy, and Bennett? Shaw did.

G.B.S. turned up even on the hellish and unnecessary front at Gallipoli. Retrieved from a trench there was a postcard addressed to Private T. Eardley, "A" Company, 7th Manchesters:

A man who goes on calmly hunting autographs with all civilisation crumbling around him, and the Turkish enemy not far below the horizon, really deserves to succeed. So here goes.

G. Bernard Shaw[21]

It was lonely for the outspoken that summer in London, and Shaw looked for other voices to sound his brand of common sense about the war. Ever since the Cabinet crisis of mid-May, when Asquith, in a rare retreat from inaction, reshuffled his coalition in order to prolong his lease on No. 10 Downing Street, demoting some ministers and jettisoning others, Shaw had hoped for some statement from his old friend Lord Haldane, a former War Minister and, suddenly and surprisingly, now an ex-Lord Chancellor. The portly and hard-working Haldane was a shrewd choice on Asquith's part to drop. He was not prone to intrigue, and as the Prime Minister explained to the King's unflappable private secretary, Lord Stamfordham, "not in all cases" were ministers selected "for their fitness for office" and that certain ones were chosen or retained because "they are safer *in* than out of office!" (Thus the potentially dangerous Churchill was punished for his costly Dardanelles adventure by being shifted from the Admiralty to the limbo of the chancellorship of the Duchy of Lancaster, eventually resigning on his own in the autumn to take up the command of a battalion in France.) To Haldane, G.B.S. wrote hopefully on August 3:

Now that you are disentangled from the party machine on suspicion of intellect, I hope you will give the country a bit of your mind. . . . You have only to let yourself go to be a much greater power outside the Cabinet than you were as a purple patch on that fearfully inadequate body. They are dear creatures, and to know them personally is to be hopelessly incapacitated from sentencing them as they will be sentenced at the bar of History; but their attempt to enlist you was an attempt to mix up the Old Bailey with the Judicial Committee, or to make an Ecclesiastical Commissioner of Martin Luther. You remember St. Luke's story about Peter when the Lord sank his boat by the miracle of the fishes. Well, I have an improbable vision of Asquith falling on his knees and saying "My dear Haldane: depart from me; for I am a sinful man."[22]

Although his pride had been wounded, Haldane kept his feelings private. Asquith could not last in office forever, and Haldane intended to re-emerge.

The summer of 1915 was also the season of the "Thousand Million [Pound] War Loan Campaign," and it did the war loan no harm when somehow the news leaked that Shaw had subscribed £20,000. He would not comment to the press about his own finances,* but when asked whether it were "wise or right" for posterity to be burdened with paying the war loan off, considering that it was not responsible for it and had no voice in waging it, Shaw responded that nothing about a war was wise or right except stopping it, yet that once it was being waged, necessity became more important than wisdom or rectitude. He answered questions about how he would finance the war (by confiscating income not engaged in maintaining a reasonable standard of living) and about war indemnities (it would not pay to

---

* His ledger lists the amount of £18,000.

bankrupt England's best customers). When he was asked what steps he would take to bring about a satisfactory peace, he said none whatever, for the job would not be given to him. Still, he observed that no peace could be conclusive without "a supranational legislature and tribunal."

Shaw's interviews were not always that quietly received. It was while he was back at the Hydro in Torquay in August that news broke that the Germans were exploiting on posters an account of an already controversial interview with American ex-Senator Albert J. Beveridge, published the previous June in *Collier's Weekly*, in which Shaw suggested that Grey had long plotted with France and Belgium against Germany. What Shaw had not been quoted as saying was that the arrangements had been defensive, however much the French yearned for revenge and the return of Alsace and Lorraine. Nevertheless, the Germans printed a notice, in parallel columns of German, French, and Flemish, which they posted in occupied sectors of Belgium:

England and the War
Important Revelation of the
Famous English Author,
Bernard Shaw.

Then followed a truncated account of the *Collier's* interview, with the claim that it confirmed the plot the Germans saw in the incriminating documents they had found in Brussels which had linked Belgian preparedness with plans made in England and France.

Shaw had no excuse that he had been misquoted, for he had granted the interview on condition that he approve the text, and when Beveridge furnished it, Shaw revised it with great care, even to the preliminary small talk. The heart of the dialogue had concerned war guilt, and it played down the German role.

"All the European diplomatists had made up their minds that an European war . . . was inevitable," continued Mr. Shaw. "Our diplomatists decided that we must be in that war. They chose our side—the French side—on the ground that if the Germans vanquished France and Russia, they could vanquish us afterward.

"So they concerted all the necessary military and naval plans and arrangements with the French diplomatists. And when the Servian affair brought about the war, we were of course bound by these arrangements."

"But," I remarked, "I have heard that the Liberal party went into power as a peace party. I have been told that peace was its central principle."

"Not exactly," said Mr. Shaw. "When the party came into power in 1906 it was divided, and public opinion was divided between modern Imperialism and the old non-intervention policy of peace, retrenchment and reform. The difference was compromised by including three Liberal Imperialists, Asquith, Grey and Haldane, in the cabinet. They were reinforced by Churchill, a blazing militarist Junker.

"But the difficulty was that, though these ministers were convinced of the necessity of our taking sides in the European quarrel, and backing France by arms, they would have broken up their party if they had said so openly and revealed their entry into the Franco-Russian *entente*. They had even to deny that they were committed to war by any secret arrangement."

"Do you mean that they publicly told a lie?" I exclaimed.

"Not at all—technically," Mr. Shaw responded. "Mr. Asquith had taken care of that. He insisted on Sir Edward Grey asking the French to note particularly that the arrangements did not bind us to anything. The French, who understand the electioneering exigencies of democracy as well as any politicians on earth, gravely noted the statement. Thus Mr. Asquith was perfectly in order in stating repeatedly that we were bound by no secret engagements. And Sir Edward Grey confirmed him.

"That," said Mr. Shaw, "is how the Liberal party and the nation were led up to the guns blindfolded."

"According to that," I remarked, "Germany's violation of Belgian neutrality had nothing to do with England's entering the war."

"Nothing whatever," answered Mr. Shaw, "except to furnish Mr. Asquith with a perfectly presentable and correct pretext for entering on a war to which he was already secretly pledged, Belgium or no Belgium."

Shaw also pointed to deviousness in English internal politics as well, observing that an Asquith deal with conservative Unionist M.P.s to replace defectors among the outraged Liberals had resulted in bringing domestic reform to a halt.

"There was not only a secret treaty with France, but one with the Opposition as well," answered Mr. Shaw. "Mr. Asquith could not be sure that his duped followers would not rebel; and Sir Edward Grey was threatened with the opposition of the City to the war. When their perplexity was at its height, a handful of the most energetic of the younger members of the Opposition jumped into automobiles and scurried out through the country to collect the Unionist leaders to take advantage of the threatened crisis.

"When they arrived in London, they proposed a deal. The Unionist leaders agreed to supply and more than supply any Liberal defection in the House of Commons, and to see Grey and Asquith through with their war programme. And the *quid pro quo* was that Mr. Asquith should meanwhile drop the Liberal party's programme of social and industrial reform legislation. This is what was politely announced as a patriotic sinking of controversy and the presentation of an united front to the Hun. For short, we now call it The Truce."

Although Shaw had more to say about the origins of the war and the English role in it, the thrust of his argument remained the eventual peace and how to keep it; as before he insisted that Russia did not belong with the West in any League of Nations.

"Russia must become the nucleus of an eastern combination similar to the western one," declared Mr. Shaw. "You see, it is quite useless as yet to talk of a Parliament of Man, a federation of the world. The world is too big an unit to be manageable. Besides, in this sort of combination psychological homogeneity is essential to stability. The oriental peoples may be ever so much better than we are or they may be ever so much worse— I shall not beg either question; but the fact remains that they are working with different customs and traditions, different religions, and with literatures and languages utterly strange to us.

"It is not practicable to amalgamate them with us in the same supernational organization," continued Mr. Shaw. "You can get sufficient psychological homogeneity for practical purposes from, say, San Francisco to Warsaw; but if you insist on taking in the other hemisphere, you will wreck the whole project—in fact, you will not be able to make even a beginning. Therefore, with no hostility to Russia, and with a very keen sense of the complications in which England will be involved by the fact that she is in two eastern places, Egypt and India, where she has no business to be, I leave Russia out of the western supernational organization, and invite her to make a separate supernational unit of the Slav states and the Asiatic Powers."

. . . . .

"It is a big idea, but is it practical?"

"It is better, at all events," said Mr. Shaw, "than making elaborate secret conspiracies against our neighbors because we are afraid they will make war on us, and then drifting helplessly into war after all, with the conspirators piteously protesting that they have striven for peace all their lives, like the Kaiser, and Bethmann-Hollweg, and Sir Edward Grey. Anyhow, it is the only way out I can see; and I am still waiting for any one to point out a better one."[23]

It was a far-reaching and prophetic anticipation of a polarization of powers that was only beginning to take shape when Shaw died, at ninety-four, in 1950. But patriots and adversaries alike saw only as far as Belgium, although Shaw had carefully designed the Beveridge interview to range far beyond the Belgian stick each side shook at the other. He could never be careful enough about his interviews. A *Daily Sketch* reporter, for example, elicited from him the comment that joining the Army was "a serious question which every man should decide for himself," and that compulsory soldiering was tantamount to slavery. With the Asquith government busy preparing the nation for conscription, the observation that summer provoked new patriotic outcries against Shaw in the press.

The first anniversary of the beginning of the war found G.B.S. beginning to write for the theatre again, although he knew there were no audiences for anything as serious as the play he had had in mind and put aside when the war began. Through the censorship he told Siegfried Trebitsch about a new playlet, a satire on the Kaiser, about which he wondered facetiously whether it could be produced in Germany. It was a tomfoolery, he confessed, his worst play, but only meant as a curtain raiser for *Great Catherine*, to fill out that pre-war farce into a full evening. As an added tomfoolery, he noted that if Trebitsch were sent to the front by the Austrian authorities, the English press would take it as evidence of the enemy's exhaustion. Perhaps Shaw guessed that the Germanic mentality might actually take him seriously and spare his translator, but it would be a long time until Trebitsch would be able to see *The Inca of Perusalem*.

An outgrowth of his visit to Lady Gregory earlier in the year was another playlet he worked on at Torquay to help her financially hard-pressed Abbey Theatre. (The idea for the play may have come from Shaw's protesting the jailing of Sheehy Skeffington, an Irish nationalist who had made an anti-recruiting speech.) War and threat of civil war had thinned theatre audiences in Dublin, and Shaw saw in Lady Gregory's request an opportunity to aid her while encouraging Irish enlistments in the British Army through a play paradoxically calculated to appeal to Irishmen through its satire of Englishmen. On both counts Lady Gregory was the appropriate destination for the play, for she symbolized Irish loyalty through her son Robert, an officer in the Royal Flying Corps. Shaw had promised it for the fall, and he wrote *O'Flaherty, V.C.* so quickly that he told Lady Gregory to put it on the Abbey's schedule, after which he wrote to Ann Elder in London, sending her the remainder of the play and urging speed, "as Lady Gregory is rather hung up for it."[24]

At Torquay Shaw continued to receive requests for interviews, prefaces, and book reviews, almost all of which he turned down, including a teasing offer to review the Bible, proposed by the imaginative literary editor J. C. Squire when the *NS* acquired a review copy of *A Literary Man's New Testament*. Having just published a lengthy preface to *Androcles* consisting largely of a discussion of the Gospels, Shaw declined and went swimming. He received visitors, too, including Barker (without Lillah), back from France and en route to the United States for the touring company of *Androcles*. After he left, his fur-lined coat was discovered at the Hydro, and G.B.S., concerned about how Barker would survive a New York autumn without it, investigated the shipping schedules until he found a way to send it across the Atlantic on a safe Dutch boat, the *Nieuw Amsterdam*.

If not his major accomplishment, at least his most frustrating one that summer was yet another manifesto, a draft submitted to the British section of the International Socialist Bureau, meant as a reply to another manifesto published on June 23 by the German Social-

Democratic Party. A conference to draft a response from Britain came up with one full of "amiable generalities" and "Pacifist principles," which Shaw felt were useless. Rather than merely not sign it, he drafted and had printed for distribution a pamphlet of eleven closely printed pages of text that substituted "hard fact" for "general principles of International fraternity." One hard fact he presented was the impossibility of assuming that the war, however long, would end in stalemate. Fraternity had to wait, and Shaw proposed the usefulness of calling upon belligerent governments to state the concrete conditions that could be the basis for negotiations to end the war. The end would not come, he predicted, with some decisive victory, "but by capacity to maintain a blockade [of Germany] by sea and an obstinate resistance on land until the enormous expenditure of men and money involved in the process renders the enemy bankrupt." In the meantime Shaw suggested that German Socialists use their voting power and their influence on public opinion to bring about an "International Diplomatic Congress in which the questions at issue between the belligerent powers can be defined and discussed," for no nation or alliance could defy public opinion by ignoring it. Until such a congress brought not only peace but a permanent international peace-keeping organization, Shaw foresaw wars inevitably recurring, "because the sword will remain the only arbiter to which nations can appeal."

Years later Shaw wondered what had happened to his proposal, for it had died so utterly of indifference. He had not even remembered writing it until a copy turned up a decade after Versailles.[25]

Toward the end of his stay at Torquay, Shaw put aside his work to spend all his available time with a stunned and grieving friend whose son, from whom—as in so many cases—great things were expected, had just been killed at Hulluch, near Loos.[26] His Guards unit had been rushed uselessly into the breach left when the inexperienced and unprepared British 21st and 24th Divisions, newly arrived in France, were marched almost directly into battle and had panicked, then stumbled back in confusion. Kitchener had told both Sir John French and Haig that the British army had to act energetically to help relieve pressure on the French even at the cost of "very heavy losses indeed."[27] He had his losses.

The offensive had opened with a bombardment that included, at Haig's insistence, gas. By nightfall on September 25, the first day the infantry moved to the attack, there were 15,470 casualties. By October 16, because the battle had not been broken off after the first failure had doomed the entire operation, British casualties had risen to 50,380. Even so Haig planned a new offensive which weather conditions prevented him from carrying out, although two weeks before, when it had become clear that the attack had failed, the demoralized Sir John French had confided to him (as Sir John's subordinate) that "we ought to take the first opportunity of concluding peace, otherwise England would be ruined."[28] Among the dead were Harold Chapin, a young actor-playwright who had worked with Barker, and Charles Hamilton Sorley, a twenty-year-old poet of remarkable powers and unfulfilled potential, who had already written, with a *Shropshire Lad* realism,

> . . . Earth that never doubts nor fears,
> Earth that knows of death, not tears,
> Earth that bore with joyful ease
> Hemlock for Socrates,
> Earth that blossomed and was glad
> 'Neath the cross that Christ had,
> Shall rejoice and blossom too
> When the bullet reaches you.
>   Wherefore, men marching
>   On the road to death, sing!
>   Pour your gladness on earth's head,
>   So be merry, so be dead.[29]

It was early October, when the bathing at Torquay was "becoming rather stern," that Shaw returned to a London changed by a year of war. Patriots were pressing the public to abstain from meat on Thursdays and alcoholic beverages on Mondays, practices the vegetarian, teetotaling G.B.S. found easy to maintain. City lights were more dimmed than before, a result of the June Zeppelin raids on London, and gold sovereigns, which had been circulating side by side with paper money, were disappearing, altering even the feel of a transaction. Newspapers were full of implacable casualty lists, but little criticism of the war, while journals like *Forward*, the *Labour Leader*, and *Tribunal* (the publication of the newly founded No Conscription Fellowship) were beginning to fall under the censor's interdict. Shaw told the Webbs that Massingham's *Nation* was "doing the war far better" than the *New Statesman*, by which he meant "getting in more criticism of the Government," but the *Nation* would inevitably be restricted by censorship, not permitted to ship or sell copies outside the British Isles, and before the end of the year even the *Times* was denounced in Parliament as "encouraging the enemy" and "hardening neutral opinion against us."

Shaw had come back from Torquay this time with more than merely war-writing accomplished, although the two playlets he had completed had war settings. He had prepared *Pygmalion* for publication not by supplying the expected lengthy preface, but by adding a brief nondramatic epilogue meant to put the quietus on the improvised and infuriatingly popular Mrs. Campbell-Beerbohm Tree romantic ending. She could never act up to the new material, Shaw taunted Stella, sending her a wildly exaggerated résumé.

I have passed *Pygmalion* for the press among the sheets of my new volume of plays; and it now has a sequel, not in dialogue, but in prose, which you will never be able to live up to. It describes in an absolutely convincing manner how Eliza married Freddy; how she realized her dream of a florist's shop; how neither of them knew how to keep shop; how she had to beg from the Colonel again and again to avert bankruptcy; how the wretched pair had to go to shorthand and typewriting commercial schools to learn; how they went even to the London School of Economics and to Kew Gardens simultaneously to learn about business and flowers and combine the information; how Eliza wrote such a shameful hand that she had to abase herself to Higgins to be taught his wonderful Italian handwriting; how Clara was converted by H. G. Wells and Galsworthy and went into a shop herself and saved her soul alive; how the flower shop began to pay at last when they tried asparagus and Freddy became Mr. Hill, greengrocer; how Eliza never got out of the habit of nagging Higgins that she acquired in the fourth act, and, though deeply interested in him, did not quite like him any more than she liked her father, who was rejected by the middle classes and forced into the highest society, where he was a huge success but poorer than he had ever been in his life before on his four thousand a year. The publication of that sequel will be the end of the romance of Sir Herbert Tree; and you will have to play Eliza properly and seriously for ever after, which is impossible.[30]

One of the changes in the London scene was the increasing lameness of the voluntary recruiting system, which had resulted in the Cabinet naming an old-style Lancashire magnate, Lord Derby, to be director-general of recruiting that October. Embarrassed by his new job of ending the shortage of manpower in the trenches because he had faith in no other recourse but conscription, he nevertheless concocted a plan on Asquith's promise that, if it failed, the government would introduce compulsory service. By a mixture of persuasion and threats, men, divided for the purpose into annual classes by birthdates, would "attest" willingness to serve if called, only those with insistent national or personal reasons for deferment being excluded. The Derby Scheme—afterwards called "a gigantic engine of fraud and moral blackmail"[31]—failed to maintain the façade of voluntary enlistment even temporarily, and, walking one day in late October by Trafalgar Square's recruiting platform, Shaw paused to listen to bellicose clergymen denouncing both the Germans and the many young men within hearing who had not enlisted on the spot. All they had produced were two recruits, "and these two, duly posted on the plinth of Nelson's monument as heroic examples to British youth, were a couple of deplorable down-and-outs so obviously untouchable" that Shaw understood why their patriotism had magnetized no one. "I'll Make a Man of You" ("And on Saturday I'm willing/if you'll only take the shilling*/to make a man of any man of you!"), the ribald recruiting song then so popular in the music halls, had no relevance to the quality or potential of Derby Scheme enlistees. Recruiting posters were full of pugnacious sentimentality that was equally tasteless, one

* Accepting the King's shilling was the traditional symbol of enlistment.

of them calculated to shame the reluctant citizen into joining the Army through the device of the young daughter on her father's knee, asking, "Daddy, what did YOU do in the Great War?" Another, "Go! It's your Duty, Lad," was illustrated by a little but determined old lady steering her proud and eager young son into the awaiting ranks. None of the recruits on the square looked anything at all like the debonair and patriotic civilian of the poster.

Leaving the dreary exhibition, Shaw walked back to Adelphi Terrace and wrote to Lord Derby, suggesting that he costume his most attractive young recruits as civilians, with instructions to return repeatedly to the square to enlist ostentatiously, "care being taken at the same time to hurry away all unpleasant looking heroes to barracks before their appearance could act as a deterrent."[32]

Back from the War Office came a reply:

I quite agree that what you mention is an example of appalling bad stage management, and I will give a hint to the people who go to Trafalgar Square not to do it again. It is very good of you to take the trouble to let me know about these sort of things, otherwise one never would hear. Don't you think you could be tempted to come to me here in the official position as Stage Manager of Trafalgar Square Recruiting Meetings[?] . . .[33]

"I had other fish to fry," Shaw observed afterward, "and had to excuse myself from this job: the only one offered me in those days of voluntary service."[34] His other fish to fry, however, had even less to do with the stage. As he wrote Stella, "The theatre is passing away from me as a sort of wild oats; I go back to politics, religion and philosophy. They give me frightful headaches, but satisfy my soul."[35]

When his interest in a major work for the theatre would return it would be as a vehicle for expressing his politics, religion, and philosophy, but at the moment those extracurricular concerns* were making

* Extracurricular concerns which nevertheless did not prevent his being the most active nonofficer member of the Society of Authors, working on both the committee of management and the dramatic subcommittee. That October he even revised, for Herbert Thring, the secretary, a communication to members on changes in the operating methods of the Society and in its fee structure.

him *persona non grata* among many of his playwriting colleagues. Their unhappiness with him which had smoldered since the appearance of his *Common Sense* pamphlet finally flared up with symbolic appropriateness at a meeting of the Dramatists' Club (to which he had carefully not been invited) on October 27, forcing H. M. Paull, the secretary, to write to him later that day:

I regret to say that at today's meeting of the Club I was instructed (as the secretary) to write to you to inform you that several members of the Club have intimated that they refrain from attending the meetings as they do not wish to meet you, owing to your attitude with regard to the war. In these circumstances the members present presumed that you will prefer that the usual notice of meetings shall not be sent to you for the present.[36]

It was no difficult feat to guess the source of the trouble, and Shaw sent Paull's letter to Henry Arthur Jones, scrawling at the bottom

My dear H. A. J.
    I hope *you* are not one of the "several members," though in these raving mad times it is hard to know.
    Cheerful sort of club, isn't it?[37]

Then Shaw sent a long letter to Paull, pointing out that he enjoyed the company of his fellow members and had no intention of depriving himself of the pleasure of their company. To accept the invitation to dissociate himself, he added, would in effect turn a professional group into a political club; thus he would not do so voluntarily, but instead would insist upon a full hearing, with an appropriate resolution of expulsion to be moved and debated in his presence. He outlined the parliamentary procedure involved, and its implications, in what he hoped would be intimidating detail to Paull, but Paull was only following his instructions, as was made clear from a scolding reply Shaw received from Jones.

In reply to yours, I was present at last Wednesday's lunch, and I strongly supported the proposal that Paull should write to you in the terms of the letter you enclose.

I believe that England's cause is a most righteous one. I am sure that England did not provoke this war. I am sure that Germany did. These are, to me, not matters of opinion, but clearly established facts.

Your writings on the War have done great harm to our cause in America and neutral countries. Germany is everywhere making use of your utterances to justify her own actions and to befoul and slander England. Whether you know it or not, and whether you care or not, you are one of our country's worst enemies. And you are an enemy within our walls. . . .

Even if what you said was true, it was yet a foolish, mad, and mischievous thing to say at that moment. . . . If you do not allow that our cause is just, do you wonder that every Englishman is against you? Do you wander that you are regarded as a man who, for the sake of showing his agility, kicked and defamed his mother when she was on a sick-bed? You will say that England is not your mother—well then put it that Englishmen regard you as a man who kicked and defamed *their* mother when she was on a sick-bed. . . .[38]

Shaw responded the next day in a long letter in which there was no trace of resentment. Asking for his old friend's *personal* opinions, he warned, jovially, "If you think you are going to put ME off with a sheet of notepaper containing extracts from the Daily Express copied with your own fair hand, you have mistaken your man."[39] But neither Jones nor most other members of the club were in a mood for laughter, and Shaw's forced lightheartedness in letters to his playwright colleagues only resulted in such laconic comments as Arthur Pinero's "I am very sorry, but the facts are as stated by Paull."[40] Shaw argued to Pinero that no one attended the club anyway except those to whom he was only a bloody schoolmaster, but it was that very group which then called a meeting without notifying Shaw and solemnly expelled him. In vain Shaw protested that the proceedings were without legality and that he was still a member of the club, but that in protest at the organization's having become "a political and not a professional club" he would resign.[41] A few others volunteered to join him, notably Granville-Barker (who never attended anyway), Alfred Sutro, Jerome K. Jerome, and Israel Zangwill, who wrote Paull that the club was not a collection of grocers or colonels "but men of letters, who should be the last to cramp healthy diversity of opinion. . . ."[42] Zangwill had been leading a campaign to permit membership of women in the club, and Shaw prevailed upon him to remain to see his fight through.

Next it was the membership of the Society of Authors—or at least a noisy minority—that rose up to protest at Shaw's presence, although he had been its leading spirit for years. At a committee meeting, bestselling novelist W. J. Locke arose screaming, "I will not sit in the same room with Mr. Bernard Shaw," and left, banging the door behind him. The *NS*'s Jack Squire was equally nasty, but soon afterward that phase of war delirium passed, and both men came to Shaw and mutely offered to shake hands. He did.[43]

5

Shaw *Redivivus*

LATE IN October 1915, G.B.S. found himself in the unexpected position of preparing propaganda for the British cause. Not
content with using his Beveridge interview against the Allies in
Belgium, the Germans had circulated a document in Arabic throughout Morocco and Algeria to the effect that Shaw was a great Western
prophet and that he had told an American senator that violation of
Belgian neutrality was only a technicality, since there would have
been war with England and France without it. The aim was to help
stir the French colonies into rebellion and to prod the Spanish into
assisting any uprising. Heading for Gibraltar to initiate counterpropa-
ganda in the Mediterranean was novelist—then captain—A. E. W.
Mason, who before leaving wrote his friend Shaw* that he needed
help. "If you will let me have a very short statement, just three or
four lines, not arguing, but declaring in the simplest way that you
wish whole-heartedly for the victory of your own country and the
defeat of Germany in this war. I will take care that it is printed and
circulated. . . ."[1]

* In whose play *Arms and the Man* he had acted in 1894.

Shaw convinced Mason that conciseness was no virtue in addressing shiekhs. "Also," said Shaw afterward, "I am not the man to lose an opportunity of preaching at the utmost admissible length when I find myself installed as a great prophet. Mason and I were not men of letters for nothing. We combined the style of our Bible with that of Burton's Arabian Nights in a prophetic message which will, I hope, find a permanent place in Arab literature as an additional surah of the Koran. It was, I assume, duly translated and circulated; anyhow, the Moors lay low and did nothing."*[2]

The epistle to the Moors was composed only a few days after Shaw had made his first appearance on the lecture platform since the winter of public discontent about *Common Sense* nearly a year before. "Riots were expected," Shaw wrote Mrs. Campbell, "but the result was three hundred people turned away, and only two questions, both about Jesus Christ."[3] It was true that there was great anticipation about his first appearance, the opening lecture in the annual Fabian autumn series of six, collectively titled in 1915 "The World after the War." Many Englishmen really thought Shaw's name had become a reproach throughout the empire, that his house was guarded to protect him from assassination, that his plays had been banished from the stage, and that sales of his books had ceased. Actually the Press Bureau had tried to suppress reports of the new Shavian appearance in hopes of making the rumors appear accurate while limiting the impact of Shaw's words; yet the number of reporters present at King's Hall, Covent Garden, when Shaw—in soberly dark suit and carefully trimmed beard—spoke on "The Illusions of War" on October 26, was the largest he had ever seen from the platform. Since his head was not carried off on a platter at the end of the meeting, the censorship apparently felt it necessary to suppress all accounts, with only the *Manchester Guardian* and a few provincial dailies—in Liverpool, Sheffield, and Cardiff—

* According to Mason's less romantic account, his request was followed within two hours by a "most ample" typewritten statement in which Shaw declared not only his hope that the Allies would win, but his prediction that they would win, "and a warning to all whom it might concern not to be led into any doubt of that." Mason had a suitable version rendered into Arabic and delivered to General Lyautey in Morocco.

defying the ban. "Fair sprinkling of reporters at Press table," jibed the weekly *New Age*: "In view of subsequent silence of the daily Press, one assumes that most of these represented 'The Grocer's Gazette,' 'The Mark Lane Express,' and other more or less impartial journals."

In the chair to introduce Shaw was Bertrand Russell, already *persona non grata* with the authorities for his pacificism and anticonscription activities. Russell had asked Shaw what he might say in the introduction, and Shaw told him to say whatever he pleased. As for himself, Shaw added, he was not going to be conciliatory and bland. He meant to be listened to and hoped to establish the right key from the beginning—"as much ostensible defiance of the lightning as possible."[4] Lytton Strachey was there, eager for a militantly pacifist oration, but with disappointment he recorded instead "poor dear Mr. Shaw talking about 'England' with trembling lips and gleaming eyes, and declaring that we should first beat the Germans, and then fight them again, and then beat them again, and again, and again! He was more like a nice old-fashioned Admiral on a quarter-deck than anything else. And the newspapers are so stupid that, simply because he's Mr. Shaw, they won't report him—instead of running him as our leading patriot."[5] But Shaw had not changed. Public opinion was beginning to shift in his direction, and Strachey refused to see through his dislike of Shaw to the reasonableness G.B.S. often disguised with abrasive rhetoric. This may have been the censorship's real reason for persisting in suppressing reports of his speeches, for Shaw's attacks were not upon the government but upon the Anti-German League and other advocates of vindictiveness. He suggested that the real gentleman in wartime was the one who refused to hate his enemy and that war was tolerable to honorable soldiers only when it was not a matter of spiteful and vicious hatred. In a real sense, he said, the brave man was the man who loved his enemy. "It is time," he urged, "for the gentlemen of England to take the upper hand." A G.B.S. note card prepared for the lectures suggests that his aim was to puncture the major clichés by which the war was being fought:

1. The judgment of God is an Illusion.
2. The destruction of Germany is an Illusion.

3. The notion that we can never again be friends with the Germans is an Illusion.
4. The conclusive peace is an Illusion.
5. The inviolability of Neutralized Buffer States is an Illusion.
6. The sacredness of treaties is an Illusion.
7. The War to End War is an Illusion.[6]

The major illusion Shaw set out to dispel was what he called the "ecstatic" view of war, recalling for his audience the terrible scene in *The Bacchae* of Euripides, where the Bacchante Agave, who thinks that she has torn a wild beast to pieces while in the grip of Dionysiac frenzy, discovers that the dripping head she is carrying in triumph is that of her son. Many an English mother, he predicted, would wake from her patriotic delusion to a similar horror. As a result he could see only lack of proportion in the rage at the sinking of the *Lusitania* or at Zeppelin casualties at home when there were far more terrible losses in Flanders.[7]

The *New Age* carped about Shaw's "sonorous closing periods" and the "sensible remarks here and there, like a few currants in a cake," and Manchester *Sunday Chronicle* cynically pronounced the ninety-minute address as a self-advertising failure, "for only one London paper considered it worth notice." But "Dangle," the *Chronicle's* columnist, felt that the lecture had been important for what it revealed to him of Shaw's dark motives. Shaw, he asserted,

has always found his spiritual home in Germany. He has been the interpreter to British readers of three representative Germans, Wagner, Nietzsche, and Schopenhauer. His Fabian ideas of social reconstruction are inspired by Berlinese notions of symmetry. His sneering perversity is evidently of the same family as Goethe's Devil. That is probably why his popularity has been far greater in Germany than in his own country.

For many years the high-browed Teutons have established Shaw among the prophets, have made an aureole of his flaming whiskers, and enshrined his snuff-coloured Jaegers in metaphoric stained glass.

Naturally, Mr. Shaw is grateful. Naturally, he reciprocates. Naturally, he thinks they must be jolly nice and clever and worthy people who have found him so nice and clever and respectable.

For after all, despite appearances, and though it is difficult to suppose

that he ever had a mother, there is reason for the belief that Mr. Shaw
is partly human.

But while Mr. Shaw's human attributes naturally incline him to a grateful regard for the Germans, we others whom the Germans have not
deified, but only "strafed," have cause to scrutinise his views on the
war with suspicious watchfullness. . . .

Three weekly lectures were to intervene before the press could
have another turn at G.B.S.—Beatrice Webb on "War and the Spirit
of Revolt," Sidney Webb on "War and the Control of Wealth," and
Beatrice again on "The War and the Demand for 'The Servile State.'"
For Shaw it became a busy and difficult month. On October 30 "Way-
farer" in the *Nation* had reported, "Mr. Shaw's new play for the Irish
Theatre, called 'O'Flaherty, V.C.', is an entirely fresh and delightful
frolic." It was exactly that, but not to the authorities in Dublin
Castle. "Incomprehensible as it may seem to an Englishman," said
Shaw, "Irish patriotism does not take the form of devotion to England and England's king."[8] Unable to understand this, the War Office
attempted to encourage recruiting in Ireland by covering walls with
placards urging "REMEMBER BELGIUM," discouraging the forma-
tion of Irish units, and refusing commissions to Roman Catholics who
lived in Ireland. Shaw had subtitled his playlet "a recruiting pamphlet,"
and thought of it as "a recruiting poster in disguise." To stimulate an
Irishman's loyalty to Ireland would only encourage him to stay on
the native soil and die for it, he thought, while a better device to get
him to want to leave Ireland was to "appeal to his discontent, his deadly
boredom, his thwarted curiosity and desire for change and adventure. . . ." There was another, unmentionable, inducement to recruiting, Shaw added—the conviction that the "happy home of the idealist" was an uncommon thing. "No one will ever know how many men
joined the army in 1914 and 1915 to escape from tyrants and taskmas-
ters, termagants and shrews, none of whom are any the less irksome
when they happen by ill-luck to be also our fathers, our mothers, our
wives and our children."[9]

Private Dennis O'Flaherty, a winner of the Victoria Cross, has come
home to his native village as part of a recruiting campaign that has
taken him wearily about Ireland. He is nervous about meeting his

formidable mother because he had led her to believe that he had been fighting in the German army, her loyalties making it impossible for her to believe that an Irishman could do anything else except fight against the English. The presence of English General (but Irish landowner) Sir Pearce Madigan notwithstanding, she flies at him in rage, for she had learned the truth when the news of his V.C. was released, even to his shaking hands with the King. His explanations leave her cold:

> "I didn't shake hands with him: he shook hands with me. Could I turn on the man in his own house, before his own wife, and his money in my pocket and in yours, and throw his civility back in his face?"
> "You would take the hand of a tyrant red with the blood of Ireland—"

O'Flaherty adroitly mollifies her by declaring that he joined the Army that would pay her the largest allowance. Tessie, his girl friend, is more interested in his prospects for a pension and in a gold chain taken from a German prisoner, evidence to Dennis that the interest shown in him by both women is primarily mercenary. Furious with both of them, he threatens to marry a Frenchwoman and leave Ireland, where he had been "imposed on and kept in ignorance," for good. Knowing his mother would refuse the offer, he even suggests that she go with him. "Ask me to die out of Ireland, is it?" she cries, "and the angels not find me when they come for me!" Rather, she hopes that the war—and thus her dependent's allowance—will last a long time. There is a row, and the two women, unwilling to quiet down, are pushed into Sir Pearce's country house and the door shut on them, leaving O'Flaherty in peace to ruminate to the General:

> O'FLAHERTY [*idyllically*]. What a discontented sort of an animal a man is, sir! Only a month ago, I was in the quiet of the country out at the front, with not a sound except the birds and the bellow of a cow in the distance as it might be, and the shrapnel making little clouds in the heavens, and the shells whistling, and maybe a yell or two when one of us was hit; and would you believe it, sir, I complained of the noise and wanted to have a peaceful hour at home. Well: them two has taught me a lesson. This morning, sir, when I was telling the boys here how I was longing to be back taking my part for king and country with the others, I was lying, as you well knew, sir. Now I can

go and say it with a clear conscience. Some likes war's alarums; and
some likes home life. I've tried both, sir; and I'm for war's alarums
now. I always was a quiet lad by natural disposition.

The play was too strong politically for the timid English authorities
in Ireland, and Shaw must have realized it, although hoping to evade
censorship through production out of the Lord Chamberlain's jurisdiction. Nothing else could have been reasonably expected for a play
which had its hero confess that he killed so many of the enemy
"because I was afeard that, if I didn't, they'd kill me," and who responds to the General's talk of the "sacred right for which we are fighting" and appeal to the newspaper view of the war. "There's not many
newsboys crying the evening paper in the trenches. They do say,
Sir Pearce, that we shall never beat the Boshes until we make Horatio
Bottomley Lord Leftenant of England. Do you think that's true, sir?"
Sir Pearce's explosion that in England the King is Lord Lieutenant
and that the war is a simple question of patriotism only leads to
O'Flaherty's "And what good has it ever done here in Ireland? . . .
The Boshes I kilt was more knowledgeable men than me; and what
better am I now that I've kilt them? What better is anybody? . . . No
war is right; and all the holy water that Father Quinlan ever blessed
couldn't make one right."[10]
The paradox that one might get unsophisticated Irishmen to fight
on England's side while suggesting that England, not Germany, was
the enemy, was viewed without humor at Dublin Castle, Augustine
Birrell, Secretary for Ireland, declaring to Shaw, "I have read your play
with interest, but it won't get a single recruit unless you are thinking
of joining up yourself. And as for my doing away with oaths [to the
King], you might as well ask me to do away with the Thirty-nine
Articles or the 'not's' in the Ten Commandments. Do use a little common sense." Further, the Commanding General of the Dublin District sent an intimidating letter to W. F. Bailey, a trustee of the Abbey
Theatre, while the play was already in rehearsal for a November 23
opening. While not suppressing the play outright, the General made
it impossible to stage it. "My recollection of the letter," St. John
Ervine (then the manager) wrote, "was . . . that, knowing the sort

of man G.B.S. was, he wished to warn us that if there were a riot in the theatre as a result of the production, the theatre's license would instantly be cancelled." Since the Abbey existed from one night's box office takings to the next, summary closure would have meant ruin, and Ervine, seeking advice, found that Yeats was in London and Lady Gregory in America. There was only Bailey, an excitable little man whose opinion was a foregone conclusion. Timidly Ervine took it.[11]

Shaw had offered the playlet free of royalty, but even so the Abbey proved unable to benefit from it. Commiserating with him, Horace Plunkett wrote from Dublin that he could understand why the play would be unsuitable, given "the present state of feeling," for either side could use the occasion for a demonstration that would only provoke counterdemonstrations. When the conscription question ceased to trouble Ireland, Plunkett hoped, "all could laugh and learn" from Shaw's play.[12] Sarcastically, Lucy Shaw, who had written to Ann Elder asking for a copy, returned her reaction to G.B.S.'s secretary while misnaming the playlet in the process.

Thank you for *Michael O'Flaherty*: it is obviously a play that could not have been produced during the war. It can easily be made into a three act play by additions that I shall humbly submit to the author when I see him, if I ever do again.

Why does he not offer himself as Lord Lieutenant for Ireland, he would soon make it anything but the figure head it has always been. He could have Horace Plunkett as Chief Secretary and McNulty as Under Secretary, and between them they could soon finish off Ireland.*[13]

Just after *O'Flaherty* "poster in disguise" was suppressed by the military in Dublin, Shaw received a paradoxical appeal from Lieutenant Colonel Matthew Nathan, then Undersecretary at the Viceregal Lodge, Dublin, asking help in counterbalancing the failure of official recruiting and War Loan propaganda in Ireland. Shaw pointed out that appeals to English patriotism were useless in Ireland. "I drafted a

---

* Lucy, no Irish patriot, nevertheless thought herself more one than her brother. G.B.S.'s boyhood friend, Edward McNulty—then a minor Bank of Ireland official—and his current closest Irish friend, Horace Plunkett—an Irish Commissioner—hardly represented nationalistic aspirations.

poster for him . . ." Shaw recalled, "and told him to print it on green paper and stick it up all over Ireland with instructions to the Royal Irish Constabulary to see that it was not torn down. He replied that the R.I.C., being a picked Protestant force, would themselves tear it down. . . ."[14] There the matter rested, and the conscription question never ceased to trouble Ireland during the war, for although the British eventually passed a conscription bill which included Ireland, threats to enforce it there became increasingly empty, especially after the events of Easter 1916. Shaw's recruiting playlet remained unperformed and his poster never printed.

At the same time, Shaw was having problems with another playlet on the war, *The Inca of Perusalem*, intended as a satire on the Kaiser and with a plot too complicated and too trivial to precis, but intended to make fun of Junker pomposity. Gertrude Kingston (who had played the Russian empress in Shaw's 1913 farce, *Great Catherine*), intending to act in and produce *The Inca*, had sent the text to the Lord Chamberlain's office for the usual clearance from the censor of plays and received a reply that requested, among other things, "Would you also kindly see that the make-up of the Inca does not too closely resemble the German Emperor." Indignant, Miss Kingston wrote to Shaw, "Apparently we are on the eve of concluding peace since we are not allowed to parody the German emperor! . . ."[15]

To get the play approved for production, Shaw had to respect the injunctions of the Lord Chamberlain, something he had not had to do for *O'Flaherty*, because by a technicality in the law the jurisdiction of the Censor's Office did not extend to Ireland, an opening effectively closed in any case by Irish prudery and the powers granted the government under DORA—the Defence of the Realm Act of 1914. However deadly an enemy, the Kaiser was after all a nephew of Victoria and a cousin of George V; thus Shaw had to alter his initial description from "The Inca, in a German military uniform . . ." to "The Inca, a handsome gentleman . . . in a military uniform and military moustaches." In his own printed rehearsal copy, Shaw lined out a number of speeches and stage directions, noting next to them, "cut to comply with license." One concerned the English way of getting rid of incompetent admirals by kicking them upstairs; another equated bravery with not having "sense enough to be afraid to die." To Robert Loraine in France, Shaw a few days earlier had sent an unamended copy, identified on the title page only as by "a member of the Royal Literary Society." He inscribed it, "from the Mysterious Author 12 Nov. 1915."[16]

Although Shaw's writing for the *New Statesman* had trickled to almost nothing, and the *NS* had refused his *Common Sense* sequel, he remained a loyal stockholder and director, and among his other activities was a mid-month *NS* directors' meeting. Afterward Shaw walked away with Arnold Bennett, who had become a director when it appeared as though Shaw would sever his connection with the paper and someone would be needed to purchase Shaw's shares. But G.B.S. had refused to sell, explaining to the other directors that if the shares were worthless he would not want to take Bennett's money for them (and that if they were to become valuable he would rather have retained the investment). Bennett's money meant then—as Shaw really wanted it to be—additional financial support for the young journal.

The meeting had not been a harmonious one. Pleased with himself, Sharp had reported cautiously that losses were running somewhat less than expected—only £800 in the first six months of the year—although the war had sent advertising revenue down to nearly nothing. To Sharp's horror, Shaw—knowing however that he had no chance of carrying his point—suggested that the *Statesman*'s situation made it all the more desirable that it take some editorial risks on the chance of winning more audience and more influence. "He had talked like that," Shaw explained of himself afterward in the street to Bennett, "as a 'hygienic operation,'" for "it was necessary to exaggerate in such hygiene . . . to bolster Sharp up." Bennett, whose sympathies lay with the pragmatic Sharp, nevertheless noted in his journal that "the fundamental decency and kindliness of Shaw was evident throughout."[17] Desmond MacCarthy, who was on the *New Statesman*'s staff at the time, agreed that Shaw bore Sharp's slashing and cutting of his material and the ignoring of his point of view, "with extraordinary patience," and that when he eventually gave up on getting a hearing in the *NS*, "it was without resentment. . . . I know of no other literary man of anything like his eminence who would have taken such treatment so good-naturedly."[18]

While G.B.S. and the *Statesman* remained in head-to-head combat, the *NS* nevertheless was reprinting as a sixpenny pamphlet Shaw's *Common Sense* supplement, which it had marketed as a back number until April, when stock ran out. In October it was again on sale, Shaw having written a new, brief preface for it. It was not that Sharp and the Webbs wanted it back in print, but the *NS*, which owned the plates, needed the money a reprint would earn, and there was a continuing demand for *Common Sense* because so many who had not read it originally sought it out. It had acquired such a mythic reputation that available copies were read until the coarse paper crumbled.

Although Shaw embraced the opportunity of the reprint to further expound his point of view, his preface became no substitute for the rejected "More Common Sense." Since he was not pressing to have it published elsewhere, he was technically correct when he wrote in the preface to the reprint, "If I be asked why I have not brought my 'Common Sense' up to date, I must reply that I have actually done so, but decided to keep the results to myself for the present. . . . As I do not wish Potsdam to win this war, I deliberately refrain from giving [the British newspaper press] fresh opportunities of making senseless mischief." But it was that very reason that made it necessary, he was convinced, to reissue *Common Sense*, for when it went out of print "the misrepresentations"—that he was "a declared partisan" of Germany—"began to gain on the truth."

As an example of the need to tell the truth to neutral nations bewildered by propaganda from both sides in the early months of the war, Shaw noted that he knew at the time, although the public did not, that "our searching of American and Swedish trading vessels and occasional confiscations of their cargoes, had led to strained relations with those countries. . . ." How *Common Sense* was to put that right Shaw failed to make clear, but he did insist, alluding to the behavior toward him of a "professional rhetorician" friend who claimed melodramatically that Shaw had kicked his mother in her deathbed, that the pamphlet had "still its work to do in getting rid of this silly and dishonourable travesty" about England's role in the war.

With the reprint in the press, Shaw prepared for his second Fabian lecture—fifth of six in the series—which he had titled "Diplomacy after the War." The printed syllabus indicated that he would discuss how diplomacy might reconcile the British claims for hegemony of the sea with German claims that her national interest required her to dominate the states that cut her off from the sea. It also said that he would point toward the postwar necessity of an international tribunal and an international legislature. He would, in fact, go further: "As soon as there is a war, the first thing should be to establish a Peace Council to decide what we are fighting for." According to the unsympathetic Labour *Sunday Herald*, "All the young women in 'arty' blouses and the young men with bangles on the left wrist enjoyed it hugely." The press corps was there again in full strength, causing Shaw to preface one remark with the mock aside, "I can tell you this, because I know it won't go beyond these four walls," and another with, "I don't mind saying this in the privacy of this meeting."

Mary Macarthur had provided the introduction, suggesting that pacifism become militant and positive and proposing that the Ministry of War be replaced—after the war—with a Ministry of Peace, the minister to be shot for his lack of success if war should break out during his tenure. Mr. Bernard Shaw, she added, should be the first peace minister! Shaw showed marked disinclination for the post, ignoring the suggestion and beginning his talk with some gibes at the occupants of the press table, then going on to outline again his proposal for a League of Western Civilization to embrace lands from the American Pacific Coast to the Carpathians, thus pointedly excluding Russia while including Germany. A question period followed, during which he was asked a question about German aims. "I don't like talking much about German diplomacy," he said, "because the Germans are an intelligent people, and take notice of what I say. I am constantly volunteering to be Prime Minister and Foreign Secretary of this country, and it takes no notice, but you may depend that if I make a similar offer to Germany that offer will be accepted." Initially an exasperated member of the audience had risen to ask, "When is Mr. Shaw going to deal with diplomacy after the war?"

"A gentleman asks me," Shaw responded, "when I am going to deliver the lecture on 'Diplomacy after the War,' as set forth in the syllabus of this series. I did not write that syllabus with the intention of speaking to it. I have never spoken to a syllabus in my life, and probably never shall. The object of that syllabus was to induce you to come and hear me talk about something else."[19]

There was no cause for audience concern about fidelity to the prospectus in the next (and final) lecture in the series, for it would be delivered by Sidney Webb, who was sure to remain undeviatingly close to the syllabus. As earnestly humorless as he was encyclopedic, the swarthy, bespectacled, and goateed Webb looked—and spoke—like a caricature of a German professor. There were consolations in his style, said one paper on announcing the lecture: "Even Shaw cannot be as wise as Webb looks."[20]

It was a busy week for G.B.S. The next day he and Charlotte entertained Sydney Cockerell, Mr. and Mrs. Vandervelde,* and Mrs. Lion Phillimore for lunch, after which the Vanderveldes went off to a meeting in behalf of Belgian relief at the Royal Automobile Club, and Cockerell, Mrs. Phillimore, and the Shaws traveled to the new Roman Catholic Westminster Cathedral to see former Fabian Eric Gill's controversial reliefs of the Stations of the Cross. Less than half of them had been sculpted and fixed by the end of 1915, and two more years' work lay ahead, but they had already attracted substantial attention. It was too misty to see Gill's work at its best, but all were more impressed than they had expected to be. Luncheons such as this were the Shaws' habitual method of entertaining, G.B.S. happier hosting a lunch than being a difficult guest at a dinner party, where a special vegetarian meal had to be prepared and where he and Charlotte would be expected to stay later than either enjoyed doing.

The mist turned to fine drizzle and lasted into the next day, but Shaw's weekdays in London were too full of meetings and social obligations to spend them at Adelphi Terrace. This time he went to a concert and conference on the relation of art to music and the drama. A trio performed old music; solosits sang Greek and Indian songs; and there were speeches, among them one by Lena Ashwell and another

---

* Lalla Vandervelde was the daughter of Edward Speyer, a banker and music dilettante; her husband was the Belgian Minister of Justice.

by Shaw.[21] Mornings (after going through the newspapers) and evenings, if possible, were devoted to writing; most of all Shaw counted on writing during long Thursday or Friday-to-Monday weekends at Ayot St. Lawrence, including working in a shorthand notebook between jolts from King's Cross station to Hatfield on the London, Midland and Scottish Railway.

The next week Shaw was back on the platform, this time speaking at a crowded meeting sponsored by the East London Federation of Suffragettes, held at the ornate Portman Rooms in Baker Street. It was not the hall at first advertised for the lecture, for the proprietors at the originally advertised location canceled the engagement after growing alarmed at the prospect of militant patriots and antisuffragettes breaking up the meeting—and the hall. No harm was done to the take, however, for there was a full house at the Portman Rooms at ticket prices ranging from five shillings to sixpence, the proceeds going to support "The Mother's Arms." (The public-house allusion in the name was intentional because Sylvia Pankhurst had converted one into a school for mothers.) As usual G.B.S. took no fee.

In the chair to offer the traditional introduction was Sylvia Pankhurst, the only one of the three militant Pankhursts who had not impugned his patriotism when *Common Sense* appeared. But Shaw sheltered few grudges, realizing that the suffragettes were playing sensible politics by accruing to themselves whatever advantage might come from the patriotic frenzies attendant upon the outbreak of war. Eventually their war fervor cooled, and Shaw could write to Mrs. Pankhurst such lines she approvingly quoted as "The men of this country are being sacrificed to the blunders of boobies, the cupidity of capitalists, the lusts and lies and rancors of bloodthirsts that love war, because it opens up their prison doors and sets them on the throne of power and popularity."*

For those expecting the G.B.S. of press accounts, his suffragette talk came as a surprise, as it was—or seemed—no less militant than a speech by Horatio Bottomley. Peace was not going to be achieved by

---

* The lines are quoted in the play *Oh, What a Lovely War* in a street corner speech by Mrs. Pankhurst which is greeted with derision at worst and misunderstanding at best.

England alone, he had come to realize, and it was certainly not going to be achieved by pacifism, however militant, for public desire to win the war increased with each additional commitment in resources and casualties and with public realization that any settlement based on the battle lines would be a German victory, however the circumlocutions of propaganda phrased it. Said Shaw, "All the conquests were on one side, and it was not on our side. We were loth to back out, and as a matter of fact we would not do so. The other evening a meeting was announced by a body calling itself the Union of Democratic Control, but it was broken up. It was perfectly clear that the persons who objected could have no objection to democratic control, because the breaking up of a meeting was the most crude form of it they could imagine. The reason was that this meeting was unfortunately announced by handbills headed by the word "Peace," and we as a nation were in such a temper at this moment that we were determined not to have peace, because that would mean we were vanquished. . . ."

Yet the militants on the home front (including those in Parliament), Shaw told Frank Harris afterward, reminded him in their posture just short of panic "of a certain prize fighter who flourished when I was a boy. His skill and power were such that he was always victorious at his weight; but he was so nervous that they had to keep a mirror in the ring to shew him his face between every round to disprove his piteous pleas that his features were obliterated and that they must throw up the sponge for him, as he would surely be killed if he went on."[22]

The pacifist meeting that nervous militants had suppressed had been scheduled for the evening of November 30 at Memorial Hall, Farringdon Street, an old building often pressed into service in radical causes. The U.D.C. had been formed in November 1914 to bring together Liberal, Socialist, and independent groups that viewed the war as a ghastly mistake and sought a negotiated peace and an open, democratically controlled foreign policy thereafter. Shaw had no doubt that they were theoretically right, but he saw no hope for such prospects in the immediate future and was concentrating instead on the redefinition of war goals toward ends he felt made the waste at the least more justifiable.

"Summer skies may come more than once before we see peace again in Europe," he warned those expecting a negotiated settlement. Even if the Germans withdrew to their frontiers and announced that they were ready for arbitration, he said, the Allies had to fight on, for they were fighting "a romantic dream from which it is absolutely necessary that the German peoples should be awakened." Meanwhile, he pointed out—his topic was "The Nation's Vitality"—war was not nearly as great a drain on national vitality as peace, for the drain of war to date had been 2½ percent of men under arms, while infant mortality and childhood malnutrition took a far greater toll. At the end of his address he picked up his watch from the table and paused. "Since I have been speaking, ladies and gentlemen, ten babies have died. I do not mean that there has been a Zeppelin raid. While I have been speaking, ten children have died, and nine of them have been murdered by you and me, by our neglect. If the war does wake us up on the subject, it will have been worth while."[23]

The Zeppelins were only part of the problem. It was a time of hysterical civilian militancy fanned by propaganda posters, the hardly less sensational press, the embarrassing failure at Gallipoli, the lengthening casualty lists from France, the collapse of the Asquith Cabinet and rise of the demagogic Lloyd George, and the first substantial Zeppelin raids on the populous Southeast of England. Pacifist meetings and anticonscription meetings were now broken up regularly while the police not only failed to intervene, but often arrested the most intractable opponents of the war, beginning for them—under the authority of the Defence of the Realm Act—the "dismal treadmill of arrest, court-martial, imprisonment, release, arrest, court-martial, and so on,"[24] until the unarrested G.B.S. began addressing usually futile appeals for the release of some of the victims. Later one of the better known civilian militants, Sir Arthur Conan Doyle, noted that "Had Shaw said in America what he said in England about the war whilst it was in progress he would have been in personal danger,"[25] and a German-American propagandist (known to G.B.S., however, only as a journalist) afterward was sufficiently suspicious of Shaw's freedom to utter wartime heresy to wonder whether Shaw had been, all the while, cynically exploited by the government. "Wells, it seems to me," George Sylvester Viereck wrote to Shaw a decade after the war, "made himself deliberately a British propagandist. You were yourself, but the British cleverly exploited the fact that you were permitted to speak with so much candour. This induced the illusion that freedom of speech was safe only in England. Consciously or unconsciously, you yourself were part of the elaborate liberal window dressing of the British Government. Behind this window dressing were the secret treaties, and in the intervals between your own explosive articles and detonations from Wells, the trained ear could discern the muffled roar of the British lion."[26]

Late in December 1915, Maxim Gorki wrote to Shaw to congratulate him on managing to stay aloof from the usual wartime passions, and Shaw answered that one had to accept madness as sanity when all the world had gone mad, for sanity, after all, was only the madness upon which the world happened to agree. In the madness Shaw's box office appeal had plummeted—on both sides of the ocean—and although he would have blamed overexposure of the plays as the sole reason, the Barker company of *Androcles and the Lion* and the Mrs. Campbell company of *Pygmalion* had both been grimly touring to half-empty houses. Shaw bluntly criticized Mrs. Pat for playing to houses of thirty pounds in cities incapable of filling a house in order to keep the play running. Great successes like *Pygmalion*, he warned her on December 19, were extremely dangerous, for they tempted producers to run them on until every farthing made in the successful months was lost in the downhill months. "If you cannot find a new play [in New York or London], go live in a cottage until you do find one," he scolded, adding that she was playing dangerous games with her prestige, for "the Shuberts and Klaws and Erlangers . . . know what business you are doing, and value you accordingly."*

On the last day of the year, co-producer of the *Androcles* tour, Percy Burton, wrote to Shaw from Toronto that the only one likely

---

* Mrs. Campbell dragged her feet over Shaw's warning and closed the tour only after fulfilling commitments through March in such cities as Lorain, Ohio; Fort Wayne, Indiana; Port Huron, Michigan; London, Ontario; Poughkeepsie, New York; Atlantic City, New Jersey; Punxsutawney, Pennsylvania; and Parkersburg, West Virginia.

to make any money was the author, who was paid his royalties whatever the production losses. Audiences were very poor, Burton reported, putting the blame upon Shaw's wartime stand. "They don't seem to like you or your works up there at present at all, at all. However, I don't suppose you will worry much, if at all. . . ." He closed sardonically "With all good wishes for the New Year and for your conversion. . . ." With that Burton called an end to the tour.[27]

6

Helplessness

ON JANUARY 3, 1916, early in the evening, Lillah McCarthy received a long letter from Granville-Barker, written from New York. He was not coming back to her and wanted a divorce. Although it was what she had been fearing for months, the news left her shaken, and she knew the place she had to run to was No. 10 Adelphi Terrace. In a version of her memoirs she never published, she described what happened:

I went, all frozen on a cold January night. . . . I found myself at the flat. . . . Shaw greeted me very tenderly and made me sit by the fire. I was shivering. Shaw sat very still. The fire brought me warmth. . . . How long we sat there I do not know, but presently I found myself walking with dragging steps with Shaw beside me . . . up and down Adelphi Terrace. The weight upon me grew a little lighter and released the tears which would never come before . . . he let me cry.[1]

Emotionally spent, she realized that there was more to living than feeling sorry for herself, and went on with rehearsals for a Stage Society play in which she was involved. Only Shaw knew of the situation, Lillah telling no one else, but instead returning quietly after the play to her country home at Stansted. Bypassing England, Barker returned to Red Cross work in France, writing Shaw where he was going. For G.B.S., who for a dozen years had been a surrogate parent to both, the breakup of the marriage was a calamity, and he tried to do whatever he could to ease an outcome that had been inevitable since Barker had first met Helen Huntington. After seeing Lillah once more, Shaw wrote a long letter to her on the nineteenth, recommending (with some psychological sleight of hand) that she "get rid of Harley":

He has gone to France; and I have now no belief that you and he will ever patch it up again. If I am right, then the sooner you set yourself free the better for you, and the more creditable for him, as you are now at the height of your powers, and not soured or aged by your disagreement with him. I don't know whether either of you is to blame, or, if either, which; and it doesn't matter anyhow; but it seems to me that if you come together again you are more likely to drive one another mad than to settle down happily. I don't see why you should not be happily married; but I gravely doubt whether Harley is fit for married life at all: and I certainly do not advise you to push the experiment beyond the ten years in which you have already had the best of such capacity for domesticity as he possesses.[2]

In the meantime Shaw wrote to Barker, for whom his affection was tried but undiminished, that he should send Lillah a letter that could be shown to a lawyer; Barker did. "I cannot express to you how futilely intrusive I felt the other night," Shaw wrote her. "But what could I do? An Englishwoman can . . . be consoled with a little sentiment; an Irishwoman (which is what you essentially are) does not want to be humbugged. . . ."[3]

To help get Lillah's mind onto something else, Shaw began reworking for her an essay he had been writing for the *Nation*, a belated review of Arnold Bennett's *The Author's Craft* that he had turned into a spoofing of Bennett's assertion that play-writing was easier than novel-writing. "I am not going to argue," Shaw had written. "I never do. I will simply take one of the shortest, most intense, and most famous scenes in English dramatic literature and rewrite it as a chapter in a novel in the style of my friends Bennett and Galsworthy when they are too lazy to write plays."[4] The scene was the fight with Macduff in the last act, which Shaw parodied in the undramatic clichés of the new realism in fiction. With that as springboard, he produced for Lillah and Gerald du Maurier a modern colloquial parody of *Macbeth* that began with the fifth scene, a paste-up version that included patches of Shakespeare and additions by Shaw. Where Lady Macbeth is given the Bard's lines, Macbeth is baffled by them, and (in Shaw's lines) protests being ordered to kill Duncan. "You see, dearie . . ." he says, "I enjoy being popular. You dont, I know; but I do. It may be a weakness; but if I were to murder the old man the very first night he is staying with us, I should lose sympathy. I really dont think people would like it." The skit was never produced. "Gerald would not burlesque himself," said Shaw. "Probably he considered himself an ideal Macbeth."[5]

For Lillah the insubstantial skit may have provided some brief cheer. For Bennett, victim of the piece that had started it all, it would have provided no cheer whatever to know when he was invited to luncheon at the Shaws at the end of January that a parody of his fiction style was in a desk drawer in the next room, awaiting publication in March.

Writing for the stage—or at least writing seriously for the stage— was without the incentive of foreseeable production, the change according to Shaw being "not in the theatres or in the management of them, nor in the authors and actors, but in the audiences." Throughout the war the theatres were crowded, but crowded with soldiers, many on leave from the front. He observed, "These soldiers were no seasoned London playgoers. . . . In 1915 I saw in the theatres men in khaki . . . [who] had never been in a theatre before and did not know what it was. At one of our great variety theatres I sat beside a young officer, not at all a rough specimen, who, even when the curtain rose and enlightened him as to the place where he had to look for his entertainment, found the dramatic part of it utterly incomprehensible. He did not know how to play his part of the game. . . . In his presence I realized how very sophisticated the natural man has to become before

the conventions of the theatre can be easily acceptable, or the purpose of the drama obvious to him.[6]

For the serious playwright, the prospect of a wartime audience was inhibiting, since the theatregoing novices in khaki, "accompanied by damsels (called flappers) often as innocent as themselves, crowded the theatres to the doors. It was hardly possible at first to find stuff crude enough to nurse them on. The best music-hall comedians ransacked their memories for the oldest quips and the most childish antics to avoid carrying the military spectators out of their depth." Although he thought the playgoing novices could have used the lessons in sophistication and would have gone to the theatre no matter what the fare, Shaw better understood what he was up against after talking to more cultivated members of the military, who confessed that they, too, at first to their own astonishment, were "thirsting for silly jokes, dances, and brainlessly sensuous exhibitions of pretty girls." One young playwright told him that "after enduring the trenches for months without a glimpse of the female of his species, it gave him an entirely innocent but delightful pleasure merely to see a flapper. The reaction from the battle-field produced a condition of hyperaesthesia in which all the theatrical values were altered. Trivial things gained in intensity and stale things in novelty." The result was that the West End had little more to do than "exploit the bliss of smiling men who were no longer under fire and under military discipline, but actually clean and comfortable and in a mood to be pleased with anything. . . ." Thus Shaw wrote pamphlets on the war instead of plays, leaving the stage for bedroom comedies and song-and-dance men.

You cannot make war on war and on your neighbor at the same time. War cannot bear the terrible castigation of comedy, the ruthless light of laughter that glares on the stage. When men are heroically dying for their country, it is not the time to shew their lovers and wives and fathers and mothers how they are being sacrificed to the blunders of boobies, the cupidity of capitalists, the ambition of conquerors, the electioneering of demagogues, the Pharisaism of patriots, the lusts and lies and rancors and bloodthirsts that love war because it opens their prison doors, and sets them in the thrones of power and popularity. For unless these things are mercilessly exposed they will hide under the mantle of the ideals on the stage just as they do in real life.

And though there may be better things to reveal, it may not, and indeed cannot, be militarily expedient to reveal them whilst the issue is still in the balance. Truth telling is not compatible with the defence of the realm. . . .[7]

In early 1916 even *O'Flaherty* was still too extreme. Shaw wrote to producer Arthur Bourchier that he had written two farcical playlets on the war, but had concluded that even they were currently "unbearable." Even the 1894 period piece, *Arms and the Man*, "jars," he now realized. "It was played on New Year's Day in Scotland before— among others—a colonel home on leave from the front. He said it was quite extraordinary how I knew all about it without any experience, and that Loos was just like the charge at Slivnitza as I described it: 'simple suicide': only the pistol *did* go off (in the play it didn't); but for that very reason he could hardly stand it. The touch of our art makes the thing live. . . ."[8]

Conscription still hung fire in January, stimulating Shaw to a different kind of writing about the war, eleventh-hour appeals to stave off the inevitable, addressed to his most responsive vehicles, the *Daily News* and the *Nation*. Asquith had introduced a military service bill on January 5 that declared that all single men would be deemed to have enlisted and to have been transferred to the Reserve, from which they would be called up as needed. On the same day, Shaw published a long letter in the *Daily News* attacking Asquith and insisting that conscription was not proved necessary merely because the generals wanted it. The débacle at the Dardanelles and the attrition in the trenches were not conducive to voluntary enlistment, however, and although protests had a braking effect, they only delayed consideration of a bill in Commons. With little hope that it would help, Shaw nevertheless dispatched another letter on the subject, this time to the *Nation*, pointing out the need to retain skilled industrial manpower, that it was not necessary as France's ally to share France's economic ruin. The change in England being brought about by conscription, Shaw thought later, was more profound than any other wartime act, for it brought the war literally home, not by an occasional bomb from a Zeppelin, but by ending the rhetoric about individual liberty that had withstood the centuries. "No article of faith was better established than that Englishmen would never stand conscription, whatever spiritless Frenchmen and Germans might put up with."

Shaw's public activities ranged from serious to silly. Labourite Fenner Brockway had published a one-act play, *The Devil's Business*, that was primarily an interview between members of a fictitious English Cabinet and an armaments salesman, a touchy matter at any time, but more so during a period when the Army in France was being plagued by ammunition shortages and by inferior ammunition to such an extent that the news leaked into the papers. The police seized all copies on sale in London, successfully claiming in court that actual Cabinet personages were thinly caricatured. Brockway appealed to Shaw, who answered that under DORA the government could do what it pleased, but since the magistrate who had heard the case claimed that there was actually no trial, there could be no contempt of court in reprinting the play as if nothing had happened. The important thing, Shaw warned, was not to appeal. "At the present pass . . ." he added, "it is more important to get plenty of munitions than to bother about the shareholders who are making money out of them." Brockway reprinted and sold copies in Manchester while others lay impounded in London, and Lloyd George, caricatured harmlessly in the play, went on building his reputation by becoming the efficient dictator of the domestic munitions industry.[9] Shaw would later caricature Lloyd George in a play himself. Meanwhile his vendetta against vaccination inspired one of his sillier letters to the editor, as the next day there appeared one under his name in the Dublin *Evening Telegraph* supporting a local society that had protested compulsory vaccination. It was an axe G.B.S. ground with tiresome regularity, never—after contracting smallpox in his twenties—having forgiven the doctor who had vaccinated him as a boy. The previous year he had written two antivaccination letters, one to the *NS*, which Clifford Sharp felt was harmless enough to publish, and another to the *Times*, which it refused.

Although he offered his public—and often trivial—letters unstintingly, he remained niggardly about public appearances, making them only when the spirit moved him, and absolutely refusing princely sums from America. In February 1916 one American agency offered him a minimum of fifty lectures and fifty thousand dollars, expenses paid. Another suggested that Shaw accept 75 percent of the gross for as many lectures as he cared to deliver, while a third simply asked if he would come when the war was over, details to be worked out later. He rejected them all.

From his own rejected "More Common Sense," Shaw had been lifting material to be reworked as articles, preferring to lecture the public when possible in the press rather than from the platform. Speaking to an audience in a hall might raise funds for a worthy cause, but it was no longer, in his case, assured of being reported at length in the newspapers, and it was also preaching to gatherings of the saved. What Shaw wanted most was to reach out to the most articulate and influential part of society, the group to whom he appealed in a "More Common Sense" spin-off in the *NS*, entitled "Wanted: A Coalition of the Intelligentsia":

Perhaps the grimmest feature of this war, as all wars, is the helplessness of the Intelligentsia. In vain do we play at being romantic schoolboys, stupefying ourselves with Quixotic reveries, lashing ourselves into virtuous indignations, and calling the clay we were born on our Mother. We loathe war as an abomination forced on us by crude and corrupt people long after we have morally outgrown it. Being unable to suppress it, we would like to obtain control of it sufficiently to dictate its aims and define its limits. But, though we write the most intelligent and interesting and suggestive articles, we might as well discharge popguns. If it were not for the attacks we make on one another, our utterances would pass without notice. They remain in any case without effect. Intelligence is not organized: everything else is, more or less. The War Office has not so much brains as the brim of Mr. Chesterton's hat; the Cabinet has not as much knowledge of political science or even of the everyday facts of four-fifths of English society as Mr. Arnold Bennett's umbrella; Maxim Gorky and Romain Rolland and H. G. Wells know more of the real needs of civilisation than all the Governments of Europe. Yet these clever persons count for nothing out of it except as more or less amusing cranks. . . . [Some] are actually proud of their futile isolation, and call it their originality. . . .

Now the question is, is the world which neglects us right? Do we matter, we literary sages, except as newsmen and story tellers?[10]

It was clearly a cry from the heart, and although G.B.S. had left his own name, but for by-line, out of the article, it could have been substituted not only for any other name he mentioned, but for all the names. No one however, was listening to him. Barker and Lillah paid no more attention to his advice than Asquith and Lloyd George, and even the apparently loyal Webbs seemed to think that on the subject of the war he was a crank who daily became less amusing and more damaging, by association, to Fabian domestic causes. When he was approached by a friend about Shaw's "coalition" idea, Arnold Bennett dismissed it as "idiotic," praise of him in the piece notwithstanding.[11] Since he was not a pacifist, Shaw had few supporters in that quarter either, and since he subscribed to no point of view around which any anti-Establishment group rallied, his position remained a lonely one. It came as a surprise to an American college professor working on a biographical study of Shaw that the great man responded to his queries rapidly and at great length; but such interest in him was what Shaw needed at the time, and Thomas Denis O'Bolger elicited revealing confessions[12] about the *ménage à trois* in which Shaw grew up in Dublin, confessions he afterward refused to let O'Bolger publish.* His authorized biographer (of a 1911 volume), Archibald Henderson, also entered into discussions, which Shaw encouraged, about a revised edition; Shaw, already thinking of his post-war reputation, told him that any new book would have to have a chap-

---

* In 1919 and again in 1921, Shaw torpedoed publishing agreements O'Bolger had made by refusing to permit his letters to be quoted (except, apparently, as he intended to edit them, *ex post facto*). Eventually Shaw had his way. O'Bolger died a disappointed man, and Shaw published some of his letters to O'Bolger in expurgated form in *Sixteen Self Sketches* (1949), when he was ninety-three.

ter about his entry into foreign affairs before the war and his activities since, chapters which would be difficult to write, especially the one about *Common Sense* and its aftermath. He felt harassed in many ways, he confided to Henderson, and thought there was something symbolic about his having returned to him by the censor each picture postcard he sent out of England together with a copy of the obtuse regulation forbidding it.[13] (These theoretically gave the enemy information about sites and topography in England.)

Still unable to get going on any extensive writing project, Shaw kept busy in a variety of trivial ways, even judging an essay contest for the suffragette *Women's Dreadnought*, explaining that the first prize had gone to Miss Crutchfield "because she has not made a single mistake. . . . I think she must have got the clergyman to write it for her." It was an awkward winter for Shaw.

Early in February Barker returned to London and met Lillah at Shaw's flat. He made no excuses, but insisted that Lillah release him to remarry. Lillah, after asking him vainly what she had done to cause him to fall out of love, stubbornly insisted that he was victim of an infatuation that would pass. Shaw had failed with both of them. Afterward he took Barker with him for the weekend at Ayot St. Lawrence, but it was not to reason with him. A few days later, Barker was back in Boulogne en route to his Red Cross public relations duties, work he did halfheartedly to keep out of England and Lillah's paths. The immediate result was a mediocre propaganda work, *The Red Cross in France*. As Shaw realized, Barker was lost not only to Lillah, but to the theatre.

On March 4, 1916, Shaw began writing the first scene of a new play he had had in mind for nearly three years. The words did not come easily amid the distractions, but he knew he had to make a beginning, even if it meant a few exchanges of dialogue at a sitting, and those unsatisfactory.[14] There were emotional scenes with Lillah. A conscription bill was about to be rammed through Parliament, making Barker, at thirty-eight, draft-eligible. Loraine, once wounded, was back in action. Shaw's sister was so ill that when Mrs. Pat soon afterward asked for her address, he wrote chillingly, "Lucy's address for the moment is 2 Grover Park, Camberwell Grove, S.E. Later on, The Crematorium, Golders Green."[*15] As for his own speeches and writings, he wondered whether he was deluding himself into believing that anyone was paying attention, since so little seemed changed; except for the loyal Charles Macdona, no company in England was doing Shaw, Macdona trying to take up the slack by playing in repertory throughout the provinces, often to lean receipts. (In the neutral countries, G.B.S. was still popular.) There was new trouble in Ireland, where extremists considered Shaw disloyal, while adherents to the Crown found his alleged pro-Germanism even more likely to render him untrustworthy than his Irish birth. The symbolic absurdity in his case occurred in March when the offices of the Gaelic Press in Dublin were raided by the authorities, and the most heralded of the suspect matter seized was a copy of Shaw's *Three Plays for Puritans* (1900). The puzzled manager of the press, recalling the fuss over *O'Flaherty, V.C.,* wrote to Shaw inquiring whether the book contained "seditious matter or matter likely to prejudice recruiting." Shaw, correctly, replied that he did not think the raid was planned with the object of seizing his book, although some references might have been mistakenly thought to be contemporary. There was a reference in *The Devil's Disciple* to "a pigheaded lunatic like King George," but the action of the play was 1777, and the George was the Third rather than the Fifth.

Other English authorities were deliberately overlooking a traffic in German books Shaw had established directly with an enemy company, S. Fischer Verlag of Berlin, publishers of his books. German war prisoners in England wanted books to read, especially *Pygmalion,* and Shaw first supplied prison camps with books from his own col-

---

* Lucy herself, writing to Shaw's secretary Ann Elder, on March 2, 1916, reported upon the toll the war—and time—had taken from Shaw's greying mane, her condition having inspired a rare visit from her brother. "What has the 'Super-one' done to his hair? I intended to have asked him, but other things ousted it from my mind. It looks as if it were all worn away from the front, and he had such beautiful thick hair."

lection, then imported them from Germany by whatever indirect means S. Fischer could devise. At the same time, G.B.S. was receiving mail from both English and French prisoners in German camps who had less difficulty obtaining German editions of his plays and wanted to discuss their finer points with the author, a situation that caused him to assume that their treatment was not as bad as English newspapers led the public to believe.[16]

The fiscal year 1915–16 ended for Shaw on March 31, with earnings he noted in his ledger as £8938.8.7, barely half his income of the year before.[17] He needed no prompting to figure out the causes for the decline. Receipts for the new year were not aided by such performances as that of *You Never Can Tell* in Alexandria, Egypt, early in April, where the imperious Mrs. Clandon was played by a fat Syrian who did not understand her lines and put her emphases in the wrong places. The rest of the cast was little better, although one spoke good English, thus sounding out of tune with the others. Having filled the front rows with friends of the cast who cheered and threw bouquets at the curtain, the management was certain that the play would be considered a success.[18] Shaw, however, was not in the management's plans. He never saw any royalties.

Easter holiday time for schoolchildren during the war often meant an excursion to a neighboring farm to help in planting or picking. One group of girls went in 1916 to Kendala, the Hertfordshire estate of Robert and Lion Phillimore, to dig potatoes. An elderly man visiting the Phillimores watched them dig and sort the potatoes by size, wrinkling up their noses at the decaying ones they had to discard.

"Do you know what you must do if you sell these potatoes in the City?" he asked. "You must carefully put one foot on the scale behind the potatoes—just like this—to increase the weight. But if you're *buying* potatoes"—and he made a different sort of wiggling motion with the toe of his shoe—"you must try to put your foot *under* the scale instead."

The girls were baffled by the advice. They came from a fashionable school. None had ever bought potatoes, and none was ever likely to sell them. The tall old man, who had never had school-age girls at home, was G.B.S.*[19]

During Easter week Shaw also traveled to Glastonbury, in Somerset, where his composer-friend Rutland Boughton had his Glastonbury Festival School. Boughton was to sing Orestes in a performance of Gluck's *Iphigenia in Tauris*, his principal singer having "gone to face a sterner music in Flanders," and Boughton, who had expected to conduct, found himself without a conductor. Writing about the opera in the *Nation*, Shaw wrote—was it kindly?—that "some of the freshness and excellence of the performance were due to the fact that there was no conductor." Further, Shaw added, "There was fortunately no scenery and no opera house: in short, no nonsense." There was not even, it seemed, a voice on Mr. Boughton's part. "I do not know," Shaw wrote, "whether Mr. Boughton's voice is a tenor or a bass, nor even whether he can be said to have any voice at all for *bel canto* purposes; but it was all the more instructive to hear how he evaded such questions by attacking the part wholly and simply from the dramatic point of view." Somehow Shaw's friendship with Rutland Boughton survived the brief return to music reviewing.

Shaw had also returned in April to his vain entreaties to the Irish about remaining loyal and united, publishing a piece in the *New York Times** aimed at counteracting revolutionary and separatist rhetoric. The large Irish-American population was a source of financial and political support to the nationalists, who if successful, Shaw insisted, would make Ireland independent and simultaneously utterly insignificant—a "cabbage garden." (The Irish separatists might have answered that at least it would be their own cabbage garden.) "The

---

* In the spring of 1917, Arnold Bennett complained in print about a photograph in a London newspaper of Eton boys preparing a field for the planting of potatoes, disapproving of the master's posture and of the unprofessional way the boys held their spades and addressed the rows. When the picture was reproduced on the Continent, "where digging is understood," he warned, it would create a bad impression.

* A second G.B.S. article, "The German Case against Germany," appeared in the *Times* a week later, April 16, 1916.

cry that England's Difficulty is Ireland's Opportunity," Shaw wrote, "is raised in the old, senseless, spiteful way as a recommendation to stab England in the back when she is fighting someone else and to kick her when she is down, instead of in the intelligent and large-minded modern way which sees in England's difficulty the opportunity of shewing her what a friendly alliance with Ireland can do for her in return for the indispensable things it can do for Ireland." Appealing to reason, yet unable to conclude without the touch of levity that often defused the trenchancy of his argument, Shaw observed that "even an Irish patriot must not be surprised at not having it all his own way. He must console himself by considering that, in the words of a deservedly celebrated Irish dramatic poet,

> Fate drives us all to find our chiefest good
> In what we can, and not in what we would.

The poet was Shaw, in Cashel Byron's lines from the 1901 farce, *The Admirable Bashville.*

On Easter Monday the Abbey Theatre was scheduled to premier a new play by T. H. Nally, *The Spancel of Death.** It never opened, and no attempt was afterward made to stage the play. At eleven o'clock that morning, a party of twenty Irish revolutionaries shot and killed an unarmed policeman at Dublin Castle who refused them admittance to the Cork Hill entrance to Upper Castle Yard. When the shots brought out the other half-dozen unarmed men on duty at the Castle, the Volunteers fled, assuming there were still more troops. There was never another chance to capture the seat of British rule, but the first shot in the revolt had been fired. The battle plan of the Irish Citizen Army had been to seize and hold the center of the city while—they hoped—their comrades all over Ireland would throw off their fetters and rise in rebellion, but in the end (a week later) they held only a shell of a building—the General Post Office in what was then called Sackville Street.

Watching the activity near the Post Office on Tuesday had been Shaw's friend Francis Sheehy-Skeffington, a colorful Dublin character

---

* *Spancel:* British for a noosed rope used to fetter an animal.

addicted to humanitarian causes. With his beard, spectacles, umbrella, cloak, and knickerbocker suit with a "Votes for Women" badge on a lapel, he was clearly not a rebel, but had technically a prison record, having served time in 1915 for making a pacifist speech. That evening he addressed a meeting he had called on the need for cooperation to stop the looting of stores in the battle zone and was arrested and shot the next morning by a firing squad. Less than three weeks before, he had written to Shaw enclosing a copy of a letter he had sent to several London newspapers warning the English of the gravity and explosiveness of the Irish situation. "I think it quite likely that none of them will publish it," he told Shaw, "so I am sending you a copy for your personal information, that you may understand how critical the position is here. It will require all the efforts of all men of goodwill to avert bloodshed in Ireland; and perhaps you, having the ear of the press, may be able to intervene effectively."[20] In his innocence "Skeffy" had no idea how difficult it was for Shaw to be heard in the press on unpopular sides of unpalatable subjects, especially in the land of his birth. Shaw, in fact, had just been forced to direct his appeal to reason to Irishmen in Ireland by way of the *New York Times*.

The indefensible execution of Sheehy-Skeffington outraged even the English, and the officer who had ordered it was subsequently court-martialed and declared insane. The widow was offered an indemnity by the government, and Shaw pressed her to be sensible and accept it. She refused.

There were other executions. Twelve authentic leaders of the rising had been executed by the tenth of May, when a Shavian letter of protest appeared in the *Daily News* defending the right of Irishmen to resort to arms to achieve the independence of their country. "I remain an Irishman," he wrote, "and am bound to contradict any implication that I can regard as a traitor any Irishman taken in a fight for Irish independence." Inevitably he made his case with what had to be for an Englishman an unpalatable paradox—that the Irish were doing "only what Englishmen will do if it be their misfortune to be invaded and conquered by the Germans in the course of the present war." More executions, he warned, only created more martyrs and heroes. Further, he noted in another paradox calculated to make

Englishmen squirm, an Irishman was "as much in order morally in accepting assistance from the Germans in his struggle with England as England is in accepting the assistance of Russia in her struggle with Germany." It was an argument he would have to face again in short order, for Sir Roger Casement, landed in Ireland by German submarine to help foment rebellion, had been captured almost immediately on stepping ashore and was in the Tower of London awaiting a trial that was almost certain to end the way it had in the past for so many notorious occupants of the grim Tower.

At least one of Shaw's arguments was effective. He had warned the authorities that they were "canonizing their prisoners," and as shock over the rising gave way to anger against the government and admiration for the rebels, the government suddenly listened. Two days after Shaw's widely publicized letter to the *Daily News* appeared, there were two more executions, one of the victims the leader of the Irish Citizen Army, James Connolly.* But after that the remaining ninety-seven death sentences were commuted to prison terms, and before the middle of May, Asquith himself hurried to Dublin to try to restore confidence and establish goodwill. But, as one Irish historian had put it, "it was already too late. Ireland was quickly passing under the most dangerous of all tyrannies—the tyranny of the dead."[21]

On the twelfth the Shaws had W. F. Bailey, the Irish Estates Commissioner and Abbey Theatre trustee, to lunch and invited the Webbs and Sydney Cockerell to meet him and listen to his tales of the Rising. Cockerell was thrilled to hear Bailey's view that there were only three or four miscalculations between what happened and a major rebellion that might have taken a hundred thousand troops to put down. Shaw was sick at heart.[22] A fortnight by the sea in April to help him recover from influenza had done little good, and the jollity of his Easter return to music reviewing was spurious. The release of the book version of *Pygmalion* (with sequel) was still delayed by paper and labor shortages, as well as by the difficulty of finding transportation from Edinburgh, where R. and R. Clark printed

---

* G.B.S. later subscribed heavily to a fund raised for his wife and family, contributing more than a third of the amount collected.

his books, to London. Peace on the Continent was still as far away as ever, and however strongly Shaw had urged unity and cooperation with England upon his countrymen, his sympathies with the proponents of Irish freedom were never stronger than in the wake of the bungled Rising.

"I never felt so morose in my life," Shaw wrote Mrs. Campbell. "I cant write: nothing comes off but screeds for the papers, mostly about this blasted war. I am old and finished. I, who once wrote whole plays *d'un seul trait*, am creeping through a new one (to prevent myself crying) at odd moments, two or three speeches at a time. I dont know what its about. I began it on the 4th March: and I have hardly come to the beginning of the first scene yet." The play would become *Heartbreak House*.[23]

During the confusion and turmoil that followed the Easter Rising in Dublin, a universal conscription bill finally became law, far more quietly than it could have a week or two earlier. Since semiconscription was already in effect through the deliberate hypocrisy of the Derby Scheme of "attesting" single men on the National Register, the government was already faced with conscientious objectors of all kinds, a problem magnified by the passage of open conscription in May. For a time the Labour ministers in the Cabinet appeared to have resigned, but after a carefully choreographed period of protest their resignations were withdrawn, their fears of forthcoming industrial conscription allayed, and their jobs in the government held for them. Still, conscription was a significant turnabout for a democratic government, and as Shaw publicly had feared, it meant not only the forcible war service of unadventurous and passive civilians, but the loss of irreplaceable brainpower and skilled labor upon which the postwar economic future of Britain depended.

One of the first outgrowths of the Derby Scheme had been the founding of the No Conscription Fellowship (NCF) by Fenner Brockway, Clifford Allen, and C. H. Norman, a borderline legal organization that conducted both open and clandestine conspiracy to protest and evade the draft. Through the NCF as well as outside it, Shaw was quickly involved in anti-conscription activity, often to his discomfort. Many conscientious objectors wrote to him, as the most visible antiwar figure, from jail, one of them, a Private Owen Lewis, jailed not for refusing to be drafted, but for refusing to be vaccinated.* Shaw managed to get an M.P. to intercede, and Private Lewis returned to duty unvaccinated. In other cases he was less successful. Both Bertrand Russell and W. B. Yeats wrote to Shaw to ask his help in the case of Eric Chappelow, who had been exempted as a conscientious objector, then reclaimed anyway by the Army for noncombatant service, which he refused. Shaw interceded with a Labour member of the Cabinet, Arthur Henderson. When Henderson declined to do anything, Shaw took the case to the press[24] in the pages of the hospitable *Nation* (May 27, 1916), using Chappelow as symbol of the futility of resistance and the futility of compliance. Compulsion, if equitable, should be total compulsion, he argued. If one man is sent to the trenches, why should another man—even a priest—escape being put into a munitions factory, or a woman—even a cloistered nun—escape compulsory maternity to replace population losses? It was a deliberate absurdity, to make the point that conscientious objection "though very bad logic, is very good sense. . . ."

What Shaw called his screeds for the papers had poured out unabated that month, one of them a long, unrepentant piece on Sir Edward Grey. Not all of them were war-inspired, but none was without war allusions. For the *NS*, for example, in reviewing a book by Julius West on G. K. Chesterton, he described the author as "of Allied extraction," but only because he wanted to point out that he had "never been able to decide exactly what Mr. Gilbert Chesterton's nationality is, except that he is certainly not an Englishman; at least I take it that an Englishman would not in England seem extraordinary and even unique." On the same date in another weekly, *To-Day*, he appeared via "War Reputations," an article in which, the editors claimed, "Mr. Shaw defends England and himself." The editorial note began, "No one will deny Mr. Bernard Shaw the gift of intellectual courage and readiness to put up a vigorous defence of his ideas; yet eighteen months have passed since his famous essay on our war policy

---

* Shaw publicly denounced the fact that a conscript "may be ordered to have his blood poisoned by the most abominable inoculations. . . ."

brought down upon him the thunders of an almost unanimously antagonistic press. . . . Those who know Mr. Shaw have never doubted his patriotism, however they may have objected to his opinions. And their faith is by no means groundless. Whilst his fellow journalists were busy inventing new terms of abuse in which to describe him, Bernard Shaw was lending his powerful pen to the men who were running the war, and investing £20,000 in the War Loan. These are the facts which give the lie to all who doubt on which side are his sympathies. . . ."

Shaw's article was an updated "More Common Sense," beginning with the unnecessary boasts that his opinions had not physically endangered him, that audiences applauded him, and that "resolutions" he received "from the provinces" approved of his position. Unable to resist the introductory self-applause, he risked losing his readers before he delivered his message, which attacked the self-defeating drafting of "industrial effectives," the "insolent suppression of poor malcontents and abject truckling to rich ones," the "Pecksniffery and Podsnappery" of Fleet Street and the Front Bench.* Apart from some flashes of persuasive rhetoric, it was a chance thrown away. How much so became disturbingly apparent when there was a benefit performance at the Coliseum for a war charity, and the actors and actresses who had taken part in it assembled on the roof afterward to be photographed. Suddenly some recoiled from the cameramen with indignation: G.B.S. was present. The cameras might inadvertently record them in the company of the author of *Common Sense about the War* and embarrass them in the newspapers.

Beneath the surface, however, even the unworshipful Lucy Shaw, housebound and aware of the outside world only through letters and newspapers, could now write to a friend about *Common Sense*, "I think George is beginning to live down the *Statesman* article. People are beginning to see that he was pretty right. The more furiously he is denounced, the more complete is the surrender of the man in the street afterwards to his gospel."[25] As G.B.S. himself would put it con-

---

* The newspaper press and the government leadership in Commons.

fidently to Frank Harris, "My reputation grows with every [military] failure."[26]

Recognizing his need for new perspectives, Shaw apparently took that need literally, driving to Hendon, not far from Ayot, on May 20, with two friends, to the London Aerodrome for a ride in an airplane. "Two circuits of the Aerodrome" cost two guineas, and a flight "outside the Aerodrome in the direction of Edgeware" cost five guineas. Shaw and Charlotte's sister Mary—guests of William Robson—took the flight in a Grahame White five-seater, 100-horsepower "Aerobus," seated in one of the open cockpits under the biplane's upper wing, with the pilot up front in a cockpit in the nose.[27] In *Misalliance* (1910) he had written possibly the first play in which an airplane had a significant role, for one crash-lands just offstage, causing the arrival of one of his most interesting characters, the aviatrix-daredevil Lina Szczepanowska. Mired in his slowly developing new play, and morose over the events of May, he was again looking for something new.

At Adelphi Terrace he had a young uniformed visitor who brought him old memories. Hesketh Pearson, soon to be posted overseas, had acted in Shaw's *Androcles* and aspired to be a writer, but the only veteran editor who encouraged him was the least influential man in the world of publishing at the time, Frank Harris. Since Harris in the 1890s had briefly brought together on the *Saturday Review* Shaw, Wells, Cunninghame Graham, and Max Beerbohm, he had drunk, gambled, womanized, and defrauded his way into bankruptcies, fifth-rate journals, and near beggary. Embittered with the English and respectful of German efficiency, he had left for America in October 1914 to look for work in journalism and preach pro-Germanism. A measure of his success was that by the spring of 1916 he had completed a life of Oscar Wilde he could not sell, was reduced to printing privately, worked as an advertising agent for the Chesapeake and Ohio Railroad, and intermittently sold idiosyncratic war polemics to American magazines. When his *Oscar Wilde* came from the printer, Harris posted a package of copies to Pearson with the plea that he unload them upon eminent writers and leading newspapers for review. Joseph Conrad returned his copy with a note that he was out of sympathy with Harris "on this and on more serious matters." Kipling wrote that he disliked both writer and subject. Bennett refused to discuss the book or the author. John Galsworthy excused himself as having no opinion, while H. G. Wells called Harris a liar and had nothing else to say. Hall Caine and Edmund Gosse ignored the book. Shaw accepted it and had lunch and several long talks at Adelphi Terrace with Pearson, eventually giving him a long letter addressed to Harris in which he described his own meetings with Wilde. Shaw knew well that Harris would try to both publish the text and sell the letter, and it was exactly what he had intended in order to help his old and unsavory friend.

At Adelphi Terrace Pearson pumped Shaw not only about Frank Harris but about war and Wagner, politicians and plays. "What are you writing now?" he finally asked.

"In my spare moments," Shaw confided, "I've been working on a play in the Chekhov manner. It's one of the best things I've done. Do you know Chekhov's plays? There's a dramatist for you! . . . He makes me feel like a beginner." When he completed it, he wanted "to tackle a big religious subject. I read the Bible when I have time to read anything."

After saying good-bye to Shaw before leaving for the Middle East, Pearson was halfway down the stairs when Shaw leaned over the balustrade and called out, "The war will last another thirty years." Then he waved a cheery farewell.[28]

Two days after his airplane ride over Hendon, G.B.S. and Charlotte motored to Cambridge through a thundershower and arrived at the Fitzwilliam Museum to spend the day with Sydney Cockerell, the director, who took them to the University Arms to have lunch with "Q"—Arthur Quiller-Couch—and C. K. Ogden. Afterward, without Q, they strolled through the manicured quadrangles of Emmanuel and Christ's Colleges and then went on to something in which Shaw was more interested—the tribunal at the university where draft exemption proceedings were in progress. Afterward there was tea at Q's rooms at Jesus College and a continuation of the walking tour, including the Round Church, the bridges, and the backs. At dusk the Shaws drove Cockerell back to his house and returned to Ayot.[29] For Charlotte it was even more a change of pace than for G.B.S., who of-

ten went on visits and walking holidays while she contentedly remained home. The one exception was Ireland, where she would go
for long stays and where G.B.S. would often join her almost in time
to return.

Charlotte hardly ever went with G.B.S. when he delivered a speech,
not even to the almost traditional autumn Fabian lectures. Shaw, of
course, went alone, without fee and at his own expense to lecture, as he
did on May 24, speaking to the Women's Freedom League at the
Clapham Public Hall on "War Economy," a talk unreported except in
the local Clapham paper.*[30] The best economy, he said, would be
to stop the war, which was impossible. Most war economies preached
at the average person were suggestions for self-mortification. Belt-
tightening, for example, was ridiculous for people already improperly
fed. One of the more brilliant suggestions for economizing, he informed the women, was not to sweep or water the streets: "Any man
who supported that in the name of economy was an enemy to his
country." The efforts to limit locomotion were even more ridiculous,
Shaw said, pointing out that posters were plastered all over the pov-
erty-stricken East End advising, "Don't use your motor car for pleasure," although if laborers had automobiles, they would work more
efficiently through the week after a Sunday drive in the country.
However the authorities could be even more irresponsible: "In Rose-
bery Avenue, a thoroughfare consisting largely of workmen's dwellings,
there are, I am told, now to be seen eleven large posters warning all
and sundry that 'to dress extravagantly in war time is not only bad
form but unpatriotic.' " The Committee on Public Retrenchment was
responsible for much of the bad advice, Shaw said, including recommending the cutback in funds for education. "It would be better for
us that these gentlemen should sling a millstone round their necks and
jump into the Thames and stay there, rather than they should continue to give us mischievous advice." The real economies, he con-

---

* Lucy Shaw's nurse (part of G.B.S.'s expenses in maintaining his sister) went
to the lecture and was impressed by Shaw's arguments, Lucy reporting to Ann
Elder, "She has been intending to write to him and offer to take half her
salary, but now feels, as one of his most fanatical disciples, that there is nothing
left for her but to ask him to double it."

cluded, were to be found in large cooperative stores, in mechanization of agriculture, and nationalization of mining and shipping. The most vital industry of all in wartime was the production of babies. Then, matter-of-factly, he asked the audience, "What is the price of a baby?"

"A hundred pounds," replied a lady.

Not long before, a thirteen-year-old Brooklyn girl had protested the raising of funds from schoolchildren in America to build a battleship, suggesting that the funds would be better spent in bettering conditions under which children labored in factories. Shaw sent her a postcard: "The point about the factory children is well taken, but at present I think you had better have both a fleet and a factory act. There are too many rogues about for honest men (such as they are) to be quite safe without weapons."[31] War economy for G.B.S. was a double-edged sword.

7

Heartbreak House

On June 2, 1916, G.B.S. began a walking tour with the Webbs that would lead into the heart of the new play on which he had been struggling. The Webbs were enthusiastic trampers, often working in the mornings before they would leave, arm in arm, Sidney's graying goatee waggling as they continued their professional discussions up hills and down country lanes. When Shaw was along, the professional side of the chatter gave way, Beatrice noting in her diary a few days later—with more warmth than her wont—that he was, as usual, "a delightful companion for an outing, always amusing and good-tempered, and sufficiently exasperating in argument to avoid tenderness in companionship—the curse of the comradeship of the old. He is a delightful raconteur—a perfect gossip, elaborating by witty exaggerations the life stories of his friends into human comedies, and sometimes inhuman tragedies. . . ."*[1] By June 6 the trio were in Tunbridge Wells, and, traveling in an arc south of London, soon were settled into Windham Croft, a Sussex country house near Crawley (and

* The last of these was a reference to the breakup of the Granville-Barker marriage, which had Shaw beset by both parties to it.

the London-Brighton railway line) that the Webbs had rented for the month.

Dividing their days between working and walking, the Webbs applied themselves to their projects while Shaw attempted to add pages to his play. He had told Mrs. Campbell that since he had begun it on March 4 he had been "creeping through" it, hardly knowing what it was about. But he did have a setting, an atmosphere, and several distinct characters. One of his grandfathers had been clever with his hands, fitting out his study like a carpenter's shop and building his own boats. "He would have been a valuable member of society as a craftsman living by his talent," Shaw once wrote. "Unfortunately his station was that of a country gentleman, forbidden to make money by his gift of manual dexterity."[2] Lena Ashwell had first turned his thoughts to the play in 1913 with the story of her father, Captain Pocock, whom Shaw called a captain of souls. Before taking Holy Orders he had lived a storybook life. At eleven he was a midshipman, and his first sea adventure was the capture of a slave ship, an experience he recounted vividly many years later when he lay dying. He served in the Burmese War, then left the Navy to live first in New Zealand, and afterward on an English sailing ship that worked out of the River Tyne. The family lived on the ship, with the captain's quarters in the stern, complete to a barred-window nursery, drawing room, and flower-filled greenhouse on the upper deck.[3] The house in Shaw's play, fitted out to remind old Captain Shotover of his sailing days, owes something to old Captain Pocock as well as to Shaw's grandfather, and Shaw probably also remembered Thomas Carlyle, for whom a dominant metaphor of England was the ship which must round Cape Horn and keep off the rocks, for which navigating skill is needed the best pilot available. Carlyle (in *Past and Present*) even used a character named Undershot, whom Shaw might have remembered; Shaw's captain points out that at eighty-eight his last bolt had been shot long before.

The irascible as well as the prophetic side of Shotover had been Shaw's starting point, particularly Lena Ashwell's pre-war story of her father's blasphemously refusing communion on his death bed unless he could have had cheese with his consecrated bread.[4] "Sometimes," Shaw observed of him, "one conceives or observes or hears of a character who insists on being dramatized." Proving the point, "Lena's Father" even became his first working title. Although Shaw afterward told his biographer Henderson that *Heartbreak House* "began with an atmosphere" and did not contain "a word that was foreseen before it was written," it actually began with a character for whom Shaw had to find an atmosphere in which to breathe, a plot in which to move, and a theme toward which the dialogue had to focus. The "overheated drawing-room atmosphere" was a borrowing from Chekhov. Before the war he had been at the first performance in England of *The Cherry Orchard*, after which he had said to producer Frederick Whelen, who sat next to him, "I feel as if I want to tear up all my plays and begin all over again."[5] (Later as the play developed in a more apocalyptic manner than he had first intended, the characters in the play as well as the play's atmosphere took on some aspects of Shaw's favorite Shakespearean play, *King Lear*.*)

In its prewar Chekhovian conception, the play—which Shaw charged with symbolism and prophecy about a nation's moral paralysis—was to be about "cultured leisured Europe" as it drifted toward a catastrophe of its own making. Before he had begun setting it down, events had anticipated his scheme; however, some of his projected characters remained valid. There was the country house "in the middle of the north edge of Sussex" that suggested a ship, and the half-mad sea captain who haunted rather than possessed it. There was the fortyish and eternally feminine daughter, Hesione Hushabye, patterned—so G.B.S. confided to her—after Mrs. Campbell,[6] and her husband Hector, developed from Shaw's former friend and soldier-adventurer, Cunninghame Graham, as well as from another friend, Fabian pioneer Hubert Bland, whose swashbuckling was limited to the boudoir. At the start there was the plot device of a young and bewildered visitor to the house, Ellie Dunn, a part Shaw wrote in for actress Ellen O'Malley. It would be a picture of a comfortable civilization unaware that it had been undermined by its own apathy.

In mid-June Charlotte arrived to join G.B.S. and the Webbs, and on June 17 Leonard Woolf and his wife also came for the weekend. Woolf

* See the Appendix. "Shaw's *Lear*."

had been working on the international government study for the Fabian Research Committee, and the invitation was as much professional as social; it turned out to be more than that for Shaw, although he characteristically exaggerated when he wrote to Virginia Woolf many years later, "There is a play of mine called Heartbreak House which I always connect with you because I conceived it in that house somewhere in Sussex where I first met you and, of course, fell in love with you. I suppose every man did."*[7] He had not conceived the play there, but very likely conceived a way to continue it. Beatrice Webb had a habit, Leonard Woolf has written, "of classifying all her friends and acquaintances in a kind of psychological and occupational card index. Thus Virginia was 'the novelist,' I was 'the ex-colonial-civil-servant. . . .' "[8] If the attractive but haughty and high-strung Virginia Woolf were transmuted into the handsome, imperious Lady Ariadne Utterword, wife to Sir Hastings Utterword (who never appears in the play), "governor of all the crown colonies in succession," it may have been in part because of the occupation for Ariadne's unseen husband suggested by Leonard Woolf's more modest background. In any case, such possible development for the play would indicate that Shaw had been satisfied by little that he had written since March 4, but that the weekend in Sussex had made it possible for him to write parts of the first two acts during the summer and early autumn. Even at Windham Croft, Leonard Woolf recalled many years later, "Shaw went out into the garden every morning and wrote on a writing pad on his knee."[9] Still, although as early as the opening scenes the old captain's premonitions are ominous, Shaw remained unable as he wrote to see a speech ahead.

Among other things Shaw was then working on a *Nation* review of

* Answering Shaw on May 15, 1940, Virginia Woolf confided that the feeling was mutual. "As for the falling in love, it was not, let me confess, one sided. . . . Indeed you have acted a lover's part in my life for the past thirty years; and though I daresay it's not much to boast of, I should have been a worser woman without Bernard Shaw. That is the reason—I mean the multiplicity of your lovers and what you must suffer from them—why Leonard and Virginia have never liked to impose themselves upon you." In a postscript she added, "Heartbreak House, by the way, is my favourite of all your works" (British Museum Add. Ms. 50522, fol. 293).

Wells's nonfiction *What is Coming*, making mild fun of its suggestion that Germany turn itself into a republic to prove its good intentions. Germany, after all, was winning the war. The review was also another platform to press the idea of a postwar "Supernational Tribunal and Legislature," something his Fabian Research Committee had already spelled out in an *NS* supplement and something taken seriously not only by Wells but more importantly by President Wilson. It was, too, another opportunity to attack Sir Edward Grey, as well as to point out that such foresight and insight as had made Wells famous was wasted on politicians. "And thus, however much genius England produces, she never gets any further than she can fight. The pilots who weather the storm [at sea] never look at the stars and have never heard of the mariner's compass. Infatuated with the skill with which they can handle the little fleet of party canoes in Election Dock, they tackle the ocean with a great contempt for faddists, and, like the Irish pilot, cry, 'I know every rock on this coast [crash]*—and that's one of them.'" The metaphor stayed with Shaw, for when he wrote the last act of his play, lines he gave to Captain Shotover urged, in effect, that moral navigation was the business of every Englishman, that the skipper who trusted to Providence would end with his ship "on the rocks, the splintering of her rotten timbers, the tearing of her rusty plates, the drowning of her crew like rats in a trap."

Back in London Shaw found a thank-you letter from H. G. Wells, who had been sent a copy of *Androcles*. Wells agreed with Shaw that religion was a "here & now" problem, as well he might, having just concluded a novel that colorfully reflected English character and setting in the first year of the war, but concluded with a sentimental sermon in which what is revealed to Mr. Britling is that "Religion is the first thing and the last thing," and that it is through men that God fights against the blind forces that beset them. It was hardly the conventional Christian God, but in 1916 it would be seized upon by Englishmen hungry less for a theological explanation of what happened in Europe than for comfort. By then he had largely come around to Shaw's position, writing later of his

* Shaw's brackets.

disillusionment about the beneficence of our war-making . . . that fol-lowed my first attempt in 1914 to find a justifying purpose in "our" war. I did not become "anti-war." I found the simple solution of the conscien-tious objectors and war-resisters generally, too simple for me altogether. My brain was quite prepared for conflict on behalf of the law and order of the world-state. . . . The anti-war people made me the more impatient because of the rightness of much of their criticism of the prevailing war-motives. I was perhaps afraid, if I yielded to them, of being carried back too far towards the futility of a merely negative attitude. What they said was so true and what they did was so merely sabotage, I lost my temper with them. . . . I was reluctant to admit how gravely I had com-promised myself by my much too forward belligerence and my rash and eager confidence in the liberalism, intelligence and good faith of our foreign office and war office. . . . My pro-war zeal was inconsistent with my pre-war utterances and against my profounder convictions. . . . I re-covered consciousness, so to speak, from the first shock of the war ex-plosion. . . .[10]

There was mail from Barker also. Awaiting military service at thirty-nine, he had left word with his lawyer to cable him when the call came. Another letter also had to do with conscription. The wife of a promising young sculptor, Jacob Epstein, had written to ask for Shaw's help in getting him deferred. Conscription was only one of Epstein's problems, for failure to achieve deferment would at least have ended the interest in him on the part of the local police at Pett Level, near Hastings, who were curious about the strange man with the Germanic name who lived on the coast in wartime and kept pigeons. No intervention helped, not even Lord Beaverbrook's urging Lord Derby to employ Epstein as a war artist, for early the next year he was drafted.*[11]

More important to Shaw through the summer months was his scheme to defend Sir Roger Casement from what appeared to be inevitable hanging, not because he was a traitor, but because he was an Irishman. As Shaw knew, however, he was both. On June 26, after having been in the Tower since his arrest, Casement had been taken to the Old

---

* Epstein was offered a commission once he was in uniform, but he refused it. Soon afterward he fell ill, was hospitalized, and then discharged.

Bailey for what would be the last trial in the aftermath of the Easter Rising. A battery of attorneys defended Casement (Serjeant A. M. Sullivan of the Irish Bar, together with two English lawyers and an American legal adviser), and to newsman Henry W. Nevinson, Shaw complained that just as men felt that to die decently one needed doctors at hand, so they felt the need for lawyers in order to be hanged in a Christian manner. In this mood G.B.S., with Charlotte, attended a luncheon at the Webbs to meet their neighbor Mrs. J. R. Green, widow of the historian, who was trying to raise money for Casement's legal defense and who counted heavily on the Shaws. (So did Casement's cousin, Gertrude Bannister, a suburban London teacher, who had visited the Shaws at Adelphi Terrace and won G.B.S. over with her air of capability and good sense.) Even before Alice Green's invitation, Shaw had been holding meetings at Adelphi Terrace to develop a course of action with his friends, few of whom had much sympathy with what Casement had tried to do, and none of whom could stomach his pro-Germanism, but their reluctance had been in the process of being overcome when a shattering rumor reached them. The prisoner's "black" diaries had been seized, and their contents indicated that Casement had been involved in homosexual activities unmentionable before the ladies in the room.

The Adelphi Terrace committee's first thought was that the rumors were cunning attempts to discredit Casement, at worst only cheap forgeries. Massingham announced that he would use the influence of his *Nation* to find out the facts and went to Scotland Yard. When he came back it was clear to the group that Casement was lost. He had been shown the diaries, Massingham said, and their purport was as bad as could be imagined. Further they appeared to be genuinely in Casement's hand. The committee fell apart. In London clubs and drawing rooms, whispered references to the "black diaries" were the summer's most delicious gossip.[12]

In this atmosphere Alice Green's luncheon was a painful occasion, although no one alluded to the scandal, and in her diary Beatrice Webb recorded her bitterness at what she considered Shaw's callous levity:

G.B.S. as usual had his own plan. Casement was to defend his own case; he was to make a great oration of defiance which would "bring down the house." To this Mrs. Green retorted tearfully that the man was desperately ill; that he was quite incapable of handling a court full of lawyers; that the most he could do was the final speech after the verdict. "Then we had better get our suit of mourning," Shaw remarked with an almost gay laugh. "I will write him a speech which will thunder down the ages." "But his friends want to get him reprieved," indignantly replied the distracted woman friend. . . . Shaw wants to compel Casement and Casement's friends to "produce" the defence as a national dramatic event. "I know how to do it," was G.B.S.'s one contribution to the tragedy-laden dispute. . . . And yet the man is both kindly and tolerant, but his conceit is monstrous. . . .[13]

What Beatrice failed to understand was that no conventional defence could save Casement, and her reaction was to vent her private irritation at Shaw's "argumentative perversities" and apparent intellectual detachment. Shaw always had sensed the undercurrent of Beatrice's hostility, realizing that his long, affectionate comradeship with Sidney had much to do with it, but he carefully ignored the existence of any problem and managed to remain working partners with both Webbs, a relationship that would last out all their long lives. At the moment, however, Beatrice was furious, for Shaw insisted for himself and Charlotte that they would not "waste our money on lawyers"; he went back to Adelphi Terrace to write a thundering speech for Casement anyway and to prepare a legal defense that he could elect to use, all or part. Basically it claimed prisoner-of-war status for Casement, thus eliminating the capital crime of high treason without denying any of the incontrovertible facts. Then Shaw would have had Casement plead Not Guilty to the charge of high treason upon which the government nevertheless would insist, pointing out that the plea did not deny the facts stated by the Crown, but denied instead that any guilt was attached to them. For that purpose Shaw provided a speech with all the thunder he had promised, "to be made from the dock, not, of course, necessarily in my words, but in whatever paraphrase came most naturally to the accused":

It may seem to some of you gentlemen of the jury that if I ought not to be hanged for being a patriot, I ought to be hanged for being a fool. I will not plead that if men are to be hanged for errors of judgment in politics, we should have such a morality in England and Ireland that hardly one of us would be left to hang the other. . . . I am not trying to shirk the scaffold: it is the altar on which the Irish saints have been canonized for centuries. . . . Will you understand me when I say that those three days of splendid fighting against desperate odds in the streets of Dublin have given Ireland back her self-respect. We were beaten, indeed never had a dog's chance of victory; but you were also beaten in a no less rash and desperate enterprize in Gallipoli. Are you ashamed of it? . . . I hope I have spoken here today as you would desire to hear an Englishman speak in a German Court if your country shared the fate of mine. . . . Gentlemen, I have done my duty: now it is your turn.

Casement pored over Shaw's draft defense and discarded most of it, heavily annotating his copy. "My failure is my crime—not my attempt," he insisted in a margin, rejecting the idea of claiming prisoner-of-war status. It was "excellent in many respects," he noted. "Shaw's view is all right; but he does not understand one tenth of the issue the Crown had in view. They are *not* after me—except in so far as they have to keep up with public feeling. They are out to befoul Germany [by identifying Irish rebels as] . . . misled and deceived by Germany and me. . . ." For the same reason he found no hope in the proposed speech from the dock. The trial went then as expected. Sullivan pleaded Casement's cause with vigor, collapsing in the middle of his closing speech, in which he had pitted his defense on a fine point of law—that high treason could only be committed *inside* the King's realm, while the prisoner had adhered to the King's enemies *outside* the realm. The Lord Chief Justice, Lord Reading, rejected Sullivan's construction of the statute, informing the jury that "contriving to assist the enemy" was the issue. The jury then returned the inevitable verdict, whereupon the Lord Chief Justice put on the black cap and pronounced sentence of death by hanging.

"Then, if you please," Shaw recalled, "the virtually dead man got up and made his speech. A couple of members of the jury were, I am told, good enough to say that if they had heard it before the verdict they would have dissented. But that possibility, on which I had banked, had been averted by the best possible legal advice, and Casement was duly hanged. . . ."[14]

Before the sentence was carried out Shaw tried other devices, including the drafting of a petition to the Prime Minister seeking commutation, but early in August, discussing it with Clement Shorter, he said that he did not sign it himself "because my name might have frightened off some of the more useful signatures."[15] His last flurry of activity in Casement's behalf involved trying to place a long appeal asking "Shall Roger Casement Hang?" in leading newspapers. It was rejected by the *Times* and the *Nation*, and was finally published on July 22 in the *Manchester Guardian*. At the eleventh hour he published another appeal for commutation, in the *Daily News* for August 2.[16] At Pentonville Prison on the morning of August 3, Casement was hanged.

The Casement affair was hardly the only business that had been cutting into Shaw's work on *Heartbreak House*. Barker was back, staying mostly with the Shaws. He had enlisted in the Royal Horse Artillery with the hope that during a furlough at the end of his training period he could give some drama lectures to raise enough money to avoid bankruptcy. Lillah was still hysterical, both in letters and in person, Shaw hectoring her in his strongest language in the hope of bringing her around:

It is frightful to meet you flitting round the Terrace in the moonlight like a beautiful ghost, answering in unreal far-away whispers when you are spoken to, until finally one runs away from you in terror, partly terror of the ghost, partly terror of being provoked into laying violent hands on you and convincing you that you are flesh and blood still until you are black and blue.

People will presently get tired of the affair and avoid you and Harley like the plague; and serve you right! Is any man, or any woman, worth making such a fuss about? What has become of our nobility? I shall end by feeling like a dog barking at three cats on the roof. These, too, are the best years of your life. However, I know it is no use *my* talking. Go on tormenting one another, just as the rest are killing one another in France; it is the nature of the human animal. I will go on with my play and leave you all to your devilments.[17]

There was also the Fabian Summer School to prepare for at Sedbergh in Yorkshire, where the problem of conscription, not on the agenda, continued to be an issue uncomfortably close to the younger Fabians. On the premises there was even a conscientious objector on the run. Ethel Hankinson, who was in charge of accommodations, permitted him to sleep in a tent on the grounds until the day when he complained (rather than confess he was broke) that he had lost his purse. Soon the whole school, including Shaw, was off beating the hillside where the loss had apparently occurred. Eventually the truth was out and the hunt called off, Shaw chuckling, "Well! I *ought* to have been able to recognize a Dudedat!"[18]

Since 1914 differences about the war and the increasing polarization of founding members ("the old gang") and younger generation (once the "Fabian Nursery") had taken the place H. G. Wells occupied a decade before as source of internal tension. Most Fabians, particularly the older ones, accepted the war in the same matter-of-fact way they accepted the monarchy; the younger Fabian researchers (whom Shaw nominally governed) tended to be against the war, on pacifist or anti-capitalist grounds, and after conscription conscientious objectors on the run were often to be found in the back rooms of the Fabian offices in Tothill Street—and on the roof when military police came by—just as one "conshy" had naturally gravitated to the Fabian summer retreat.

Shortly before Shaw had left on his month-long busman's holiday, Ellen Terry had turned up at Ayot without warning, but rather than knock at Shaw's door she bought some picture postcards and left a message at the post office that she had been there. It was typical of that long relationship which remained almost entirely on paper, for even when they were part of the same crowd, as at the Coliseum benefit some months before, they seldom spoke to each other. Shaw playfully accused Ellen, then in her seventieth year, of barbarity, adding, "As you have ordered postcards, I send you a real Ayot album to put them in, and have filled up half the leaves with my own productions."

One specimen was a view of the Ayot graveyard, on the back of which Shaw had appended a caption:

> Tread softly, Nell. Here Ayot's deaders
> Into eternity take headers.[19]

Death seldom caught him in a sentimental posture. While away in Yorkshire, he had received news from Charles Charrington of the death of Charrington's wife, Janet Achurch, at Ventnor.* When Shaw was younger, he had written *Candida* (1894) for her and was the Marchbanks of her marriage, confessing to her what she well knew from her own experience, that "as an Irishman, an irregular artistic person, an anarchist in conduct," he was "a creator of an atmosphere subtly disintegrative of households."[20] Now to Charrington he wrote, "I dont feel any sorrow; death doesnt catch me that way, least of all when it moves me as Janet's does. Will you write her life, and yours? Mention, in that case, that I once said to her, 'Remember how I may change and deny it, that I really did love you once.' "[21]

From the White Hart Hotel in Sedbergh, G.B.S. wrote Mrs. Pat that the reason he was away for such an extended period (a month) was not to take a holiday, but to give the servants one. (Charlotte, as usual, had gone to Ireland.) Before the summer school, he had spent a week at the Glastonbury Festival, where Rutland Boughton presided while appealing to the Tribunal at Bath for exemption from military service. Boughton at thirty-eight, Shaw thought, was of considerable value to music, but of negligible utility as an infantryman, and to press his friend's cause while in the area he published a lengthy appeal in the *Western Daily Press* on August 29. "Is it true," Shaw asked wryly, "that General Haig cannot make shift without him?" But his argument was less for a friend than to make a case for the national importance of the arts, the disregard of which on patriotic grounds was "honest barbarism."

---

* Over the years Janet had been her own worst enemy, her acting talents disintegrating under indulgence with drugs and drink. On her death at fifty-two, G.B.S. paid the funeral expenses for Charrington and sent death notices to the *Nation* and the *NS*.

"The Session of 1916," the *Fabian News* reported laconically, was "as successful as any in our records. Except Lieut. W. S. Sanders, all the lecturers were able to fulfil their engagements, a matter for congratulation at a time when so many are under imperative orders in connection with the war. The school-house was full nearly all the time, and in the closing weeks many who wished to attend had to get rooms at hotels in the town." One of the attractions during the final fortnight was Shaw, who read three unpublished war playlets on three evenings and lectured on another.

At the summer school, journalists intermittently turned up, attracted by some of the newsworthy people in attendance. Among them during the 1916 session was Rebecca West, whom Shaw described to Mrs. Pat (who may have known the scandalous details but read the wrong papers) as "an extremely clever young woman whose critical writings in the papers have been startling everyone for the last few years."[22] Miss West was so attractive, he added, that he regretted that he had just turned sixty—an unnecessary regret in her case, since he knew that she had been H. G. Wells's mistress for several years and the mother of Wells's two-year-old son. The school went on until September 16, Shaw remaining there with the Webbs until the end and writing little except for letters. As a result Charles Macdona's touring company, which had planned to begin alternating performances of *Fanny's First Play* with their long-running *Pygmalion*, had to open *Fanny* on September 18 without a new prologue "in pantomime doggerel" that Shaw had promised them to help shorten the play. It was "to be substituted for the Induction when the play alone is performed," and was to be spoken by Fanny herself:

> Just think! in real life what is it touches us?
> Stories about ourselves, not about duchesses.
> If we all live by honest business, such as is
> The backbone of this town, why not insist
> On plays that shew at least that we exist! . . .[23]

Overcommitted in public business and frustrated by his work on the first serious play he had begun since *Pygmalion* in 1912, Shaw had let the prologue become a war casualty. Delivered too late, it was not used. But he had tossed off some weeks earlier, when he had begun thinking about a *Fanny* prologue in verse, ninety lines of high-spirited doggerel Macdona could not possibly use, titled "Property & Rent, or Fanny's First Poem." The kind of writing one does when appropriate words refuse to come for the task at hand, it satirized the Shaw-Hilaire Belloc controversies on economic questions, in which (as with religion and politics) Belloc was certain to be as far to the right as Shaw, usually exaggerating his position for effect, went to the left:

> Be it so, Belloc: let's rehearse
> Our economic stunt in verse:
> We'll in the style of Robert Burns
> Discuss Diminishing Returns,
> Variegating our assumptions
> With insults to each other's gumptions. . . .

It ended in similar good humor, and in no better verse:

> Hilaire: forgive my halting carol.
> I yield the floor: *à toi la parole*.[24]

Shaw returned from Sedbergh in time for rehearsals of *The Inca of Perusalem*, which after some minor Shavian surgery to avoid offending the Royal enemy had been finally passed by the Lord Chamberlain's reader of plays and scheduled for production by Barry Jackson in Birmingham on October 7, with Gertrude Kingston and Felix Aylmer. Part of a triple bill, with one-acters by John Masefield and John Drinkwater, his censorship-muted satire on the Kaiser created no sensation, which should have disappointed Shaw, but it became only a minor annoyance because he was suddenly deep into plans for what had been, until five minutes before midnight on the night of October 1, a play with no last act in sight.

The Zeppelin problem had become increasingly serious for the southeastern counties in the sixteen months since May 31, 1915, when by common report a Zeppelin passed over every house in London. Because bombsights were primitive and navigation unrefined, the Zeppelins often appeared to be dropping their bombs haphazardly when actually aiming at planned targets, resulting sometimes in their reporting (or in German propaganda inflating) explosions as having destroyed such targets as the Tower Bridge or Charing Cross Station. For a time the Zeppelins cruised almost unmolested two and one-half miles above the English countryside, their presence causing more than one mother trying to warn her unhappy child huddled in a shelter, "Hush, hush, or the Zeppelins will hear you!" Few accepted the incursions in the manner of the unflappable James Woburn, butler to Adeline, Duchess of Bedford. As the Duchess finished dining alone at Berkeley Square, Woburn interrupted her postprandial coffee, noiselessly shutting the door and approaching the correct distance, and saying, "The Zeppelins have arrived, your Grace," as if—so E. F. Benson wrote— "they were guests at her evening party, come rather early." Two years later Shaw found that raids over the nothern outskirts of London were still so commonplace that he joked about protecting himself from the enemy (who by English report still loved him) through the stratagem of having a large sign[25] inscribed upon his roof at Ayot in luminous paint:

HIER WOHNT DER DICHTER SHAW
BITTE
FAHREN SIE WEITER.

By September 1915 the raids had already begun causing spotty but sometimes considerable loss and excitement and concern all out of proportion to the casualties, although one sortie by the L-13 did start fires in London that resulted in a half-million pounds' worth of damage. In command of the clumsy sausage-shaped monster was thirty-two-year-old Heinrich Mathy, a daring and resourceful former destroyer skipper whose exploits over England had made him a leading German hero. It was a year before the British managed to bring down their first airship on English soil, at Cuffley in Hertfordshire, thirteen miles from London. Four weeks later on October 1, 1916, Mathy was over England in the L-31, a newer craft, making his landfall from the North Sea at 9 P.M. near Lowestoft and intending to look for the line of the Great Eastern Railway at Chelmsford to follow it into London.* As searchlights converged on him, he changed course to circle around the darkened northeast fringe of the city, but when the L-31 opened up its engines to again head south, four Royal Flying Corps planes took off in pursuit. Mathy jettisoned his bombs and tried to climb away from the planes, but one passed under him, banked, and fired a volley that caused the huge cylinder of hydrogen "to go red inside like an enormous Chinese lantern." The flaming wreckage of L-31 came to earth in a field near the village of Potters Bar, south of Ayot St. Lawrence. Lying on his back a short distance from the tangle of charred girders was an officer who had apparently leaped from the burning ship before it reached the ground. The first villagers on the scene were astonished to discover that he was still breathing, but he almost immediately expired. His identity disc read "Kaptlt. Mathy. L 31."[26]

The end of the L-31 had been witnessed by artists Charles Ricketts and Charles Shannon from a window in London.

Shannon, who was by the stove, cried, "Look! look!" and the room became filled with a salmon-pink glow. I imagined a searchlight breaking into the window, the Zepps being overhead. In the time it took to get to the window, Shannon had guessed at a burning Zeppelin, and there it was, hanging perpendicularly above and to the right of the steeple of the church, looking at once detailed and unreal, like a twist of burning paper in the sky. The light increased and the flames billowed out at the base. The sky became like a sunset, pieces became detached, one larger than the others, obviously the gondola. Slowly the thing descended, breaking

* Because English railroads were for the Germans an illuminated map converging on London, whenever Zeppelins were reported all trains in the affected area were brought to a halt. Their engine fires were drawn, lights extinguished, and hapless passengers forced to sit in gloomy inactivity. Even the railway stations were closed and lights put out, often for hours at a time, while the Zeppelins lingered in a slow arc overhead.

into different shapes, leaving the skeleton visible in the rack of the smoke. By it, seemingly immobile, stood a fixed light in the sky, from which dropped two bluish flames: this we imagined to be an aeroplane; and to the east a red light flashed up and out in mid-sky. Shannon and I, who watched breathless, exclaimed automatically, "How splendid! How smart! How slowly she descends! How long has she been?" Shannon looked at his watch by the glow of his cigarette, it was five to 12.[27]

For Ricketts and others, the destruction of the L-31 provided a thrilling entry for their diaries. For Shaw the incident furnished material for a long paragraph in a letter to the Webbs,[28] and much more:

The Potters Bar Zeppelin manoeuvred over the Welwyn Valley for about half an hour before it came round and passed Londonwards with the nicest precision over our house straight along the ridge tiles. It made a magnificent noise the whole time; and not a searchlight touched it, as it was the night-out of the Essenden and Luton lights. And not a shot was fired at it. I was amazed at its impunity and audacity. It sailed straight for London and must have got past Hatfield before they woke up and brought it down. The Commander was such a splendid personage that the divisional surgeon and an officer who saw him grieved as for an only son. At two o'clock another Zeppelin passed over Ayot; but we have no telephone, and nobody bothered. . . .

In the morning Shaw went to see the wreckage on his motor bicycle, although rain fell persistently and a clammy mist still clung to the muddy roads and sodden fields. Despite the weather a happy crowd had gathered around the two enormous heaps of twisted Zeppelin framework, more onlookers than the entire population of Potters Bar, which was only one long oak-shaded village street of shops and inns and houses. Someone struck up an old song with a familiar refrain, in which the others joined:

> Cheer, boys, cheer, no more of idle sorrow.
> Cheer, boys, cheer, for a free and happy land.[29]

"The police were in great feather, as there is a strict cordon, which means you cant get in without paying," Shaw explained to the Webbs. "The charges are not excessive, as I guess; for I created a ducal impression by a shilling." The nineteen bodies lay in a barn at the edge of the meadow. "May I go in?" a woman asked the sergeant in charge. "I would like to see a dead German."

"No, madam," he said politely. "We cannot admit ladies."[30]

"Corpses are extra, no doubt," thought Shaw, "but I did not intrude on the sleep of the brave." Then came a curious confession.

What is hardly credible, but true, is that the sound of the Zepp's engines was so fine, and its voyage through the stars so enchanting, that I positively caught myself hoping next night that there would be another raid. I grieve to add that after seeing the Zepp fall like a burning newspaper, with its human contents roasting for some minutes (it was frightfully slow) I went to bed and was comfortably asleep in ten minutes. One is so pleased at having seen the show that the destruction of a dozen people or so in hideous terror and torment does not count. "I didn't half cheer, I tell you" said a damsel at the wreck. Pretty lot of animals we are![31]

That war, and even home-front war, could turn ordinary citizens into a pretty lot of animals had already been pointed out in a grim story Rudyard Kipling wrote in 1915, after the first raids and civilian casualties. In "Mary Postgate" a British flier has died in a training accident, and his aunt, who cared little for him, and her passive and plain paid companion, whose devotion for him he had ignored, are distributing and destroying his personal effects. Miss Postgate's grief takes strange form. "It's a great pity," she says, "that he didn't die in action after he had killed somebody." Bombs fall nearby and a German airman is discovered by Miss Postgate in the garden, mortally injured by his fall. When he begs her for help she returns instead with a revolver for which there is no need: he is groaning in his death agony. "Stop that!" she orders him, stamping her foot. "Stop that, you bloody pagan!" That evening her mistress notices innocently that Miss Postgate is looking, for once, "quite handsome."

A symbol of wartime hatred for the enemy that rose from elemental forces beyond politics to inspire perverse gratification in once ordinary people, it was Kipling's confrontation with emotions he, too, felt. A few months later, while Kipling was touring the front lines as one of the earliest of the headquarters' guests, his only son, John, wrote to ask parental consent (he was underage) to go to France with the Second Irish Guards. On October 2 came the telegram from the War Office that John was missing in action, in the battle of Loos, which cost the British twenty thousand dead. His body was never recovered.

The world as *Heartbreak House* opens is a world on the eve of war. No hint of a war in actual progress appears in the first two acts, although the captain's forebodings are gloomy and the occupation by which he maintains his household involves the invention of more efficient explosives, antisubmarine armaments, and weapons to counter machine guns and tanks.* The first suggestion of hostile action in the play is lost on the occupants of Shotover's house, and later when they are ordered by telephone to take appropriate air-raid precautions, it occurs to none of them to question whom or what they are defending themselves against. Shaw clearly intended to keep the action on a symbolic level, yet it is equally clear from the events of October 1, 1916 (the play is even set "on a fine evening at the end of September") where he acquired his material.

The first suggestion of imminent attack from the air is Mrs. Hushabye's declaration that she has heard "a sort of splendid drumming in the sky," wrongly identified by her guest "Boss" Mangan as a "goods train." It was the "magnificent noise" Shaw described to the Webbs.

---

* At the end of Act 1, Shotover considers—on the eve of war—designing a cannon-like weapon that might "fire a grapnel and wind in a machine gun or even a tank." However the first completed machine—still a military secret —did not have its first trials at Hatfield, near Ayot, until February 2, 1916. Haig used the first forty-nine tanks available on the Somme front on September 15. (The term itself—deliberately noncommittal in the interests of secrecy —was not even used by its inventors until December 1915.)

"Sh-sh! Listen: do you hear it now?" she asks as it approaches. "It's magnificent." Overhead it becomes "splendid; it's like an orchestra: it's like Beethoven." Caught up in a similar emotion, young Ellie Dunn responds, "By thunder, Hesione: it is Beethoven." There are bright lights and explosions, which turn out not to be the destruction of a Zeppelin, but the landing of bombs nearby, one of them close enough to Heartbreak House to kill two guests, useless beings anyway, who had hidden in a pit outside.* The unidentified aircraft in *Heartbreak House* apparently slips away unscathed, but with the same emotions in the breasts of the onlookers which not only Shaw but others (as Ricketts exemplifies) found in themselves. "I positively caught myself hoping next night that there would be another raid," Shaw confessed, and in the last two speeches of the play the feeling is expressed by Hesione and Ellie:

> MRS. HUSHABYE. But what a glorious experience! I hope theyll come again tomorrow night.
> ELLIE [*radiant at the prospect*]. Oh, I hope so.

Other aspects of the Potters Bar experience also may have been worked into the play:

> Shaw's sympathy for the incinerated crew of the dirigible is echoed in the anxiety of the humanitarian Mazzini: "Think of the risks those poor fellows up there are running!" The source of Nurse Guinness's all-too-human but savage response, "Think of them, indeed, the murdering blackguards! What next?" is found in the " 'I didn't half cheer, I tell you' said a damsel at the wreck. Pretty lot of animals we are!" Shaw's surprise over the absence of searchlights to pick up the airship over Ayot is perhaps reflected in reverse in Hector's reckless outcry, "There is not half light enough. We should be blazing to the skies," in Ellie's impulsive "Set fire to the house, Marcus" (Mrs. Hushabye only a few minutes before has ironically inquired of Mazzini, "Whats the matter, Mr. Dunn? Is the

---

* Shaw may have borrowed this from another incident, when at Letchworth, where a Belgian munitions manufacturer had opened a factory, the bombs missed the town and hit a man in a field who had lit a flare.

house on fire?"), and in Lady Utterword's sarcastic suggestion to Randall that he play "Keep the home fires burning" on his flute.[32]

From the start Hector has demanded more light, even asking the captain, as the curtain descends upon Act I, "Shall I turn up the lights for you?" In Act III, when Nurse Guinness turns off all the lights in the house on the telephoned order of the police, Hector protests (*"furiously"*), and shouting "It shall be seen for a hundred miles," he dashes into the house to turn on all the lights and tear open all the curtains.

What did the L-31 episode mean to Shaw in the context of the play? Hector Hushabye calls the first drumming in the sky "Heaven's threatening growl of disgust at us useless futile creatures. [*Fiercely.*] I tell you, one of two things must happen. Either out of that darkness some new creation will come to supplant us as we have supplanted the animals, or the heavens will fall in thunder and destroy us." Shotover agrees, but in nautical terms, the danger to him being the moral directionlessness of the ship of state's crew, to which Shaw would add—in terms of his character's reactions at the end of the play— the aimless lives and jaded emotions that grasp even at the savoring of violence. In this the play (in Colin Wilson's words) "anticipates Eliot's *Waste Land* in tone and in its analysis of the problem of a civilisation undermined by triviality and 'nihilism.' . . . The affluent society is inevitably the violent society. In other words, this civilisation, which is the necessary instrument of the evolutionary force, contains within itself the seeds of its own destruction. . . . This was a new recognition for Shaw—in fact, for most of his contemporaries. It represented a complete change in the cultural climate. . . ."[33]

In the play of its wit the symbolic fantasy was intended to attract audiences, but, said Shaw, "The funny old captain, having lured them into the ship by his sallies, ties them up to the gangway, and gives them a moral dozen. . . . Then the heartbreak begins, and gets worse until the house breaks out through the windows, and becomes all England with all England's heart broken."[34] More than hearts are broken, but no one asks why a bomb should drop without warning onto the grounds of Heartbreak House killing two occupants. On the basis of their opportunistic morals—one is a burglar and the other a swindler*—the two who die might be denied pity, but Shaw rejects conventional poetic justice. Meaning lies less in who has died and more in the fact of death, as Hector emphasizes in scolding the incurably idealist Mazzini Dunn for his concern about one of the victims: "Are you immortal that you need pity him? Our turn next." Most of the inhabitants of Heartbreak House will endure. Learn navigation and live, Shotover exhorts them. Leave it and be damned. Until they begin learning, the old captain intends to remain on the bridge. So too G.B.S.

It would still be some months before G.B.S. could transform the experience of the night of October 1 into a page of play script. Six weeks later Lady Gregory visited Ayot, writing afterward in her diary, "He read . . . the first part of a play, very amusing, *The House in the Clouds*, but says he doesn't know how to finish it, it is so wild. He thought bringing my 'fresh mind' to bear on it might be a help."[35] It was the most difficult play to write in Shaw's experience, but when the ideas of four years and a night finally coalesced, the result was possibly Shaw's greatest and most difficult play. The puzzlingly titled *The House in the Clouds*† would become *Heartbreak House*.

---

* The swindler was the morally bankrupt businessman "Boss Mangan," who prior to the play's action has ruined Ellie Dunn's father. He was modeled after the well-fed, florid, grumpy, and gruff Lord Devonport, who was then chairman of the Port of London Authority and Food Controller briefly and unsuccessfully in 1916–17. To Shaw Lord Devonport was "a megalomaniac and a superficial fool" (*New Witness*, March 8, 1917, p. 522), and Shaw worried afterward that his caricature of Devonport as Mangan spoiled the play.

† Both Aristophanes' *The Clouds* (432 B.C.) and the cloud kingdom of Laputa in the third book of Swift's *Gulliver's Travels* may have been in Shaw's mind before he developed his Peacockian title. In *The Clouds* Aristophanes attacked the insidious disease that was corrupting Athens, when men— for money—argued not for truth but for victory and prided themselves on their ability to take a bad cause and make it triumph over a good one. In Laputa there is an undertone of corruption and insanity. Intellect is divorced from sense and technical skill from a sense of values, while science increasingly dominates life.

8

Floundering

W HILE G.B.S. struggled with his intractable new play, a number of the old ones were doing very well in London and in the provinces, in neutral countries, and even in Ireland, often the most inhospitable of countries to its native son's works. *Caesar and Cleopatra* was appearing in Holland, *Mrs. Warren's Profession* in Norway, and *Androcles and the Lion* in Sweden, where the first-night audience found the references to Androcles' occupation of tailor particularly funny and saw nothing unusual about a stage lion with leonine head and trunk and hairy masculine legs. A half-dozen Shaw plays were on tour in America from Boston to Palo Alto, and in England a half-dozen more toured the provinces from Plymouth to Birmingham and Hull. At Booth's Theatre in New York, William Faversham opened a production of *Getting Married* that Shaw had guided via overseas letters. Faversham sent copies of the opening-night reviews, eliciting from Shaw the reply, "First-night successes and notices leave me cold; I pay no attention until the first fortnight's returns arrive."[1]

Faversham had wanted to do *The Devil's Disciple*, but Shaw had forbade all overseas productions of it as long as the war lasted, not wanting a play about English military stupidity and other stupidities during the American Revolution to be turned into "an attempt to exploit anti-English feelings."[2] It was a side of Shaw none of his critics or admirers knew. The disappointment on Faversham's part lasted only until the first box office returns were counted, for *Getting Married* did excellent business, Shaw receiving between eight hundred and a thousand dollars in royalties each week well into the next year. However, when he saw a copy of the program, which referred to the piece as a work in "acts," although the action of the play is continuous, Shaw cabled, "You have heartlessly outraged clause ten of our agreement."

Faversham answered laconically, "Heartless never; often victim printer's error." Shaw, often outraged at printers' "corrections" of his spelling and typographical idiosyncrasies, had found his match. "Every genius meets his Waterloo some time or other," he wrote Faversham, and the performances continued with the programs unchanged.[3]

In Dublin the Abbey Theatre, trying to recover under J. Augustus Keogh from the disasters of St. John Ervine's management, was playing *Widowers' Houses* and *John Bull's Other Island*, with the latter, once rejected by the theatre for fear it would result in riots, playing to standing-room-only audiences. (Ervine was now in the Army, as was Barker, who had enlisted in the Royal Horse Artillery to spare himself from the infantry and from Lillah.) Emboldened and aware of the shifts in moral attitudes the war had already caused, Shaw tried to secure permission from the censor of plays to stage *Mrs. Warren's Profession* publicly in England, something he had not been able to do since it had been written in 1893. The reaction proved that some things had not changed in England. Lord Sandhurst, the Lord Chamberlain, not only refused to license the play, but refused even to look at it, returning the reading fee "because both my present Examiners of Plays had [previously] read the play."*

The wrangle over *Mrs. Warren* was a minor frustration compared to Shaw's continuing problems with Sharp and the *NS*, which finally had reached a point of no return after Shaw returned to London in the fall. While at the Fabian Summer School at Sedbergh, he had discussed

---

* The censor finally relented in 1925, when the play was performed with no perceptible damage to public morals.

with Rebecca West a book in which they were both interested and which he was reviewing for the *NS*, Wilma Meikle's *Towards a Sane Feminism*. Once back in London, he quarreled for the last time with what he called Sharp's "suburban-Tory" attitude, accusing him of having turned into a disciple of Cecil Chesterton. He would express his own point of view from the other side of the ocean, through the American press, he wrote Sharp, concluding with the pledge to never again plague him: "You are free for ever of your G.B.S." Shaw never again did appear in the *NS* during Sharp's tenure,* the bitterness between the two costing the struggling *New Statesman* the services of the most talented pamphleteer since Swift.

To the secretary of the New Statesman Publishing Company on October 5, Shaw forwarded a curt letter of resignation from its board, declaring that he would remain "a simple shareholder." On the same day, he wrote of his decision to the Webbs, regretting that he had not been able to turn the *NS* into a paper that "will fight for our policy; disable and discredit our opponents when it cannot convert them; use the events of every week to drive home our morals; and, above all, attack the big national idols, and do it with sufficient tact, generosity and gallantry to compel the tolerance and applause of the political world and the ideal old English spirit. I should not ask such a paper to pay dividends: the value would come in the heightening of faith and courage in the community." Beatrice responded, and G.B.S. reiterated his position.

My dear Beatrice,

It cannot be helped: it was bound to be, in the nature of things. My working relations with Sidney have always been those of a ticket-of-leave man who has forced himself on a benevolent employer by making himself useful. The benevolent employer appreciates the usefulness; but he can never trust the ticket-of-leave man, and is always surprised when his accounts turn out correct after all. This didn't matter in our Fabian work, because he never had to trust me: he had only to accept the finished work from me and wonder as its being so sensible instead of being what

* Except in the letters to the editor columns.

he expected. But a paper cannot be run on those lines. I might have wrecked the *New Statesman*: and it was psychologically impossible for Sidney to conceive that a man with my sort of mind and character, and an Irishman to boot, could do anything else. If he, as Chairman, felt this after nearly forty years' experience of me, how could novices like Simon and Bennett have any confidence in me? . . . When I tell Sidney that the sword we forged has broken in my hand, he says in effect 'So much the better: you are not to be trusted with a sword; and the broken-off point will come in handy for me as an oyster knife.' I can only reply that he will not be allowed to open oysters with it. . . . The *New Statesman*, after its little Shavian spurt, has come to heel; and that is the end of our influence on Cabinets. . . . The longer I live, the more I perceive that Napoleon's rule of six years as the effective lifetime of a general applies to all public bodies and all papers. Three years ago the *NS* was young; today it is about eighty: a comfortable age for the directors, but not a promising one for the paper. A paper, unless it is to be frankly a dull paper for dull people, like *The Spectator* (which now suits my elderly taste remarkably well) or an ungenerous paper for ungenerous people like the *Saturday,* must live by advertures. The amazing journalistic feat of sacking Bernard Shaw does not indicate much taste for that sort of thing at Great Queen's Street. . . .

Unhappy about the break, Beatrice reproached Sharp for losing Shaw to the paper, and Sharp defended himself.

Dear Mrs. Webb,

Your letter rather demands an answer. It is one thing to be criticised by Shaw, another to have *you* supporting him. I don't think I have failed to do justice to Shaw's 'lack of practical egotism' (as you call it—though *I* shouldn't). I have always been amazed by his willingness to go on supporting a paper which obviously represented his views in scarcely a single particular, and, of course, he has always been extraordinarily nice to me personally—so much so that I never felt inclined to resent in the least the good-humoured contempt which he never concealed. I think he is much the most generous and sweetest-tempered person I ever came across.

But that does not affect the fact that he is intellectually the most grossly egotistical and unreasonable of beings. I cannot imagine anyone more perverse than he has been in his dealings with the editor of the *N.S.* He has never shown the smallest sympathy or understanding of the difficulties of the job of maintaining a coherent line in the paper, but, on the contrary, he has always apparently made it a point of honour or dignity not to compromise on the smallest point. A tentative criticism of mine on a particular sentence of his, for example, has always meant that the sentence would be underlined and strengthened in the proof. . . . I've no desire at all to have a *personal* organ, my whole object has always been to express a policy which shall command the widest possible measure of agreement amongst our supporters (the Board on the one hand and the readers on the other)—and, as a matter of fact, I should have been very glad to have incorporated in the policy and personality of the paper a dash of Shaw—such as has run through so much Fabian work. But it has not been practicable because he would not co-operate. I daresay it would have been possible if we had met every week, because he might have been induced to meet one half-way. But as it was, his stuff has always been quite incompatible with the rest of the paper—and all the more troublesome because it attracted so much attention. . . .[4]

Since he considered Arnold Bennett the most important member of the *NS* board (after the Webbs), Shaw explained himself separately to Bennett, restating his concern that English foreign policy could drive Germany into the arms of Russia and Japan after the war, and America into a balance-of-power alliance against England as well. He believed that what was needed after the war was a combination of states from the Pacific to the Carpathians to protect European civilization from the Orient—in which he included Russia. It was a foreshadowing of the NATO alliance that followed a second world war, but Bennett—whose "Sardonyx" column in the *NS* Shaw praised—was not interested, as Shaw understood in advance when he ended his letter with the realization that he and Bennett and others like them would go on "ploughing our lonely back gardens."[5] Bennett's response was laconic and unsympathetic. He supported the *Statesman*'s policy as shaped by Sharp, although conceding that "in some ways" G.B.S. had had "an excellent influence upon the opinion of the enlightened."[6] Shaw was not interested in saving merely the already converted, and only Beatrice Webb—belatedly—seemed to understand the magnitude of the blunder that had cost the *NS* Shaw's services.

Even so she confided her view only to her diary* and let the matter drop. With Shaw busy preparing the annual autumn Fabian lectures with the Webbs, it was a time for healing of divisions.

As usual Shaw led off the series, which had as its general theme the melodramatic "The World in Chains." Of the six lectures, Shaw offered both the initial and the concluding ones, the first—"Life"— given at King's Hall, Covent Garden, on Friday evening October 27. According to the syllabus, Shaw intended to speak on "how far the sacrifice of liberty to the emergencies created by war is really necessary," but according to one of the few reports of the meeting in the press, the syllabus remained "an independent document, having much the same relation to the lecture as Mr. Shaw's prefaces have to his plays."

Mr. Shaw spoke mainly about biology, theology, and the super-man or super-Prospero, Zeppelins, Plato, poverty, the intelligent parent, and—himself. The result was a very brilliant lecture, upon which the best critical comment would be that made by Dr. Johnson after dining upon a haggis —that it had given him "some fine confused feeding." The hall was quite full, and judging by the congestion in the entrance and the excitement of the stewards, a considerable number of people had neglected to book their seats and had to be turned away in the rain.[7]

Although the evening had gone well and every seat sold, Shaw was concerned that he had felt the strain of keeping the audience "up to concert pitch" for ninety minutes and realized that he would not be

* "G.B.S. has definitely severed his connection with the New Statesman. The immediate and real reason—not mentioned to the Press—is an adequate one— Sharp's refusal to insert his articles, signed or unsigned. Clifford is a hard-minded conservative collectivist, who obstinately refuses to condemn either measures or men unless he has an alternative plan or an alternative Government to propose. He is also a materialist, a despiser of all ideals which cannot be embodied, in the near future, in social machinery to improve the conditions of life. Sentimentality is said to be the Emotion of the Unimaginative—but Sharp has neither imagination nor emotion. Unless he can see through a question and all round it with his intellect he refuses to admit that the questions exists. Above all, he loathes the professional rebel. . . ." (diary entry for November 3, 1916).

able to do it any better as he grew older. Reaching sixty had been a symbolic event for him, and he wondered in a note to Beatrice whether the Fabians ought to keep counting on him year after year as star performer and chief fund raiser.[8]

The four lectures between Shaw's two were by the Webbs, Graham Wallas, and (on art) Clutton Brock. Roger Fry introduced Brock and acted as chairman for him when he fielded questions from the audience afterward, a task that proved to be more difficult than usual when Shaw arose to attack what he understood to be a perversion of William Morris's attitudes toward "machine-made ornament." A machine, Shaw insisted, *is* capable of making beautiful ornament, and as Brock began to defend himself he became so confused that he had to call on Shaw to explain what Morris had really done. The last lecture—Shaw's —was on religion, a subject that in a third year of wholesale and violent death had become of obsessive interest to him as it had to Wells and others. Shaw had been determined for some months to dramatize his ideas on religion as soon as he had satisfactorily completed *Heartbreak House*. The European war, he was convinced, was "essentially a Darwinian product"—a reaction in political terms to the belief that the dynamic quality in the universe was a result of the operation of "apparently blind and purposeless forces such as polar magnetism, natural selection and high explosives." A belief in trial and error led to deicide, Shaw told the last audience of the series, "reducing civilization to a mere struggle of blood and iron." But it only killed the old God belonging to "those who believe that there is nothing further to learn than the Book of Books has revealed; that man cannot add a cubit to his stature; and that we are all merely rival courtiers of a universal throne." His lecture summed up ideas he had been maturing since *Man and Superman* toward an opus to come:

The religious man is no longer the man who has hidden his eyes in the bosom of a Church, but one to whom God (if he uses that term at all) is an overwhelming intention in the world which he feels mysteriously interested in and impelled to carry out even when it is contrary to his immediate personal interests and intentions. He is no longer an Agnostic, because he recognizes a creative will in the world which can and does produce actual material live cellular tissue when it wants it, and because he not only recognizes a biological movement towards a destination, but perceives that the direction of that movement is always towards higher organization with the apparent object of becoming capable of greater knowledge and power: in short, towards Omniscience and Omnipotence. And as that destination is at an infinite distance, he is not troubled with the horrible fear that we shall presently arrive there and have nothing else to do for the rest of our lives.

It was the wrong time for anyone, let alone Frank Harris, to suggest that he wanted to write about Shaw's "inner life" and wanted Shaw's help in doing it. "I want to know why you did not marry early and beget children," he noted, and among other queries wondered, "How did you come to be a vegetarian? Was it through indigestion?" To Harris in America Shaw warned, "You had better avoid the subject as you will certainly botch it frightfully." It was as difficult a time to be patient with parasites as with patriots. Numbed by wholesale death and feverish journalism, people could look neither life nor death in the face and resented the few who publicly could and did. As Shaw had just told an audience, Englishmen were brave enough on the battlefields of France or Mesopotamia, but dared not allow Bertrand Russell to speak in Glasgow. The sons of his friends were being wasted in battle—if not their lives, their talents. Lady Gregory, then en route to visit Shaw, had a son flying for the British in Italy and had lost a young nephew (and surrogate son), Sir Hugh Lane, on the *Lusitania*. (Shaw, who knew Lane well and also mourned him, had not let the loss alter his sense of proportion over the greater carnage in the trenches.*) G.B.S. had just watched two protégés go into uniform, Barker and Ervine, and a surrogate son closer to him than anyone but

---

* Lady Gregory was appointed sole trustee to carry out his will, which included an unsigned codicil offering the art collection he had bequeathed first to the National Gallery in London to the city of Dublin instead. A bill had already gone through Parliament to legalize the unwitnessed wills of soldiers who had died on active service, but Lady Gregory's suggestion that legislation could be had to legalize the shift in destination of Lane's paintings from England to Ireland prompted Shaw's comment to her that he was reminded of the country saying that it is hard to get butter out of a dog's mouth. His prophecy proved correct.

Barker, the twice-wounded Robert Loraine, was with a flying unit in France. Shaw's neighbor James Barrie, one of whose godsons had already been killed at Ypres, had another, Peter Llewelyn Davies, evacuated home as a shell-shock victim. Other friends and friends' sons were at the front or en route there, where expectations for survival were no better than expectations for peace. By the end of November, British casualties in the newest push, in which Haig and his generals deliberately sacrificed mobility for mass, were over 400,000. At the maximum the Germans had been temporarily pressed back in a few places as much as seven miles. The London press hailed it as a great victory.

Trooper St. John Ervine, unable to live on his serviceman's pay and with a novel he was counting on postponed by the publisher, wrote to Shaw soon afterward. He needed £50 to keep his wife going until January. Shaw sent a check by return mail.[9] The same month another request arrived from one of his earliest girl friends, Alice Lockett, with whom he had been infatuated when she was a young nurse in the early 1880s. Her physician husband was an Army officer with a much diminished income, and Shaw guaranteed for her the renewal of a loan.[10] Such expenses—which Shaw seldom expected to be returned—were not the reason he asked for high fees for his writing, but with his own income much reduced he nevertheless needed them, turning down an invitation from the American humor magazine *Puck* for a series of articles, partly on the grounds that it could not afford him. "My articles for America are longer and more ponderous than the sort of thing you need," he wrote the editor. "You want young men with light hands, and light purses, not spoilt elderly gentlemen who expect to be paid immoderately for being dull."[11] One of several of his articles for America at the time—for the *New York Times* of October 22—paid him £100 (before Paul Reynolds deducted his agent's fee) and was typical of much of Shaw's writing for the press then in not being exactly dull, but in being self-consciously serious in a way to prevent readers from construing wit with triviality. As a result, although he began his view of Anglo-American relations by comparing them to the Chuzzlewit cousins as described by Charles Dickens, Shaw went on to again argue the necessity of a Western postwar alliance embracing the United States as well as Germany.

The world is growing smaller; and the saying that Great Britain is no longer an island will soon apply to the whole North American continent. When the bridging of the sea by aircraft and submarine has gone a little further we shall become acutely conscious of the fact that the belt of habitable land round the waist of the globe is now practically continuous; and that the hemming-in process, by which we in England have so craftily and successfully circumvented the Germans, has possibilities perilous both to ourselves and to our American cousins.

Much of the piece was prophecy in the style of his off-and-on friend Wells. Wells himself was too preoccupied for prophecy, being busy as a war tourist in northern Italy. In the same issue of the *New York Times* with G.B.S.'s piece was Wells's "Italy's Picturesque Mountain War." Arnold Bennett, after a carefully guided tour, had already reported on the war in France. Others—Belloc, Masefield, Conan Doyle, and even Mrs. Humphry Ward—had made similar jaunts. But it required being invited, and being invited was predicated upon being safe. Ironically, a piece Shaw was then sending to the printer, the one-act satire on home-front ineptitude, *Augustus Does His Bit*, would alter opinions of him in the military. Shaw ordered one hundred rehearsal copies on October 10, subtitling it "An Unofficial Dramatic Tract on War Saving and Cognate Topics. By the Author of the Inca of Perusalem."

One of Shaw's visitors at the time was Cecil Chesterton, who turned up "in khaki, a sturdy, jolly, deeply sunburnt, hopelessly unsoldierlike figure," Chesterton, lumpy and—fond of a pint—red-faced under normal conditions, was a "C" class draftee, a term indicating the lowest degree of physical fitness acceptable for the Army. He had been extricated from the editorial chair of his *New Witness* to become a private, a thoughtless exercise in democracy by the conscription, for no one—unless it were his older brother G.K.C.—was as jingoistic and anti-German in print. Shaw thought that Cecil, as a soldier, could—merely by standing still—camouflage himself as a beet upon a sack of potatoes. "I have come here to tell you," he announced to Shaw, "that it is not true that I have given up beer. I am told that beer will shorten my life by ten years; and I am prepared to pay that price cheerfully."[12] Few people were as contrary in their views and styles of living as G.B.S. and the Chestertons, yet Shaw loved them almost as brothers and admired their brilliance with the pen, although it was almost always put to use in ways he disapproved.

Cecil's real reason for visiting was to ask Shaw to review *The Perils of Peace*, an expansion of his *New Witness* polemics, then in press. Although he knew Shaw would disapprove of everything in a tract aimed at averting a laying down of arms, the publicity would be good for it, and he was certain more people would agree with him than with Shaw anyway. Shaw eventually did place a lengthy review of the book in the American *New Republic*, from which large extracts were quoted elsewhere, especially since Shaw insisted on the curious title for his piece, "On British Squealing, and the Situation After the War."[13] In it he warned,

There are two main facts to be grasped before any sensible criticism of the war can be delivered. The first is that the judgment of international relations by the ordinary morality of personal intercourse between fellow citizens in peace is as idle as taking the temperature of molten steel by a common bath thermometer. . . . The second fact to be kept steadily in view is that as fear is the most universal of emotions, and the war raises fear beyond all self-respect in weak men as it raises valor above all self-respect in strong ones, every war produces a Reign of Terror in which the government must either rise to the occasion or sit trembling on the front bench, a row of two-penny Robespierres, not daring to shriek for its blood at the next rumor of disaster.

Finally Shaw came to his point and made his title more understandable:

From the things that Mr. Chesterton must not say let us turn to the facts that he must face. First, the fact that nothing has happened in this war as yet that should make any man who knows what war means turn a hair. Atrocities in Belgium, pogroms in Galicia, Lusitania sinkings, bombs falling like the rain on the just and on the unjust, the old and the young, the male and female, Lille deportations, shootings of Nurse Cavell and Captain Fryatt and Sheehy Skeffington and the Baralong crew, the Wittenburg funk and the Ruhleben food, starvation blockades, violations of neutrality and tearing up of scraps of paper, poison gas and liquid fire and Juggernaut tanks: none of these raise any new moral question nor throw any new light on what human nature is capable of or on what war involves. If you go to war, you engage yourself not only to fight, but not to squeal. The Germans are out to shake our nerves; and the symptom of such shaking is squealing. Well, nobody can deny that the Germans have succeeded in shaking our civilian nerve, to an extent very disgraceful to us. We have squealed shamelessly. The submarine and Zeppelin campaigns have been enormously encouraged by our squealing. If a member of the German General Staff shook his head over their slender physical results, and asked was it worth while to spend so much and run such risks for so trifling a bag, the reply must have been, "Never mind the bag: read the English newspapers. Read the *New Witness*, written, not by twopennyhalfpenny journalists, but by some of the ablest writers in England; and see how it squeals. We are frightening them: their shrieks for revenge will presently become shrieks at their government for peace at any price." How infinitely more prudent as well as more becoming was the wreath sent by our Royal Flying Corps to the grave of Immelmann, whom our squealing civilians would have buried at the crossroads with a stake driven through his body.

By the time the review appeared, Cecil Chesterton was in France, and long afterward Shaw recalled with deep emotion that unexpected final good-bye from Cecil. "It is impossible to describe what I used to feel on such occasions. It was hard enough to see any young man thrown into the common heap of cannon fodder . . . but when the young man, possessing a rare and highly valuable talent, was not replaceable, one's hatred of the war bit fiercely in. However there was nothing to be done but keep his spirits up. . . . So we parted gaily. . . ."[14] A few weeks after the war ended, Cecil Chesterton was dead of trench fever in a French hospital. He was thirty-nine.

Lady Gregory had arrived at Adelphi Terrace in mid-November to tell Shaw in person of the Abbey successes of *John Bull's Other*

Island, Widowers' Houses, and *Arms and the Man.* At lunch the conversation turned to spiritualism, which had become the solace of so many the war had bereaved, and Shaw, reminded by his play of an incident about Ireland, recalled that his mother had become in her later years a table-rapping enthusiast, particularly successful in summoning up a spirit who identified himself as Matthew Haffigan, a name Shaw afterward used for a character in *John Bull.* The spectral Matthew Haffigan had been a consistent liar, his statements, when checked out by G.B.S., proving always to be false. But Lucinda Shaw went on happily with Haffigan, and her son humored her by becoming adept at cheating at séances.

They went on to Ayot for the weekend in the midst of an early snowfall. In the house, "warm and bright with fires in every room and pots of chrysanthemums," Shaw reminisced to Lady Gregory of William Morris and read to her some of his recent writings, including something in a form rare for him—the short story.[15] The next weekend, after a few days in London, he was back at Ayot with another guest, Granville-Barker, who with the help of friends more influential in the government than G.B.S., had been released from artillery training and given a commission on the General List for the purpose of special duties in the Intelligence. Barker was on his way to a nonarduous assignment in America and had been pressing Shaw and Barrie to persuade Lillah to agree to begin divorce proceedings. Finally she agreed, and Barker left in December with the welcome news that his freedom would be forthcoming.

If he had any premonition of what Barker's new freedom and impending attachment would do to their relationship, Shaw did not show it in his continuing warmth toward Barker. In America Barker continued to hear from Shaw, not only to keep him apprised of the legal situation (the divorce became final in April 1917), but to encourage him to stay with the theatre. There were, he wrote, "serious official leanings toward an attempt to convince the neutrals of Europe that we can outdo [Max] Reinhardt when it comes to high [theatrical] art by sending out a specimen of our best, and that it is understood for a wonder that this conviction cannot be carried out by the admirers of Reinhardt or by Sir H[erbert] T[ree]." Shaw urged Barker to take the job if he were asked, but no one was asked, and the propaganda-through-theatre project fell through.[16] Helen Huntington, waiting for her own divorce in order to marry Barker, had entirely opposite ends in mind, never losing an opportunity to express to Barker her abhorrence of the theatre in general and Shaw in particular.

Beginning in the December Barker left for America and left the G.B.S. orbit forever (as both he and Shaw realized but left unsaid). Shaw had impressed upon him ideas that he could not have known would become the nucleus of a new play, one a dozen years away in the writing. Ironically, too, it would be a play in which people would see the influence of one Barker himself was to write and that was never performed, *His Majesty* (1923–28), a play about an abdication. In the preface to *The Apple Cart* (1929), Shaw mentioned a curious genius who was already completely forgotten, Alfred Warwick Gattie. In 1896 in Shaw's days as a *Saturday Review* critic, he had favorably reviewed a Gattie play, but years later had apparently forgotten all about it, only mentioning Gattie's failed aspirations as a playwright while detailing his frustrated achievements as an engineer. Early in December 1916, Shaw was persuaded by Henry Murray, a friend who knew both men, to investigate what appeared to be a Utopian project on which Gattie was working. Gattie himself, a volcanically emotional man, left it to one of his engineers to explain that adoption of the labor-saving invention "would release from industry enough men to utterly overwhelm the Central Empires with whom we were then at war."

Still Shaw approached his investigation with skepticism, almost afraid to tell Sidney Webb he was going across the Thames to a warehouse on the Battersea docks to see the invention in operation. The visit convinced him, and on December 9 he wrote to Webb to urge him to see a demonstration of the Gattie machinery, for Gattie had proven to be more than "a crank with a crane," as Webb had dismissed him. Afterward Shaw described his experience.

I found a workshop, duly labelled as the premises of The New Transport Company, Limited, and spacious enough to accommodate a double railway line with a platform. The affair was unquestionably real, so far. The platform was not provided with a station: its sole equipment was a table with a row of buttons on it for making electrical contacts. Each line of railway had on it a truck with a steel lid. The practical part of the proceedings began by placing an armchair on the lid of one of the trucks and seating me in it. A brimming glass of water was then set at my feet. I could not imagine what I was expected to do with the water or what was going to happen; and there was a suggestion of electrocution about the chair which made me nervous. Gattie then sat down majestically at the table on the platform with his hand hovering over the buttons. Intimating that the miracle would take place when my truck passed the other truck, he asked me to choose whether it should occur at the first passage or later, and to dictate the order in which it should be repeated. I was by that time incapable of choosing; so I said the sooner the better; and the two trucks started. When the other truck had passed mine I found myself magically sitting on it, chair and all, with the glass of water unspilled at my feet.[17]

What Gattie seemed to have accomplished was a system of loading and unloading container cargo that was not only automated, but safe for fragile and dangerous goods, even explosives. What Gattie could not do was convince anyone who counted that what Shaw called "the enormous saving of labor and smash" was worth accomplishing, and with each rejection he had become progressively more undiplomatic. The hidebound officials were perceptive enough to recognize that the transportation revolution of Gattie's Clearing House would threaten thousands of jobs, including perhaps their own, and while the helpless inventor berated them as corrupt idiots, they saw in him (in Shaw's words) "an enemy of the human race, a wrecker of homes and a starver of innocent babes." An unknown soldier of automation, Gattie is memorialized only in one place. "The Apple Cart," Shaw wrote, "is his only shrine; and . . . it does not even bear his name."[18]

The "villain" of *The Apple Cart* is Breakages, Ltd., a monolithic monopoly that controls the nation's business and sums up for Shaw all that was wrong with a system that exploited the many for the profits of a few. Private capitalism, Shaw wrote, consisted of "huge vested interests in destruction, waste, and disease. The armament firms thrive on war; the glaziers gain by broken windows; the operating surgeons depend on cancer for their children's bread; the distillers and brewers build cathedrals to sanctify the profits of drunkenness; and the prosperity of Dives costs the privation of a hundred Lazaruses."[19] It was no monolithic monopoly, but only the accumulated self-interest of Englishmen who had much to lose in the short run by efficiency, which dogged Gattie. His proposed Central Clearing House —with seven times the interior space of St. Paul's Cathedral—would have replaced seventy-four London freight stations and untold numbers of loyal labor unionists. Its heavy glass roof would have doubled as landing strip for aircraft, particularly mail planes, and would have been lit from underneath for night flights.[20] It was clearly a Wellsian dream almost come true, and Shaw urged Wells to see it and convince him that he was not mad.

Almost no one came to Battersea for a demonstration. Fortunately for the British, it was not until June 1914, that the German Ministry of Transport became interested enough in Gattie's proposals to send an official to examine the system, and it could never follow up the official's initial favorable impressions. The chief of the Railway Department of the Board of Trade, however, only as far away as the other side of the Thames, remained too busy throughout the war to visit the Battersea docks. Sidney Webb apparently never went either, perhaps because Shaw warned him to take an overcoat, since the warehouse was draughty and cold. Not giving up easily, however, Shaw urged the Clearing House scheme upon the Chairman of the Board of Trade as an urgent wartime labor-saving possibility, but was told that the enormous expenditure of men and materials necessary to test the project's practicality on a large scale, even if the foul and abusive Gattie personality were no obstacle, made it impossible under wartime conditions.[21] A victim of the vested interest in inefficiency, Gattie was finally given a formal "no" by a Board of Trade committee in 1919, after the war. Automated handling of container cargo was eventually proved practical, but the same forces that frustrated Gattie still prevented its use on the scale he envisoned, and Gattie lives on only in the "Breakages, Ltd." of the Shaw play he never saw. He died in 1925.

Other aspects of *The Apple Cart* seem traceable to the same period. One of the elements of the futuristic play, in fact its climax, is the facing down of his Cabinet by a Republican-minded King who, although constitutionally weak, has his way by threatening to abdicate and then run for a seat in Parliament as a commoner and leader of his own party. Popular with his people, he might succeed in turning an electoral victory into a Prime Ministership for himself, a possibility not lost on the incumbent Prime Minister and his Cabinet, who give way. There had been Republican talk by some disgruntled Englishmen through the war, and on April 21, 1917, H. G. Wells had followed up his proposal that Germany indicate its sincerity about peace by throwing out the Kaiser and installing a republic with some Republican noises about England. "Our Monarchy is a peculiar one," he wrote, "the general Republican feeling has found satisfaction in the assertion that the British system is in its essence a 'crowned Republic.' . . ." What Wells was actually opposing was the setting up of puppet monarchies in freed countries of eastern Europe to fill discredited and vacant thrones, but Shaw applauded the general sentiments, which had echoed what he had written a few months earlier, when he had alarmed the Fabian Executive Board with the text of a proposed Republican manifesto.*

To the *Times* G.B.S. wrote a letter congratulating the editor on his courage in printing Wells's letter about a "Republican" monarchy, but the monarchy, he admonished the *Times*, was "a popular and convenient institution" that had been insulted by the *Times*'s leader on Wells's observations. In effect the *Times* had said that since the King was a nobody as far as real power was concerned, there was no cause for serious concern. What the King should do, Shaw suggested, is sell his crown to a theatrical costumier and get himself elected to Parliament by a comfortable majority from the Royal Borough of Windsor. Shaw's letter was returned with the usual printed slip in such cases: "The Editor of the Times presents his compliments and regrets that he is unable to avail himself of the communication kindly offered him."

---

* A worried board met on January 17, 1917 to attempt to figure out what to do with Shaw's proposal and watered it down into a committee project to discuss "Empire Reconstruction," to which Shaw agreed. It eventually produced a book under the authorship of H. Duncan Hall, *The British Commonwealth of Nations* (1920).

The idea was too good to waste, and what Shaw had described as "this king business"[22] to Arnold Bennett a few months before eventually matured into one of the best plays of Shaw's later years.*

Quietly working away at *Heartbreak House* and other projects, Shaw intended to close the year out of the newspapers, but the futile wooing of his services for the American lecture circuit, which had promised to become an annual ritual, came even earlier, not even waiting for the beginning of 1917. More wishful thinking than anything else was the report to the *New York Times* by a George H. Brennan, who claimed he was to manage Shaw's American lectures. It created a sensation on both sides of the ocean:

* Shaw might have also heard of the apparently real-life equivalent of his plot in an incident that occurred in mid-1914, when George V attempted to get all parties to agree on Irish Home Rule. According to Ford Madox Ford, (in *Return to Yesterday*, 1932) who had heard about it from his friend C. F. G. Masterman,

The King was acting almost—oh but only just almost—unconstitutionally. He had asked all the leaders of all the Irish parties to meet in a Round Table conference at Buckingham Palace under his own Presidency. The *Daily News* said it was a really very naughty King.

I imagined I knew all about that. I had seen Masterman a month before really angry for the first time in my life. He said that the King was impossible to get on with. He was as determined that the Irish Question should be settled to the satisfaction of all his Irish subjects, as his father had been to have the Entente Cordiale with France. The Cabinet was unanimously against the Buckingham Palace conference. They wanted to do nothing that could enhance royal prestige. The matter had come to an absolute impasse.

Finally, according to Masterman—and I made a note of his words immediately afterwards. It was the only note I ever made, but the occasion seemed very extraordinary—the King had said:

"Very well, gentlemen. I am the richest commoner in England. If you wish me to abdicate I will abdicate, supposing that to be the will of the country. But before that we will have a general election and I have not much doubt as to the results as between you and me." So he had his conference.

But the conference went nowhere and was indefinitely postponed after the war began.

Mr. Brennan said yesterday that the British War Office has taken up the matter of the Shaw tour and that the correspondence with the author has practically ceased. He said he believed Shaw's projected visit here had been disapproved by his Government.

Letters and cablegrams between Mr. Shaw and Mr. Brennan have been held up, and the small amount of correspondence allowed to trickle through has been severely handled by the censors. The only mail received recently from the author consisted of postal cards, on which he made it a point to show his contempt for the censors.[23]

Too obtuse, or optimistic, to realize that there were no eager letters and cablegrams, but only the characteristic and mostly irrelevant postcards, Brennan persisted, and when a London reporter finally caught up with G.B.S. he was told that the Shavian reply "could not without incivility be made public" until its recipient released it.

"I have received," he added, "a cutting from a Glasgow paper, which has been extensively reproduced in this country. It says: 'George H. Brennan, who is promoting a lecture tour for Bernard Shaw in America declared yesterday that fear of the British authorities of Mr. Shaw's views on war is preventing the well-known author from obtaining permission to leave Great Britain.'

"There is not a word of truth in this statement. George H. Brennan is not promoting a lecturing tour for me, though, like many other people, he has tried to persuade me to allow him to do it. I have not applied for permission to leave Great Britain. There is no reason to believe that the British authorities have the slightest fear of my views on war, nor, on the other hand, that their personal attachment to me is so uncontrollable as to tempt them to retain me in this country by violence if I had any intention of leaving it."[24]

The Shavian reply to Brennan was apparently not one likely to do the American agent any good. It was never released, and G.B.S. himself kept his peace. To keep the pressure up, however, the New York chapter of the Drama League of America sent Shaw an invitation signed by distinguished men of letters and of the theatre, among them William Dean Howells, James Huneker, Nicholas Murray Butler, William Lyon Phelps, Winthrop Ames, Otto Kahn, Daniel Frohman, and Walter Pritchard Eaton. Shaw politely declined and then continued at length in his characteristic fashion:

Every year the papers announce in desperation that I am actually coming; and every citizen of the United States writes me a cordial private invitation to stay at his house. . . .
I cannot help asking myself whether it is not now too late. I could have come when I was young and beautiful. I could have come when I was mature and capable. I did not. I am now elderly and doddering. Could I live up to my reputation? Have I any right to bring my white hairs and my crowsfeet to blast the illusions of the young American women who send me my own photographs of thirty years ago to be autographed, and to address American audiences with a fictitious clearness of articulation that is due wholly to my dentist? If I were a modest man I should not think of such things. Being notoriously an extremely vain one, they daunt me. Authors, unlike good little children, should be heard, not seen. I shall leave America its ideal unshattered. . . .[25]

But he did not. In March, 1933, in his seventy-seventh year, a ship on which he was making a cruise stopped briefly in San Francisco. Shaw paid a hurried visit to William Randolph Hearst, at his nearby San Simeon barony. Hearst had earned the honor, having long published Shavian screeds. On April 11 the *Empress of Britain* reached New York, where Shaw spent one day, and where—for the American Academy of Political Science—he delivered a lecture that evening at the Metropolitan Opera House, afterwards published as *The Political Madhouse in America and Nearer Home*. Then he returned to the ship and went home. The lecture agents still had not lured him. He never came back.

In mid-December there was a Cabinet crisis that ended not in the unlikely exit of the King as would be threatened in *The Apple Cart*, but in the predictable exit of Asquith and Grey and the entrance of Lloyd George as Prime Minister. Shaw saw little difference, and in writing to Sidney Webb about the changes in Downing Street again importuned him to visit Gattie's Clearing House model, one of the few interesting things in a London that grew greyer all the time. The streets were full of drably clad troops, and Trafalgar Square no longer echoed with the exhortations of the recruiting sergeants who claimed to be straight from the trenches and warned, in those days of the Derby Scheme, "Come in or be fetched."

The day before Christmas the Shaws visited their new Hertfordshire neighbor, Apsley Cherry Garrard, a survivor of the Scott "Terra Nova" expedition to the Antarctic. Scott's young widow had been invited to the Cherry Garrards for the holidays, and at lunch, Lady Scott, who had known G.B.S. only vaguely before, noted in her diary later, "Shaw was enchanting; told me I had the blue eye of genius, what he called the Strindberg eye."[26] On Christmas day she took several books to Ayot as gifts for the Shaws, and G.B.S. asked Lady Scott and her small son Peter to stay so that he could read to them "what he called a children's story, [although] it was a hyper adult story. . . ."[27] It was an imaginary scene between the Kaiser and a little girl at night on a Flanders battlefield, which Shaw had written for a gift book for a Belgian children's charity, the Vestiare Marie Josef. When he had delivered it, the lady who had solicited the story was reluctant to bury it in a gift book after all and sold it instead—for the charity—to Mrs. Whitelaw Reid of the *New York Tribune* for £400. It had already appeared in America on the front page of the *Tribune*'s Sunday magazine on October 22, 1916, with an illustration by Boardman Robinson and a sentimental caption beneath.

"It is not my doing," said the Emperor helplessly, when the little girl put questions—Shavian questions—to him. The little girl, of course, was but one of the waifs of the War Zone; the Emperor was the Kaiser; and they met at night, between the lines, and talked. It is a subject and a situation for the great British satirist to revel in, and perhaps as you read it the thought will come that the Kaiser himself is but a child, for all his hapless majesty; as lacking in understanding as was she who found freedom in the bursting of a shell.

It was almost as if Shaw had suggested an answer to speculation about what Joan of Arc was like when she was a girl. Simple, yet shrewd, and irreverent about authority, the child is the Kaiser's intellectual match in their brief exchange, and the monarch is seen as the helpless pawn of his position. Another shell explodes nearby, obliterating the child and rendering her a disembodied voice, in which fashion she reappears to him as if in a dream he is having. The bewildered and bespattered Kaiser is left alive and alone while the little girl has been "set free by the shell" from the pain and privation of existence much in the manner the lively Joan of the epilogue of Shaw's play (1923) is freed from the body by her burning. The Kaiser's officers eventually find him, and—observing his condition—assume, one to the other, "The All Highest is as drunk as a pig." But the Kaiser does not overhear.[28]

It is more than possible that a play about France's patron saint (formally canonized only in 1920) was in the back of Shaw's mind during the war years, for in the year before the war he had visited "the Joan of Arc country," writing from Orléans to Mrs. Campbell that he would do a Joan play some day and describing his proposed epilogue for it, complete to English soldier rewarded in heaven for two sticks he tied together and gave Joan for a cross as she went to the stake.[29] Several years later, according to Miles Malleson (then a young actor-playwright), he met Shaw on a London street and was invited to Adelphi Terrace to talk. "Then he went on to say that he was writing a play about St. Joan. . . . He described his play, walking up and down the room with long strides. . . ."[30] Supporting evidence is lacking, but ideas for a Joan play had clearly been going through his mind even before the war, and the renewed agony of France may have stimulated additional ones.

Sixty years old but younger in heart when it came to attractive women, even when he thought of them more as daughters than anything else, G.B.S. was in his element when reading his story to the attractive, if mannish, sculptress and her fatherless little son. He would see much more of Kathleen, Lady Scott through the war years and after, even after she married again and became Lady Kennet, once telling her as she sculpted him, "No women ever born had a narrower escape from being a man. My affection for you is the nearest I ever came to homosexuality."[31]

As 1916 ended and 1917 began, Shaw heard from one of the earliest women in his life, Florence Farr, whom he had loved when he was a young playwright and whom he had put, along with himself, into his second play, *The Philanderer* (1893). She had been the epitome of the emancipated woman, detaching herself from a husband of minor talents and making her own careers as actress and writer, and mistress first to Shaw and afterward to Yeats. When she had gone to Ceylon several years before the war, becoming principal of Ramanathan College, a Hindu school for girls, people wondered whether it were merely the logical outcome of her long interest in Eastern thought, but when she received news from home of the death of Aubrey Beardsley's sister Mabel, she wrote back, "I am always glad to hear of someone making a good end. I came here to make mine brave." To G.B.S., after years of silence, she wrote from a hospital bed in Colombo that she was to undergo surgery for cancer the next day and although she was not going to tell her people about it, wanted to confide in him. "I shall like to get a letter from you someday. . . . Goodbye. Remember me to your people."*³² It was a desolate ending to another desolate year.

* Florence Farr Emery died in Ceylon on April 27, 1917.

9

War Tourist

On New Year's Day, 1917, Shaw decided to try to keep a diary for a year, "as a sample slice of my life." Initiated piously that Monday, it faltered to nothing in a fortnight, yet even the fragment gave an intimate glimpse into how the Shaws lived at Ayot. In his first entry, Shaw reported finishing the Republican manifesto that would startle the Fabians and—with a covering letter to veteran Fabian secretary Edward Pease—putting it in the mail. Calling for republics to replace discredited European monarchies, a cause the Fabians could have supported, it also suggested a Republican party in England, an idea the social-reformist but otherwise conservative Fabians could view only with embarrassment and horror. At their usual hour, 1:30, the Shaws lunched and then rested, after which they went out into the garden for their traditional exercise of sawing and splitting logs for the Ayot fireplaces. Charlotte did the sawing, and G.B.S. split them with a mallet and wedges. At four-thirty (16.30 in Shaw's twenty-four-hour reckoning) they had tea, which meant hot chocolate for the abstemious G.B.S., after which he went off to write, mostly letters, until dinner at seven-thirty. After dinner he would read (the current book was Madelin's *French Revolution*) or go to the piano to play, often singing robustly to his own accompaniment. That evening he performed for himself the second half of *Die Meistersinger*, an exhausting enterprise that left him ready for sleep.

Tuesday and Wednesday were devoted mostly to "What is To Be Done with the Doctors?"—a multipart series Shaw was writing for the *English Review*, again permitting his crotchets to cut deeply into his creative time. It was not that he sapped his creative energy with polemics and journalism, for when he was between major creative projects and had not yet focused upon a new one, the professional writer in him sought other expression. Thursday he made "a Sunday of it," writing only letters, altering his wood splitting to the morning hours and going off on a thirteen-mile motorbike trip to send a reply-paid cablegram (cost: £1.12.6) to Florence Farr in Ceylon. Afterward he read Havelock Ellis's *Essays in War Time* and played Liszt's piano transcription of Beethoven's *Ninth Symphony*. It was probably a relief for the household staff: on the previous evenings he had sung scenes from Richard Strauss's avant garde *Electra* and "a lot of songs by Gounod." By the afternoon post on Friday he was busy answering the letters forwarded from London by Ann Elder that had been delivered in the morning mail. "It is one of my troubles," he observed in his diary, "that I have so much business to do in connection with my former work that I have less and less time to work seriously in the present. As I grow old, I find for some reason that I attend to business the first thing in the morning, whereas formerly I always devoted the morning to my creative work, and attended to my business at long intervals, if at all." Before lunch, too, he had done his log splitting and afterward worked in the garage tightening the front wheel of his motorbike, a tedious job since he was without the special tools he needed. He could have left it for Kilsby, the third of the three-person Ayot staff, who doubled as assistant gardener and chauffeur. (The other two, Henry Higgs and his wife, Clara, had worked as gardener and housekeeper for the Shaws since 1901 and continued in his service until 1943.) After tea it was back to the medical articles, and after dinner—and the remainder of Ellis's *Essays*—the household heard "a lot of Mozart's Idomeneo."

Since he had been a young man, Shaw suffered regularly from migraine headaches. On Saturday the 6th his first migraine since November 29 (he kept careful personal medical records) cut down on his volume of work. After tea he dozed in his chair by the fire until called to dinner, and, after eating, realized gratefully that the headache was gone. But the evening energy usually put into music had been sapped, and he resorted to the lazy man's device of the pianola. Sunday meant a heap of weekly newspapers to read, which he interrupted for a mid-day drive to the Phillimores at Elstree, where the Webbs were staying for the weekend. It was so cold that Shaw took a walk round his garden to warm his feet before driving, but once at Elstree the heat of discussion made him forget the chill in his limbs; "the Webbs and I disputed about republicanism with our customary violence, so astonishing to people who are not used to it."

Monday was spent working grimly at the article on doctors, while outside the grey skies discharged a fine wet snow that was close to rain. The only lengthy respite came when Edward Claypon, the local rector, and his brother Joe, a soldier, came to lunch, after which G.B.S. read them his home-front playlet *Augustus Does His Bit*, which was scheduled for its first production later in the month. On Tuesday he pronounced the medical polemic finished and ready for typing. "I grudge the time it has cost," he noted in the diary unconvincingly. "I have been tired of the controversy for years. I could have written a play in the time this article has cost me." The afternoon suddenly free, he took the household Highland terrier, Kim, for a walk, although the weather was still bad and the dog an unpleasant "growler and fighter" who nevertheless was spoiled by everyone. After tea there was the daily correspondence, which included the proofs of his *Nation* review of *Men of Letters*, by the late Dixon Scott, a brilliant young critic who had already become a war casualty and whose literary journalism—including a shrewd and irreverent essay on G.B.S.—had been posthumously collected. (As "The Artstruck Englishman" the review would appear in the *Nation* for February 17.) Shaw put off correcting the proofs until after dinner.

When Charlotte went to bed to rest a bruised knee, Shaw went to the pianola and pumped out Elgar, Berlioz, and Schumann until it was time for bed.

When I went into Charlotte's room to bid her goodnight, and manipulated her damaged knee for her, we fell to talking about a matrimonial scandal in musical circles in the provinces, of which I have just heard. As Charlotte has no charity for the polygamists of the artistic temperament, and attributes the fact that I not only tolerate them as inevitable, but even accord to them a certain degree of respect and sympathy, to the deplorable looseness in my own character, the subject is a dangerous one; and discussions of it have to be stopped when they threaten to produce personal recriminations. So we stopped just in time, and I went to bed and read Pigou's article in the Economic Journal on the export of capital after the war.

On the 10th Shaw noted that he drove Charlotte to Hatfield to catch the 12:17 to London. It was the last entry in the abortive journal[1] that was the most detailed record he ever set down of his life at Ayot St. Lawrence. It also closed one of the longest periods he had spent continuously at Ayot. *Augustus* had to be rehearsed, and that meant returning to London.

There was another opening the evening before *Augustus*, but Shaw had nothing to do with it, as it occurred amidst the enemy at the Lessing Theatre in Berlin. *John Bull's Other Island* had never been staged before in Germany, and its continued indefinite postponement would have been for the best, since the belated production of his 1904 play about Ireland completely misread his ironic intentions, giving the Berlin critics cause to complain patriotically that Shaw had made Broadbent, a pompous ass of an Englishman, the "triumphant hero" of the play. G.B.S. was no longer *persona grata* to the *Berliner Tageblatt*. "For this Anglicized Irishman," it observed, "it is quite sufficient to hear anybody pronounce anything black immediately to jump up and shout that it is white."[2]

While rehearsing *Augustus*, his satire on the red tape and pomposity of officialdom, Shaw received a more than usually pompous letter from Frank Harris, still loudly and ineffectively pressing the Kaiser's cause in New York. Hard-up, Harris was publishing a commentary on his life of Christ that Shaw had charitably sent him for the purpose, and he had sent galley proof as well as a rejoinder and a pro-German sally. The rejoinder rankled Shaw. Harris was always certain that he had produced the first word on any subject and had provided the helping hand to every current literary reputation; Shaw determined to play schoolmaster at Harris's expense.

If he ever wanted hospitable criticism for his books again, Shaw warned, he had better not infuriate arbiters of taste by implying that he had been sponsor of the Wellses and Conrads and Kiplings of Europe. Shaw went on to develop a mock "Contemporary Portrait" in a parody of the egotistical and inflated Harrisian style, "How I Discovered Frank Harris." In it G.B.S., the "champion feuilletonist" of the London press corps, seeking an editor up to his own high standards, befriends a penniless, homeless outcast he finds wandering on the Embankment, presses a shilling into his hand and hurries in a hansom to the *Saturday Review* office where he proposes to save the faltering weekly by filling two pages of any paper that is edited by Frank Harris. The conclusion is equally inescapable Harris. When Shaw leaves it for playwriting, the paper disintegrates at once, "and Frank returned to the Embankment until he emigrated."

The tone of such a piece, Shaw wrote, would be as false as the facts, and if it were true it would be even more unpleasant. He concluded with a moral—that in one's biographical pieces about contemporaries, "dont dwell too much on what you did for them; they would much rather hear about what they did for you, if they ever did anything."[3] The knuckle rapping must have tantalized Harris: it was good copy and might be turned into additional coin, but it was too dampening to the ego. Eventually he did get his hands on a longer and safer Shavian parody of a "contemporary portrait"—of Shaw himself. "How Frank Ought to Have Done It" was published in 1919.

Augustus had its Stage Society opening at the Court Theatre in Sloane Square on January 21. Unfortunately it was paired with *The Tinker's Wedding*, Synge's grim farce about rural depravity in Ireland, leaving the audience with the impression that the Shavian part of the program was insufficiently serious. Perhaps the most serious part of the program was the portion between the two plays, when Lalla Vandervelde—who played "the Lady" in *Augustus*—recited poems by the Belgian poet Cammaerts and the French poet-dramatist Claudel. Shaw saw a good deal of the half-Belgian (and thus half-exiled) Vanderveldes during the war, once, soon after *Augustus*, lunching with them when Roger Fry and Sir Edward Elgar (a great friend of Lalla's father) were there. With Fry, Elgar, and Shaw representing the arts, the subject at the table was an obvious one. "Elgar," Shaw afterward told Virginia Woolf, "talked music so voluminously that Roger had nothing to do but eat his lunch in silence. At last . . . Roger . . . began in his beautiful voice . . . 'After all, there is only one art: all the arts are the same.' I heard no more; for my attention was taken by a growl from the other side of the table. It was Elgar, with his fangs bared and all his hackles bristling, in an appalling rage. 'Music,' he spluttered, 'is written on the skies for you to note down. And you compare that to a DAMNED imitation.' There was nothing for Roger to do but either seize the decanter and split Elgar's head with it, or else take it like an angel with perfect dignity. Which latter he did."[4]

In subtlety Shaw's farce was on a par with "How I Discovered Frank Harris," but Shaw's Lord Augustus Highcastle should have been taken seriously. His type, the conscientious but obtuse and egotistic home-front bureaucrat, however broadly sketched, had added a new horror to war. He displays a bullet that flattened upon impact with his head when he served on active duty and comments with complete seriousness, "Nothing has ever penetrated to our brains." When he is complimented on the mellifluousness of his voice, he responds, "What you hear, madam, is the voice of my country." Real concern develops from another of his many boasts: "Whilst England remains England, wherever there is a public job to be done, you will find a Highcastle sticking to it." The problem, Desmond MacCarthy wrote in the *Statesman*, was a failing in both the audience and the playwright: "People won't take Shaw lightly enough when he is doing the Dan Leno stunt, nor seriously enough when he is serious. I am not saying it is not partly his own fault, for he claims that he is always serious, and he cannot resist a joke whatever he writes."[5] It also took too much detachment to make fun of the home-front effort while it was going on, especially since life was becoming more and more grim as losses of shipping and the demands of the military eroded everyone's standard of living, and the newspapers published numbing lists of the dead.

In the morning mail on Saturday January 6, Shaw had received a letter from Lieutenant Colonel R. H. Hutton Wilson, press chief with the British armies in France, containing an invitation from Sir Douglas Haig to visit the front and write about it. Although his first reaction was negative and he quipped to a friend that it was either a compliment or a design on his life, Charlotte insisted that he had "to see this terrible thing" for himself. Grumbling that he would be permitted to see nothing except the conventional round on which all visiting journalists were escorted, G.B.S. nevertheless noted in his diary at the end of the day, "I suppose it will end in my going."

It took some days to procure the passports and official documents and make arrangements for transportation to the Flanders front, and Shaw found himself treated by the bureaucracy with courtesy and consideration unusual even for Very Important Persons. Finally he learned the reason. The Stage Society had just presented *Augustus Does His Bit*, and it had opened the hearts of officialdom still helpless as to "how to win the war with Augustus on their backs, wellmeaning, brave, patriotic, but obstructively fussy, self-important, imbecile, and disastrous." As one bureaucrat put it to Shaw exasperatedly, "We are up against Augustus all day."[6]

More than notebook and passport were required for correspondents. Shaw checked with writer-friends who had already been at the front and learned from Massingham (who had just returned) that khaki tunic and breeches were necessary and that he had almost been turned back because his black civilian clothes showed for an inch beneath his long military overcoat. Wells recommended trench boots to better wade through the knee-deep mud.[7] He was the knowledgeable veteran of three fronts, having observed the comic opera of the Italian mountain war with Austria as well as the trench fighting and artillery duels of the French and British sectors, returning home frustrated that the tanks he had invented in a *Strand Magazine* story in 1903 ("The Land Ironclads") had been reinvented less effectively by his compatriots only to bog down in Flanders mud. One night in the British sector in the late summer of 1916, Wells had tumbled out of bed with an idea he sketched for a mobile apparatus to transport equipment through the trenches on a conveyor wire rather than on the backs of overloaded Tommies, but even Winston Churchill, who had forced the tank upon the skeptical Kitchener, failed to convince the brass hats about Wells's "telpherage system," although a working model actually worked. Shaw, having experienced the massive official disinterest toward Alfred Gattie's automated dock, would have understood.

Toward the end of January, the khaki-clad Shaw crossed the Channel to Boulogne well protected from a bitter northeasterly gale by a warm, private cabin. At Boulogne he was met by a staff captain in a private car and driven to a lush compound of three chateaux near St. Omer, one of which housed Haig, the Commander-in-Chief, and his staff. Another billeted the accredited war correspondents. The Château de la Tour Blanche housed the distinguished visitors, who ranged from Harry Lauder to Mrs. Humphry Ward and her daughter Dorothy, from Horatio Bottomley to Arthur Conan Doyle, as well as delegations of Welsh miners, Japanese royalty, members of Parliament, and high personages from neutral and Allied nations. Sixty miles away was the war.

In spite of the pervasive military presence, largely well-dressed and beribboned officers and their aides, few could have reconciled the scene with newspaper accounts of devastation and carnage, and no writer dared file a story to an English paper contrasting these two inevitable faces of war. (As Shaw told *Daily Chronicle* correspondent Philip Gibbs there, "While the war lasts one must put one's own soul under censorship.")[8] The stately old country houses were in a park-like setting and approached by tree-lined avenues. Inside, the appointments were splendid and the food plentiful. Even Shaw's dietary crotchets were anticipated. At the chateau in a small triumph of military intelligence, there were provided for him eggs and cheese (prepared in a variety of ways), bread and butter, and dried dates and figs. It was not so easy elsewhere. "Awful ass!" complained one officer whose unit Shaw had visited at the front. "He was no end of nuisance for us. Why, when he got out here we found he was a vegetarian, and we had to chase around and have omelets fixed up for him every day."9

The first morning he was at G.H.Q., Shaw was asked what he most wanted to see, and said it was Ypres. The devastation there was legendary and visitors were discouraged, but Shaw insisted, recalling his last visit just before the war when he passed the time between Calais and Boulogne "inventing a play on the Rodin theme of The Burgesses of Calais, which . . . I have never written down, and perhaps never will." This time he jotted down the idea for passing mention when he wrote his report of what he had seen. (In 1934 he finally wrote the play, the one-act *The Six of Calais*.)

One newspaperman—a regular at headquarters—complained afterward that Shaw had gone about the business of being a visiting war correspondent the wrong way. "He told me, 'When I want to know about war I talk to soldiers.' I asked him: 'Do you mean officers or Tommies?' He said that he meant Tommies. Now you know how much reliance you can put in what a Tommy says. He'll either say what he thinks you want him to say or what he thinks you don't want him to say. I told Shaw that, but he paid no attention."10 It was what the War Office had guarded against at the outset of the war by providing its own communiqués from G.H.Q. and occasional, and anonymous, "eye-witness" reports often referred to in Fleet Street instead as "eye-wash." Public pressure eventually forced Lord Kitchener to back down, and the first accredited, but carefully shepherded and censored, correspondents had gone out in March 1915. It was often out of order for them to mention the weather, although it was being shared by the enemy. It was usually out of order to mention the filth and the fear that were the common denominator of existence in the trenches, because recruiting might be discouraged. It was definitely out of order to describe the traffic of war, from refugees to replacements, because Rule 17a prohibited all mention of movements of troops.

To minimize the conflict between the professional aims of the press and the eagerness of the military to protect its own interests, G.H.Q. gave war correspondents (carefully limited to five Englishmen, to which were later added two Americans) officer status—honorary rank as captains—and saw to it that they were piloted about by officers. They lived in the staff world, and writer C. E. Montague, a friend of Shaw's and then one of the officer-escorts for reporters, afterwards explained[11] the value of the system for Headquarters.

> The Staff was both their friend and their censor. How could they show it up when it failed? One of the first rules of field censorship was that from war correspondents "there must be no criticism of authority or command." And how could they disobey that? They would visit the front now and then, as many Staff Officers did, but it could only be as afternoon callers from one of the many mansions of the G.H.Q., that heaven of security and comfort. When . . . twilight came down on the haggard trench world of which they had caught a quiet noon-day glimpse they would be speeding west in Vauxhall cars to lighted chateaux gleaming white among scatheless woods. Their staple emotions . . . were of necessity akin to those of the Staff. . . .*

Although he had been warned that Ypres was an "unhealthy place," Shaw was escorted there anyway, protected from possible shelling when he arrived not only by helmet, but by ear plugs. The scene might have reminded him of the *Punch* cartoon in which one soldier asks, "D'you remember halting here on the retreat, George?" and the

---

* Arnold Bennett, who had the traditional tour of the chateaux and the trenches, complained privately about press restrictions in a letter that apparently replied to a friend's puzzlement as to why Shaw's own war articles had not created a greater impact. "If you knew G.B.S. as I know him," he wrote Oswald Davis, "you would understand why he is not taken more seriously. I quite agree that he often says very wise things, and things that need to be said. The press-correspondents are not a very brilliant lot perhaps: but have you ever seen them at work? They are kept together all the time, practically under lock and key, always under the eye of a Staff officer. They are told what they can say and what they can't say, and you will find that they all say practically the same things. Often they are deliberately hoodwinked by the soldiers whom they meet. P. Gibbs is a very conscientious man; I know him and I like him; but his reputation is a mystery to me. I think he is incurably sentimental and therefore false. The best of the correspondents, easily, is Tomlinson" (June 8, 1917, Hepburn, *Letters of Arnold Bennett*, Vol. 3).

other, looking down on the unidentifiable rubble and devastation, answers, "Can't call it to mind, somehow. Was it that little village in the wood there down by the river, or was it that place with the cathedral and all them factories?" For Shaw, who had been to Flanders a few years before, everything was different. "The language of the country was English in all its dialects. The farm houses and villas had no roofs, no floors, large holes in the walls, and no inhabitants." As they entered the Ypres salient Shaw observed a headless body lying by the roadside and heard the *Boche* "'sending them over' as persistently as the gentleman next door to Mrs. Nickleby sent cucumbers and marrows over the garden wall."

Ypres itself was quiet, but the major in charge of the gutted town, an immense Irishman who kept a visitors' book as a hobby, was dubious about exposing Shaw, finally sighing, "If you want to see it all, I'll show you, though I expect I'll be stopped by my own police— but we'll get round." At the main square the major insisted upon full speed to cross the open space in the shortest possible time, driving rapidly by the shattered tower and "the twenty or thirty yards sample of facade that was once the Cloth Hall." According to his newspaper piece on Ypres, Shaw was never in any difficulty, but on his return he apparently told his wife a different story, Charlotte writing to her sister that "when they were getting near the big square—bang! a shell exploded in front of the car! . . . It frightened the chauffeur & he stopped. The Town Major yelled 'Go on, man, go right on. A shell never comes in the same place twice.' So they went on."[12] What Shaw actually wrote for publication was that he had been warned to "Go flat on your face if anything comes over," and that he had "a wild hope that Brer Boche would send over something that would give me an excuse for exhibiting this accomplishment. . . . But nothing came over. . . ."

From shattered St. Eloi south of Ypres, Shaw, with Philip Gibbs, surveyed the bleak battlefields of the Vimy Ridge to the east, quiet on a cold winter evening just after sunset but for a lone shell that burst below them in Neuville St. Vaast. It was the only shell the Germans fired, and the party took cover in vain, but the British seemed to be firing intermittently at nothing most of the time, while the enemy conserved his munitions, an unrealized portent of things to come. "The artillery major who obligingly blew half a field to bits for me to shew me how it is done, assured me that he was doubling the value of the farmer's land by a super-ploughing which no farmer could afford. 'But,' said I, 'how are these pits to be filled up and smoothed over for the tillage?' 'I could shove them together with a few charges of dynamite,' he said. . . ."

Shaw pitied the boredom of the artillerymen, who fed the camouflaged cannon with shells they had fused, closed the breech, and fired absurdly in the direction of the enemy without the slightest idea where their explosives were landing and to what effect. Even reminding himself that across the line was another similarly employed group of men who had unknowingly fired at him and might fire again stirred in him no excitement, and he wondered how the newspaper correspondents could pump thrills into such events. It pressed upon him "the utter divorce of the warrior from the effects of his soulless labor. He has no sight or knowledge of what he is doing: he only hands on a shell or pulls a string. And a Beethoven or a baby dies six miles off." It was a thought he could not print, and it waited for expression until midway through another war.

Gibbs lamented the cold while Shaw found the snowy landscape beautiful and was happy to find the mud frozen over. Happily, too, there was no need to stay there overnight. A staff car returned them to quarters a world away from war.

At Arras farther south along the line, Shaw observed that the shelling had done the town some good, as the cathedral, "a copy of a copy, looked better as a ruin than when it was intact."* His irony was lost on his companions. "I heard him out there," said one officer, "and he talked no end of rot. He said the Germans had made a botch of destroying towns. He said he could have done more damage to Arras with a hammer than the Germans did with their shells. Of course, he couldn't begin to do it with a hammer, and, anyway, he wouldn't be

---

* H. G. Wells thought that the obliterated villages he saw during the summer of 1916 left him "far more desolated" than did the wreckage of churches and monuments. "I suppose that one is a little accustomed to Gothic ruins . . . it is only a question of degree whether they are more or less tumble-down."

let. I suppose he never thought of that. Then he said that the Germans were doing us a great favor by their air-raids. He said they were smashing up things that were ugly and unsanitary.* That's silly. We could pull them down ourselves, you know, and anyhow, in the last raid they hit the post-office."

"The old boy's got nerve, though," said another officer. "I was out at the front with him near Arras, and there was some pretty lively shelling going on around us. I told him to put on his tin hat, but he wouldn't do it. I said, 'Those German shell-splinters may get you,' and he laughed and said, 'If they do me in, then there is no gratitude in this world.' He doesn't know the *Boche*."[13]

To another correspondent at Arras, novelist H. M. Tomlinson, sighting G.B.S. was more of a scoop than anything the censors had permitted him to write about in a long time. In a dispatch he filed to his paper he observed that "When, a day or two since, I saw a tall and alert figure in khaki, with beard and mustache terribly reminiscent, overlooking with disfavor what affairs of war happened to be about him at the moment (to be precise, his army chauffeur was kneeling in the snow trying to persuade a frozen radiator), I wondered whether the war was beginning to affect my mind. You never can tell." The car would not be persuaded, and Tomlinson offered his own, becoming in the process "the chronicler of an historic episode in the war. I was not at Mons; but I was present when Shaw looked first on Armageddon."

Tomlinson asked G.B.S. how long he thought the war would last.

---

* In his newspaper account Shaw remained consistent with this view, writing, "The devastations of war are not all to be deplored. I shall not attempt to console those mourners for the Louvain library who have always voted against a penny rate for a library in their own parish; and I will not pretend that Ypres and Arras are as pleasant to see as they were when I saw them in peace. But I have been a member of a sanitary authority concerned with the clearance of slum areas and the administration of Building Acts; and the tragedy of the Somme district began for me in some of the villages which have not been demolished, not in those which have. A comparison of what the Germans have done to Albert with what I should like to do to London or Manchester would make the Kaiser seem a veritable Angel of the Passover beside me."

"Thirty years," said Shaw. "You see, war creates its own resources. The resources grow less on both sides, and each combatant improvises with what he can get. If these are pretty well balanced you can foresee the result—if you have the courage to look at it. Each side must continue to strive for victory to prevent the other side getting it." A gas alert was sounded—a false alarm. Then their car went past a barrier leading "to a foreboding town. I feebly told Shaw that usually the *Boche* put some stuff into this place each day, and to get his tin hat ready." Shaw declined. While British guns hammered, they peered into the wreckage of a once picturesque town, Shaw commenting that Wigan could have been better spared. Back among the young officers, Shaw was asked, as he turned down a tin of baked meat and a whisky, "What do you think about peace?" Picking up a biscuit and cheese instead, he told them, "What the nations of Europe really want is an early and dishonorable peace." Once they understood his intent, Tomlinson reported, "Youth with its military crosses leaned back in its chairs, and its laughter rolled down the ruined corridors of the deserted town."[14]

When an invitation came to lunch with the Commander-in-Chief, G.B.S. had to cancel other arrangements. What happened that day could not be deduced from the laconic entry in Sir Douglas Haig's diary for February 1: "Mr. Bernard Shaw (the Author & Playwright) came to lunch. An interesting man of original views. A great talker! On sitting down to lunch, I at once discovered he was a vegetarian. As if by magic, on my ordering it, two poached eggs appeared, also some spinach and also macaroni, so he did not fare badly."[15] G.B.S.'s opinion of Haig was less enthusiastic, but not then for publication. "He seemed to me a first rate specimen of the British gentleman and conscientiously studious soldier, trained socially and professionally to behave and work in a groove from which nothing could move him . . . always steadied by a well-closed mind and an unquestioned code. Subject to these limitations he was, I should say, a man of chivalrous and scrupulous character. He made me feel that the war would last thirty years, and that he would carry it on irreproachably until he was superannuated."

Apparently more exhilarated by Shavian conversation than can be inferred from his journal, Sir Douglas after lunch countermanded plans already made for him and offered to take Shaw on an examination of experimental weapons then being tried out in a secluded sector to the rear. They went off in an immense closed Rolls Royce, with Shaw treated for the only time during his stay in France to the luxury of a warm rug over his chilled knees. There were new tanks to see and one to ride in, the terrible clatter suggesting a speed far higher than the turgid crawling they were actually doing. There were also thermite incendiary shells and the "appalling volcano" of the primitive flame thrower, already in use by the Germans as the terrible *flamme werfe*. The first time the flame thrower was operated nothing happened, and the man responsible for it murmured, "How amazing, it's worked every time I've tried it until now." But an old general called out, "It's done exactly that every time *I've* seen it." Shaw wondered aloud, "But it's all snow and ice, and yet that shall set the furze on fire?" "Oh," explained the general about the frozen but inflammable furze, "they soaked it in paraffin."[16] Haig, Shaw thought, seemed "disconcerted and distressed" by the military novelties and skeptical of their military value.

That night Shaw slept in Amiens because it was too far to return to his chateau and because Haig wanted him to meet Sir Henry Rawlinson, commanding general on the Somme front. It was Shaw's introduction to the furthermost sector of British responsibility, near the junction of lines with the French. Rawlinson's handsome Fourth Army headquarters northeast of Amiens, on the road toward Querrieux and Albert, had probably survived because the generals on both sides coveted it—an old chateau by a meandering stream among pleasant meadows. The next day Shaw had a long talk there with Rawlinson, whom he found (but not for publication) as unlike Haig "as it is possible for one British officer to be unlike another. . . . He was frank; his manners were his own; and he had no academic illusions about the situation, which was not then a very rosy one; for the recent Somme offensive had come to nothing but a very superfluous

demonstration of the homicidal uselessness of sending waves of infantry to attack barbed wire defended by machine guns, even after
the costliest bombardments and minings."

In the aftermath of the offensive, the signposts that had survived
directed one to places since obliterated. On the Somme Shaw found
their irony "immense":

"To Maurepas"; and there was no Maurepas. "To Contalmaison"; and
there was no Contalmaison. "To Pozières"; and there was no Pozières. I
went to the windmill of Pozières, and saw a little mound on which the
windmill may have stood. . . . On the road to Ypres the trees had stood, an
unbroken Old Guard lining the road, with hardly a gap in their ranks. But
here! With every limb shot to bits, beheaded, halved, cut off at the shins
or torn out of the earth and flung prostrate, these woods seemed to scud
with bare poles or broken jury-masts before the wind as our car passed,
all their rigging blown and shot away. Of houses, except in one strangely-
spared place, not a trace. And I knew from what I had seen in Ypres that
this meant that almost every square yard of brick had received a separate
smashing hit. As to the ground, you cannot find enough flat earth in a
square mile to play marbles on. The moon seen through a telescope, or a
slice of Gruyère cheese, is a tennis lawn by comparison. From the small
pit made by the funny little Stokes gun that spits out shells as fast as you
drop them in, to the dew-pond made by the medium trench mortar,
culminating in the incredible crater made by the subterranean mine, the
land is humped and hollowed continuously everywhere. Such ploughing
and harrowing was never seen before on earth.

The Somme front was then the most active, with the British "blazing away industriously at imaginary Germans." Shaw, guided there
by C. E. Montague, then a white-haired captain, inquired why the
Germans were not replying in kind and was told that they were expected to shell Albert at three o'clock that afternoon, but the usually
punctual Germans left the red brick tower with its famous statue of
the Golden Virgin alone. (The Virgin and Child already hung head-
downwards from the broken tower of the church, which had been
within sight of the enemy the previous June. Since then the British

had advanced as much as eight miles in as many months, inheriting vast useless stretches of rubble and pock-marked meadow.)

As we walked up towards the windmill at Pozières a solitary German shell exploded harmlessly half a mile ahead of us. Montague stopped dead, and surveyed a Roumanian general who was with us, wearing a gorgeous uniform. "I ought not to take you up to the windmill," said Montague; "you are not in khaki. They may see you and have a shot at you. And I am responsible for you." Giorgescu grinned: "Let me point out, gentlemen," he said, contemplating our khaki with amused contempt, "that as the whole country is frozen white, you are [all] much more likely to be conspicuous than I." This was obviously true. Montague shrugged his shoulders; and we went on. The Germans must, I think, have left behind them one of the patent scarecrows advertised in Stores catalogues, which fire a shot automatically every fifteen minutes; for they did send over one more aimless shell, which impressed the general sufficiently to make him insist on a young friend of his who was also present retiring behind a knocked-out tank. . . .[17]

In the car the gorgeous Roumanian general quaffed Shaw's wine ration while, coming from the trenches on the far side of Contalmaison, men being relieved stumbled along in such extremity of exhaustion that their mouths hung open; Shaw felt ashamed of the very conspicuous sandwich in his hand and the fact that what he was really seeing was not appropriate for print.[18] That evening he again slept at Amiens, and in the morning was driven back to his chateau.

The next phase of Shaw's first-hand look at the war took him to Major Robert Loraine's 40 Squadron, at its base at Trezennes, a collection of huts huddled close to a landing strip. It seemed even colder there than it had been on the Somme, Charlotte writing dramatically to her sister afterward that when G.B.S. "was dressing in the morning in his hut . . . he could not button any button without holding his fingers in a jug of hot water they brought him. The men's clothes freeze to the ground. . . ." It was a bleak period for Loraine, who had left active flying (after being recommended for a D.S.O.) for the organizational and administrative work of commanding his squadron. With his wounds healed as well as they would ever be, he was more useful at a desk, where his seniority and experience were valuable to the fledgling service, but it meant substituting for the exhilaration of flight and danger the bottle of whisky before him on his desk as he wrote to the next of kin of downed airmen and tried to find something consoling to say when he could find no consolation himself.

Loraine had become a martinet for efficiency and duty in an attempt to provide a substitute for self-pity, and after the notes of the Last Post concluded each funeral ceremony for a downed flier, Loraine would urge on the nightly merrymaking in the mess, shepherding his young officers to the piano and commanding, "Sing! Sing!" With an actor in command, it was inevitable that fragments from plays would be part of the entertainment, and Shaw arrived in time to see the dress rehearsals, although he could not stay for the finished performances, of *The Inca of Perusalem*, done by the men, and *O'Flaherty, V.C.*, done by the officers. Loraine had been using his dog-eared rehearsal copy of *Inca* for more than a year, the Lord Chamberlain not being present to proscribe the *verboten* lines. *O'Flaherty* came next in the nearly empty mess, with Shaw laughing throughout the rehearsal and enjoying himself enormously. A major sitting behind him, finding it a curious sight to see the famous author laughing at his own jokes, leaned over and said to him, "I'm glad you appreciate our poor efforts at your play, sir." Shaw could scarcely speak for laughing. "Do you know," he said, "if I had thought the stuff would prove to be so poor as this, I'd never have written it."

Loraine's squadron was engaged neither in artillery spotting, reconnaisance, nor ground support, its mission restricted to intercepting enemy aircraft. The fliers were, Shaw wrote, "pure duellists. Their machines carry one man only; and he, with one hand on his tiller and the other on his machine gun, throws himself on any German he can find in the air, and intimates, like the Shakespearean warrior, that 'for one or both of us the hour has come.'" To warn his men into the air, Loraine had a "great, loud, braying horn" activated by an electric button, and in pointing it out to G.B.S. he accidentally sounded it. Before he could explain that it was a false alarm, one plane was already in the air; it spent more than an hour searching for the elusive *Boche*. When the puzzled airman finally came down Loraine praised him for having got off the ground so rapidly.[19]

The next day Shaw was driven in Loraine's car on an hour-and-a-half ride away from the war to Wimereux and to Boulogne, Channel ports where Shaw's friend Sir Almroth Wright—the original of Ridgeon in *The Doctor's Dilemma*—superintended military hospitals. At Boulogne where the hospital was located in the converted Casino, "wounded men were being operated on in all sorts of odd corners, and those who had been attended-to and were safe in bed seemed so glad to be there and not in the trenches that nothing that the operating surgeons could do could dispel the general cheerfulness." Sir Almroth, Shaw recalled, was "extraordinarily interesting," but Shaw failed to indicate exactly how interesting, for one night there (he overstayed an extra night by missing the boat back) he and Wright were deep in discussion in front of the fireplace when the chimney caught fire and filled the room with smoke. While others ran outside to see if the roof was alight and attempted to put the fire out, Shaw and Wright went on with their discussion apparently undisturbed.[20]

"When I was home again and had presented my trench boots to a clergyman," Shaw wrote, "I had to consider how to fill a dozen columns of The Daily Chronicle with an account . . . which would tell the enemy nothing that he did not know already better than I, and that would help the general reader, by this time badly discouraged by the duration of the war and the absence of any prospect of its ending, to stick it." It was not easy, for his trip had confirmed the waste of lives and material and the likelihood of a long war becoming still longer; he did publish three articles on the 5th, 7th, and 8th of March, doing his own censoring "so effectually that only two objections were raised by the authorities. One led me to change a word which had a technical military sense with which I had been unacquainted. The other was a description of some German prisoners which suggested that they had been sent to work. A change of another word or two got over that. The rest was unchallenged." For his "Joy Riding at the Front" articles the *Chronicle* paid him £200.*

There were two useful results of his trip to France, Shaw thought. He had had an opportunity to look at the war and present his findings to the many whose consciences were unsatisfied by patriotic rhetoric, and he was able to provide an amusing diversion for the few troops whose paths he crossed, "performing"—he wrote Barker—"stupendous conversational feats at all the mess tables from Bailleul to Amiens."[21] He had underestimated the potential the excursion had for self-education. In several ways he had surprised himself, and in at least one of them was willing to confess as much to *Chronicle* readers, saying in public what he was already saying in private. Having surveyed "all this ruin . . ." he wrote, "I am bound to state plainly, as a simple fact to be exploited by devils or angels, according to its true nature, that I enjoyed myself enormously and continuously. . . ." Before he attempted to explain that phenomenon he attempted what he hoped was a valid yet publishable scrutiny of what he had seen. For one thing, war was costly; the way the British waged it was also wasteful, and not only on the evidence of the daily casualty lists that he carefully did not mention. He explained the pocketbook effects of British prodigality with artillery, "showering shells on the enemy as if they were eggs at 16 a shilling" because the big guns could only be aimed crudely, and one had "to send a thousand bombs to do the work of one." In a way, he thought, it was reassuring for those having loved ones at the front and who were tormented by the fear that nothing could escape the enemy's shelling. Most explosives landed harmlessly. "Life is very uncertain at the front," he observed, "but so is death." Man, he concluded, was "still the instrument of precision par excellence," but the inference could have been that the only effective fighting was being done with a bayonet.

---

* Horatio Bottomley went to the front later in 1917 to see "whether, perchance, I might for one short moment be permitted to look beyond the veil," and came back to report, "I have been in Hell—and from its depths have seen the striking splendor of Heaven. In the scorched and blackened track of the Devil—I have met with God." For his five mostly ghost-written articles in *The Sunday Pictorial,* he was paid £1000. His own journal, *John Bull,* paid all his expenses.

A second and related point he wanted to make was not reassuring to the British taxpayer, who had to reconcile himself to the fact

that war is not precise and economical. It is almost inconceivably wasteful and extravagant. It burns the house to roast the pig, and even then seldom roasts him effectively. It is a gamble in which the German citizen and the British citizen must play the impossible martingale of double or quits. The German is economizing his ammunition only that he may waste it madly when the battle is joined again. We are damning the expense and hammering away because it is a poor heart that never rejoices; also no doubt because we have calculated that extravagance pays. But calculation or no calculation, waste is the law of modern war; and nothing is cheap on the battlefield except the lives of men. Give your soldiers trench mortars enough; and no enemy can live in his trench or escape being buried alive in his dug-out. But the Kaiser can say as much with equal truth. Therefore, my taxpayer, resign yourself to this: that we may fight bravely, fight hard, fight long, fight cunningly, fight recklessly, fight in a hundred and fifty ways, but we cannot fight cheaply. That means that we must organize to increase our production. Mere saving wins no battles. If we are to destroy with one hand we must create with the other.

Another observation may have come as a surprise to those who still thought of G.B.S. as what he never had been—a pacifist or pro-German. War, he continued to insist, was an offense to human morality. "But it is too late to consider it when the sword is drawn. You cannot vindicate outraged morality by surrendering or allowing yourself to be beaten." It was the reason why, he said, the many "Socialists, internationalists, haters of war" who were in the front lines fought to win. Moralizing stopped at the trenches' edge for other reasons as well.

The soldier says that war is hell; but he does not say that it is a crime. We make many accusations against Germany, some of them ridiculous enough in view of similar exploits of our own; but when a man becomes a soldier he ceases to blame her for bringing war upon Europe, though that is the real grievance of pacifist morality against her. Therefore the moralizing which represents the waste and destruction, the tortures and terrors and sufferings of the war, as quite unmixed horrors, may be edifying and human; but it is not true to nature at the front. The strange satisfactions and fascinations which men find in war may be rooted in that part of their nature which is common to the paleface, the redskin brave, and the Zulu warrior. They may be largely a reaction against the dullness of a civil life that satisfies none of their heroic instincts. I do not justify them; and I know that they must finally be satisfied in nobler ways or sternly repressed and discarded; but I should be foolish and dishonest if I attempted to ignore them.

He could not ignore them in himself either. It was "a hopeless moral muddle," Shaw confessed, "a diabolical phenomenon," that "whether I write as a human being or a fiend . . . I shamelessly avow that I enjoyed my week at the front much more than I enjoyed my last week at the seaside." The war was still largely in the hands of the politicians who were responsible for it, he concluded in his final article, and

if even one shot too many be fired the fault will lie on them and not on the soldier. For at this rate of destruction the prayer of the people must be, not "Give us peace in our time" but "Give us peace in all time." As to the heroes who do not desire peace, there will be for them the "mental fight" of William Blake, who, long after Waterloo, did not let his sword sleep in his hand. His Jerusalem is still to be built; and it will not be built with howitzers. They are too easy to fire.

One outraged citizen, on reading that G.B.S. had been at the front, called the War Office to account for their sending him out. Two weeks later he received the results of their investigation:

War Office. Whitehall S.W. March 24.

Dear Sir,

I am directed to acknowledge the receipt of your letter of the 6th March 1917, and to inform you that the case has been investigated, and that nothing is known against this Officer.

I am, Sir, your obedient servant,
E. W. Engleheart, S.C.
(For Lieutenant-General, Military Secretary).

Outraged sensibilities did not stop there, for there was a question in Commons, which, according to the daily Parliamentary Report in the *Times*, was better fielded by the spokesman for the government than the earlier inquiry had been by the War Office:

MR. BERNARD SHAW'S VISIT TO THE FRONT

Replying to Major Hunt (Shropshire, Ludlow, U.), Mr. Macpherson (Ross and Cromarty, L.) said "It is the accepted policy to ask distinguished publicists and authors to visit our front. These invitations are issued by the Department of Information and General Headquarters. In accordance with this policy Mr. George Bernard Shaw recently visited the British Front in France."

Major Hunt asked whether the hon. member was aware that Mr Bernard Shaw was the gentleman who advised British soldiers to shoot their officers, as reported in the San Francisco Bulletin of November 2, 1914, and whether he thought that this was the sort of man who ought to be allowed to go to the front.

Mr. Macpherson. "I was not aware of that particular fact; but I have always found that when any gentleman visits the front in France he comes back with an added desire to help the British Army and is proud of it." (Cheers.)

If permitting the nation's leading gadfly to have a first-hand look at the war had been a calculated risk, it had paid off.

10

The Old Dog Barks

WHILE G.B.S. was at the front, the irrepressible Frank Harris mailed another pro-German letter to him from New York, exhorting him to see the other side as Harris did—to see a people who loved art, encouraged education, and thrived on hard work. "I would like you to see the German soldier as I see him, patient, strong, obedient, decent; and his officer, burning with patriotism, feeling in some dumb way that Prussia has done great things in the world and that he is part of the great work and willing to die at any time for that consciousness and its fulfilment."[1] Although Harris in his paranoia would not have agreed, many Englishmen still considered Shaw a dangerous crank because he *did* attempt to look at both sides, and shortly after his well-publicized return from France he was greeted by an editorial in the *Morning Post* entitled "The Jester's Dilemma," which attacked him for supporting the German cause "upon minor points" and because German propaganda in neutral countries was quoting him for its own purposes. "After all," cracked the *Post*, "it is impossible even for a vegetarian to be neutral in a war in which his country is engaged." After two columns of polemic the *Post* wondered why "the shooting of a pheasant by an Englishman moves him to savage indignation [while] the shooting of a peasant by a German seems to him all in a day's work. Is it because he is endeavouring to be absolutely neutral in this war, or is he influenced by some faint yet fragrant memory of the triumphant runs enjoyed by his plays in the cultured capital of Germany?"[2]

Shaw responded; the *Post* followed with another editorial blast at him; Shaw again answered, this time noting that no one was safe from quotation, "Sidelights on England" being just as popular a feature in German newspapers as "Sidelights on Germany" were in the England press. He wrote specifically with that in mind, he declared. "But the *Morning Post* is much more quoted in Germany, no doubt because it writes without regard to that possibility."[3] The last word on Shaw's neutrality was left by the *Post* to an indignant correspondent who signed himself from the New Century Club, Berkeley Square, and offered the quotation, "because thou wast neither hot nor cold . . . I will spue thee out of my mouth."[4]

The Crank, a playlet of the period by one of the rare pro-G.B.S. Members of Parliament, Arthur Ponsonby, was an implicit commentary on the continuing press war against the outspoken minority. In it a merchant complained to a professor (a friend and intermediary) about his nephew Walter, who also happened to be his secretary:

MERCHANT. Well, to be a crank over politics or religion or what they call social reforms is all very well. . . . To be a crank now when the country is in danger is another thing altogether. It is . . . unpatriotic, it is playing the enemy's game. . . . But really I am not much concerned with theories and motives and views and opinions just now. It is his action, or rather inaction, that offends me. He goes about talking or writing. He has spent his holiday doing nothing else. That is all very well in peace time but this is not the time for airing theories. . . . It is the duty of every man to come forward for active service one way or another. . . . Our only job now is to kill Germans.

PROFESSOR. What did he say to that?

MERCHANT. Oh, something about his being more concerned about how many British lives were sacrificed. But what I say is that every man ought to help either to make munitions or to fire them off. . . . So when I see this chap just talking and arguing I cannot control myself. I despise such conduct. It is unpatriotic and mischievous. To put this briefly, the fellow is pro-German.

PROFESSOR. You mean by that, he actually wants the Germans to win?

MERCHANT. No, not that, but what he does helps them.

PROFESSOR. How? I don't quite see.

MERCHANT. Well, the nation is united, isn't it? There is no party standing out against the war, only a few individuals of no account who are well-known cranks. But what they say gets quoted in Germany. . . . Anyhow the newspapers will call them pro-Germans.

PROFESSOR. Which newspapers?

MERCHANT. Oh, the *Morning Post* and the *Daily Express* and—

PROFESSOR. And I suppose *John Bull* and the something *Witness*. . . .[5]

In mid-February the new Prime Minister, Lloyd George, reorganizing another of his predecessor's staffs, came to the [Postwar] Reconstruction Committee, which had consisted of Cabinet ministers and private secretaries, and asked Edwin Montagu for alternative suggestions. Montagu came up with more of the same, and Lloyd George snorted, "This is a mere shadow of Asquith. Bring me a list of persons with ideas." Hastily a list was drawn up, including Shaw, Wells, and the Webbs. The Prime Minister spent ten minutes going over it, striking out both Shaw and Wells. When he came to the Webbs he pondered briefly and then chose Beatrice, saying, "Mrs. Webb I think. . . . Webb will be angry, Mrs. Webb won't."[6] It was the closest G.B.S. had come to official service, and the unpredictable part of it was not his removal from the list but his being on it in the first place. That Wells had also been eliminated was an index of how far he had moved from his earlier position on the war.

At least one success could be scored for Shaw that February—the first public production of his banned religious drama *The Shewing-Up of Blanco Posnet*, refused a license by the Lord Chamberlain on grounds of blasphemy in 1909. The Abbey Theatre Company had performed it in Dublin, where the powers of the censor did not extend, and it was not until April 1916, seven years later, that they were

permitted four guest performances in Liverpool. But until a technically private production of a "hole and corner" variety was arranged, London had not been able to legally see the play, a curiously
moving melodrama of the conversion of a horse thief in an improbable Shavian "wild West." Not until 1921 was a London license
granted.

Toward the end of the month another controversial religious play
was produced by the Stage Society, John Masefield's *Good Friday*.
Shaw, who had pressed Masefield into playwriting a decade earlier
during the Court Theatre seasons, was there, as was Arnold Bennett,
who complained that it was "dull and portentous" and was irritated
"that all the elite said they liked the damned thing." Afterward Bennett and Shaw had tea with the Stage Society's Lee Mathews, and
Bennett, who harangued G.B.S. about the war rather than the play,
noted with satisfaction in his journal, "I shifted Shaw a little in the
end."[7] From the Somme front, where the blasted trees were "like fig-
ures come up out of hell," Masefield wrote to scene designer Charles
Ricketts that the play had been "only the draft of a play" he had
meant to recast, "but the war broke out and I had to leave it as it
was."[8]

In March G.B.S. seemed to be appearing everywhere—reviews in
the *Nation*, a teasing piece in the Chestertons' *New Witness* accusing
Wells (in his new *War and the Future*) of borrowing the Shavian
religion of the superman, medical articles in the *English Review* in-
veighing against inoculation, and war-tourist columns in the *Daily
Chronicle*. And there were also speeches and new productions of old
plays. Even the *Daily Express* reported one of his speeches, a plea for
spiritual power in politics, on the evening of March 9. As Shaw had
said—through his character Cusins—as early as *Major Barbara* (1905)
in the great munitions town scene in the last act, "I think all power is
spiritual: these cannons will not go off by themselves." "If a man has
spiritual power," Shaw asserted at King's Hall, Covent Garden, "people can't help noticing him. Since the war broke out we have hardly
had a good speech made on the war by an English official person.
What is wanted at the present time is a body of statesmen who will

not play to the gallery. . . . Side by side with the feeling that we want to get the bishops out of the House of Lords is the feeling that we want to get some saints into the House of Commons."

Acknowledging that progress was being made, Shaw insisted that it was happening too slowly and at too great a price. "All great reforms," he observed, "have had at their back some calamity like a war or a cholera epidemic." The mass of people who stood most to benefit were the most hesitant about change. "The great purpose of democracy," he concluded, "is to prevent you from being governed better than you want to be governed." An insight he was fixing upon reluctantly, based upon the experience of a disappointingly sluggish civilian population under the stress of war, it would become the focus of a number of his postwar plays.

In Ireland in March 1917, Shaw was undergoing a surprising apotheosis. When the Abbey had reopened in the aftermath of the failed insurrection, its first three offerings were *John Bull's Other Island*, *Widowers' Houses*, and *Arms and the Man*. For the September 25 opening night of *John Bull*, Shaw's satire on Anglo-Irish manners, the queue extended into the Marlborough Street pit entrance, with many unsuccessful ticket seekers turned away long before eight o'clock. In February the Abbey had staged *Man and Superman* and in March was producing *The Inca of Perusalem*, while *The Doctor's Dilemma* was scheduled for May. It was a Shaw festival of a magnitude unseen since the 1904-07 repertory of the Vedrenne-Barker Royal Court Theatre in London, and undoubtedly Shaw's outspokenness on Irish matters had had much to do with it. "The repatriation" of G.B.S., J. M. Hone reported to the *New Statesman* from Dublin, was proceeding swiftly:

There was a time when Mr. Shaw could not lecture in Dublin, even on the Poor Laws, without a section of his listeners rising to leave the house; but his action last spring, when as an opponent of Sinn Féin he explained Sinn Féin better than its exponents, seems to have led to a change; at all events, the Irish National Theatre is now in the midst of a peaceful Shaw season. . . . Nothing is more curious than to observe the difference between a typically Irish and typically English reception of one of Mr. Shaw's plays. It is not that the standard of intelligence of Abbey Theatre audiences is abnormally high. For there are certain well-known plays in the repertory of that theatre which invariably produce Irish laughter at precisely the wrong moments; only Mr. Shaw's plays are not among these, which is the more remarkable, since in London cackling so commonly greets his most profound lines. While in England Mr. Shaw has had to struggle against the reputation of being a mere farceur. In Ireland he is too exclusively regarded as a commentator on politics—a good commentator if his sayings fit in with the popular mood, a bad [one] if they do not.[9]

The Inca of Perusalem, then, was received "exactly as an Irish audience might have been expected to receive a topical play by Mr. Shaw—*i.e.,* in silence, save for an occasional political cheer." The cheers were not in appreciation of the Shavian lampoon of German royalty, in the form of a stage Kaiser that would have horrified the Lord Chamberlain because of an authenticity in mustaches and mannerisms forbidden in London; for its most enthusiastic applause, the audience waited for that moment when the Inca contrasts his country with others that have *not* kept the peace for forty years. Clearly, the Irish Nationalists felt, Shaw was pointing to England.

While the Shavian box office success continued, the Dublin diehards complained that it was at the cost of the native drama. Architect and theater hanger-on Joseph Holloway, a conservative influence at the Abbey, complained that Shaw was the fetish of J. Augustus Keogh, St. John Ervine's successor as manager. "And when I chanced to remark," he noted in his diary, " 'We have had far too much of Shaw of late at the Abbey, and many are saying so to me,' " Keogh was furious, becoming even more enraged when Holloway suggested that Irish plays had failed to draw as well as Shaw because they were poorly played, "as the Irish acting did not take kindly to the English methods. . . . When I said that the Gaiety or the Royal were the proper places for Shaw's plays and not the Abbey, Keogh could have slain me on the spot." But Holloway's kind would have padlocked the Abbey rather than play "English" plays by an Irishman, and Keogh paid the price for his advocacy. While *The Doctor's Dilemma* played that May, Keogh was sacked by the Abbey board of directors, Holloway gleefully writing a friend that "a love of Shaw and a hatred for Irish drama and Irish acting were, I am sure, the cause. Keogh from the first wanted to make it a sort of Shaw playhouse, and not caring a tinker's curse for the traditions of the little theatre. . . ."[10]

Although he had become the whipping boy for the superpatriots, Keogh had had little to do with the choice of repertory, other than his fatal accident of reopening the crisis-closed Abbey—as a private speculation, since he was not yet paid by the Abbey—with Shaw's *Widowers' Houses*. As Lady Gregory had written G.B.S. the previous August, Keogh, an unknown who had taken Ervine's place because there was no one else to be had, acquitted himself well not only as director but in the Dickensian comic role of Lickcheese. "There was a good audience and it went extremely well, every point taken up, and great applause on the slum question. So a brilliant thought struck me · . . . our peasant plays for the moment knocked on the head, to do an autumn season of G.B.S.—our Irish Shakespeare. . . ." She had her ideas about which plays would fare best—*John Bull's Other Island* "(written for us and never acted by us)," *The Devil's Disciple, The Doctor's Dilemma*, and *Androcles and the Lion* ("if we could borrow the lion—it is so delightful, and religious discussion should be popular here").

As far as G.B.S.'s new-won status in Ireland was concerned, the band of small minds at the Abbey who had overruled Lady Gregory and deposed the hapless Keogh made little difference. Shaw was again *persona grata*, something his persistent paradoxes about Ireland now failed to shake. In the *Nation*[11] early that spring, for example, he noted about the inability of Ulster and the rest of Ireland to live in peace that "civil war is one of the privileges of a nation," as was the possibility "that they would exterminate one another." "Mankind still longs for that consummation; but it has never happened, and is too much to hope for." He doubted that Ireland would lapse into civil war, but added, as he would not have a year earlier, "I do not deprecate that method; for if hatred, calumny, and terror have so possessed men that they cannot live in peace as other nations do, they had better fight it out and get rid of their bad blood that way." That it would not happen, he thought, had been made clear by the restraint of Irishmen north and south when, at the Easter Rising, England "supplied a sensational bombardment and a Reign of Terror to

impress the imagination of the world with the heroism of the patriots
and the magnitude of their blow for independence. . . ." Shaw
had labeled his article "Brogue-Shock," a reference to the Government's having been rattled by the noisy but "depopulated little
island." A sudden Irish patriot and rebel, he hardly realized the extent of his own, and very different, brogue-shock.*

Under Shaw's signature as chairman, the Fabian Research Department issued its annual report for the year ending March 31, 1917.
After pointing out the difficulties in finding volunteer help in wartime, it noted that its most important work completed during the previous twelve months was "the formulation of a definite scheme for a
supernational authority, as the best hope of preventing future war . . .
a 'League of Nations.' " It had also produced a booklet called "How to
Pay for the War," which already had gone into a second printing, and
an investigation "into the organisation and working of Professional
Associations . . . dealing with the legal, medical, engineering, artistic,
and other professions, drafted by Bernard Shaw, Sidney Webb, and
Beatrice Webb. . . ." Shaw wrote the entire section on Literature and
the Fine Arts, but for a single blank before a reference to "Engineers."
In the margin at the left was Shaw's note: "Mrs. Webb please fill in
the title of the Engineers Association."

A landmark study in its field, the finished version appeared in two
lengthy parts in the NS on April 21 and April 28. Shaw did not let
his personal refusal to appear further in the NS complicate matters.
It was still a Fabian organ, and his loyalties were firm. At the same

---

* The Easter Rising and subsequent executions also moved the essentially
nonpolitical W. B. Yeats. He had been for Home Rule without independence
and since 1914 had turned down all suggestions that he write war poetry or
Irish poetry of a political slant. Even after the rising, he wrote to Lady Gregory
of "the heroic, tragic lunacy of Sinn Féin." But after he became aware of the
executions and long prison sentences dealt the rebels there was a transformation.
Within a few weeks of the sentencings he wrote "Easter 1916," with its famous
refrain "A terrible beauty is born," and three other poems on similar themes,
"Sixteen Dead Men," "The Rose Tree," and "On a Political Prisoner." By the
end of the war he was for complete separation.

time, Massingham's *Nation*, to which Shaw submitted screeds once directed to the rival weekly, had fallen under the interdict of the War Office, having been informed on April 5 that its export and sales out of England were forbidden on the ground that a previous issue had been exploited by German propaganda. "The mischief of suppressing the export of a whole newspaper issue," Shaw pointed out, "is that nobody knows which article in it is being suppressed; and wrong guesses may run through Europe with consequences undreamt-of by the censors." Actually it turned out months later, when the *Nation* was still under indefinite export prohibition, that the censor had confided the reason to a New York *Tribune* correspondent: "since December last *The Nation* has preached peace by Negotiation."

Officially no one knew the cause of the suppression, and the infringement of the freedom of the press spread outcries across the entire political spectrum. Publisher Cecil Harmsworth suggested "inviting the War Cabinet . . . to study John Milton's 'Aereopagitica' " over the weekend, and Winston Churchill delivered a brilliant condemnatory speech in Parliament, parts of which sounded like his friendly enemy Bernard Shaw. "The administration of this country in regard to newspapers," he insisted, "cannot be based on the caprice of a Munchausen department which collects tit-bits for the German wireless telegraphy." Even Chesterton, who disagreed with all of the *Nation*'s policies, protested, as did Wells, Bennett, Galsworthy, "Q," Sturge Moore, and H. de Vere Stacpoole. The worst of it, Shaw declared, was that "all the raving Jingo papers . . . are left free to provide Berlin with 'Sidelights on England.' " To a letter to the editor of the *Nation*, he appended a postscript after the War Office had explained its action: "I am much impressed by the Government's explanation that the foreign circulation of your issue of April 7th was prohibited lest your already exported issue of March 3rd should discourage the Army. After this, our gallant fellows can never again doubt the lucidity of our Organizers of Victory."[12] Late in October 1917, the War Office ban was finally, and quietly, removed.

Two shocking turnabouts had altered the face of the war in the early spring of 1917. In Russia the Liberal revolution unseated the

Czar, and in the United States, the President who had been elected months before on the slogan that he had kept the country out of the war exhorted Congress to declare war on Germany. For Shaw it meant suddenly embracing two unexpected allies, for he had, almost alone, rejected Imperial Russia as an ally to nations claiming democratic ideals, and he looked on America's neutrality as a good thing, enabling her to be the eventual mediator in a hopeless stalemate. The truth was, Shaw told the press, "that although we could not afford to dispense with the military assistance of the Czar, our alliance with him was felt to be a disgrace in Liberal circles, while even our reactionaries found it extremely embarrassing." To Frank Harris he wrote, "Good news from Russia, eh? Not quite what any of the belligerents intended, any more than Bismarck intended to make France a republic in 1870; but the Lord fulfils himself in many ways. It is probably not the least surprise He has up His sleeve for us."[13]

The entry of America into the war found Shaw in the unusual position of being quoted favorably by the entire spectrum of the press, as he praised the move as a "first class moral asset to the common cause against junkerism." The change in attitudes was two-sided, for although critics of the war like Shaw began to see that the two great events of March and April had made it certain that there would be no stalemate, the public found little to cheer about after the initial hurrahs, and opinion continued shifting in the direction of Shaw's once heretical points of view. In mid-April the country, even London, was still frostbitten and in places snowbound, Easter week one of the most inclement in living memory. Amid the frost there was public indignation over the stupid suppression of the *Nation* and burgeoning sympathy for the conscientious objectors given prison sentences at hard labor. For those fortunate enough to enjoy the appalling boredom and creeping privations of being at home and out of uniform, there were, even among the privileged, vast losses of relatives and friends in battles that even the most careful communiqué prose failed to conceal had gained at best only a few yards of mud. Even the Zeppelin raids had created no acute sense of danger at home, and gradually the feeling had come, however yet unspoken, that the war was being fought over nothing. However mischievous Shaw's paradoxes appeared earlier to have been, there was now an awareness that they had not been composed with easy hindsight.[14]

The realization produced no satisfaction in Shaw, and in any case his awareness of the shift in opinion was slow in penetrating his profound disillusion about English apathy. That there was a change was being made clear by the lessening public hostility toward such organizations as the Union for Democratic Control, and by the popular success of the first mass meeting sponsored by the League of Nations Society once it felt it could emerge safely from its wraps. Even crafty Lloyd George began suggesting vague agreement with the idea that peace was a good thing and that an international organization to help keep it might be a good thing, too. As one historian saw it afterward, "The old cries of honour and duty were wearing a little hoarse, the memories of the outrage inflicted upon Belgium rather hoary; it was becoming difficult for the human frame to bear all the slaughter and sacrifice and not believe that it was for something which was at the same time bigger and more precise."[15] Thus G.B.S. on April 23 could appear without shocking any sensibilities at an Aristotelian Society symposium in Albemarle Street on "Ethical Principles of Social Reconstruction" and on the same day receive an invitation to visit the Italian front. To General Dalmé-Radcliffe Shaw responded that although the Trentino in the spring was a pleasant thought, he had no desire to go where he could be of no use. Few Englishmen were involved in the fighting there, and few were interested in that sideshow of a war; he could not even amuse the troops, as his few words of operatic Italian were good only for expressing murderous jealousy or for making love. What, then, could he do that Wells had not done earlier? He could keep silent, he concluded, for Wells's interview with the King of Italy had resulted in a Wellsian manifesto suggesting a republic there, and it was unreasonable to subject the King to an Irish republican as well.[16] Shaw had had all the war-touristing he wanted.

From Russia Shaw received another proposal he quickly rejected. On May 2 Gorki had cabled from revolutionary Petrograd inviting Shaw to be joint editor with him of a Socialist Russian daily, *New Life*, to be published by the Council of Workers, Soldiers, Deputies and

Writers. It was impractical, Shaw thought, and he would not be merely a façade,[17] but it was an index to his stature outside England. Production and publication were another index, and the annual accounts rendered in April showed strong sales of his books, while his columns from France were being published from Stockholm to Buenos Aires, and the William Faversham touring company of *Getting Married* in America was furnishing box office receipts that eclipsed the many scattered productions of *Pygmalion* and other plays in Holland, Sweden, Denmark, and elsewhere among the dwindling neutrals.

On the other side of the ledger the outgo included some unusual entries, the most curious of them the £300 debt G.B.S. cleared up for his sister Lucy, who was leaving for Devon, out of range of the Zeppelins. Lucy had only recently moved to a London suburb after complaining of "Zepps which terrify me." Yet the house she chose, she wrote Ann Elder, was comfortingly beside a country lane near an antiaircraft searchlight battery, "so we shall always know when the Zepps are on the way. The light station is near enough to hear the officer giving orders." She and her nurse moved in with great difficulty during the Easter frost and planted potatoes "in the wilderness of a small garden." Sussex Lodge, Champion Hill, S.E.5, was a fine, scenic location, except for the antiaircraft guns planted nearly as close to the house as Lucy's potatoes; when a fresh spate of air raids followed the spring weather, the guns shattered Lucy's peace as well as the windows and her crockery. Suffering from shell-shock, she escaped to a furnished house in Devon that G.B.S. leased for her and her nurse, the transfer complicated by the red tape connected with another change of address for her nurse, who remained an "alien enemy." "The crowning horror," Eva Schneider wrote later, had been when Lucy, "from her French window . . . saw a Zeppelin descend in flames, after many anxious nights waiting for its attack." It was a different reaction from that G.B.S. observed at Potters Bar.

To a friend Lucy explained,

The fact is I have run away from the air raids which threatened to 'do for me' altogether. My nerves seemed to have collapsed, and set up a form of very distressing dyspepsia which would give way to nothing, and so there was nothing for it but to fly. The constant apprehension was almost as bad as the raids themselves. One of the biggest defence guns was in a field beside our garden, and it really seemed as if the house must be blown away every time it went off. In addition we were near a bombing exercise ground on one hand, and within sound of the gun testing at Woolwich [Arsenal] on the other, so that we didn't know whether a raid was on or not, except by our big gun. . . . Confined as I am to sitting in a chair all day, with nothing to do but listen for bombs, I could not stand the strain, so fled here to Dartmoor. The journey was a great trial, but terror lent energy to my weakness. I had not been away from home, even to go to town in a taxi, for over two years.

She did not expect to ever return to London, for she had no wish to be there again until the war was over and saw no prospect of surviving that long. Maintaining Sussex Lodge via a caretaker while in exile in Devon made her, she admitted, "a very expensive person," but, she added with a wry reference to her diminishing needs, *"my brother indulges me in any extravagance I express the least wish for."*[18]

Lucy never got over the experience and was failing when G.B.S.— immediately after the armistice—leased a house for her across the road from Sussex Lodge* and had her moved back in stretcher and ambulance, as she had expressed the hope that she would not die far off in Devon. One afternoon more than a year after she took up residence on Champion Hill, Shaw came on one of his rare visits—Mrs. Pat had written about Lucy's condition with great anxiety—and found his sister in bed. She was dying, she told G.B.S. "Oh, no: you will be all right presently," he assured her and took her hand. They both fell silent, the only sound coming from a piano being played in a house nearby until Shaw heard a faint flutter in her throat. Her thumb straightened in his hand.

When her doctor arrived to certify the death, Shaw asked what cause he would assign, knowing that she had suffered from tuberculosis during the years since she had given up her stage career. "Starvation," the doctor said, and Shaw protested that he had provided

---

* The owner, African explorer Sir Harry Johnston, wanted it back for his own use.

for her better than that. Since the war, the doctor explained, he had
never been able to make Lucy eat enough. Shell-shock had affected
her appetite, and peace had brought no improvement. Her will, dated
February 14, 1918, specified, "No funeral, no flowers, no mourning,"
but Shaw, arriving at Golders Green for her cremation, discovered
that the chapel was crowded with her friends. "With all those people
there," he realized that he "could not have her thrown on the fire
like a scuttle of coals; so I delivered a funeral oration, and finished by
reciting the dirge from Cymbeline because

> Fear no more the lightning-flash,
> Nor the all-dreaded thunder-stone

so nearly fitted what the doctor told me."[19]

When G.B.S. went off with the Webbs for a holiday early in June
at Logan Pearsall Smith's Elizabethan manor house in Sussex, it
was with his work on the long and intractable play completed. Lucy
had written a friend about it, on Shaw's report, on April 4, 1917. "He
is writing a new big play in which he says he is letting himself go for
all he is worth. I expect he will have to build a theatre, for no manager would dare to produce unlimited and uncontrolled Shaw."[20]
From March through May, working at a high pitch in spite of his other
activities and distractions, he had managed to coalesce his ideas for
what he now thought of as a "dramatic fantasia," and it was fitting that
he should relax from the effort at a country house and in a setting
not unlike that around which he had constructed his play. Charlotte
wasted no time in providing Shaw with a trial audience for his lines,
now turned into typescript from his shorthand by Ann Elder. She
wrote friends that G.B.S. would read his new play to "a select few"
the following Friday.[21]

The select few gathered at Adelphi Terrace at a quarter to four on
the afternoon of the eighth of June, among them Sir Sydney Olivier,
H. W. Massingham, Gilbert Murray, and Lady Scott, who had left
her work* at the Ministry of Pensions early for the occasion. G.B.S.,

---

* She was private secretary to the Minister of Pensions.

who warmed to the task of reading all his roles, was at the height of his form. "Very, very funny," she noted about the first act, which has only a foreshadowing of the heartbreak of the later scenes. After the reading of the opening act came tea, and the remainder of the play followed, but while the others stayed for the entire reading, Lady Scott had to return to her office to work until 9:30.[22] The next day Shaw traveled to Lamer with her, and after Peter Scott had gone to bed that evening read parts of what she had missed. She was baffled. "All the people develop as you least expect." Shaw could not stay for late dinner and complete the play, explaining that Charlotte was waiting for him at Ayot and "gets awfully annoyed if he leaves her alone."[23]

On Sunday Lady Scott and Peter went to lunch at the Shaws, and afterward while she dozed contentedly in the garden G.B.S. finished his reading, more for himself, it seemed, than for her.[24] He was clearly pleased with the outcome, yet had no idea what to do with the script other than let it become known privately. He had usually published his plays *after* performance rather than before, yet it was clearly an inauspicious time to produce a serious play that ended with falling bombs, even a play in his unique blend, serious farce. It was just as poor a time to publish such a play, but Shaw determined to have a "rehearsal copy" set in type by his usual printers and publishers. In the interim he read the play again later in June, to Stella and George Cornwallis-West. Having told her in advance that the leading role was that of an "inspired half-wit," she suggested—half-seriously—Beerbohm Tree for the role, and an autumn opening at Tree's His Majesty's Theatre. Shaw, however, was only interested in reading the play, not in producing it, warning Stella that it required five hours.[25] As he told Graham Wallas, the play was a terror to read, having nearly killed him while leaving his audience prostrate. Realistically, he thought, a reading of *Heartbreak House* should be spread over a week.[26]

For his reading to Mrs. Pat—in a single evening—Shaw had gone to the Cornwallis-Wests' London home in Kensington Square, possibly wondering as he read, with all the stops pulled for her, whether Stella recognized her former self in Hesione Hushabye, the shrewd and exotic enchantress who keeps Heartbreak House for her aged father and keeps a romantically handsome husband in a manner that suggests a harem of one. Again the play proved baffling. The setting became unrealistic. The characters became eccentric. The events became fantastic. "You beget your dramatis personae like a God," Stella wrote G.B.S. afterward in a thank-you note, "—but as you went along you lost respect for their bones. . . . Your pen makes you drunk. . . . I feel *disorder* where you probably feel 'there I was inspired.' . . . But I am so grateful to you. I wish I was a man and old enough for Shotover. . . ."[27]

Afterward Stella—now past fifty—suggested unrealistically to G.B.S. that she play the youngest woman in the play, Ellie Dunn, and it was not until 1929 that Shaw told her that she had been his prototype for Hesione, the oldest, who at forty-seven is the age at which Stella almost wrecked Shaw's marriage. Lillah McCarthy, too, wanted to play the eighteen-year-old Ellie and talked Shaw into letting her read the script. "There is something about the play that makes me extraordinarily reluctant to let it go out of my hands," he wrote her. "I suppose I am not quite convinced that it is really finished. You are the first to extract it. . . ." Lillah was even more eager after reading the play, but Shaw was adamant. All the conditions were wrong, he insisted. The play was too long to play under the blackout and austerity rules that required theatre lights to be out at 10:30, and even if people would come to a theatre early enough to sit through a long play, there would not be enough of them for more than a fortnight's run. *Heartbreak House* would just have to "lie there to show that the old dog can still bark a bit."[28]

Trying another gambit, Lillah offered to produce the play, although she had no means to do so, assuming that backers would follow if she could acquire the rights. As gently as he could, Shaw deflated the proposition, pointing out that he had written an unpleasant play that horrified everyone who had heard him read it and that it was an unsound commercial proposition, too long and too loaded with roles for aging players, having been written without regard to theatrical circumstances in order to prove to himself that he could still write an extended, serious drama.[29] For more than a year Lillah kept trying to coax the performing rights from Shaw, certain that the play was his *Lear*, and that in its very chaos and formlessness—qualities sometimes pointed to afterward by critics to discredit the plays—Shaw was mirroring his time. Technique had become theme. "I see in Shaw's doubt about the play a sign of disagreement between Shaw's art and his personality. He is a tidy man. . . . He likes to make his plays tidy too. And *Heartbreak House* is untidy: untidy as the waste places of the world.* It has, however, a quality which only once before an English playwright had contrived to give the drama he has written. The quality which *King Lear* has: spaciousness. In *Heartbreak House* there is no stage. It is life speaking from the stage of life, a voice crying in the wilderness."[30]

For Lillah—in part as compensation for refusing her *Heartbreak House* and in part to keep her mind off Barker—Shaw wrote a potboiler, explaining imaginatively that he needed to get something into production because the war had wrecked his income. The "bravura" playlet took its cues from the events in Russia and on the surface is about a grand duchess who is reported to have eloped with a young officer but turns out to have joined the Revolution. The setting is a thinly fictional east European monarchy where the government, beset by dissension, has faltered into chaos, while the imperial general is too baffled about what to do to be able to do anything at all. Suddenly he is confronted by the once unworldly Grand Duchess Annajanska, who he does not know has joined the Army (as well as the burgeoning Revolution), convinced that the corrupt court must be replaced by a regime more worthy of popular support. She has been arrested as one whose activities run counter to the national interest, but when accused of uttering political blasphemy insists con-

---

* Very likely Colin Wilson did not know of Lillah McCarthy's observation made a generation earlier when he wrote, in *Bernard Shaw: A Reassessment* (1969), "*Heartbreak House* anticipates Eliot's *Waste Land* in its tone and in its analysis of the problem of a civilisation undermined by triviality and 'nihilism.' But Eliot arrived at the conclusion that the answer lies in a return to traditional Christianity, and Shaw was quite certain that it did not."

fidently, "All great truths begin as blasphemies." Further, she points out, she is on the side of the "energetic and capable minority" that must govern when people cannot govern themselves.

Although she is able to convince General Strammfest that war will paradoxically unite the revolutionaries on behalf of the nation, the General yearns for a man who can provide and embody the necessary leadership. "I have won no victories," he explains helplessly: "they will not rally to my call."

"Suppose I find you a man and a soldier?" Annajanska offers, and to his shock (as well as that, presumably, of the audience), she throws aside her cloak and reveals herself in resplendent military attire, ready to lead the forces of the future into battle.

In some ways the melodrama was another embryonic suggestion of a later play, where another misleadingly innocent young woman in love with war and soldiers' uniforms confidently assumes military command and leads her disorganized nation into the future, although she is accused of blasphemy and afterward imprisoned. *Saint Joan* was to continue to evolve, apparently subconsciously, under pressure of war.

First *Annajanska, the Wild Grand Duchess*, it was retitled by Shaw afterward—taking advantage of events—to *Annajanska, the Bolshevik Empress* when he revised and published it in 1919. He had hardly expected a Bolshevik coup to upset the new Kerensky regime, but few knew how faltering the revolutionary government was, a group of "representative Englishmen" including Shaw making hopeful noises about it in the July 1917 *Anglo-Russian Review*. Lord Bryce, G. K. Chesterton, Jerome K. Jerome, W. J. Locke, and others contributed idealistic paragraphs on "What We Expect from Russia," while Shaw expected "a vigorous prosecution of the war, as I unfortunately know no other method of binding a nation into a politically conscious and strenuously coherent whole after the dissolution of its traditional constitution except a war which threatens its existence as an independent State." His Russian farce for Lillah, meant for a variety bill at the Coliseum, was praised by a friend when it was first performed (on January 21, 1918) as "the only one of your works that is not too long." Its running time was twenty minutes.

On Saturday July 7, twenty-one huge, ungainly German airplanes crossed the North Sea from Belgium and flew in two clusters over the South of England, crisscrossing London repeatedly while antiaircraft fire burst harmlessly below them. Unaware of their actual dimensions, observers below thought they were flying far lower than they were. "For fifteen or twenty minutes," Sir Hall Caine wrote, "they did not appear to move. Against the gray banks of clouds they looked precisely like a collection of cholera germs on a glass disc. . . . It was an example of the most brutal bullying." These were the new twin-engined Gotha biplanes, with a wingspan of seventy-eight feet, larger than any aircraft the Germans sent against England in World War II. Their bombs unloaded, mostly over the East End, they turned back toward the Kentish coast while a motley assortment of ninety-five Royal Flying Corps machines belatedly took after them, downing one Gotha which, its engine faltering, had straggled behind the rest.*

The casualties in London (57 killed and 193 wounded) were smaller than some previous raids had caused, but the consternation was acute and humiliating, the enemy having demonstrated the vulnerability of the island to aircraft not as sluggish in performance or as easily brought down as the dreaded Zeppelins. The British had been forewarned, a statement issued in Berlin toward the end of June advising, ominously, that populations be moved from areas of military production and warehousing, such as London. "The German people, under pressure of English starvation and the war, has become a hard race with an iron fist. . . . The hammer is in our hands, and it will fall mercilessly and shatter the places where England is forging weapons against us." In the House of Lords, Lord Montagu of Beaulieu agreed, candidly warning that the Germans "had a perfect right to bomb London" and urging an adequate air defense force for the city. Although he was denounced in the press, after the Gotha raid Fleet Street decried the "shame" and "dishonour," and angry mobs in the damaged northern and eastern sectors of London demolished shop windows

* The British claimed five kills, and the actual German loss was that number because four Gothas crash-landed in Belgium, accidents due to their nose-heavy design, particularly when empty of bombs.

bearing names that seemed to them to be Germanic, throwing equipment and merchandise into the streets.

The next day the Sunday newspapers featured stories about "fearless Londoners" and "intrepid British airmen," and the *Times* on Monday editorialized that air defense needed "fresh investigation." The affair was quickly toned down in the daily press in the interest of supporting shaken civilian morale. Certain that there were more urgent considerations, that the war of the future would be air war upon civilian populations and that those civilians, especially children, had to be protected, Shaw sent a long letter to that effect to the *Times*, which shrank from printing it, alarmed that it would cause alarm. Yet after the first Gotha raid (the July 7 embarrassment was the second), a mass meeting sponsored by the *Daily Express* at the London Opera House, with the Lord Mayor presiding, had protested "the brutality and horror of high explosive bombs being dropped upon small children who were blown about like bundles of bloody rags. . . ."[31]

After the *Times* rejection, Shaw sent his manifesto to the *Daily Chronicle*, which also refused it, declaring that the letter could not be published in any civilized country. Stubbornly, Shaw then sent it to Massingham, who published it in the *Nation*:[32]

Sir,—The correspondence on this subject in the daily papers only demonstrates for the thousandth time how few civilians in this country have any notion of what war means. . . .

This sort of amiable silliness has to be endured as long as it is not allowed to distract the attention and waste the time and material of our forces. But it is not clear that even our military commanders have grasped the fact that the way to win any war is to kill civilians. Even editors of London dailies will not face it, though they should be braver than soldiers.

What is an army for? Simply to prevent the enemy from slaughtering the civilian population until it buys its life by consenting to the terms of peace imposed by the slayers. That is what war is, and nothing else. Why will the Germans be beaten if we break through their lines and shatter the resistance of their army? Solely because we shall then be in a position to slaughter them if they refuse the ransom we demand. Does anyone imagine that if they refused, we should only say, "Very unkind of you," and come home? Suppose the Germans sink our fleet and annihilate our army, will the alternative to our submitting to their terms of peace be nothing worse than a remonstrance? Would any commander waste his time killing soldiers if he could get at the civilians over their heads?

Well, that is just exactly what the British and German commanders have been enabled to do through the invention of the heavier-than-air flying battery. If Hindenburg can get London at his mercy, or if Sir Douglas Haig can get Berlin at his mercy, the war is over, and the gigantic operations at the west front are mere waste of life, time, and powder. And yet on the morrow of the last raid, The Times, in a long letter which it evidently wrote to itself, declared with an axiomatic air that the protection of our soldiers in Flanders must of course be put before the protection of civilians in the capital. . . .

I am not now thinking of the moral effect of the air raids. It is true that ever since an appalling slaughter of our soldiers at Festubert and there-abouts produced no effect on us except one of exhilaration at their courage, whilst immediately afterwards the sinking of the Lusitania, a trifle in comparison, elicited a squeal that rent the heavens, we have been steadily impressing on the enemy, apparently without realizing it ourselves, that the moral effect of killing a single baby in arms is greater than that of annihilating a whole battalion in the field. But we shall get over that. Squealing does not lead to surrender; and the Germans are not raiding us merely for the fun of making us squeal, any more than we are raiding them to make them call us baby killers and so forth. They are doing it, and we are doing it, because it has a genuine military effectiveness which needs only sufficient extension to supersede the warfare of the trenches. War is going into the air; and the side which realizes this first will be the winner. There is no longer any question of reprisals for outrages: we might as well talk of Waterloo as a reprisal for the outrage of Austerlitz. We have to make war on German cities from the air, and to defend our own cities from German attacks from the air; and the sooner we make up our minds to it the better. . . . We in London must set ourselves to provide shelter for ourselves as soldiers do. In London the tube railways act as dug-outs. The War Office, Buckingham Palace, and the National Gallery are protected by umbrellas of netting supposed to be bombproof. In Arras a whole population lives in the cellars. In Rheims and the champagne country the wine vaults are used. But modern London is practically cellarless; and tubes are few and far between. We cannot spread netting over the whole metropolis; but we can net the school playgrounds, and send the children there when the alarm is given. At present we refuse to give the alarm because the people have nowhere to go for safety. Other open spaces can be protected in the same way. Large buildings, strong enough to bear sandbags, can be fortified against the sky and thrown open in case of need. When the buildings are not strong enough, elephant dug-outs can be used. Ypres has been made habitable in that way under years of heavy artillery fire. Some approach can be made to providing every neighborhood with refuges sufficient at least to save the children and those who are too nervous to take their chance without going distracted.

It must be remembered that the present amateurish attitude of the civilian who, when he hears of a raid, jumps into a taxi and tells the driver to make for the bombs, will not outlast a little experience of what bombs can do. Soldiers do not crowd to see the fun: they scuttle for the nearest cover whenever they can; and that is what we shall all do when the war becomes frankly a war on civilians, and the blows are struck at the head and stomach instead of at the far-flung limbs. The demand for cover will become irresistible; and if it is not forthcoming it will change into a demand for peace. Defensive air squadrons and aircraft guns are all very well if they prevent the arrival of the enemy; but once he gets over us, our own machine-gun and shrapnel bullets are as dangerous as his bombs, and will remain so even when we all wear helmets and carry gas-masks.

I suggest that we begin *to-day* with the school playgrounds. It is really no use shaking our fists at the sky and shrieking that it is murder to kill a civilian. We shall get killed all the same. I do not think we shall even get the sympathy we so confidently claim. If it be true that our best men are in the trenches, I had rather see a street bombed than a trench; and if I thought the contrary, I should at least have the decency to keep my selfish civilian opinion to myself within hearing of our soldiers.—Yours, &c.,

G. Bernard Shaw.

By the end of July a London Air Defence Area was established to augment and coordinate protection of the city, including an improved warning system. Until then the government had been more concerned that news of approaching enemy bombers would cause panic and create work stoppages in critical war industries, but a new warning system combined the firing of booming "maroon" signal flares from the roofs of fire stations with the sending of self-conscious policemen, wearing fore-and-aft placards reading, "Police Notice: Take Cover," down the streets of London on bicycles. By the end of the summer there were, on the nights of some raids, as many as three hundred thousand Londoners bedding down overnight in the tubes of the Underground, complete to baskets of food, dogs, cats, and caged birds. Trains ran as usual, but at some stations passengers could neither get on or off, as the platforms and stairways were choked with people fleeing the Gothas.[33] It was a foreshadowing of 1940.

As the war dragged on toward a fourth year, the position of the conscientious objector became more confused, in part because of the frightening example of pre-Bolshevist, revolutionary Russia. In Leeds, for example, the National Labour and Socialist Convention opened on June 4 and immediately passed a resolution moved by future Prime Minister J. Ramsay MacDonald that congratulated the Russian people on its revolution; when Mrs. D. B. Montefiore rose to second it, amid cheers she invited the delegates to "fetch out Clifford Allen—and do as the Russians have done." Allen was one of the living martyrs of the pacifist cause, and as Shaw put it, "as far as the question was one solely of courage the Conshy was the hero of the war; and the man who would not enlist until he was forced was the coward." On Allen's behalf on June 12, G.B.S. published a letter to the editor in the *Manchester Guardian* protesting the inhumanity of his imprisonment. Not only was the frail Allen (afterward Lord Allen of Hurtwood) jailed for two years at hard labor—a sentence generally reserved for the most malicious of offenders—but the sentence was renewed on expiration if the offence of conscientious objection continued. The lack of any protest on the part of the press was to Shaw just as staggering as the punishment, which for a sick man he considered virtually a sentence of death. "Is this," Shaw asked, "the intention of the Government, the military authorities, and the nation? If so, there is nothing more to be said. It may be so; for it is a matter of daily experience that many people who are taking advantage of their age and sex to do not only less public work than Mr. Clifford Allen and Mr. Stephen Hobhouse* did long before the war put any pressure on them, but no public work at all, think that such a death is too good for a conscientious objector, and do not hesitate to say as much. But are these vicarious zealots in the majority? May not the absence of protest be merely the ignorance of the respectable man who knows nothing of prisons and criminal law and has no idea that Mr. Allen is being treated with a new and quite abnormal frightfulness? . . . Anyhow, here are two gentlemen in a fair way to be killed because the public has no knowledge and the authorities no sense. If we wish to kill them, cannot we shoot them out of hand and have done with it, Dublin fashion?"

The problem of protesting the conshy's lot was a delicate one, Shaw realized, for the objectors ranged from sheer shirkers and cowards to determined martyrs as unwilling as St. Joan to submit their private judgment to any external authority. His own contribution to the causes of those whose motives he respected ranged from speaking and writing in their support to testifying at their trials, one such appearance being unexpectedly successful "because, although I told the exact truth and nothing but the truth, my evidence convinced and was meant to convince the court that the prisoner was an Evangelical fanatic, whereas he was as a matter of fact a Freethinker. His case was quite genuine as a case of conscience; but a military court would not have held that a Freethinker could have a conscience; consequently it was necessary in the interests of justice to produce the evidence of fanaticism, of which there was plenty, and leave the court to infer that a fanatic must be a hyperpious Quaker."[34]

Most of the summer of 1917 was passed by G.B.S. as a bachelor. Charlotte had deserted the heat of London, which troubled her back, to visit with her sister in County Kerry. She was suffering from an

* Stephen Hobhouse (1881–1961). Member of a wealthy Quaker family, he worked in the Board of Education, 1905–1911. During this time he renounced his heirship to his father's estate and worked for the poor in London's East End. He undertook relief work in the Balkan Wars, 1912–13. Imprisoned as a conscientious objector, 1916–1918. With Fenner Brockway he edited *English Prisons Today.* His autobiography was published in 1951.

assortment of minor but chronic and uncomfortable ailments, one of which doctors had diagnosed as lumbago, but which was actually the onset of the *osteitis deformans* which gradually bent her back and turned her into an octogenarian invalid. For Shaw the months in Kerry would have been a surfeit of leisure. "I get miserably unhappy if my work is cut off," he insisted. "I get hideous headaches after each month's bout: I make resolutions to break myself of it, never to work after lunch, to do only two hours a day; but in vain: every day brings its opportunity and its temptation: the craving masters me every time; and I dread a holiday as I dread nothing else on earth." Both in London and at Ayot he had his work, and nearby in both places there was always Lady Scott, who had emerged as a daughter figure in whom he could confide those things he was reluctant to tell Charlotte. There were also the insistent calls upon his services at public meetings, which took several of his afternoons and evenings each week. He was at the "Fabian Nursery," that organization of second generation junior Fabians, on June 6, for example, to speak extempore on current issues. The audience chose the Russian Revolution and its possible effect on the duration of the war, the Irish Convention, and H. G. Wells's newest book, *God, the Invisible King.* There were few topical subjects on which he would refuse to venture to speak; on July 5 at Central Hall in Westminster, he urged a state-supported program that would ensure that no mother would be "prevented by economic stress from caring for her children adequately and well." Among other things Shaw had been made chairman of a Fabian study group on the representation of the Empire in a League of Nations, titled pretentiously the Empire Reconstruction Committee. It had begun meeting on May 18, when Shaw was elected chairman, and met on June 1 and July 6, both times at five in the afternoon when presumably all its members would have already done a day's work.

It was not the only way in which Shaw passed his evenings. He had also returned, briefly and somewhat nostalgically, to music criticism, possibly in relaxation from the strain of completing *Heartbreak House.* *The Marriage of Figaro* was so botched, he protested in the *Nation,* that beginning the performance with the National Anthem was "almost high treason." And *Il Trovatore* was produced so shabbily that it was a waste of his six shillings and sixpence. After these, Sir Thomas Beecham's version of *Figaro* at Drury Lane later in July was "the most delightful entertainment in London," although it was "Mozart with Mozart left out." Yet, Shaw confessed, "As I am only half a critic now, I act up to that character by going to only half an opera at a time. As in the case of *Il Trovatore*, I did not see the first two acts of Figaro's Wedding." But he did return the following Thursday night to hear the first two acts.[35] ("Shaw grumbled much at the performance," Arnold Bennett noted in his journal the next day, although Bennett privately thought that the acting was not up to the musicianship.)[36]

Bennett had seen more of G.B.S. that week than was usual, for when he had had dinner at James Barrie's on July 24, two days earlier, with Thomas Hardy and his wife as the only other guests, Barrie decided to enliven the conversation when the aged Hardy began to wear down by telephoning Shaw and the Wellses to join them. At dusk they looked out on what Bennett called "the finest view of London I ever saw" and watched the antiaircraft searchlights. It was too much for Hardy to stand out on the balcony in the breeze from the Thames, and he put a handkerchief on his thinning pate to keep out the chill. Then Shaw and the Wellses arrived, and in Bennett's words, "Hardy seemed to curl up. He had travelled to town that day and was evidently fatigued. He became quite silent. I then departed and told Barrie that Hardy ought to go to bed. He agreed. The spectacle of Wells and G.B.S. talking firmly and strongly about the war, in their comparative youth, in front of this aged, fatigued, and silent man —incomparably their superior as a creative artist—was very striking."[37]

Wells and Shaw could talk "firmly and strongly about the war"[38] because they had been drawing together in their views, views not shared by the less compromising Bennett and Hardy. Shaw was more reluctant to air his opinions on the war for the newspapers, although the requests were insistent and continuing. One the following week from the Northern Newspaper Syndicate offered ten guineas for one thousand words answering six questions:

Has the war been worth it?
How will the war help democracy?
Is state control becoming a menace?
Has the war made us more religious?
Who is paying the war bill?
What will become of the neutrals?

Shaw refused to answer any of the questions, although adding that for £1000 he would have answered all six.[39] He was worried over his income taxes and somehow was sure he would soon be paying more in tax than he earned, having just received a bill for arrears of American income tax amounting to £600. The obsession with the tax collector would grow through two world wars until Shaw, who eventually left one of the largest literary estates on record, was sure that he was being taxed into poverty.

The end of August, war or no war, meant the annual Fabian Summer School, in advance of which Beatrice Webb in 1917 decided there had to be a special "at home" for the younger Fabians, which she held not at her own Grosvenor Road residence, but at the Fabian offices. It became "a scandalous orgy," one he might want to expose in the *New Witness*, Shaw wrote Chesterton on August 6:

You know that there is a body called The Fabian Research Department, of which I have the hollow honour to be Perpetual Grand, the real moving spirit being Mrs. Sidney Webb. A large number of innocent young men and women are attracted to this body by promises of employment by the said Mrs. S. W. in works of unlimited and inspiring uplift, such as are unceasingly denounced, along with Marconi and other matters, in your well-written organ.

Well, Mrs. Sidney Webb summoned all these young things to an uplifting At Home at the Fabian Office lately. They came in crowds and sat at her feet whilst she prophesied unto them, with occasional comic relief from the unfortunate Perpetual Grand. At the decent hour of ten o'clock, she bade them good night and withdrew to her own residence and to bed. For some accidental reason or other I lingered until, as I thought, all the young things had gone home. I should explain that I was in the two pair back. At last I started to go home myself. As I descended the stairs I was stunned by the most infernal din I have ever heard, even at the front, coming from the Fabian Hall, which would otherwise be the back yard. On rushing to this temple I found the young enthusiasts sprawling over tables, over radiators, over everything except chairs, in a state of scandalous abandonment, roaring at the tops of their voices and in a quite unintelligible manner a string of presumably obscene songs, accompanied on the piano with frantic gestures and astonishing musical skill by a man whom I had always regarded as a respectable Fabian Researcher, but who now turned out to be a Demon Pianist out-Heroding (my secretary put in two rs, and explains that she was thinking of Harrods) Svengali. A horribly sacrilegious character was given to the proceedings by the fact that the tune they were singing when I entered was Luther's hymn *Eine Feste Burg ist Unser Gott.* As they went on (for I regret to say that my presence exercised no restraint whatever) they sang their extraordinary and incomprehensible litany to every tune, however august its associations, which happened to fit it. These, if you please, are the solemn and sour neophytes whose puritanical influence has kept you in dread for so many years.

But I have not told you the worst. Before I fled from the building I did at last discover what words it was they were singing. When it first flashed on me, I really could not believe it. But at the end of the next verse no doubt or error was possible. The young maenad nearest me was concluding every strophe by shrieking that she didn't care where the water went if it didn't get into the wine.* Now you know.

I have since ascertained that a breviary of this Black Mass can be obtained at the Fabian Office, with notes of the numbers of the hymns Ancient and Modern, and all the airs sacred and profane, to which your poems have been set.

This letter needs no answer—indeed, admits of none. I leave you to your reflections.

Ever

G.B.S.[40]

The good humor on Shaw's part reflected no feeling that all was right with the world, but it did suggest his changed position in it.

---

* The refrain from a poem in Chesterton's *The Flying Inn.*

There was just as much cause for despair as before, but he was no longer a lonely voice, and his completion of *Heartbreak House,* his own plunge into pessimism, seemed to have acted as a catharsis. As an American weekly reported early in August, his views at the outbreak of war had "cost him the support of many admirers who felt that he was unpatriotic and disloyal. Now we learn from a London correspondent of the New York *Tribune* that his 'army of followers' is returning to him though he has not changed his attitude in the least. He defends the conscientious objectors and held that Casement should have been treated as a prisoner of war, and the correspondent indicates that it is hopeless to try to classify Shaw, who is not a pacifist, or a peace-by-negotiation advocate, or a fight-to-a-finish warrior. He is 'just Shaw,' and thoroughly acquainted with all phases of the war-situation." As for the average person's understanding of the military situation, Shaw expressed "a feeling very much like contempt, for he holds that they do not know what war is and are not told. . . ." Rather, " 'They are deluded with lies, official and unofficial, to keep them in a manageable temper. Their ignorance and thoughtlessness make this seem necessary, and the result is that they pass from mere ignorance to illusions and false hopes, the inevitable occasional disappointment of which may produce panic. . . .' " Thus G.B.S. was an advocate of bringing the war home to the Germans, not in reprisal for Zeppelin raids on England, but because "all wars are decided by breaking through a military barrier and getting a bayonet or bomb against the brains and stomach of the nation as represented by the civilians of the capital." Let Haig have Berlin, he suggested, and Hindenburg could have the entire Western Front for all the good it would do him. On the other hand, he said, let Hindenburg have London and Sir Douglas "may as well pack his soldiers in boxes and sell them to the toy-shops," for it was Shaw's belief, said the *Tribune*'s correspondent, "that the war will be won in the sky and not in the trenches, and he says that all London has seen yet is 'an experimental rehearsal or two.' "[41] It was a lesson Adolf Hitler would attempt to apply in 1940 and 1941 and for which Germany was less ready than Shaw thought in midsummer of 1917, but it was also an implicit lesson of *Heartbreak House* and the experience that gave it its ending.

11

Saints and Practical Men

"I LEARNT to dance for the first time last August. Or stop! Was it really the first time? I recollect that when I was a very minute kid indeed, a lady named Magrae, who lived a few doors off, taught me the five positions; and I can still remember three of them. That is what they did in those days: they taught you positions but did not teach you to dance. Thus I learnt the positions at, say, seven and how to dance (rather like a tank) at 61."[1] The confession to Ellen Terry was further evidence of change in G.B.S., one he described elsewhere as a return to his second childhood through a phase of "retrograde juvenility." *Heartbreak House* had been a catharsis, and the experience of writing it, bisected by Zeppelin bombings and a trip to the front, had brought him through his worst months of despair.

The Fabian Summer School in late August of 1917 had borrowed the facilities of a girls' school near Godalming in Surrey. As became his years and reputation, Shaw was accepted there as a sort of Fabian bishop, but he soon discovered that after the business of the day was done, particularly after 8:30 P.M., intellect was put aside in favor of other accomplishments and that he would have to retire at that hour or stand aside as a social failure while a phonograph ground out waltzes and country dances. After lumbering through several lessons, he accepted invitations to waltz with the fairest Fabians and decided that although he had commitments in London, he would return to Godalming for the entire second week of the school.

Briefly on his first day in the city, G.B.S. saw Granville-Barker, by then a lieutenant. Officially Barker was in France, doing intelligence work, while actually he spent a good deal of time in London, where his chief activity seemed to be avoiding Lillah. For this purpose, whether or not the Shaws were there, he spent his weekends at Ayot, where he kept a spare set of civilian clothes. The divorce from Lillah had become final the previous April, but she still brooded over it, Shaw insisting all the while that it was "a thing that happens" and that no one was to blame. Somehow Lillah remained hopelessly convinced that the break would heal, although Barker had covenanted to pay her £600 a year for life and Helen Huntington was arranging a divorce from her wealthy husband. Barker apparently expected to afford the payments to his ex-wife via substantial income from his anticipated wife.

The business which had brought Shaw back to London was the August 28–29 Inter-Allied Socialist Conference, in which there were as many points of view as delegates, with Shaw, Beatrice Webb, Edward Pease, and Susan Lawrence representing the Fabians. Beatrice's diary entry for September 1, based heavily upon two unacknowledged and anonymous paragraphs in the "Events of the Week" department in the *Nation* of that date—and written by G.B.S.—summed up the meeting cogently:

The Inter-Allied Socialist Conference was a fiasco. The French delegation was made up of equal numbers of the "majority pro-war" and minority, "stop-the-war" parties. The "majority" led by Thomas and Renaudel, had come to obstruct and prevent a pro-Stockholm* decision—and they

* A conference in Stockholm to develop a peace formula along international Socialist lines was planned by Dutch and Scandinavian Socialists, but after preliminary talks in June, it foundered on the refusal of Britain and Germany to grant passports to prospective delegates.

used every device of delay and denial they could invent. The Russian delegates were tiresome and childish in their insistence on their own importance and their long-winded revolutionary pedantry; the Italians were "impossibilists"; the Belgians were hostile in a dignified and eloquent manner; the Greeks were represented by an absurd and fussy little English spinster; the Portuguese, thanks to the fact that they could speak neither French nor English, were silent. The British, made up of four mutually contemptuous sections—all alike contemptuous of the foreigners—were well-behaved but divided in opinion. The foreigners wrangled for two days with each other and the Conference finally broke up into two separate and informal meetings—the British and French majority parties and the Belgian delegation at the Waldorf Hotel, and the British and French minorities and the Russian and Italian delegations at the Fabian Hall. From these meetings will issue, I assume, separate reports. One wonders what Stockholm would have been like! The British and Germans might have found themselves trying to do business together with the Latins and Slavs storming around them. There is a real cleavage of temperament between the British and the French and one wonders whether it does not show itself at the front. One notable distinction is the British dislike of rhetoric and delight in a joke—the worse joke the better. Any attempt to relieve the tension by a joke gives dire offence to the French, and when G.B.S., impatient at Renaudel's blatant use of rhetoric to obstruct progress, asked what was the French word for "obstruction" and Longuet* shouted back "Majorité" Renaudel threatened to leave the Conference. Not being allowed to laugh, the British delegation settled down to a grim silence.
Result—Nil.

Stubborn idealists of every stripe, the conferees spent so much time arguing over the ground rules for the second day's sessions that formal proceedings could not begin until after lunch, and even then the only resolution carried, over many protests from the French, was

* Albert Thomas (1878–1932). French Socialist, friend of Jaurès; later moved rightward and became Minister of Munitions, 1916–1918. Secretary of the International Labour Organisation, 1920–1932.
  Pierre Renaudel (1871–1934). Leader of the French right-wing Socialists; editor and manager of *L'Humanité* from 1906 to 1918.
  Jean Longuet (1876–1938). Grandson of Karl Marx and leader of the minority in the French Socialist Party.

an unrealistic proposal by Ramsay MacDonald that delegates vow to go to Stockholm without passports if necessary. A resolution Shaw had carefully drafted to reconcile differences proved too objectionable to even introduce on the floor. He had pointed out that the forces they represented were as powerless to stop the war as they had been to prevent it and that they could not hope for a settlement without either military victory by one side or the mutual realization that such a victory was no longer possible. A realist, Shaw put his resolution aside while suggesting that any statement that included continued allegations of moral responsibility for the war served only to deepen postwar bitterness. That had failed, too.

Despite the acrimony in which the conference ended, the Webbs grimly went ahead with the scheduled reception at 41 Grosvenor Road on the evening of its second day and discovered that the bad feeling among the conferees did not extend to eating and drinking. G.B.S. had to rush home to Adelphi Terrace during the festivities to bring Beatrice two additional pounds of priceless sugar. Immediately afterward he left for Godalming on the 8:30 train, having had enough of the delegates during the day.

It took Shaw all his first day back—August 30—to transcribe and condense his shorthand notes of the fiasco into a report for the *Nation* and an evening lecture to the Fabians at the school, all this in addition to the set pieces he had promised to deliver during the sessions, which included the ironic "The Romance of War" and "Our Own Imperialism, which in Others We Call Prussianism." The titles alone made it clear that his point of view had altered little from 1914. The *Fabian News* was ecstatic about the 1917 sessions, reporting in its September issue in colorful detail about the school:

The experiment of holding the School near to London has proved an unqualified success. Prior's Field is the largest house we have ever taken, and it has been full during the whole period, which has never happened before. The only complaint of the guests has been that they were usually unable to prolong their stay beyond the time for which their rooms were booked. In addition to the lectures on the programme, Bernard Shaw, who spent three weeks at the School, has given addresses on "Equality" and "The Evolution of the Drama," Emil Davies on "The Financial Aspects of the War" and on "The Labour Party Conference," and Geoffrey Pike on his escape from Ruhleben. On August 23rd a cricket match was arranged between a mixed eleven and a team of Canadians from the camp at Whitley, which ended in a severe British defeat. August 24th was devoted to a programme of sports. Miss Hankinson's birthday was celebrated by a procession of the whole School bearing lanterns, an exhibition of living statuary, a concert, and a dance. In the early weeks of the School Mr. and Mrs. Clutton Brock were constantly present, and introduced the visitors to the district, and especially to the Watts Gallery at Compton, close by. Later on other visitors from the district, including Roger Fry, Lowes Dickinson, and Godfrey Blount, have attended the School.

The exhibitions of living statuary—there were two of them—Shaw attributed uncomfortably to the "normal establishment" and not to authentic Fabians. One was witnessed by baffled Canadian soldiers who had come up from their camp expecting something much different, as— for example—a lecture on "Is the Church necessary to the establishment of the Christian Ethic?" Shaw accordingly gave it to them. It was what a Fabian Summer School was supposed to be and they were satisfied.[2]

By the fifth of September, Shaw was grateful he had returned to the relative quiet of Surrey, for at eleven the night before German aircraft had come to the Adelphi. Flying up the Thames, one of the five Gothas unloaded its four 110-pound bombs along the Victoria Embankment, hoping to hit Charing Cross Station. One bomb exploded just outside the Charing Cross hospital in Agar Street, blowing in the front door and hundreds of windows. Another exploded in the Embankment Gardens near the Hotel Cecil, temporary headquarters of the Air Board, and a third in the road opposite Cleopatra's Needle on the Embankment, scarring the obelisk and killing two passengers in a passing tram.* The fourth made a shambles of

* A plaque on the pedestal commemorates the incident but with erroneous information which remains uncorrected after more than half a century: "The scars that disfigure the pedestal of the obelisk, the bases of the sphinxes and the right hand sphinx were caused by fragments of a bomb dropped in the roadway close to this spot in the first raid on London by German aeroplanes a few minutes before midnight on Tuesday 4th September 1917." The second German raid on London by Gotha aircraft had occurred on July 7, when the East End, rather than central London, suffered most of the damage.

the Little Theatre in John Street, just to the rear of G.B.S.'s home in Adelphi Terrace, shattering all the windows at No. 10. By the time he left Godalming for Ireland on Friday, September 7, the Embankment roadway, where gas had been escaping from a blasted main, had been reopened, and the Underground beneath was running again. But the massive job of window replacement, including his own, was far from over.

While at Godalming Shaw had waited hopefully for a summons that never came, his new-found Irish identity inspiring the expectation that Sir Horace Plunkett would make it possible for him to fill one of the five government-appointed positions on the Irish Convention still vacant. Crossing to Ireland, he joined Charlotte at the plush Great Southern Hotel in Parknasilla and waited, but nothing happened. As Shaw put it, "Believing that I might be of some service on the Convention, I conceived it to be my public duty to take steps to have it suggested to the Government and to the Convention itself that I should be nominated or co-opted as a member. By doing so I brought the British Government and the Irish Convention nearer to unanimity than it was supposed possible at the time."[3] What had happened was that as soon as the Lloyd George government had announced a Home Rule convention to resolve Irish differences, G.B.S. bluntly offered himself as one of the fifteen eminent Irishmen from public life who would serve as delegates along with local officials, labor union representatives, and political and religious leaders. "It is perfectly clear," he had written Lord Haldane, "that I ought to be in the business, not only by pre-eminent celebrity but because I am the only public person who has committed himself to the only possible solution: to wit, federation of the four home kingdoms. . . . I am prepared to demand a nomination."[4]

The best he could do after he and Charlotte left Parknasilla on October 13 was to remain in Dublin as Horace Plunkett's guest as the Convention began, in an attempt to exert some indirect influence, but even this was useless as the Sinn Féin party, unwilling to concede any limitation to complete independence, refused to participate, leaving the Convention with no broad moral authority in Ireland. While on the outside looking in, Shaw was invited by Ralph D. Blumenfeld, editor of Lord Beaverbrook's *Daily Express*, to publish his views on the Irish problem in their usually inhospitable pages. When he quickly rejected the offer, Blumenfeld answered persuasively that he appreciated Shaw's frankness about *Express* policy. "In the columns of the *Daily Express* you preach to a new audience. You are quite wrong in labelling my clientele as a 'mob.' It is most responsive—and again you may laugh—but I can assure you that it is intelligent, and effective in its conclusions. In the *Daily Chronicle* you will be preaching to the converted. Why not have a try at missionary work? I'll give you the run of my columns in a serious attempt to reach a solution of the problem. It may not do anything of the sort but, at least, it will be a contribution to the literature on the Eternal subject."[5]

Within two weeks in the middle of November, Shaw had drafted a lengthy three-part article which appeared simultaneously on November 27–29 in the *Express* and in the *Irish Independent* (Dublin), the Cork *Examiner*, and the Belfast *Evening Telegraph*. A month later it was published as a pamphlet in London and Dublin, and as a series in the New York *American*. Coverage and reason were useless, however, against what he called the "Sinn Féin idiots" and the "Ulster impossibilists." It was good political sense, he thought, to demand "Federal Home Rule" within a single United Kingdom for not only Ireland, but Scotland, Wales, and England as well. Within each he saw room for regional units of local government that could satisfy the impossibilists on all sides. "Dreamy Ulster," he suggested, "steeped in its glorious, pious, and immortal memories, has not noticed that there is a far stronger case for giving separate provincial legislatures to the industrial north and the residential south of England than for doing as much for the north and south of Ireland."

However persuasively he argued the case for a politically and economically united Ireland, the die-hards were not listening; nor were they listening to the delegates at the futile Convention Horace Plunkett still doggedly chaired. After eight stormy months, the delegates recommended by a vote of 52 to 19 part of what Shaw had wanted, an Irish Parliament that would encompass all of the island. No one in or out of the government ever did anything to implement it.

Once he was back in London, he was pressed to enlist in another

Irish campaign, this time by an American judge, Henry Neil of
Chicago, who had visited the Dublin slums and was appalled by what
he had seen. Not a sentimentalist, Shaw saw the enthusiastic Judge
Neil as "a sort of American Pickwick, a great deal of a simpleton and
nothing at all of a fool." What he wanted was Shaw's help in touching
the consciences of Americans to the tune of twenty thousand pairs
of shoes and socks for the children of Dublin. Shaw told him he
was out of his mind, that the shoes and socks would be immediately
pawned by the parents and the children barefoot the next day, with
a few of the better-off children in somewhat cheaper shoes.

"Very well," said Neil stubbornly. "Say that. That will do as well
as anything else. I don't care about the shoes and socks; but I know
that nothing will get at an American like children having no clothes.
I've seen the poverty and I'm out to advertise it. That's what the shoes
are for."[6]

With that, the judge managed to extort the appeal he wanted from
Shaw, but it was one loaded with Swiftian irony, with advice to Americans "not to send a single cent to Ireland ever again, for shoes or anything else" as Ireland was "perfectly able to feed and clothe her children if she chooses. It is a mistake to suppose that she is poor; she is
only an incorrigible beggar, which is not the same thing." What Shaw
wanted for Ireland was justice rather than charity, and a climate which
would encourage Irish self-respect.

The Judge says that it is the bare feet that get at an American; but I
am a Dublin man and think nothing of bare feet; if you give a country girl
in Ireland a pair of good boots she will carry them in her hands for miles
to the fair or the market town, and then put them on to make a fine show
with. What got at me when I walked about the slums of Dublin lately were
the young women with the waxen faces, the scarlet patches on the
cheeks, the pink lips, the shuffling, weary, almost ataxic step, representing
Dublin's appalling burden of consumption. They are not the product of
bare feet, but of wet feet in broken boots, of insanitary poverty generally.

When the police were driven from the streets by the week-long struggle
for an Irish republic in Easter 1916, these people came out and began to
pillage the shops as naturally as their neighbors a mile or so away pick up
cockles on Sandymount strand. Civilization is nothing to them: they have

never been civilized. Property is nothing to them: they have never had any. The priest came and drove them away as if they were flies; but the moment he passed on they came back like flies. Civilization means "Respect my life and property and I will respect yours." Slumdom means "Disregard my life and property and I will disregard yours."

Giving money is no use.

It is like people at a railway accident offering surgical instruments and splints and bandages to one another when there is nobody who knows how to use them. If you give shoes to a hungry child, it will eat them (through the medium of the pawnbroker) and be just as hungry next week. And the person who gives the money or the shoes, instead of feeling like a scoundrel because the children were in misery, feels saintly because he has played the generous sailor of melodrama.

Until we all acquire a sense of social honor and responsibility as strong as our present private family sense (and even that is not very strong in many of us), the children will shock that social conscience in Judge Neil.

I do not object to his shewing up Ireland, which poses as warmhearted, affectionate, impulsively generous, chivalrous, and all the rest of it. I am fed up (unlike the children) with these professions. If the United States, instead of asking its immigrants silly questions as to whether they are anarchists and the like, so as to make sure that all her foreign anarchists shall also be liars, were to refer to the statistics of infant mortality in the country or city from which the immigrant came, and send him back contemptuously if the rate were anything like so infamously high as it is in the slums of Dublin, such a step would do more to call the attention of Irishmen to the disgrace of their annual Slaughter of the Innocents than all the shoes that ever were pawned.[7]

Neil, Shaw thought, was "just as pleased as if I had written the most impassioned appeal. . . ." The Judge had reason to be, for in Shaw's paradoxical way it was exactly what he had done.

In September, while Shaw was in Ireland, the first American production of his 1910 play *Misalliance*, produced by William Faversham, had opened at the Broadhurst Theatre in New York. Faversham had engineered a highly profitable *Getting Married* a season earlier, and Shaw found it easy to direct *Misalliance* at long distance in the same way, via three or four typewritten pages of instructions, interlarded

with caustic comments about everything in general. It was important, he warned Faversham at the start, not to let the backcloth get too
detailed, "or the people on the stage will be practically invisible." It
was unimportant, he advised, to seek realism in the scene where an
airplane crashes into a greenhouse at the edge of the garden. "All that
is needed for the airplane is the good old hamper full of broken glass.
In this matter you must sit hard down on the producer's head, as he
will think of nothing but rigging up an airplane descent to be featured
on picture posters. Even so clever a man as Dion Boucicault* insisted
on doing that in London. He spent days in rigging up an absurd and
rather dangerous contraption by which [Charles] Bryant and Lena
Ashwell had to slide down. . . . Fortunately nobody saw them, as they
shot past before the audience were aware of them. I had not the heart
to veto this asburdity, as Boucicault loved it as a child loves a toy; but
you had better be more hard-hearted. The effect is produced to perfection by all the people looking up and shouting, and by the final crash."

Ruling out benefit performances for war charities, Shaw pointed
out that it was only the actors and writers who worked for nothing,
the management and all the tradesmen feeding off such productions
never contributing their services. The same had been true of the
wartime gift books, he added, forcing the Society of Authors (partly
as a result of Shavian pressure) to ban its membership from further
charity book activities, as the printers and publishers benefited, while
the writers sometimes had to appeal to the Society for financial aid
to tide them over income-barren periods of writing for charity. That
Rudyard Kipling had tendered his resignation from the Society in
protest at such hardheartedness failed to move Shaw. If Faversham
were to make any statement to the press on the subject of the ban
on benefit performances, he added, with an eye toward what newspapers were likely to pick up and print, "please say that nothing would
surprise you about such a shark as Shaw, and that it is I and not
Hindenburg who deserves to be stuffed with nails."[8]

---

* Dionysius George Boucicault (1859–1929), actor, director, and playwright,
was the son of the prolific Irish playwright, Dionysius Lardner Boucicault.

Late in September the first proofs of *Heartbreak House* had been forwarded to Shaw in Ireland. A veteran of the proofreading experience, he knew that a text could look far different in print than it did when it first came from the typewriter, but even with that allowance Shaw could not make up his mind as to its quality, worrying that it had a good opening spoiled by the plunge into war and by the caricature of Lord Devonport as Mangan. He was concerned, too, about the Empire Reconstruction Committee, wondering whether Leonard Woolf could do for its findings what he had so skillfully done for the earlier League of Nations report. With *Heartbreak House* in galleys, his thoughts were turning to new projects, particularly one that might salvage his maltreated writings on the war. Before he and Charlotte had gone on to Plunkett's home in Dublin, this took shape in his mind as a postwar volume to be called *What I Said During the Great War*. He was more certain than ever that his position would stand up.

The western coast of Ireland, Shaw wrote Beatrice Webb before leaving County Kerry, was ironically reaping great benefits from the German submarine campaign. The details were left to Beatrice's imagination, but undoubtedly he could see the effect of the salvaged goods washed ashore from torpedoed ships on the otherwise chronically impoverished population. It was not the way he wanted to see material well-being come to Ireland.

From Parknasilla, too, he wrote a propaganda piece for the American press urging citizens to subscribe their funds to the Liberty Loan. America could no longer stay aloof from Europe, he declared, for the Atlantic was "no longer an ocean, but a bridge. . . ." He added a last word: "War is a horrible business, and to contribute money to its prosecution wrenches the best instincts of the best men as no other sort of financial transaction can. But there is no way out of war but the fighting way until the establishment of a supernational court of justice, a supernational legislature, and a supernational police, makes an end of the existing international anarchy. America did not make this war; but she cannot stand by and look on it as if she had no interest in its issue. . . ."[9]

To the *Observer* in London, he forwarded a review puffing Gilbert Chesterton's *Short History of England*. There were few judgments in it with which he agreed, and G.K.C. was fast and free with his facts, as always, but Chesterton was a valued friend and, as always, in need of money, while his book at the least had the virtue, like most of his writings, of being consistently entertaining. "Something Like a History of England at Last," Shaw headed his notice.* Also from Parknasilla he wrote to St. John Ervine, then about to embark for the front, wishing him a safe, inglorious berth in France. Later Shaw had to write to him again, this time consoling him on the loss of a leg in combat. Every tree is better off for a little pruning, he wrote Ervine on a postcard. It sounded remote and cynical, but the convalescent knew better: "It was his way of telling me not to dwell too much on my troubles."[10]

Before the end of October, Shaw was back in London to prepare for the annual Fabian lecture series in which he would be giving two of the six Friday evening lectures on "The Britannic Alliance and World Politics." The first, on October 26, 1917, at King's Hall, Covent Garden, was delivered by Liberal Party younger statesman Herbert Samuel, and the second ("The Coloured Races and the Commonwealth") by world traveler and colonial expert Sir Harry Johnston. Shaw gave the third and sixth, separated by Sidney Webb (on international trade) and historian Graham Wallas, once a Fabian pioneer. On November 9 Shaw spoke on "Heredity and Democracy," a subject only peripherally related to the theme of the lectures, but one that was at the core of his thinking at the time. As usual, although the hall was full, the event went unreported in the press except in minor journals few people read, and those the already converted. The lone full-length coverage appeared in the *Christian Commonwealth*, a small-circulation weekly long hospitable to Shaw and self-proclaimed as the "organ of the World-Wide Progressive Movement in Religion and Social Ethics." Somewhat irreverently it reported that the substance of G.B.S.'s long lecture appeared as an answer to the last question he dealt with that evening. "For more than an hour he spoke with his usual brilliance upon spiritual and temporal power, government by superior persons, revolution, the superlative merits of the Fabian Society,

---

* It was published in the *Observer* on November 16, 1917.

federal parliaments, peace diplomacy, the Press, and himself. In this mass of luminous irrelevancies one definite assertion arose like a rock above the mist and foam—that the saint or the superior person ought never to be trusted with the business of government. . . . Mr. Shaw contemplated, and indeed advocated, the entrance of the saint and the superior person into politics, but he solemnly warned his hearers against giving them the right to vote. There were several long parentheses in the lecture, but this was the main theme."[11]

Within the parentheses Shaw, whether he knew it or not, was building the intellectual scaffolding for the plays of the last phase of his life. From *Saint Joan* (1923) and *The Apple Cart* (1929) to *In Good King Charles's Golden Days* (1939), G.B.S. would apply to the problem of government the irreconcilability of the saint and the philosopher with the successful practical man. He had dealt with the dilemma before in other ramifications—in the saintly unfrocked priest, Father Keegan of *John Bull's Other Island*; in the Salvation Army's Major Barbara and her armaments-maker father, Andrew Undershaft; and in the heretics, emperors, and warriors of *Androcles and the Lion*. A few years after his King's Hall lecture, preparing what would amount to a preface to the collected edition of his works, he would write that there was "no place in ordinary society for extraordinary individuals. For the worldly wiseman, with common ambitions, the matter is simple enough. . . . But what about people like St Francis and St Clair? Of what use to them are the means to live the life of the country house and the West End mansion? . . . It is true that those who are called saints are not saintly all the time and in everything. In eating and drinking, lodging and sleeping, chatting and playing: in short in everything but working out their destiny as saints, what is good enough for a plowman is good enough for a poet, a philosopher, a saint or a higher mathematician. . . . Besides, to sample society is part of a prophet's business: he must sample the governing class above all. . . . But he can never feel at home in it."

St. Joan, who in her unorthodox way manipulates kings, cardinals, and generals, is then destroyed by coming into conflict with their collective self-interest, and who returns as a saint to ask whether she would now be more welcome and is rejected by a world still unready for her, would become Shaw's classic working out of the theme.

It is assumed erroneously, Shaw told his King's Hall audience,

> that the government should represent the highest thought of the community and should enforce the highest life. It takes people a long time to escape from that error. They ultimately learn, however, that to be governed by a body of great spiritual geniuses who brought all their powers to bear upon the elevation of the race would be intolerable. It would be the worst kind of tyranny. We can get on if we are governed by people a little worse than ourselves, but to be governed by people better than ourselves would be a calamity. . . . How, asked Mr. Shaw, would the audience like to be governed by a man like himself—a person of great spiritual force, of large views, of great genius, and high character? How would they like to be compelled to live in the way he thought good for them? They would not like it at all. They would fall back from him upon the most dastardly politician they could find. The great purpose of democracy is to prevent that calamity. The great purpose of democracy is to prevent your being governed better than you want to be governed.
>
> Even if we granted that the State should be governed by saints and were prepared to accept such rulers, one difficulty still confronts us. Saints cannot be produced to order. . . . There are not enough saints to go round.

One aspect of the problem would be worked out by Shaw in his futuristic fantasy, *The Apple Cart,* and its preface on the inadequacy of choosing a nation's rulers at the ballot box. There the play's Magnus is a Platonic philosopher king who dominates through what Shaw might have labeled spiritual power an elected prime minister and his semi-Socialist cabinet. The "autocratic solution" had its recommendations, he had said in his Fabian lecture. "All autocracies have an element of reality in them which is absent in our pseudo-Democracy. They assume the political incompetence of the man in the street. On the other hand, they assume the political competence of the autocratic or oligarchic ruler; and though this assumption may occasionally have the good luck to be justified by the facts, no means of securing it as a permanent condition have yet been discovered. The Antonine emperors of Rome tried to secure it by adopting their successors.* . . . Napoleon shamelessly fell back on heredity; and heredity is the practical alternative to democracy today. Heredity implies the theorem that one man governs as well as another, provided he is brought up to it. In a sense this is the most democratic of doctrines; and it is far more hopeful and reasonable than the popular quasi-democratic doctrine that every mob can govern, provided it is not brought up to it."

Unquestionably part of Shaw's lecture was sheer devil's advocacy, but he was as serious when he suggested that there be sensible criteria to qualify electors and the electable as he was when later he dramatized his paradoxes about autocracy and democracy in *The Apple Cart, On the Rocks,* and *Good King Charles.*

Shaw's November 30 lecture closing the series was almost anticlimactic after the heresies of "Heredity and Democracy." "The Reconciliation of Uniformity with Diversity" dealt with the redistribution of work and leisure, how an excessively managed society, however efficient, would destroy happiness, and with neo-Bunyan thoughts about "the misery of idleness and the uselessness of leisure." Shaw's trio of "Irish Question" articles had just appeared in the *Express,* and even these had been far overshadowed by the notorious Landsdowne letter that had appeared in the press the day before and that was still causing shock waves. As Shaw put it, "only one statesman saw the danger to his side and caste. . . . He wrote to the *Times* to say 'Stop the War: it had gone far enough.' The *Times,* in one of its occasional fits of lunacy, refused to publish the letter, which appeared at once in the *Morning Post.*† It was denounced as a German Peace Offensive; and the wheels of the war chariot went over old Lord Landsdowne; but he lived to see three more empires crash in the ruin he had tried to avert, and the seats of the mighty occupied everywhere by persons who in his youth could hardly have aspired to black his boots." The fifth Marquess of Landsdowne (1845–1927), a former Foreign Secre-

---

* In *Major Barbara* each Andrew Undershaft adopts a successor (who must be a foundling) to take his name and inherit his industrial empire.

† Actually, the *Daily Telegraph,* on November 29, 1917.

tary and Viceroy of India, had not said anything that others had not said before, but it was an indication of the change in climate that it was now said by a respected Establishment figure. His suggestion was that "an immense stimulus" might be given to the peace advocates in Germany if it were understood that the Allies did not aim at the annihilation of Germany, the ruin of her commerce, or the imposition upon her people of any government not of their own choice; and that the British government was prepared to enter into an international treaty for the settlement of disputes by peaceful means. He was one of those, Landsdowne wrote, "who look forward with horror to the prolongation of the war, who believe that its wanton prolongation would be a crime, differing only in degree from that of the criminals who provoked it. . . ."

From August until mid-November, British casualties in Flanders were 244,897, as a result of which a few miles of churned mud changed hands. Haig's saturation artillery bombardments contributed to the difficulties of his weary troops by making the ground even more impassable and even less worth occupying. The "wearing down" policy, Churchill charged soon afterward in a private memorandum to the War Cabinet, was one of "exchanging lives upon a scale at once more frightful than anything that has been witnessed before in the world, and too modest to produce a decision."

The *Daily Express,* so broad-minded about commissioning Shaw's heterodoxies on Ireland, returned to form the day after the last Shavian article appeared by describing Landsdowne's heresy as a "national misfortune. . . . No wonder that the German newspapers have reprinted Lord Landsdowne's letter and have declared that it is a sign that Great Britain is growing 'reasonable.' "[12] The *Daily Mail* published an abusive editorial headed "The White Flag. *Lord Landsdowne's Surrender,"* while the *Morning Post* observed that "saner people do not disguise their disappointment. . . . The people really pleased are the pacifists. They are dancing a Turkey-trot all over the place." No one in public life had been so vilified by the press since Shaw's *Common Sense about the War* exactly three years before, and in private Shaw was bitter toward men in high places who stubbornly resisted the ideas of those who had followed him as visible spokesmen for reason. At a dinner he gave at Adelphi Terrace for Massingham, he listened to the editor's outrage at the government that had harassed and suppressed his journal* and had called the tune for most of the popular press. Asquith, he declared, was a drunken pantaloon and Lloyd George a counter-jumping swine; and he had other uncomplimentary adjectives for personalities then conducting the war. Shaw added none of his own, although at a dinner not long before he had called Asquith "a drunken old sluggard."[13] He would take out his deeply felt vindictiveness toward both men in a play.

A gentler side of Shaw appeared when he visited Lamer for tea, and remained for the evening, telling bedtime stories to Kathleen Scott's small son. Ever since he was very little, he told Peter Scott, he always told himself a story each night before he went to sleep, some of them continuing as serials over several nights, but his favorite stories he told himself over and over again. After Peter went off to bed and G.B.S. and Lady Scott had dinner, Kathleen offered to give Shaw a dancing lesson, and he glided across the floor with her, pleased with himself. In mid-November, three weeks earlier, he had been to Lamer with Charlotte and the artist pair Ricketts and Shannon, and Kathleen had urged Shaw after dinner to demonstrate his dancing achievements. Charlotte was content to watch, while G.B.S. happily went through his paces. "To begin to learn to dance at sixty-one is rather delicious," Lady Scott wrote in her diary that night. "I love old Shaw."[14]

Early in December when he was rehearsing *The Inca of Perusalem* for its opening at the Criterion Theatre, taking longhand notes in a large spiral notebook and explaining to Randle Ayrton, who played the Inca, how to speak like the Kaiser, a reporter for the New York *Tribune* lay in wait for him. At the first break in which he could draw G.B.S. aside, he queried him about the Landsdowne letter and Shaw's own public statements. "By all means, as Lord Landsdowne says, win your victory if you can," said Shaw. "But the more glory you get by it the more will the glory of a future victory over the victor dazzle the military imagination." Since he expected that "If the Germans win

* The War Office ban on overseas shipment of the *Nation,* in effect since April 5, was not removed until late in October.

they will pocket their winnings; if we win we will pocket ours, in spite of all the philanthropists and Socialists and Stockholm conferences in the world," he forecast that the Allies would have to take on Germany again in due time and would have to be ready for it as long as a League of Nations were unavailable to keep the peace. "From the moment we flinch from this attitude we are beaten morally, and the physical consummation is only a matter of time." It was something Shaw failed to remember when he hobnobbed in the 1930s with the Cliveden Set, which advocated, until it was almost too late to rearm, appeasement of Hitler's Germany.

"Finally, Mr. Shaw," the *Tribune* reporter (F. V. Conolly) flattered, "if the various nations had the excellent sense to appoint you, as a man possessing that extremely rare attribute, common sense, as president of the delegates appointed to discuss peace terms, what proposals for a settlement would you be inclined to propose?" "Place me in the position you describe and I shall, no doubt, make the requisite effort of thought," Shaw said, "but your desire to be amused does not supply pressure enough to nerve me to it." Having brushed aside the question, he then attempted an answer, suggesting that only a stalemate in the field could cause a return to the *status quo ante bellum* until a supernational council could decide the unsettled questions and develop a League of Peace. Both would be opposed, he thought, by those who preferred to negotiate "on the old diplomatic lines, the powers bargaining and buying one another off in the usual way. In fact, this is already the real issue. If the democrats win we may get rid of war. If the diplomatists win, the fight for the balance of power will go on, and the peace they will negotiate will be only the interval between the rounds.

"And it will not be an interval of a century next time."[15]

He went back to his notebook and the rehearsals.

The "almost historical comedietta"—produced by Edith Craig, Ellen Terry's actress daughter—opened on Sunday, December 16, and was distinguished by being one of the rare occasions when both parties in the longest-running paper courtship in the theatre were in each other's presence. It had happened only once before since the war had begun, and then they never spoke to each other. "You looked very nice, and very young at The Inca," Shaw wrote Ellen afterward. "I scan the rising generations of women for another Ellen; but Nature seems really to have broken the mould this time: nobody replaces you in my heart."[16] She was nearly seventy-one.

By the opening of *Inca*, Shaw had finished *Annajanska* and returned the proofs to R. and R. Clark in Edinburgh in time for copies to go to Lillah for rehearsal in January, having added and altered passages to account for the Bolshevik overthrow of the Kerensky regime and revised his transparent pseudonym to "From the Russian of Gregory Biessipoff." He had first identified the author as the even more transparent "G. B. Sipoff." On Christmas Eve he charitably sent Frank Harris a license to publish a long Shavian letter on Oscar Wilde as an appendix to an edition of Harris's life of Wilde. To A. M. Thompson, editor of the pro-war but Socialist *Clarion* to which Shaw had contributed over many years until *Common Sense about the War* had come between them, Shaw answered, just before Christmas, a request that he visit factories to exhort disaffected workers to greater production efforts. Of what use would it be, he wondered, when the *Clarion* had been assuring its readership that he was a pro-German traitor? The *Clarion*, while not reporting his wartime speeches, had abused him with regularity even when the *Express* had not. Tell them, he told Thompson, that it was their duty to exploit their value to the war effort to see that the redistribution of wealth, which was becoming one of the few positive by-products of the war, would not become a casualty of the peace.[17] Having battled almost alone for more than three years of war, Shaw felt few debts to old and estranged allies.

12

Notes from the Madhouse

"My beloved Beo is killed," Stella wrote G.B.S. in the first week of 1918, "—you have seen it in the papers. I feel he is asleep, and will wake and come to me if I am quite strong and calm."[1] Her son, Lieutenant Commander Alan Campbell, had been killed when a shell burst at the entrance to his dugout. Letters from Barrie and Shaw in response to her news illustrated their contrary approaches to the war.

"I am sad that you should have this ordeal to go through," wrote Barrie, who had lost adopted sons in France, "and I wish I knew any way to comfort you. How much rather would you have had this sorrow than never had a son who would go to the war and die fighting gallantly for his country. How good that you have had a son who stood the supreme test of manhood. And in those three years he lived thirty of such lives as mine; he had in them the work he was so fitted to do superlatively well, all the joys that come to most lives that are spread over many years. He died in great honour. Surely you are a proud woman as well as a sad one." And Barrie offered to come to see Stella "any time you want me."[2]

To Shaw she had added that she wanted him to read the letter she had received from the chaplain of his son's unit: "It is full of tragic gentleness and praise of my brave son." The suggestion, on top of the news itself, was more than he could take.

10, Adelphi Terrace, W.C.2.
7th January 1918

Never saw it or heard about it until your letter came.

It is no use: I cant be sympathetic: these things simply make me furious. I want to swear. I *do* swear. Killed just because people are blasted fools. A chaplain, too, to say nice things about it. It is not his business to say nice things about it, but to shout that "the voice of thy son's blood crieth unto God from the ground."

To hell with your chaplain and his tragic gentleness! The next shell will perhaps blow *him* to bits; and some other chaplain will write such a nice letter to *his* mother. Such nice letters! Such nice little notices in papers!

Gratifying, isnt it. Consoling. It only needs a letter from the king to make me feel that the shell was a blessing in disguise.

No: dont show me the letter. But I should very much like to have a nice talk with that dear chaplain, that sweet sky pilot, that—

No use going on like this, Stella. Wait for a week; and then I shall be very clever and broadminded again, and have forgotten all about him. I shall be quite as nice as the chaplain.

Oh damn, damn, damn, damn, damn, damn, damn, damn, DAMN

DAMN!
And oh, dear, dear, dear, dear, dear, dearest!

G.B.S.[3]

The death of Beo was the first of several heartbreaking losses of sons that Shaw shared with their families in the early months of 1918. Distant young cousins had been on the casualty lists since 1915, but the more affecting losses were those whose parents had lived lives intertwined with his. Within the month came the news that Major Robert Gregory, flying for the British in Italy, was dead, and Shaw quickly sent a letter of consolation. "I was hoping for a letter from you," Lady Gregory answered. "I knew it would be helpful." Like Stella she drew a picture from reports she had received of instant and heroic death. "I have been more serene since we have had letters—he was I think happy to the very last—for they were coming back from patrol over the enemy's lines and they say he fainted in the air & never recovered consciousness—here it has taken away the horror. . . . But I have missed already [for] these 2 or 3 years his right judgment & clear thinking & intellectual grip. I am maimed without him."[4]

Robert Gregory (who had thought of himself as a painter) had had an Elizabethan versatility of talent that W. B. Yeats, another writer-friend of his mother, celebrated in several ironic and elegiac poems, notably "In Memory of Major Robert Gregory" and "An Irish Airman Foresees His Death." In Robert Gregory's person in "Airman," Yeats wrote:

> Those that I fight I do not hate,
> Those that I guard I do not love . . .
> Nor law, nor duty bade me fight,
> Nor public men, nor cheering crowds,
> A lonely impulse of delight
> Drove to this tumult in the clouds;
> I balanced all, brought all to mind,
> The years to come seemed waste of breath,
> A waste of breath the years behind
> In balance with this life, this death.

Neither Yeats, nor Shaw, nor Lady Gregory, apparently, ever knew that the young man they mourned had been shot down in error by an Italian pilot.

One of Shaw's oldest friends, drama critic and Ibsen translator William Archer, became another of the bereaved. His only son, whom Shaw had called from childhood "Tomarcher," had rushed home from a law firm in America to become a lance corporal and at the Messines Ridge was severely wounded. After he recovered he returned as a lieutenant, and while on leave in February 1918 married a cousin of a comrade who had fallen at Messines. "Then," Shaw wrote, "the war still dragging on, he hurled himself into the gulf again; and this time, at Mount Kemmel, it closed on him, and his father saw him no more. He left his young widow. . . ." Later it was discovered that he had died in a German hospital and was buried at Courtrai. "Yet Archer was loth to let the son go. He renewed an old interest in super-rational research . . . and even experimented unsuccessfully in those posthumous conversations in which so many of the bereaved found comfort."[5] Archer, meanwhile, continued the militant propaganda work for the government that had become his full-time occupation in 1914. When the French, at Haig's pleading, took over seven miles of front from the beleaguered British, it took them only two hours to lose Mount Kemmel to the Germans.

Another kind of casualty was Kathleen Scott, who had fallen ill from overwork, having often stayed at her desk at the Ministry of Pensions far into each evening. On January 8, G.B.S. came to visit and remained for a long time at her bed, returning two days later, after which she was well enough to note in her diary, "Still in bed, fainting a good deal. Bernard Shaw came, and we discussed dreams, deliriums, and happiness."[6] The rehearsals for *Annajanska* on the 9th and 10th had kept him in London, Shaw sitting through them with his notebook and making as meticulous an appraisal as he would have done for a longer and more serious play. They also kept him in London for the end of the fracas over a clumsy bureaucratic attempt to pre-empt Shaw's university, the British Museum, for war purposes. He had, shortly before, written a preface to the *Workers Educational Association Yearbook* for 1918 in which he condemned the "astounding" cultural ignorance of the governing classes exposed by the war. After a recital of revealing incidents, from the country houses to the cities, he came to his most conclusive example.

We have seen, even as I write, a gentleman who was appointed to control the Air Service because his brother is a rich newspaper proprietor beginning [his duties] by making a speech in which he described his own official business as murder . . . and following this up by demanding that the British Museum be cleared out to make room for him and his staff.

He did not ask for Westminster Abbey to store petrol in; but it can hardly have been any cultural consideration that hindered him. And the working classes can hardly reproach him after handing over Ruskin College for war purposes with an alacrity which suggested that they were glad of an excuse to get rid of it.*

Not finished with Lord Rothermere, Shaw accused him in the *Nation* of conceiving the British Museum as "a comfortable place for his armchair and Turkey carpet," and went on to describe his brother, *Daily Mail* proprietor Lord Northcliffe, as one who "makes and unmakes ministers and commanders as Warwick made and unmade kings" and "establishes his brother, in the middle of an epoch-making war as chief of a national service on which our fate in the war will probably depend, without having to offer the public the smallest evidence that the said brother is capable of conducting a whelk-stall successfully."[7] The *Nation's* circulation was small but select, and the indictment did the new Air Minister no good in London.

There were other protests, including one in the *Daily Telegraph* by Charles Ricketts, and when the Cabinet could no longer count on public apathy, Lord Curzon initiated a motion to drop the idea of moving the Air Board into the British Museum. After a short but decent interval, Secretary of State for Air Lord Rothermere quietly resigned.

The major alteration in Shaw's own life early in 1918 was the loss of his secretary, Ann Elder, who took a job with the Theosophical Society and left her sister-in-law, a Mrs. Elder, to cope with Shaw's shorthand. She had never before handled a typewriter and had a shorthand expertise of three weeks. It complicated Shaw's letters as well as his literary production, but it was not apparent from what actually appeared in print, for lengthy pieces written long before

---

* Ruskin College, Oxford, established for the education of the children of workingmen, closed its doors early in the war, its Executive Committee announcing in the *Times* of September 15, 1914, that "owing to the war, the college shall not be open for resident students during the session 1914–15, and that the college shall be offered to the Government for hospital purposes." (It did continue its correspondence department.)

were then appearing, particularly his four-part series in the *English Review*, "What is to be done with the Doctors?" The first part had been published in December, and the last would appear in March, a book-length* polemic on medicine as a "professional conspiracy" to suppress, out of self-interest, a public medical service. Although such of his doctor-friends as Colonel Sir Almroth Wright were serving in France, Shaw suggested that whatever the military operations of Field Marshal Hindenburg had left of the British Army the operations of its own medical staff would wipe out. A storm of abuse descended on Shaw in angry letters to the editor and in angrier private letters to him at home. It was hardly worse than what Siegfried Sassoon, a young officer at the front, had published in a poem entitled "The General," which closed,

> "He's a cheery old card," grunted Harry to Jack
> As they slogged up to Arras with rifle and pack....
> But he did for them both by his plan of attack.†

"Fortunately," Shaw wrote about military medicine, "nothing is more false than the proverb that when doctors differ patients die. On the contrary, when doctors differ wounded soldiers get well. . . . When doctors agree we are face to face with a conspiracy of pretentious ignorance. . . . As long as we are fools enough to make healing and hygiene a matter of commerce . . . serve us right!"[8]

On January 12 he published "The Falling Market in War Aims" in the *Daily Chronicle*, an examination of the growing realization that peace aims were as necessary as war aims, but that they were unlikely to be realized unless neither side won the war. An imposed peace, he thought, would not last. He also went off to the law courts and spoke to a student debating society in the common room of the Middle

---

* It became the major section of a weak patchwork book in the later collected edition, *Doctors' Delusions, Sham Education and Crude Criminology*.

† Winston Churchill was quoted afterward as saying, "In the recent war we politicians had only two duties. The one was to persuade our admirals to put to sea, the other to persuade our generals to stop killing their own men. In both we were quite unsuccessful" (C. M. Bowra, *Memories* [London, 1966], p. 205).

Temple. Preceding G.B.S. was the formal debate "that the solution of the Irish problem is Home Rule for England." For the *Nation* he reviewed Hilaire Belloc's pamphlet, *The Free Press,* declaring that "It takes a very hardy constitution to stand the truth" and that Englishmen were "between the nether millstone of the press that is too poor to tell the truth and the upper one of the press that is too rich." For the March *Eton Review*—unlikeliest of all places for a piece by G.B.S. to appear—he contributed an article on the Etonian "as others see him," ridiculing the tradition of "the ugly Penguin costume" of school dress. He also found time to produce a wry *Daily Chronicle* piece on a favorite subject, his ascetic diet, beginning, "It is my patriotic boast that from the day the war began until the present hour I have abstained rigidly from consuming flesh, fish, fowl, alcohol and tobacco. These envious detractors whose yelp follows every utterance of mine like an obscene echo, have objected that as I had abstained equally for the 33 years preceding the war, I deserve no credit for my conduct. This is obvious nonsense. . . ." If he could not urge life without mean and artificial stimulants upon Englishmen on patriotic motives, he had another approach in his closing paragraph. "Think of the fierce energy concentrated in an acorn! You bury it in the ground and it explodes into a giant oak. Bury a sheep and nothing happens but decay."[9]

It was an amiable piece, suggesting a kind of personal and professional contentment he had not evidenced in the earlier years of the war. He found it, for example, difficult to be angry with Lillah McCarthy for having botched her producer's role in *Annajanska* to such an extent that—having ignored Shaw's advice on contract terms—she, rather than the theatre, had to pay Shaw's author's fee of £50 a week and Charles Ricketts's designer's fee besides. For the first three weeks of the run, Lillah sent Shaw a check for £150, and Shaw wrote to Ricketts on February 6, "I propose that we share this and take £75 apiece. This is not so fair as it looks as I have a continuing interest in the play. But it seems the most natural way of settling it." His public reputation as a hard bargainer belied his private one, but he enjoyed his newspaper role as one who squeezed the last penny in the pound out of producers and publishers.

"I should have written before," Shaw added to Ricketts, "but I have been knocked out for a week by ptomaine poisoning and a fall on my precious head down a flight of stairs—a form of exercise which I have somewhat outgrown. Therefore, now that I have got over it I find that it has bucked me up remarkably; and the bumps on my head are taken for intellect."[10] What had happened to him is that a hostess solicitous of his vegetarianism had served him liberally of a wartime compound supposed to be synthetic egg, and Shaw had reacted to an overdose of the phosphorus in it. The aftermath was "intoxication and colic and horror," in the process of which he fell down the stairs and injured his head so severely that he had to lie still for several days, his activity restricted to reading in bed an American author he had heard of but not read—O. Henry. He found him a first-class storyteller.

Before long, his head swathed in gauze, he was up and again active in attempts to broaden the base of antiwar feeling, which often meant turning the younger generation from being merely anti-conscription to being positive about peace strategy and aims. Not everyone considered the search for reconciliation a betrayal of the dead, particularly some of those who felt they were next in line for a headstone in Flanders. One of them was a young officer named Osbert Sitwell, who when previously in London had read his *Telegraph* and rushed to the Guards Club to write a letter to Lord Lansdowne congratulating him on his courage. The man in public life Sitwell admired most for his courage at the time was G.B.S.—"almost the only famous writer who at this time did not betray truth, reason, and his contemporaries and juniors in order to march with the band." One Sunday evening that winter* he had his first opportunity to meet Shaw, at a dinner given by H. W. Nevinson and Massingham, to whose *Nation* Sitwell had begun submitting pseudonymous satirical poems signed "Miles":

I was twenty-four now, and still unused to meeting men of Shaw's genius. It seemed to me the culmination of all for which one could hope. The rest of us waited in the hall at Romano's until the great playwright

---

* Sitwell recalled the incident as happening in the autumn of 1917, but the context makes it clear that it should have been dated *after* Shaw's accident.

made his appearance, a few minutes late. He entered, a tall figure, broad-shouldered, with . . . easy, loose-limbed gait . . . and in his usual warm, rough suit, while, in addition, and rather unexpectedly, a white bandage encircled the crown of his head. I had never seen Shaw previously, though of course I knew him well through photographs, paintings, and busts: but I had been unprepared for his genial presence, his fine manners, his great stature, and his typical Irish voice, generous and compelling. In spite of this last attribute, which should call out a responding fire in others, when we had gone upstairs and sat down at our table in the gallery, I remained for long mute, bound fast with wonder—with wonder, but not with awe: for Shaw's natural courtesy would have put anyone younger and less celebrated than himself at his ease. Merely, I wanted to listen, not to talk. He spoke much that evening of the great Duke of Wellington, a fellow countryman in whose exploits and conversation he had always been greatly interested: he told us the story of how, on one occasion, when the Duke was asked by an admirer, "How did you really manage to beat Napoleon?" he replied simply, "Well I'll tell you. Bonaparte's plans were made in wire, mine were made in string"—a very good simile to convey strategic flexibility to a lay mind.* When there came a silence, I had mustered sufficient confidence to say something. My eyes reverted to the great man's bandage: it worried my curiosity.

"I'm sorry, Mr. Shaw," I observed, "to see you've hurt yourself: I hope not badly?"

"Well, you see," Shaw told the young man with mock solemnity, "I'm a teetotaler, and my wife got in a new kind of nonalcoholic drink for me to try. As soon as I had the first glass, I became intoxicated, and in going downstairs, fell and cut my head open!"

Sitwell accepted the account, thinking however, what "a feeling of relief" it had been that evening "to find people in whose presence any idea, whether original or conventional, whether accepted or rejected by the world, whether condemned or derided, or praised, could be discussed on its own merits, without anger. This, though an at-

* Speaking of the French Marshals, Wellington had once said, "They planned their campaigns just as you might make a splendid set of harness. It looks very well, and answers very well, until it gets broken; and then you are done for. Now *I* made my campaigns of ropes. If anything went wrong, I tied a knot; and went on."

mosphere entirely new to me, after my upbringing, and in the environment I had so far known, was one, withal, in which I felt immediately at home."[11]

In February Bertrand Russell, who had already been expelled from his lectureship at Trinity College, Cambridge, because of his pacifist activities, had been arrested for publishing, in the pacifist journal *Tribunal*, an article that argued for a negotiated peace that included not only Germany and Austria, but that Allied outcast, Lenin's Russia. He had long been in danger of prosecution for his outspoken views on conscription and war aims, but when the actual moment came the intellectual community reacted either by paralysis or by sending him letters applauding his courage, one from E. M. Foster informing him, "In the middle of a six course dinner at the Club last night I was told that you were in prison. This is to send you my love. I suppose they will let you have it when you come out."[12] As the case dragged on, a young Fabian schoolteacher admirer of Russell's who had already lost her fiancé in France appealed to Shaw for help. Shaw's reaction, as in the much more serious case of Roger Casement, was to recommend that the accused, clearly more intelligent than his lawyers, should plead his own case, and as he had done in the affair of Sir Roger, he offered a draft defense through Dorothy Mackenzie:

Russell is not an imbecile who cannot defend himself. He is not a poor man who cannot afford a strong bar. He is practically a nobleman with a tremendous family record on the Whig side as a hereditary defender of popular liberties. . . . The only matter that is really in doubt is whether Russell should conduct his own case or employ counsel. In his place I should unhesitatingly do the job myself. A barrister will put up some superficially ingenious plea which will give him a good professional chance of shewing off before the Court of Appeal, one which will not compromise him by any suspicion of sympathy with Russell's views, and the failure of which will be a foregone conclusion. Russell will have no preoccupations of that sort; and he can, as an amateur, take liberties with court procedure which a barrister cannot. He is accustomed to public speaking, and therefore not under the necessity of getting another man to speak for him simply through nervousness and inexperience.

His case is not by any means a weak one. . . . The war is full of ironies: the belligerents claiming to be the defenders of liberties which they have all been engaged at one time or another in vigorously suppressing. . . . All these ironies have been pointed out again and again in the bitterest terms by philosophic journalists, except the last which Russell was the first to hint at very mildly in *The Tribunal.* Immediately some foolish censor, knowing nothing about irony or history or anything else except the rule of thumb of his department, pounces on the allusion as something that has not been passed before, and therefore must be challenged.

But the main point is that if Russell, in spite of his social and academic position, is to be savagely punished for writing about the war as a Pacifist and a philosopher, the intimidation of the Press will be carried thereby to a point in England which it has not yet attained in Germany or Austria; and if it be really an advantage to be a free country, that advantage will go to Germany. We are claiming the support of the world in this war solely on the ground that we represent Liberal institutions, and that our enemies represent despotic ones. The enemy retorts that we are the most formidable and arbitrary Empire on the face of the earth; and there is so much to be said for this view in consequence of our former conquests that American and Russian public opinion is sorely perplexed about us. Russell can say, "If you like to persecute me for my Liberal opinions, persecute away and be damned: I am not the first of my family to suffer in that good cause; but if you have any regard for the solidarity of the Alliance, you will take care to proclaim to the world that England is still the place where a man can say the thing he will &c. (peroration ad lib.)."

This is the best advice I can give in the matter as Russell's friend.[13]

By April it was clear to Shaw that Russell saw no way to legally escape prison and had no desire to awaken the kind of vindictiveness in a judge that would not only gain him headlines in the press but extra time in jail. But having failed with Casement, G.B.S. tried again:

I have an uneasy feeling that you will take legal advice on Wednesday, and go into prison for six months for the sake of allowing your advocate to make a favourable impression on the bench by advancing some ingenious defence, long since worn out in the service of innumerable pickpockets, which they will be able to dismiss (with a compliment to the bar) with owl-like gravity.

I see nothing for it but to make a scene by refusing indignantly to offer any defence at all of a statement that any man in a free country has a perfect right to make, and declaring that as you are not an unknown person, and your case will be reported in every capital from San Francisco east to Tokyo, and will be taken as the measure of England's notion of the liberty she professes to be fighting for, you leave it to the good sense of the bench to save the reputation of the country from the folly of its discredited and panic stricken Government. Or words to that effect. You will gain nothing by being considerate, and (unlike a barrister) lose nothing by remembering that a cat may look at a king, and, *a fortiori*, a philosopher at a judge.

G.B.S.[14]

Russell spent almost all that was left of the war in Brixton Prison.

Early in May G.B.S. was the featured speaker at the annual meeting of the Society of Authors in Central Hall, Westminster, a sign that his heresy was becoming more tolerable or that he was too internationally visible to be cut down as was Bertrand Russell. It was a professional meeting, and he remained in tune with professional problems, pointing out the economic straits of authors whose works were going out of print or were not being published because of wartime shortages of paper. One of his own productions, "of the greatest value to society at the present moment," he claimed, could not be got out in proper form for the want of paper. Yet for any other purpose than literature there appeared to be an unbounded supply, evidence to him that the "practical businessmen" who ran the war on the home front were culturally illiterate, unconscious of the importance of the intellectual life of the community, and ready to sacrifice education or literature for any immediate war purpose. Canon A. C. Deane, the chairman, followed by suggesting that the Society of Authors impress upon the government that literature was not a luxury at any time, least of all in wartime, and that fact had been obvious ever since the early months of the war when publishers had timidly and mistakenly canceled books for which they thought there would be no sale. There had never been such a demand for reading matter, but unfortunately never had the quality denominator been so low.[15]

Also in May Shaw gave one of the longest speeches of his life, one that he had taken great pains to prepare. The Fabian Society, in the midst of arranging closer ties with the Labour Party, had presented three lectures on "The Labour Party; Its Programme and Its Possibilities"—by Arthur Henderson, Sidney Webb, and G.B.S.—at King's Hall, Covent Garden. Shaw's was the final offering, on May 10. "The Climate and Soil for Labour Culture," ran to fifty-seven typed pages, pointing out the war-enhanced potential for political change and going beyond to matters more philosophical and futuristic. "When we are told that Europe has been in Hell since August 1914," he told his audience, "we who are Socialists and know the truth, must answer, 'Do you suppose it was Paradise in 1913?'" It was his rallying cry for the postwar era of reconstruction, but he was then more interested in religion than in socialism, telling Fabians and Labourites that their task would not be "passing this measure or that for the immediate relief of the poor," or to be negative in a Tory regime, or to seek quick and peaceful revolution within the system. "You cannot overthrow the Church of England or any other Church by simply putting out your tongue at it. If you ask a man to come out of it, he will refuse until he finds another lodging for his soul; and if that lodging is either some conventicle ten times more narrow and stifling and ugly than the Church, or some Secularist Hall where nothing of the Church teaching is discarded except faith in miracles, and the Individualism and Materialism which is only the Old Testament half of the Church doctrine is made the whole duty of Man, you will have taken your proselyte farther from Socialism instead of nearer to it."[16]

Shaw had been working on that lodging for the soul, a dramatic parable of what he called creative evolution; he had done so quietly, however, unsure of the direction it would take. Man, he was convinced, not only needed a more honest and relevant religion; he needed to live long enough to learn from his many mistakes. As he wrote afterward in the preface to the dramatic cycle that resulted, "All that is necessary to make him extend his present [life] span is that tremendous catastrophes such as the late war shall convince him of the necessity of at least outliving his taste for golf and cigars if the race is to be saved. This is not fantastic speculation: it is deductive biology, if there is such a science as biology. . . . To make the suggestion more entertaining than it would be to most people in the form of a biological treatise, I have written *Back to Methuselah* as a contribution to the modern Bible."

One of the earliest indications that he had been working on a major new work came when Charles Ricketts met Shaw on the day before his King's Hall speech. They were on the stairs, leaving the music room at Mrs. Lee Mathews's house, when G.B.S. stopped and said with apparent irony, "Tell me, is the war inspiring you? Are you doing big things?"

"No, my dear chap," said Ricketts. "It is a nightmare, a bore. I view it as I would an earthquake."

"I am like you," said Shaw, confiding that any attempt on his part to find creative inspiration in the war had been disastrous.

Politely Ricketts rationalized their different problems. "But in your case it might not have been so, your work is in touch with reality, mine as a painter is in a backwater; for years I have absorbed only what interested me, or was needful to my work. Were I young, I might respond to events, but I am too old by this time: if I did, it would be too late, life is too short."

"Curious," said Shaw; "I am at work on that subject—the shortness of life. I deal with the future, the secret of longevity has been discovered, men have time for adventure, discovery, and work. There are very funny things: my hero, or one of them, is a survivor in the Colonies from our times; he hates all he sees, yet people are kind to him, he is given a home as he is unable to fend for himself; he takes up a sheet of notepaper to write to his wife, and discovers from it he is in a madhouse."*

As they continued down the stairs Ricketts added, "Life is too short, I wonder if time slows down later?"

---

* In A.D. 2170 (part III of the cycle) Englishmen actually select their parliamentary candidates from the lunatic asylums and rely on the efficiency of an industrious civil service run by Chinese. "The English always did elect parliaments of lunatics," says the presidential secretary, Confucius. "What does it matter if your permanent officials are honest and competent?"

"Yes, I think it does," said Shaw. "I am sixty-one, and feel from time to time that bland sensation one experiences in autumn afternoons—one becomes a spectator as one was in childhood."[17]

Much altered as he worked, the play Shaw described on that May afternoon would become the fourth part of what he later called his "metabiological pentateuch," *The Tragedy of An Elderly Gentleman.*

13

Back to Methuselah

Born of war, *Back to Methuselah* is a mirror of the 1914–18 experience, the major theme having already been struck in the unforgotten *Common Sense about the War.* The danger to the general improvement of the human condition through science, Shaw had warned, was "the danger created by inventing weapons capable of destroying civilization faster than we produce men who can be trusted to use them wisely. At present we are handling them like children. Now children are very pretty, very lovable, very affectionate creatures (sometimes); and a child can make nitro-glycerine or chloride of nitrogen as well as a man if it is taught to do so. We have sense enough not to teach it; but we do so. We have sense enough not to teach it; but we do teach the grown-up children." Further, the war had convinced Shaw, as was clear from lines he had given Hector in *Heartbreak House,* that if man failed to heed "Heaven's threatening growl of disgust at us useless, futile creatures . . . one of two things must happen. Either out of that darkness some new creation will come to supplant us as we have supplanted the animals, or the heavens will fall in thunder and destroy us."

The intellectual base for the cycle had been laid as early as 1906 in a lecture for the Fabians on Darwin and evolution, and in 1912, in a lecture called "Modern Religion"[1] in which Shaw had already concluded,

> We have to face the fact that we are a very poor lot. Yet we must be the best that God can as yet do, else he would have done something better. . . . Modern science shows that life began in a small, feeble, curious, blind sort of way as a speck of protoplasm, that, owing to some sort of will in this, some curious driving power, always making for higher organisms, gradually that little thing, constantly trying and wanting, having the purpose in itself, being itself a product of that purpose, has by mere force of wanting and striving to be something higher, gradually, curiously, miraculously, continually evolved a series of beings each of which evolved something higher than itself. What you call evil is nothing but imperfection. . . .

Man, Shaw went on, was not the fulfillment of purpose in the universe, but the way that purpose did its work, and man's mission in life was "simply to help on the purpose of the universe. By higher and higher organization man must become superman, and superman super-superman, and so on." He had an answer, too, for the obvious question as to where it would all end. "There need be no end. There is no reason why the process should ever stop, since it has proceeded so far. But it must achieve on its infinite way the production of some being, some person if you like, who will be strong and wise, with a mind capable of comprehending the whole universe and with powers capable of executing its entire will—in other words, an omnipotent and benevolent God."*

War and the mood of despair that enveloped Shaw during its first years tested his personal religious faith more severely than had

---

* The two lectures, March 23, 1906, and March 21, 1912, each an extension of ideas dramatized in the "Don Juan in Hell" scene of *Man and Superman* (1903), were heavily borrowed from for Shaw's 1921 preface to *Back to Methuselah*.

anything else in his life. Creatively, the first result of that inward crisis had been *Heartbreak House*. *Back to Methuselah*, begun in reaction to his own play, was his attempt to keep from falling into "the bottomless pit of an utterly discouraging pessimism." It took all of his resources, as he drew imaginatively upon Genesis, Plato, Swift, Wagner, Ibsen, and dozens of other sources,[2] including the war in progress, to create a parable that was his vision of life as it was and as it might be. Originally it was to be a huge work in four parts, playable, like *Man and Superman*, over a single evening, but by July 25, 1918, he was writing to Major Robert Loraine (about whom as "next of kin" he had just received another wounded-in-action telegram), "I have written a play with intervals of thousands of years (in the future) between the acts; but now I find I must make each act into a full-length play. And this is the time you select to stop another bullet! The devil take the war!"[3]

War proved a grimly useful and omnipresent touchstone to validate Shaw's thesis about the need to find new directions by which to achieve the age-old goals of bettering the human condition in the race between Utopia and catastrophe. It became one of the chief motifs in the long work, appearing in all five plays in the cycle, the first four of which were all either underway or completed in first draft before the war had ended. Only *As Far as Thought Can Reach* was not begun until after the war. Shaw's original intention had been to create "a huge tetralogy, like Wagner's Ring."[4] A 1920 afterthought, the fifth and most futuristic play was begun on March 16 and completed in London on May 27.

An unlikely motif for a play set in the Garden of Eden, war is part of the universal irony Shaw sets out to elucidate, for without death there is no dynamism. *In the Beginning*, based on Genesis yet like a medieval morality play, is one of Shaw's most poetic and most profound dramatic works, one that has not yet found its time. It is Shaw's answer to John Milton's *Paradise Lost*, which he described through the Devil in "Don Juan in Hell" as written by a fool of an Englishman who "described me as being expelled from Heaven by cannons and gunpowder; and to this day every Briton believes that the whole of his silly story is in the Bible. What else he says I do not know; for it is all in a long poem which neither I nor anyone else ever succeeded in wading through."

The temptation of Eve takes up the first act of the play, with Adam, Eve, and the Serpent the only characters. The conflict is that between Adam, who discovers (through the accidental death of a fawn) a way of escaping burdensome immortality, and Eve, who seeks to prevent extinction of the human species. The Serpent has the answer—that "imagination is the beginning of creation. You imagine what you desire; you will what you imagine; and at last you create what you will." Eve asks for one word to encompass it all, and the Serpent responds with "to conceive. That is the word that means both the beginning in imagination and the end in creation." When Eve seeks the secret of creation, and the Serpent whispers it to her, *"Eve's face lights up with intense interest, which increases until an expression of overwhelming repugnance takes its place. She buries her face in her hands."* The result, however, is Cain, the first aspiring Superman.

"Anybody," Cain jeers at his father, "could be the first man: it is as easy as to be the first cabbage. To be the first murderer one must be a man of spirit." Thus when the second act opens *"a few centuries later,"* we have on the scene what has been called "the first military aristocrat . . . the Superman of this society: he is a romantically dashing figure, full of high spirits and vaunting bravado, who has been goaded by his mother's discontent with his stick-in-the-mud father to surpass his parents. In doing so he has introduced first murder, then organized warfare, and finally exploitation and slavery into the social system. In the name of progress he has instituted class privileges, ostentatious wealth, passionate love, luxurious idleness for spoiled wives, and a penchant for blood sports, and in the process developed a contempt for his father's manual labor as beneath the dignity of a landowning fighter. . . . Shaw in creating Cain, presumably had in mind feudal Europe as it existed in its prime from Charlemagne to Richard III. . . . But Shaw did not see Cain simply as a social anachronism. What Shaw elsewhere calls the Junker spirit was not totally dead in 1914—it lingered on. . . ."

Afterward Shaw made it clear that he had exactly this in mind, by advising the actor who created the role to play it "in quite a modern vein, with the high-pitch and haw-haw of a stage cavalry officer, and with conceited superiority and self-satisfaction. He is not a savage."[5]

The Prussian Cain defends the murder of his sensitive and peace-loving brother Abel with the clichés of extreme Junker militarism. He tells Adam, "He who has never fought has never lived. He was not my keeper any more than I was his: why did he not kill me? There was no more to prevent him than there was to prevent me: it was man to man; and I won. I was the first conqueror. . . . Without danger I cannot be great. . . . Danger and fear follow my footsteps everywhere. Without them courage would have no sense. And it is courage, courage, courage, that rises the blood of life to crimson splendor. . . . Death is not really death . . . it is the gate of another life: a life infinitely splendid and intense: a life of the soul alone. . . ."

Eve castigates him as anti-man when he comes to her with "your stupid fighting and destroying, and your foolish boasting; and you want me to tell you that it is all splendid, and that you are heroic, and that nothing but death or the dread of death makes life worth living." Death plays its part in life, Cain insists. The terror of eternity is too great a burden to bear, as his father, who formulated the concept, should understand. "But if you invented death, why do you blame me who am a minister of death?"

Too weary to cope with Cain, Adam leaves the last words to his wife. "Through him and his like," Eve understands, "death is gaining on life. Already most of our grandchildren die before they have sense enough to know how to live. . . . Man need not always live by bread alone. There is something else. We do not yet know what it is; but some day we shall find out; and then we will live on that alone; and there shall be no more digging nor spinning, nor fighting nor killing."

Shaw had the tetralogy (as it was then) roughed out by the summer of 1918, but the first public reading of *In the Beginning* took place at the Fabian Summer School in 1919. Act I was completed in final form on February 14, and Act II on February 23, in 1919. No beginning date appears on the manuscript. Afterward Shaw wrote the Theatre Guild's Lawrence Langner about the first reading of *In the Beginning* in terms of that event. "As to the first play," he told Langner in 1921, "it produced such an astonishing effect when I read it to an audience consisting mostly of women that I never ventured on the experiment again. . . . I assure you it *can* explode with shattering consequences."[6] The audience, if largely composed of women, almost certainly included many whose fathers, husbands, brothers, and sons had, in the previous four years, met sudden and violent death. To such an audience of Eves, *In the Beginning* had to have been a shattering experience.

Later when the play was in print Shaw's old friend and critical adversary, Max Beerbohm, would write him that posterity would consider *In the Beginning* the best thing Shaw had ever done, and that the first Adam and Eve scene possessed high imagination and thrilling and tender beauty. "You must be glad and grateful that it has been reserved for you to do at your age. . . ."

The first portion of the play Shaw had begun was the most contemporary one, set "in the first years after the war." *The Gospel of the Brothers Barnabas*, intended to be second in the sequence, had been begun at Ayot on March 19, 1918, and was completed on April 9, with revision started on May 1. It would be the only part with a country house setting, establishing its continuity with *Heartbreak House*; the Barnabas house can be thought of as cultured, leisured England *after* the war in the way that *Heartbreak House* had represented that society on the eve of war; it can also be thought of as Shaw's bitter commentary on the catastrophe the inhabitants of Heartbreak House proved unable to prevent and in which they took perverse joy. "A world without conscience," observes Franklyn Barnabas, "That is the horror of our condition." One did not live long enough, Shaw thought—and Franklyn is Bernard Shaw's spokesman in the play—to develop a well-tempered conscience.

Despite revision throughout the year, including a change in title from the provisional "The Adelphians," he remained dissatisfied

with the play and tinkered with it, adding postwar details right up
to the time of its first production in 1921; but toward the end of
1918 he felt it was ready to be unveiled to friends, and after a reading in the now rare presence of Barker and his new wife, the atmosphere tense with everyone's unspoken awareness of Helen's hostility
toward Shaw, G.B.S. apologized that the play had never seemed so
tedious to him before. He was "bored by the Brothers Barnabas . . ."
he confessed.

I shall have to get the picture better composed; but I don't think it
will come to a Socratic dialogue pure and simple. The idea is not to get
comic relief (they are not really comic, if you come to that); but to ex-
hibit the Church, marriage, the family, and parliament under shorthand
conditions before reproducing them under long-lived conditions. The
stuttering rector develops [in the next, and futuristic, play] into an im-
moral archbishop and the housemaid into a Minister of Public Something
or other. . . . To this end I may have to disregard the boredom of the
spectator who has not mastered all the motifs, as Wagner had to do; but
I daresay I shall manage to make the people more amusing, some of them
more poetic, and all of them more intelligible than they now are in this
first draft.

A surprising admission followed, suggesting that Shaw had read
the play earlier in the presence of the deposed (and in G.B.S.'s case,
despised) Prime Minister. "The girl who jars on her father (and
you)," he wrote Barker, "justified herself by jarring very surprisingly
on Asquith."[7] If the final version of the play is any clue at all, any other
reaction on Asquith's part would have been surprising. "The girl"—
Franklyn's daughter Savvy—is an early flapper type, high-spirited,
frank, unconventional, and almost certainly (since Shaw afterward
confessed as much) a newer-generation version of Margot Tennant,
the ambitious, sharp-tongued, convention-defying, and flirtatious
second wife of the widowed Prime Minister, who married her the
year after she had achieved literary notoriety. (In 1893 E. F. Benson,
son of the Archbishop of Canterbury, had made her the heroine of
his best-selling society satire, *Dodo*.) Another character in the
play must have jarred even more, for the two political leaders caricatured are recognizable to the point of questionable taste, one of

them an urbane and amiable former Prime Minister named Henry Hopkins Lubin (with a politically tenacious wife named Mimi), born in the same year as H. H. Asquith. The other, and first on-stage, happens to have a birth date coincident with that of Asquith's demagogic successor, Lloyd George. He is Joyce Burge, characterized by the Brothers Barnabas as a man who "has talked so much that he has lost the power of listening" and one of the cynical party politicians who "have managed to kill half Europe between them."

Stage directions provide a vivid description of Lloyd George—"a well-fed man turned fifty, with a broad forehead, and grey hair which, his neck being short, falls almost to his collar." Even more vividly, and libellously were it not scandalously true, is the description of him as having "a reputation as a profligate," something the accuser—and thus Shaw—quickly and carefully withdraws in a way to force Joyce Burge's realistic response, "You are destroying my character in the act of pretending to save it." (Later, defending his portrayal, Shaw wrote to the *Times*, "My play, as far as it goes outside the public history of public men, contains not a word against the private honour of any living person. . . ."[8]) Accused of lack of principle in heading a government "formed largely of men who regarded you as a robber of henroosts, and whom you regarded as enemies of the people," Joyce Burge counters with his usual sentimental eloquence, "The Hun was at the gate," a line from Kipling's 1914 "For All We Have and Are," often quoted in patriotic oratory during the war. "Our country, our lives, the honor of our wives and mothers and daughters, the tender flesh of our innocent babes, were at stake. Was that a time to argue about principle?" Further, he argues, recalling to us the fact that Lloyd George's early wartime reputation was made by the scandal of a shortage of shells and his overhaul of the lagging munitions industry, "It wasnt principle that won the war: it was the British fleet and the blockade. America found the talk: I found the shells. You cannot win wars by principles; but you *can* win elections by them."

What Shaw had captured was the essential Lloyd George. "England has scarcely known a greater demagogue," George Dangerfield has written in *The Strange Death of Liberal England* (1936). "His face, in its rare moments of repose, was elfin and commonplace, like a Barrie play: animated, it was something between an incomparable drama and a high-class vaudeville act. It was tragic, and sorrowful, and charming and comic by turns; it was lofty and it was low: emotions chased themselves across it like wind across a rain puddle, breaking it up into a hundred images. Without the magic of face and voice to support them, his speeches are not likely to survive; and one can only imagine the effect." A half-century later a critic would write that in performance the play could "send our eyebrows shooting up at such fearfully outspoken portraits of what were, when the play was written, living politicians. . . ."[9]

Franklyn's accusation that a politician's chief aims are to gain, and remain in, power, recalls Shaw's accusation, in his 1915 interview with Senator Beveridge, about Asquith:

> FRANKLYN. When the terrible impact of real warfare swept your parliamentary sham warfare into the dustbin, you had to go behind the backs of your followers and make a secret agreement with the leaders of the Opposition to keep you in power on condition that you dropped all legislation of which they did not approve. And you could not even hold them to their bargain; for they presently betrayed the secret and forced the coalition on you.
> BURGE. I solemnly declare that this is a false and monstrous accusation.
> FRANKLYN. Do you deny that the thing occurred? Were the uncontradicted reports false? Were the published letters forgeries?
> BURGE. Certainly not. But *I* did not do it. I was not Prime Minister then. It was that old dotard, that played-out old humbug Lubin. He was Prime Minister then, not I.

Joyce Burge is, of course, correct. It was Asquith, not Lloyd George, who had made the deal, and on his entry Lubin (Asquith) confirms all the allegations against him, and more. He admits his hostility to the suffragettes, who often "had to be carried out kicking and making a horrid disturbance" when they attempted to petition him, and confesses the truth of an accusation made against him in 1916, when his overthrow was plotted, that he busied himself playing bridge with three ladies throughout a working Monday, while Bonar Law tried vainly to see him on business:

> BURGE. I wish youd be serious, Lubin. God knows we have passed through times terrible enough to make any man serious.
>
> LUBIN. I do not think I need to be reminded of that. In peace time I used to keep myself fresh for my work by banishing all worldly considerations from my mind on Sundays; but war has no respect for the Sabbath; and there have been Sundays within the last few years on which I have had to play as many as sixty-six games of bridge to keep my mind off the news from the front.
>
> BURGE. [*scandalized*]. Sixty-six games of bridge on Sunday!!!!
>
> LUBIN. You probably sang sixty-six hymns. But as I cannot boast either your admirable voice or your spiritual fervor, I had to fall back on bridge.

That Asquith casually played bridge on Whit Monday in 1916, while his Cabinet awaited a decision on who would succeed the drowned Kitchener at the War Office, was disputed a generation later, long after Shaw satirized the episode, but as the *Times* pronounced, "Posterity unfortunately often seizes upon some easily related and striking contretemps to fix an historic figure's character."[10] Fixed in a major play, it is likely to survive the revisions of historians and biographers; however it is overshadowed by the most terrible of all wartime accusations, leveled at Lubin (and by implication at Asquith as well)—that although he survived the war, his son was killed in it. "To me," adds Haslam, the parson, about wartime politicians in general, "the awful thing about their political incompetence was that they had to kill their own sons." Asquith's brilliant eldest son Raymond *was* killed during the battle of the Somme on September 15, 1916. It had shattered the Prime Minister, weakening his hold upon the government and marking the beginning of the end of his struggle to retain the premiership. The tasteless allusion could have escaped no one, and Shaw failed to escape criticism in the press when the lines appeared in the London production of the play.

Edward Marsh had written an emotional letter to the *Times* on the subject that by his choice of words left Shaw room to weakly wriggle out of an uncomfortable situation. Marsh had accused him of "pouring scorn on a politician who actually allowed his son to be killed in the war." Shaw asked (February 25, 1924),

> In what sense did any man "allow" his son to be killed in the war? Would any man have allowed such a thing if he could have prevented it? Many men, who were more or less responsible for the war, had that responsibility brought home to them by the loss of a well-beloved son; but they will hardly, I think, regard that as a fact to be suppressed as shameful, or deny the son his right to his record and his share in the moral of the greatest tragedy of his time. Does Mr. Marsh really believe that his delicacy is greater and more consoling than mine when he dismisses the son with the remark that 'somebody must be killed in a war,' and treats his fate as a mere personal episode. . . . In the framework of my play such phrases would be heartless nonsense; the case is bigger and deeper than that.

The point Shaw was making, in heavy-handed criticism that reflected his bitterness at the human cost of the political cynicism and military ineptitude he had seen since 1914, was that if the ruling classes represented the best the race had to offer, the human race was a failure. What he had said before in lecture and in dramatic dialogue, and as recently as *Heartbreak House*, is repeated by Franklyn Barnabas: "We shall not be let alone. The force behind evolution, call it what you will, is determined to solve the problem of civilization; and if it cannot do it through us, it will produce some more capable agents. Man is not God's last word: God can still create. If you cannot do His work He will produce some being who can." The reason for the failure had been pointed out to the statesmen earlier by Franklyn: Lubin and Joyce Burge were only two of "a European group of immature statesmen and monarchs who, doing the very best for your respective countries of which you were capable, succeeded in all-but-wrecking the civilization of Europe, and did, in effect, wipe out of existence many millions of its inhabitants." He was not blaming them, he adds, for it was beyond present human capacity "to control powers [of destruction] so gigantic that one shudders at the thought of their being entrusted even to an infinitely experienced and benevolent God, much less to mortal men whose whole life does not last a hundred years."

Conrad Barnabas agrees that the war had established the point beyond argument: "It is now absolutely certain that the political and social problems raised by our civilization cannot be solved by mere human mushrooms who decay and die when they are just beginning to have a glimmer of . . . wisdom. . . ."

Thus *The Gospel of the Brothers Barnabas*, a "serious farce" in the *Heartbreak House* manner, is set in the heartbreak house of the immediate postwar world, played against those persistently erupting memories of the war which justify the quest for the new "metabiology" Shaw sets out in parable form in the futuristic plays which follow in the cycle. No parable to the war's survivors, the play was inevitably shunned by the victors and embraced by the vanquished, who with the blinders of defeat saw in it not a sharing of their guilt, but only new objects upon which to fasten it. "In Germany," Shaw recalled later, "the Barnabas scenes—thanks to Asquith and Lloyd George—were such a success that the manager [of the first postwar production] broke his contract and ran Barnabas as a single play, dropping the rest."[11]

In the futuristic third play (written second), *The Thing Happens*, two of the Barnabas characters reappear, although it is A.D. 2170.* With his war fury somewhat spent by his having written it out in *Barnabas*, Shaw was able to complete a less bitter first draft by May 16, but Asquith and Lloyd George were still too much with him to discard, and they reappear in composite as the weak President of the British Islands, their stoutish, breezily genial descendant, Burge-Lubin. Two characters—the rector Haslam and a Barnabas housemaid—survive as early longlivers, Haslam confiding that he had not been able to prove his age for two centuries, because "the register of my birth had been blown to pieces by a bomb dropped on a church . . . in the first of the big modern wars." The world has been much altered because of the 1914–18 war, Archbishop

---

* Originally the time of the play was to be A.D. 2068, 150 years after the end of the war.

Haslam explains. "Before the few changes we were forced to make by the revolutions that followed the Four Years War, our governing classes had been so rich . . . that they had become the most intellectually lazy and fat-headed people on the face of the earth."

Little else to recall 1914–18 appears in *The Thing Happens*, but in the next play, *Tragedy of an Elderly Gentleman*, the "Four Years War" is pervasive, although the action of the play is set on "Burrin pier on the south shore of Galway Bay in Ireland, a region of stone-capped hills and granite fields . . . [on] a fine summer day in the year 3000 A.D." Shaw knew the stark hills well, since Lady Gregory's estate at Coole—as forested as the face of the Burrens is bare—was nearby, and the bleak lunar landscape suited the futuristic aspect of his play. The new longlived race has populated key sectors of the earth, has overawed such dwindling subject races as are represented by the Elderly Gentleman, and has lived peacefully and responsibly without the coercions and inhibitions of a codified system of law and order, while a decaying but tolerated remnant of the British Empire has moved its seat to Baghdad. Defending his race to a young, longlived Oracle, the more childish Elderly Gentleman boasts of the great ancient teachers of his civilization and the "galaxy of Christs" that arose in the twentieth century. The Oracle shrugs off the claim, knowing the response of that war-happy civilization to pacifists and conscientious objectors:

But did any of their disciples ever succeed in governing you for a single day on their Christ-like principles? It is not enough to know what is good: you must be able to do it. They couldnt do it because they did not live long enough to find out how to do it, or to outlive the childish passions that prevented them from really wanting to do it. You know very well that they could only keep order—such as it was—by the very coercion and militarism they were denouncing and deploring. They had actually to kill one another for preaching their own gospel, or be killed themselves.

One of the militarist leaders of the vestigial old world is a descendant of Cain—Cain Adamson Charles Napoleon. An anachronism like his people, he explains proudly the self-defeating success of his leadership in 1914–18 terms, his followers going off to war because their love of fighting, their desire for glory, their shame of being branded as dastards, their instinct to test themselves in terrible trials, their fear of being killed or enslaved by the enemy, their belief that they are defending their hearths and homes, overcome their natural cowardice, and make them willing not only to risk their own lives but to kill everyone who refuses to take that risk. But if war continues too long, there comes a time when the soldiers, and also the taxpayers who are supporting and munitioning them, reach a condition which they describe as being fed up. The troops have proved their courage, and want to go home and enjoy in peace the glory it has earned them. Besides, the risk of death for each soldier becomes a certainty if the fighting goes on for ever: he hopes to escape for six months, but knows he cannot escape for six years. The risk of bankruptcy for the citizen becomes a certainty in the same way.

Nearby, outside a temple, curious tourists see a strange monument and are informed about it by Zoo, a longliver:

All I can tell you about it is that a thousand years ago, when the whole world was given over to you shortlived people, there was a war called the War to end War. In the war which followed it about ten years later, hardly any soldiers were killed; but seven of the capital cities of Europe were wiped out of existence. It seems to have been a great joke: for the statesmen who thought they had sent ten million common men to their deaths were themselves blown into fragments with their houses and families, while the ten million men lay snugly in the caves they had dug for themselves. Later on even the houses escaped; but their inhabitants were poisoned by gas that spared no living soul. Of course the soldiers starved and ran wild; and that was the end of pseudo-Christian civilization. The last civilized thing that happened was that the statesmen discovered that cowardice was a great patriotic virtue; and a public monument was erected to its first preacher, an ancient and very fat sage called Sir John Falstaff. Well [pointing], thats Falstaff.

Begun in May 1918, *The Tragedy of An Elderly Gentleman* was not completed to Shaw's satisfaction until nearly two years later, but distance in time failed to erase bitter memories of the war or of the arms race that led up to it and that Shaw was sure would occur again and again until man either destroyed or remade himself. A British Envoy makes the recurring point:

THE ENVOY. Well, perhaps I do; and perhaps history makes me. I hardly recognize myself in the newspapers sometimes, though I suppose leading articles are the materials of history, as you might say. But what I want to know is, how did war come back again? and how did they make those poisonous gases you speak of? We should be glad to know; for they might come in very handy if we have to fight Turania. Of course I am all for peace, and dont hold with the race of armaments in principle; still, we must keep ahead or be wiped out.

ZOO. You can make the gases for yourselves when your chemists find out how. Then you will do as you did before: poison each other until there are no chemists left, and no civilization. You will then begin all over again as half-starved ignorant savages, and fight with boomerangs and poisoned arrows until you work up to the poison gases and high explosives once more, with the same result. That is, unless we have sense enough to make an end of this ridiculous game by destroying you.

"Like Swift's Superhorses," says a critic, "Shaw's Superrace [of longlivers] has no organized system of power, government, law, or punishment. Again, like the Houyhnhnms, and like Plato's Guardians, they are passionless, stern, ascetic, kindly, responsible, and unbending."[12] They are far too superior to the Elderly Gentleman for him to be able to survive among them, although, having made his pilgrimage to the Irish home of his ancestors, he begs to stay, as Gulliver begged to remain among the Houyhnhnms. His plea is accepted, but a touch from the Oracle causes him to stiffen and die. "Poor shortlived thing!" says the Oracle. "What else could I do for you?"

The imaginative fifth and last play, begun and completed in 1920, is set in A.D. 31,920, the time of the Superrace, and resembles in atmosphere the best of fourth-century B.C. Greece. Even here, in *As Far As Thought Can Reach*, there is a suggestion of 1914–18, when the She-Ancient tells the Newly Born, "There was a time when children were given the world to play with because they promised to improve it. They did not improve it; and they would

have wrecked it had their power been as great as that which you
will wield when you are no longer a child."

When darkness falls on the fifth play, which in spite of a lack of
the conflict of wills or egos—the heart of Shavian theater—is "a
remarkable triumph of imaginative drama," the ghosts of Adam,
Eve, Cain, and the Serpent materialize and speak in an epilogue, and
Lilith, forerunner of Adam and Eve, appears, too, and questions
them. When all fade but Lilith,* Shaw gives her the cycle's last
words, a long, bleakly eloquent speech in which she declares that
she has not lost faith with her erring but aspiring charges. "Of Life
only is there no end; and though of its million starry mansions many
are empty and many still unbuilt, and though its vast domain is as
yet unbearably desert, my seed shall one day fill it and master its
matter to its uttermost confines. And for what may be beyond, the
eyesight of Lilith is too short. It is enough that there is a beyond.
[*She vanishes*]."

Weakened where war fury blinded Shaw from apprehending the
inartistic, and strengthened by the emotional power generated from
Shaw's 1914–18 experience, *Back to Methuselah* is an uneven work,
compounded of greatness and silliness, enlarged as well as dated by
its topical references, ennobling as well as enervating in its vision.
The magnitude of its aim precluded perfection, and he was its most
severe critic, writing in its preface in 1920, "I am not, I hope, under
more illusion than is humanly inevitable as to the crudity of this
my beginning of a Bible for Creative Evolution. I am doing the best
I can at my age. My powers are waning; but so much the better for
those who found me unbearably brilliant in my prime." It may be
what Shaw had declared it was in 1944, toward the end of his long
life and near the end of another and more terrible war he had predicted in his play: "*Back to Methuselah* is a World Classic or it is
nothing."[13]

* Lilith derives from a legendary tradition with roots in Assyria and Baby-
lonia, and from thence into such post-Biblical literature as the Talmud, where
Lilith is a succubus in the shape of a woman with long hair. The concept of
Lilith as first wife of Adam originated in later Talmudic lore, and Shaw suggests, rather, that she is creator of the sexes.

14

Armistice

EVEN WHILE involved in peripheral activities that pushed
the war aside for a few hours and provided relief from his work on
Methuselah, Shaw could not keep the war out of mind. Early in June
he had returned to music criticism just long enough to review two
opera performances, writing in the *Nation*[1] that one of them—
Don Giovanni—"might have been an attempt on the part of the
opera company, a conductor, and a number of bandsmen, all perfect
strangers to one another and accidentally marooned in the Shaftesbury
Theatre, to wile away the time by reading at sight a bundle of band
parts and vocal scores of a rather difficult opera which they had
never heard before. . . ." For the other, Shaw ironically invoked the
despised Defence of the Realm Act, that blank check to inhibit
freedom of speech and press, for he approved of a Drury Lane production of Wagner's *Die Walküre,* conducted by Thomas Beecham,
although the work was a product of the enemy. "The house was
crammed from floor to ceiling," he reported, "and the applause
prodigious. This for a work . . . written and composed by one classed
by our patriotic papers as a congenital scoundrel with a specific lust

for the blood of women and children, would probably be accounted for by the patriots on the ground that Old Drury, huge as it is, does not hold 47,000,000 people. I will therefore conclude by mentioning that I never saw a more normal and native British musical audience in my life, or a more enthusiastic one. And now bring along your Dora and hale me to the Tower."

Wagnerian music remained in Shaw's head through the rest of the month, exorcised neither by the routine of social-professional engagements nor by his writing, which ranged from lunch with Arnold Bennett to a conference speech on "What is Wrong with Our System of Education?" to work with the Fabian Research Department, to the polite refusal of more lecture offers from America. On June 29, when he went to Lamer for a Saturday with Kathleen Scott, Shaw followed dinner as he often did at Ayot by an uninhibited performance on the piano. "He amazed me," Lady Scott wrote in her diary. "I have known him for fifteen years, and this was the first time I knew he sang. He went almost all through the score of *Rheingold* on the piano, singing in a charming baritone voice. He plays amazingly well. He is a marvellous man." On Sunday Shaw returned to spend the day, practicing his dancing with Lady Scott, and playing from memory and with lusty vocal accompaniment the entire score of Wagner's *Walküre*.[2]

June 30 was the day the Fabian Research Department officially dissolved itself and became the Labour [Party] Research Department, a transfer actively promoted by Shaw, who as chairman had the most power to lose. G. D. H. Cole, the young economist who was the operating force in the Department, agreed to stay, which meant for him a sacrifice of some of his rebelliousness and independence for the chance of larger influence. For Shaw it meant relief from a responsibility that had grown too complex and burdensome, and its transfer* to younger hands meant continuity. He could better continue work on his lengthening play.

For July and August, Kathleen Scott (no longer now at her ministry job) rented Streatley Vicarage in Berkshire, up the Thames west

---

* He stayed on, however, as titular chairman, and was again reelected in November.

of London; and G.B.S. agreed to visit and to sit for her while she sculpted a statuette of him if he did not have to dress "respectably." He was grateful for the opportunity to extricate himself from his households, for Ayot and Adelphi Terrace were both in a chaotic state, with his staff of five (two in London and three in the country) incapacitated by illnesses ranging from appendicitis to influenza. Charlotte had gone directly to Ireland, as usual, and expected G.B.S., after visits to Lady Scott, the Webbs (who had rented a house in Wales for the summer), and the inevitable Fabian Summer School (this time in Devonshire) to cross over to Kerry to accompany her home. With his play cycle going well, Shaw planned to work on his drafts wherever he went, optimistically promising Graham Wallas that in October he would look him up and read "some queer dramatic stuff" he wanted to discuss with him—something "more sociological" than *Heartbreak House* had been. He had been keeping his feelings about the war at the time mostly to himself except as he poured them out into his new play, but to Wallas he added, "We are all really dying slowly of horror; but we dont know it."[3] Four years of war would have been a sufficient reason for the remark, but the newspapers of July 1918 were full of news of the Second Battle of the Marne in which the Germans under Ludendorff had pushed a salient toward Paris and evoked Allied counterattacks that proved—at great new cost in casualties—to have taken the initiative away from the enemy for good. No one knew how close the end was.

Just as Shaw was about to leave home, a telegram arrived for him as "next of kin":

MAJOR ROBERT LORAINE REPORTED WOUNDED ON JULY 20TH PARTICULARS FOLLOW WHEN RECEIVED.*

Anyhow, Shaw found himself thinking, it meant at least that Loraine, although apparently shot down, was alive, and he thought of

* Loraine—a lieutenant colonel in charge of a training center in England after his 1917 duty in France—had asked to revert to major in order to return to head a squadron in France. In May 1918 he arrived back at the front.

lines from *King Lear,* a play that had worked on him profoundly
while he was writing *Heartbreak House;*

> Hadst thou been Gossamer! Feathers! Air!
> So many fathoms down precipitating,
> Thoudst shiver like an egg.

He rushed off a commiserating letter to Loraine, hoping it would
follow to whatever hospital he was in and wondering what were the
extent of Loraine's new wounds. "I hope they send those particulars soon," he wrote, "and that it is a cushy one this time. You are
going too far with this silly soldiering." He went on to impart some
details about the problems he was having in developing his huge,
new play, posted the letter, and packed for Streatley Vicarage.[4]

Shaw's first full day with Kathleen Scott was July 26, his sixty-
second birthday. After the telegram any acknowledgment of his
birthday would have turned sour anyway, but the day was also cold
and wet. Shaw was cross, and she was shy and dull, Lady Scott told
her diary. Worst of all, the food was "bad," and the prospects for
improvement "hopeless." Still, G.B.S. remained for ten days, swimming in the Thames when the sun shone, sitting for the statuette
when it did not.[5] Lady Scott, husbandless since Sir Robert had
been lost in the Antarctic, never seemed concerned about a chap-
erone on the premises when G.B.S. visited, their relationship being as much father-and-daughter as that with Barker or Loraine had
been father-and-son. She could be just as irreverent as an emancipated daughter, too, her diary entry for Sunday, August 4, noting
what had happened when the grave and sober Frederick Watson,
a leader in crippled children's causes, came to visit for the day
and found himself greeted by the overpowering G.B.S.:

Shaw at once took up the duties of a host, and behaved through the day
in a manner reminiscent of Queen Victoria and the annual Wesleyan Conference. Frederick Watson was frequently extremely promising in occasional asides and was instantly submerged and rejected by the reminis-
cences instantly inflamed in the mind of Shaw. There was however one

supreme moment [at dinner] when Shaw set up a strident noise for cheese when he [Watson] seemed on the point of a joke. It passed never to return.

While Shaw was being sculpted that week, supplementary information arrived from France identifying Loraine's injury as a severe gunshot wound shattering the left knee. "Oh, tell him," Lady Scott quoted Shaw as advising, "to be sure not to take any leg they recommend at Roehampton." He was attempting, with whatever good humor was possible under such circumstances, to prepare Loraine for the most extreme solution. "I trust," he added, "it is not necessary to rush to conclusions in this fashion; still, if the worst comes to worst, I suppose one can play Hamlet with a property leg as well as lawn tennis. Why the devil need they have hit you in the knee-joint? The shin would have served their purpose just as well."[6]

Later he wrote again to Loraine to point out that he had spent eighteen months on crutches himself, after a foot infection in 1898 that nearly cost him the limb and forced his retirement as *Saturday Review* drama critic. "But in that period [I] produced Caesar and Cleopatra and The Perfect Wagnerite; and I cannot remember that I was in the least less happy than at other times." Some forced humor followed, and Shaw recognized its falsity, concluding, "these are the cheering remarks one makes now to the sacrifices of this horrible war. They must make you long to bomb Britain from the nearest Handley-Page."[7]

Shaw had no idea how close Loraine had already come to losing his leg. Military doctors in France had advised amputation on the ground that it would save him from gangrene and other complications that would inevitably, after much further pain, force an amputation anyway. But Loraine, although he had completely lost his kneecap as well as the ends of the bones to which it had been attached, resisted anything more than the extraction of three flattened bullets and in agony held on to the shattered remnants of his leg.

For his brief stay with the Webbs at Presteigne in Radnorshire, Shaw had to take a bus northward as far as Oxford, where he would meet a train that would take him the rest of the way. Since it meant lunch en route, Lady Scott had asked her cook to pack cucumber sandwiches for the vegetarian G.B.S.; when Shaw opened the first one he discovered that the overly thoughtful cook had supplemented the cucumbers in the sandwiches with potted meat. Unobtrusively he threw them all away and hungered all the way to Wales.[8]

From France Loraine wrote to Shaw for advice, the letter following him to Radnorshire, and Shaw tried to blend frankness with wit. "I dont know what to say about the leg," he admitted, since it was impossible to advise another man—even a surrogate son—to acquiesce in the amputation of his own limb. "If you lose it, an artificial leg of the best sort will carry you to victory as Henry V. If you dont and are lame, it means a lifetime of Richard III, unless I write a play entitled Byron." An actor, he concluded, "may be more disabled by a crooked leg than by a cork one." As for Loraine's continuing in Air Force service, which Shaw must have understood was remote, he observed that when it came to aerial combat, very likely the more of one that was artificial the better. "Wells's Martian, a brain in a machine, is the ideal. You could carry spare limbs and replace damaged ones. . . . A dozen bullets through an artificial shin would move you to nothing but a Mephistophelean laugh." Shaw knew how unfunny that concept would be to Loraine and apologized, "If we did not die of laughter at the humours of war we should [die] of horror."

The larger question was what Loraine would do if—as Shaw was certain—the former actor would be forced to remain exactly that. He could still be a pilot, Shaw thought: "The first flight to America remains unachieved. You have done enough Richthofening for honour; and I like not such grinning honour as Richthofen hath. There still remains Columbus to emulate. You have, God forgive you, bombed enough German homesteads to fill ten pages of the Recording Angel's debit column; and it behoves you to start a credit by drying up the Atlantic for ever. The world will be full of such jobs for bold men for a long time to come. . . ."⁹

Granville-Barker and Helen Huntington were married in London on July 31, 1918, at King's Weigh House Chapel, Duke Street, off Grosvenor Square. Helen gave her occupation as "author," which was as accurate as any other occupation she might have set down, and—older than she looked—gave her age as forty-three, slashing a full decade from her surfeit of years. Barker discreetly gave his age as forty, although he had four more months to go before he reached that milestone. There were three witnesses, none of them in any way connected with the theatre. Helen was determined to cut Barker off from people who represented that phase of his life, and G.B.S. was not only not invited, but not even informed. Eventually he found out and wrote Barker an admonishing letter redolent with forced friendliness:

It would be convenient occasionally to know something about you. I surmise that you are married; but it is only a surmise. It is desirable that your friends should be in a position to make a positive affirmation on the subject. An affectation of ecstasy so continuous as to make you forget all such worldly considerations is ridiculous at your age. So just send me along any information that ought to be public, however briefly. I have refrained, with an exaggerated delicacy, from asking you questions for a year or so. Now I do ask them bluntly. People ask me questions; and there is not the same reason for not meeting them with a mystery that there was formerly for not giving them too much information.¹⁰

Barker's ex-wife was still one of Shaw's concerns, for Lillah remained convinced that the cure for her career, which had gone the way of Barker and the war, was to star as Ellie Dunn in *Heartbreak House*, an ingenue part for which she was too old in a play for which no audience was ready. "I am not deserting you: I am only facing the facts," he explained to her from Wales. "The theatre just now is impossible. You should revive 'Black-eyed Susan.' If [Henry] Ainley can dance a hornpipe well enough to produce the

proper pattern with a pair of diamond buckles, it would delight
the Tommies and ruin the carpets with their tears.

"I really dont know what is to be done. I am too old."[11]

En route to the Summer School from Presteigne, Shaw changed
trains at Hereford, taking the advice of a stationmaster impressed by
his white beard not to take the first train, which was so packed
with troops and tourists that their elbows protruded from the open
windows. An unscheduled second half followed soon after, going
as far as Newton Abbott, just north of Darmouth. It too was crowded,
but Shaw at least had a seat for the eight-hour ride through the
heat of the afternoon and into the evening. At the end he had nearly
all the seats, as the train arrived nearly empty.[12]

The next morning came the letdown. He had traveled long dis-
tances to go to the now traditional Fabian sessions only to find that
war or other reasons had depleted the school of most of his old
friends; women now predominated, and the program itself was a
hollow pretence of the old activities. Still he played his role of
Fabian bishop, he wrote Barker, "with Pickwickian geniality." The
geniality was not easy, although he swam in the channel, puffed
through Swedish calisthenics led by the school directress, Mary
Hankinson, participated in country dances in the evenings, and
slept in an unheated cottage high up a hill overlooking the sea. For
the Webbs he drew a diagram showing why it was the geography
rather than the regimen that made him feel his years. A two-story
building on a cliff overlooking the Channel housed the dining area,
while two plateaus farther up the hill, separated from the main
structure by a road, was the building in which lectures were given.
Two levels above that (the fifth floor, he called it) was Shaw's
cottage. Even without the Hankinsonian drill he was getting plenty
of exercise.[13]

Shaw's swimming, as Cyril Joad, then a young Fabian, described it,
was a curious phenomenon. "In the afternoon Shaw could be seen
bathing: it was an odd sight. His limbs seemed to me to be insufficiently geared up to their central directing agency, with the result that they appeared to be possessed of wills of their own,

striking out each in its individual direction and operating with a
fine idiosyncratic independence of one another. Shaw's dancing
gave one the same impression: whether his partners shared it, I
cannot tell; they were too respectful to say."[14] Early in his stay,
G.B.S. noticed a familiar black beard bobbing in the sea and swam
over to identify it, finding that it belonged to Fabian pioneer Sydney
Olivier. It proved too good to be true. Olivier was not staying at
the school, but at Dartmouth, having inspected Penlea and politely
departed. Even perennial Fabian secretary Edward Pease left for
Bristol for family reasons, leaving Shaw to listen, almost alone of his
generation, to a lecture by a Mr. Katz on "England's Greatest
Thinker." G.B.S. was prepared to be modest about the designation
during the question period to follow, but Mr. Katz turned out to
be referring to the imprisoned Bertrand Russell.[15]

Shaw never appeared until midday, Joad recalled, for he spent
his mornings writing, "and sometimes in the evening he would
read to the assembled school what he had written. The reading
was most impressive. Shaw sat in front of a reading-desk with a
candle on either side of him, the rest of the hall being in darkness.
Much has been written about Shaw's histrionic powers. . . . But
anybody who has not actually heard Shaw read one of his plays
can have no conception of the charm and power of his presentation."[16] At Penlea he lectured on "Dickens; and After," a discussion
on romance and realism from Hogarth through to Gissing, Ibsen
to Strindberg; he also tried out a portion of *Methuselah*. He was
glad to leave for Ireland, where Charlotte was still at her usual hotel
in Kerry with her sister.

Considering his position, as far as the English Government was
concerned, especially after *O'Flaherty, V.C.*, Shaw must have been
surprised to receive, when he arrived in Ireland, a telegram from
Colonel Arthur Lynch, M.P., urging him on behalf of the Irish
Recruiting Council to write something for publication that might
encourage Irish soldiers to fill the depleted British ranks. Rather
than dispatch a rhetorical telegram that would have fetched no recruits, Shaw thought the issues over in the leisure of Parknasilla
left to him between Charlotte's social engagements, as if the war

were likely to go on for years. He drafted a six-thousand-word appeal based upon making a case for himself as an Irishman.

What we Irish have to consider . . . is not what the kings and their councillors and their warriors intended this war to be, but what, in the hands of that inexorable Power of whom it used to be said that "Man proposes: God disposes," it has now actually become over and above its merely horrible aspect as an insane killing match. If there is anything at stake except military prestige, and the resulting Overbalance of Power, what is it? I think we must reply that the war has become a phase of that great struggle towards equality as the sole effective guarantee of democracy and liberty which is being constantly waged against the delivery of human welfare into the custody and control of privileged persons and classes: in short, against robbery of the poor and idolatry of the rich. . . . Any Irishman who will not fight for his side in the world conflict because the English are fighting on that side too has no political sense; and an Ireland composed of such men could never be free, even if the gates of freedom were open wide before her. It is a case not of refusing to help the English in a bad cause, but of refusing to take advantage of the help of the English in a good one.

Then there is the more intelligent Irishman who hopes that the war may end in the establishment of a League of Nations, and that this League may take up the Irish question and insist on Ireland having its place as a nation, and not remaining a conquered territory governed by her conqueror . . . But we must not deceive ourselves as to the interest the rest of the world takes in our little island and our little people. Those of us who talk and think as if, outside England, all the great federations, empires, and nations of the world were enthusiastic branches of the Gaelic League, or that they will put Irish interests before their own lightest advantage in the settlement after the war . . . are deceiving themselves very ridiculously. The truth is that these great European and Asiatic Powers will be hardly conscious of Ireland when the settlement comes. We are too far out of their way. We shall count for less with them in the treaty than Cyprus did in the Treaty of Berlin. We can make England feel us; and America is well aware of us; but we cannot make Europe feel us. The beginning of diplomatic wisdom with us is to realize our own insignificance outside the group of islands to which we belong.

But if we have no diplomatic importance, our sentimental importance in America and the Overseas Dominions, and our political importance with-

in the British Islands, is considerable: it is, in fact, out of all proportion to
our merits. . . .

What we *can* plead is that as, like the Americans, we did not make the
war, and are free of the guilt of bringing such a calamity on mankind, and
as we can take part in it only on what we conceive to be the side of political emancipation in spite of our intense preoccupation with our own
acute national problem, we shall be acting with complete national dis-
interestedness in the spirit of men with a duty to the world as well as to
ourselves. Unless Dublin Castle has hopelessly broken our spirits and
limited our horizon, the Irish soldier will carry the burden which war
throws on the conscience of every sane man all the more lightly because
he will be able to say honestly, "At least we had nothing to gain by it
that the whole world did not share; and we did not hesitate to risk our
lives for the national liberty of men who had denied national liberty to
us." The Irishmen who have been fighting since 1914 can already say this.
Can the rest hope to be able to say anything more honorable to Ireland?[17]

Still certain that there was plenty of time, Shaw mailed his manifesto to London to be typed by his secretary. It was then returned
to him in Kerry for proofreading and disposition. Shaw warned
Lynch in the interval that what he had to say would be unconventional and would make officialdom furious, but might work,
while a respectable text would fall flat.[18] (Privately, he felt that
nothing would work.) Captain Stephen Gwynn arranged for the
Dublin firm of Maunsel and Company to print the polemic as a sixpenny open letter to Lynch entitled *War Issues for Irishmen*, and
Shaw provided a brief preface before it was rushed (by Dublin
standards) into print. Prudently, he predated it "10 November
1918."*

With the *War Issues* pamphlet done, Shaw remained in Kerry
with Charlotte until the end of September, then went on to visit
Lady Gregory at Coole Park, Sir Horace Plunkett in Dublin, and his
own and Charlotte's relatives in the vicinity. It was turning into one
of his longest absences from London and Ayot, as he was not planning on returning until late in October unless he canceled the rest
of his Irish stay to go off again to France. W. M. Hughes, Prime

---

* It was printed but never released, the Armistice arriving before the pamphlet.

Minister of Australia, had asked him to join a special party touring the Somme front. Shaw temporized, feeling that he would be of little use there, and finally said no, deciding instead to do additional work on *Methuselah* and attend to his compulsive letter-writing in the intervals when the creative impulse was low but the need to put pen to paper remained. The Great Southern, on the rugged Ring of Kerry, was ideal for both—in good weather. The hotel, a grey Victorian pile on the broad mouth of the Kenmare, warmed by the Gulf Stream, sat amid subtropical palm trees and high flowering hedges clipped into mazes which wrapped around small secluded grassy terraces into which resident peacocks sometimes wandered and on which canvas-backed chairs were set. It was very private and very far from the war.

Yet the war continued to intrude. While still at Parknasilla, G.B.S. received additional details of what had become the continuing saga of Robert Loraine's leg. In London, where he arrived at a military hospital while Shaw was traveling, surgeons had examined the maimed leg and decided that since gangrene had not set in, it might be best after all to try to save what was left of it. Accordingly it was encased in plaster, to be kept immovable for five months. Two days later, however, Loraine learned in casual conversation with a doctor that at the end of the period of immobility he would retain his leg if all went well, but that the muscles would have knit in a way to stiffen it permanently. A leg he could not bend at the knee was of no use to an actor, and in panic and desperation, as soon as doctors and nurses were out of sight, Loraine broke the cast and tried to force his leg to bend at the joint. The attempt left him exhausted and in agony, and the medical staff only looked on him as having gone temporarily insane.

It was a coincidence that that afternoon actress Irene Vanbrugh had come visiting and heard the story of Loraine's frustration, for she was a friend of one of the most famous surgeons in London, Sir Alfred Fripp. Evading the rules by professing to be the patient's lifelong friend and former physician, Sir Alfred arrived, took new X-rays, consulted with military surgeons, and a week later proceeded to rebuild a knee joint where contemporary practice was certain none could be made. By the end of September, his patient could be transferred to a convalescent hospital (a former resort hotel) at Swanage, overlooking the Channel below Bournemouth, and Shaw was writing:

> How soon will you be able to play again if you decide to return to the boards instead of starting an Aeroplane Express? . . . The reason I ask is that as Pygmalion came off at His Majesty's at the end of the season to big business, and Tree was discussing a resumption of it when he died,* Mrs. Campbell is looking round for another go.
>
> Now, there is not the least reason why Higgins should not be lame, or Tanner lame, or any of the rest of my heroes. So long as you have a mouth left and one lung to keep it going, you will still be better than the next best: my pieces are not leg pieces. . . .

Shaw's letter from Ireland arrived just as Loraine finished reading an English translation of *Cyrano de Bergerac*. Having fought his duels in the air he could think of nothing else but, with more primitive weapons, fighting the romantic Gascon's duels on the ground.[19]

If climate were as important a factor in creativity as Shaw thought, it was fortunate that Charlotte's homing instincts did not keep her husband in Ireland any longer than it already had done in 1918. "I am writing all this drivel," he explained to Frank Harris about a letter to him, "on the coast of Kerry with nothing visible in the grey but the white horses on the waves and a blanket of incessant rain Zenith high and horizon far."[20] It was a setting to inspire a play by Ibsen or Synge, but would do little for the Shavian drama, although the fourth play in the Methuselah cycle was being set "on the south shore of Galway bay." At the end of October, as the war news began to foreshadow a German collapse, Ludendorff's troops

---

* Beerbohm Tree had died on July 2, 1917. It was unlikely that Shaw would have permitted him to play Higgins again, although he afterward wrote about Tree in a memorial volume, "A few days before his death, when he was incredibly young and sanguine, and made me feel hopelessly old and grumpy, he was discussing a revival of Pygmalion as if it promised to be a renewal of the most delightful experience of our lives."

staggering backward across French and Belgian territory they had held since 1914, Shaw was still in Ireland. (In London Lady Scott went to the pre-opening private viewing of the International Show, where her statuette of Shaw appeared "alone on the central table of the principal room, looking very small.")[21]

Companies of *You Never Can Tell* and *Pygmalion* were touring the English provinces at the same time *Blanco Posnet* was being done by the Little Theatre in Dublin, on the last night of which G.B.S. also lectured on "Literature in Ireland." Strangely, one of his chief detractors in the vicinity, Abbey Theatre buff Joseph Holloway, not only attended, but came away more pleased than he expected to be.

His discourse was quite Shavian in his findings, and he kept nagging all the while he spoke; he afterwards said he knew he was nagging, but once set going he couldn't stop. Only those who don't succeed in art or literature make good critics was his opinion; therefore, he was no critic. He didn't read critically. It was only when they went to Paris [that] Irishmen could write, and then he spoke of George Moore's and Joyce's works and their indecencies. He also said that Synge got his local colour in Paris, and that there is nothing Irish about *The Playboy*. The central idea is that the worship of crime is universal; in fact, the Irish people don't understand it. Then he went on to say that the Irish should be conscripted out of their own country so that they would learn to know what Ireland was really like. He also said they could never get anything until they ceased to have a grievance. Nobody liked people with a grievance; they were generally bores. The man who didn't leave Ireland wouldn't write like Synge. The plays that were written by Irishmen who never travelled were generally those that lacked poetic outlook and were sordid and abusive in character. . . . Shaw is always stimulating and entertaining and never dull. He mixed all he said with a very nimble wit, and his words came ever ready to his lips. He speaks excellently well always, and his delivery is clear and telling! . . .[22]

When he returned home at last, Shaw appeared still unwilling to believe a German surrender was near, continuing to insist to Lillah McCarthy that the time for production of *Heartbreak House* had not yet come. "The war is not over, the lighting order is still in force, the audiences still consist of Tommies on leave . . . and nothing is improved except that it looks as if the air raids are over at last for good. The failure of the play as a commercial speculation by a syndicate is nearly a certainty as anything theatrical can be." Lillah had acquired the backing of Sir Alfred Mond (later Lord Melchett) before entreating Shaw again, but Sir Alfred's check for £2500 failed to convince because Shaw was sure that Londoners had sufficiently jangled nerves already without having to relive their immediate pasts in his play. Besides, he pointed out, writing from Ayot on November 5, although a failure would mean little to the pocketbooks of her backers and she would get some income out of a run of a few weeks, he would be the loser. "I should lose a month's exhausting work at rehearsals, and have a big play killed. It would never revive in London in my lifetime. . . ." More important to him, he thought, with a haunting sense of the calendar, was his need—"at all hazards"—to complete the three plays in his tetralogy (as he then conceived it) which he still considered unfinished. They would be, he thought, "the end of my output."[23] It was a pessimistic outlook belied by the gay farce he was then putting together as a second act of the *Barnabas* segment of the cycle. At its center was a new character, Immenso Champernoon, recognizable as Shaw's old friend and adversary, Gilbert Chesterton.* Its good humor may have been due to its having been written during that second week of November and finished on November 12. The day before had been the last day of the war, signaled ironically from London police and fire stations by the booming maroons that, until the Zeppelins and Gothas had paid their final visits in May, had warned of air raids. In the mist and rain, not far from Adelphi Terrace, revelers in Trafalgar Square dismantled whatever temporary wooden structures remained in the area and built a bonfire at the base of Nelson's Column that would leave it permanently scarred. "Peace!" Beatrice Webb wrote in her diary. "London to-day is a pandemonium of noise and revelry, soldiers and flappers being most in evidence.

* It was dropped from the final version of the play.

Multitudes are making all the noise they can, and in spite of depressing fog and steady rain, discords of sound and struggling, rushing beings and vehicles fill the streets."[24] In Hogarth House, Richmond, Leonard and Virginia Woolf "celebrated the end of a civilization and the beginning of peace by sitting in the lovely, panelled [drawing] room . . . and eating, almost sacramentally, some small bars of chocolate cream."[25] What G.B.S.'s own attitude was to the sounds of victory may be guessed from an inscription[26] to a friend on his pamphlet, *Peace Conference Hints*, written soon after:

Dare not to rejoice when thine enemy comes to the ground; but give him food when he hungers.

Eliezer ben Isaac.
1050.

15

Apotheosis

WHEN THE war collapsed, Kaiser Wilhelm withdrew into neutral Holland, "and instead of receiving a vote of thanks from Europe for that very sensible and considerate step," Shaw wrote, "was reviled for it, apparently because he had not rushed on the enemy sword in hand and perished gloriously, like Byron's vision of the Duke of Brunswick at Waterloo. From which it is clear that even four years of sanguinary disillusion had not quite cured our romantic civilians of enjoying the war as a cinema show."[1] Even before the Armistice, the Cabinet had decided on an immediate postwar general election so that the coalition in power could acquire, out of the hysteria of a grateful electorate, a mandate for making the peace. Shamelessly, Lloyd George (as G.B.S. would characterize him in *Barnabas*) allowed the election to be fought to the cries of "Hang the Kaiser" and "Make Germany Pay." Shaw, who immediately set out to campaign for candidates opposed to the coalition, drew large crowds who looked on him not as that persecuted but proud figure, a major prophet whom his own people refused to honor, but as a confirmed oracle—if not a certified mouthpiece of the gods, at least a prophet who had survived into his time. "Why," he had queried Hesketh Pearson a fortnight before the Armistice, "did it take a colossal war to make people read my books? The whole army seems to do nothing else, except when it lays down the book to fire a perfunctory shot at Jerry, or to write me a letter asking me what I meant by it."[2] Dismissing the Shavian apotheosis, T. S. Eliot remarked a few years later that it "might have been predicted that what he said then would not seem so subversive or blasphemous now. The public has accepted Mr Shaw not by recognizing the intelligence of what he said then, but by forgetting it; but we must not forget that at one time Mr Shaw was a very unpopular man. He is no longer the gadfly of the commonwealth; but even if he has never been appreciated, it is something that he should be respected."[3] Eliot notwithstanding, what had happened by November 11, 1918, and was reinforced by the major plays which grew out of the war years, *Heartbreak House, Methuselah,* and *Saint Joan,* was "that the aged revolutionist had, quite naturally and yet quite magically, become a British tradition. He had become the official gadfly of the British state, as almost a hundred years before, the Duke of Wellington had become the official defender of the eighteenth-century constitution. . . ."[4] But on the subject of the Kaiser, he found no audience, however much he pointed out that Wilhelm II for all practical purposes was beyond the reach of legal vengeance. "As Mr. William Hohenzollern, of Amerongen, Holland, has now been promoted to the position of an ordinary citizen," Shaw explained, "he has a right to live where he pleases. If anyone is afraid of him, it is quite simple to go to the nearest [Dutch] magistrate and ask that he be bound over to keep the peace. No doubt the magistrate will comply if a reasonable case can be established. If his rights are not as sacred as those of the poorest peasant in Europe, then the war has been fought in vain."[5]

Shaw appeared for Ramsay MacDonald, Arthur Henderson, and other Labour candidates who refused to campaign as part of any coalition, speaking to ordinary election meetings in provincial town halls and public squares and—where they worked—to dockers and warehousemen warning them not to vote for so-called Labour candidates who would go blindfolded into a coalition. They would then, he argued, not be a party at all, while to play the "Parliamentary game" meant that "the Government should govern and the Opposition should oppose."[6] A real opposition, however, stifled so long by the Defence of the Realm Act, had no chance to form, and few soldiers had a chance to make their own concerns felt; an enormous coalition majority was swept into office, with almost every candidate for whom Shaw had campaigned defeated. To oppose Lloyd George's 516 seats, the Asquithian Liberals could only elect twenty-seven, and Labour sixty-two. On the credit side for G.B.S.'s efforts, it had replaced Liberals with Labour as the opposition, with the older party never again able to reform as a major force in British politics. Lloyd George, ostensibly a Liberal, ruled a predominantly Conservative government and would not survive another election. The antiwar MacDonald would be, five years later, the first Labour Prime Minister, and G.B.S. would refuse the empty honor of an earldom or even to become Sir Bernard Shaw.

"I never grieve," he wrote in 1919, "but I do not forget."[7] And the unforgetful Shaw translated his experience of 1914–18 into a dozen plays, sometimes defiantly, sometimes unobtrusively. The war was more than a journey to *Heartbreak House*. Even earlier plays were not unaffected, Shaw writing a note for a 1929 production of *Major Barbara* (1905) that added a postwar glance to the story of the cannon-making partnership in which Barbara's father made his millions. He wrote, "When the war came, Undershaft and Lazarus did not do so well as was expected of them . . . and after a frightful slaughter of our young men through insufficient munitions the Government had to organise the business. . . . But the moment the war was over, Undershaft and Lazarus came back with all their newspapers shouting that they had saved the country, and that the national factories were sinks of corruption and incompetence. They then plunged into an orgy of overcapitalisation followed by repudiation . . . so that every blunder and swindle on their part left the public more impressed. . . ."[8]

Refusing to let anyone else forget his wartime journalism, Shaw in 1931 published what he had threatened to do since early in the war, a collection of 1914–18 pieces in which the major document was the once notorious *Common Sense.* It had "no parallel in literature," he thought, "since Swift's classic pamphlet on The Conduct of the Allies,"[9] a 1711 masterpiece of argumentation the full title of which points even more in the direction of Shaw's own polemic: *The Conduct of the Allies and of the late Ministry in beginning and carrying on the present war.* Shaw's *What I Really Wrote about the War*—comprehensive although inexplicably incomplete*—became the twenty-first volume in the collected edition of his works.

One of the pieces omitted from *What I Really Wrote*—and one of the least known of Shaw's dramatic works to come out of the war—is *The War Indemnities*, a playlet he wrote in 1920 to underline the economic and political stupidity of the Allied insistence upon German reparations. Because Lloyd George and Marshal Foch, among others, appeared in it under their own names, he put it aside, but published it the next year.[10] It was no less prescient then and no less painfully funny, but like the earlier wartime playlets and such later plays as *The Apple Cart* and *Too True to Be Good,* it remains overshadowed by what are collectively perhaps the greatest creative achievement inspired in an individual by a war. Not only are *Heartbreak House* and *Back to Methuselah* the bitter fruit of 1914, but also the third of the great plays to come out of that crucible, *Saint Joan.* As with the earlier two, the concept preceded the war and was metamorphosed by it. *Joan* might have been penned less sensitively had Shaw not written "The Emperor and the Little Girl." Even the English chaplain in it, de Stogumber, seems treated with surprising gentleness and magnanimity considering Shaw's experience of anti-Hun John Bulls in 1914 pulpits. But, a critic has observed, the difference between de Stogumber and Britannus (of *Caesar and Cleopatra*)

---

* The publications he omitted from the collection by accident or design in no way alter the general picture. He excluded nothing out of any desire to show himself more favorably, for the excluded pieces could only have done so.

is Shaw's bitter experience in World War I. His story is a parable on contemporary history. He is cruel only through lack of imagination and in
the fury of patriotism. The spectacle of Joan's burning arouses in him a
mania of guilt which leaves him finally a gentle, broken, slightly crazed
old man. He worships Joan because she has changed his cruelty into kindness. But he is as terribly unprepared for her return as England, having
emerged from the madness and cruelty of war, was unprepared for anything but peace. His reply to Joan is prophetic: "You must not come
back. I must die in peace. Give us peace in our time, O Lord!"[11]

Explaining his play to the Theatre Guild, G.B.S. even argued that
the play would not have been written had he not visualized in it
relevance to "a world situation in which we see whole peoples per-
ishing and dragging us toward the abyss which has swallowed them,
all for want of any grasp of the political forces that move civilization."[12] Against one of those forces he protested not only in his
play but in his preface, for after the war the body of martyred army
nurse Edith Cavell had been brought home for a military funeral,
after which a statue of her was erected in St. Martin's Place near
Trafalgar Square. On the pedestal were inscribed the uplifting catch-
words "Humanity, Fortitude, Devotion, Sacrifice," as well as Edith
Cavell's own last words. Shaw wrote a more powerful epitaph for her
in his introduction to *Saint Joan*. "The modern military inquisi-
tion . . ." he declared, "shot her out of hand; and her countrymen,
seeing in this a good opportunity for lecturing the enemy on his
intolerance, put up a statue to her, but took particular care not to
inscribe on the pedestal 'Patriotism is not enough,' for which omis-
sion, and the lie it implies, they will need Edith's intercession when
they themselves are brought to judgment." The inscription on the
pedestal, Shaw knew, had only quoted the second half of her statement to a clergyman who had attended her just before the end,
"This I would say, standing as I do before God and eternity: I
realize now that patriotism is not enough. I must have no hatred or
bitterness for anyone."

When *Saint Joan* and its preface were published in 1924, Edith
Cavell's countrymen bowed to Shaw's rebuke and put her (and

Shaw's) plea for humanity—"patriotism is not enough"—on her statue.

In that spirit Shaw, when he was nearly eighty, confided to American playwright Paul Green that he was thinking of a new play,

". . . the biggest thing I have attempted, one in which all the facilities of the theatre will be called on to their fullest. It's only an idea yet, an idea I've been thinking about. It has to do with this childish fanaticism about war—specifically with the Unknown Soldier." He stopped and gazed before him, his hands shoved deep in his pockets and that light, almost inaudible, whistle sounding through his lips again.

"Yes, sir—" and I waited.

"I've thought of using the combination of mysticism and science in this play, making use even of an actual miracle. There's to be a big scene when all the people are gathered on a certain night around the Unknown Soldier's tomb where the sacred and mysterious light is burning. Through some proper device and in the proper mood, this Unknown Soldier will rise from the grave. I've only thought about it in dim outlines. To the horror of those assembled, he proves to be not a soldier of their own country but one of the enemy who has been buried and honored by mistake."

He snapped his fingers and whirled around, and stood with his back to the fire. "I'm only considering it, you see. I haven't thought it out clearly."[13]

The play was never written—for which more is the pity—although G.B.S. told much the same story to Cedric Hardwicke, who was not only one of the first to play Shotover in *Heartbreak House*, but one of the young officers who at a makeshift chapel at St. Pol had stood over the plain wooden boxes of unidentified dead from which the choice of Unknown Soldier was made.[14]

Heartbreak House was published in 1919, but there was no production of it in England until the fall of 1921. Even then it was too soon, and some of the roles were miscast and misunderstood. Even worse, the last scene change of the long play, timed to take four minutes, took twenty-five instead because of an electrical failure. "The delay," Hesketh Pearson recalled, "at a moment when the audience was exhausted by the length of the play, was disastrous,"[15] and the reviews were overwhelmingly negative. "Last night I had to go to Shaw's *Heartbreak House*," Arnold Bennett wrote in his *Journal* on October 19, "3 hours 50 minutes of the most intense tedium. I went to sleep twice, fortunately." In public print the *Times* was equally caustic, finding one remark of the aged Shotover particularly significant: "He says he cannot keep up a continuous train of thought. Is this a bit of self-revelation on the part of Mr. Shaw the playwright? . . . As usual with Mr. Shaw, the play is about an hour too long." In the *Daily News* E. A. Baughan called the play a failure, and reminded readers of Shaw's war record, pointing out that there was not a word in preface or play about Germany's war guilt. *Heartbreak House*, he concluded, was not "cultured, leisured Europe before the war" but "England as viewed by a man who naturally does not consider himself an Englishman. . . . I can quite conceive why Bernard Shaw is a popular dramatist in Germany and Austria."

In an unusual gesture, Shaw asked the critics back for a second look and took to the newspapers to explain the play himself; but nothing availed, and the play closed after a disappointing sixty-three performances. It would take another generation (and another world war) to understand its parable and underline its heartbreak. For Shaw the failure of what he felt was his greatest play in his own lifetime was heartbreak enough, and it was understandable that in his nineties, when in his puppet play *Shakes vs Shav* Shakespeare challenges him, "Where is thy Hamlet? Couldst thou write King Lear?" Shav replies, "Aye, with his daughters all complete. Couldst thou have written Heartbreak House? Behold my Lear."[16] But the productions of it Shaw supervised never came up to expectations, one of the early ones not even providing a sufficiently substantial last-act explosion. He demanded a bigger bang and was duly promised one by the stage manager, who warned the cast accordingly. When the cue for the bomb blast came, Edith Evans spoke her line, then prudently covered her face with her hands, but nothing happened. It was only after the curtain came down that the explosion finally came, bringing down part of the ceiling on the departing playgoers. Shaw was satisfied.[17]

Appendix: Shaw's *Lear*[1]

SHAKES. Where is thy Hamlet? Couldst thou write King Lear?
SHAV.   Aye, with his daughters all complete. Couldst thou have written Heartbreak House? Behold my Lear.

      —G. B. S. in *Shakes vs. Shav.* (1949)

Although Bernard Shaw called his *Heartbreak House* (written 1916–17) a fantasia in the Russian manner upon English themes, and echoes of *The Cherry Orchard* unquestionably reverberate through it, the play might be profitably viewed as a fantasia in the Shakespearean manner upon Shavian themes. Whether or not Shaw recalled Swinburne's curious remark that *King Lear* was the work of Shakespeare the socialist, *Heartbreak House* seems clearly to have been designed, at least in part, as Shaw's *Lear*. Earlier he had tauntingly titled part of a preface to his *Caesar and Cleopatra* (1898) "Better than Shakespeare?"—suggesting a parallel with the Bard's *Antony and Cleopatra*; yet by presenting a kittenish young queen and an aging Caesar, rather than an aging but still sultry Cleopatra

333

and a younger admirer, he had evaded any direct comparison. Like his Cleopatra play, Shaw's *Lear* was offered not in competition but as commentary.

G.B.S. waited until his nineties to point publicly to *Heartbreak House* as his *Lear*. Even then he did so guardedly through the disarming medium of a puppet play, perhaps to prevent the comparison from being taken as seriously as he inwardly still meant it to be, for in his lifetime the play's now very considerable reputation[2] had never measured up to his expectations for it. "If the critics had the brains of a mad Tom," he grumbled, using a suggestive association with *Lear*, "they would realize it is my greatest play. But they don't. They all go following after the Maid of Orleans."[3] Privately Shaw had hinted at the *Lear* connection almost as soon as he had completed the play. In 1917 actress Lillah McCarthy had asked him for details of the work, hoping to convince him to let her produce it or at least acquire a starring part in it. Shaw put her off. It was wartime, he pointed out, and the play was unpleasant, unsuitable fare for war conditions. The hero was an old man of eighty-eight, and there were no young males in the cast at all (its implicit recognition of the wartime dearth of leading men). The women were either too young or too old—an ingenue and two sisters in their middle forties. The sisters, Shaw confided—"I dont find them much more popular than Goneril or Regan"—were the old man's daughters.[4] Disgusted with the dragged-out war and its effect on theatre as well as much else, he confessed that his heart was not in a London production of a new play. And Miss McCarthy—creator of some of Shaw's greatest roles, beginning with her Ann Whitefield in *Man and Superman*—appeared neither then nor afterward in a performance of *Heartbreak House*.

"There is something about the play that makes me extremely reluctant to let it go out of my hands," he insisted on completing it, and at first he would let no one read it, and only on a few occasions would he read from it to his friends, although in his later years he had found great satisfaction in performing such dramatic readings—with all the histrionic stops pulled—scene by scene and act by act as his plays were being written. He was, as Miss McCarthy discovered, not even interested in having it produced, and when it was discussed he talked of it as having been inspired by Chekhov. Yet later he would insist, as he told Hesketh Pearson, that it was his favorite play, noting also to Pearson that old Captain Shotover was "a modernized King Lear." As for its meaning, Pearson reported Shaw's stock reply, "How should *I* know? I am only the author."[5] Lillah McCarthy felt she knew, having accepted Shaw's hints about his play. It had, she thought, a quality that she found nowhere else in Shaw—"a quality which only once before an English playwright has contrived to give to the drama he has written. The quality which *King Lear* has: spaciousness. In *Heartbreak House* there is no stage. It is life speaking from the stage of life, a voice crying in the wilderness."[6]

What was to have been his *Cherry Orchard* had been transformed almost *in utero*, by events as much as by Shaw, although the Chekhovian atmosphere remained. (Shaw, in fact, told his biographer Henderson that *Heartbreak House* "began with an atmosphere and does not contain a word that was foreseen before it was written.") Chekhov had the charm of novelty as well as a doom-ridden nostalgia, but *King Lear* had long fascinated Shaw, although not until the years of the 1914–18 war had he been confronted with a sense of helplessness and futility such as he was convinced Shakespeare had dramatized in the play. Shaw had never had the opportunity to review a production, yet he had consistently tucked into other commentaries his insistence that it was a "masterpiece," and that "no man will ever write a better tragedy than Lear." He had written of the "blasphemous despair" revealed to him by the play,[7] thinking particularly of Gloucester's dark lines, lines he quoted afterward in the preface to his next play, where, writing of Shakespeare's "religionless condition . . . of despair," Shaw added, "His towering King Lear would be only a melodrama were it not for its express admission that if there is nothing more to be said of the universe than Hamlet has to say, then 'as flies to wanton boys are we to the gods: they kill us for their sport.'"[8] "Even the fool in Lear," he wrote, "is tragic."

Lear's tragicomic aspects were also bound to attract a playwright who had been writing as though he meant his line that every jest was an earnest in the womb of time. As Shaw put it,[9] although Shakespeare had often juxtaposed passages of "downright circus buffoonery" with the "deepest tragedy," it was only in *Lear*, his "greatest tragedy," that "we find the alternation of tragic and funny dropped for an actual interweaving of the two; so that we have the tragic and the comic simultaneously, each heightening the other with a poignancy otherwise unattainable." To Shaw "the wonderful storm trio in which the king, the fool, and the sham madman have their parts 'concerted,' . . . like the statue, the hero, and the comic valet in . . . *Don Giovanni*," was "the summit of Shakespeare's achievement as poet and playwright."[10] Few plays from the pre-twentieth-century repertoire, as Jan Kott has shown,[11] insisting (like Shaw) on the play's essential pessimism and near nihilism, lend themselves so readily to interpretation as black comedy. Even the core of the play, Wilson Knight has claimed in a famous essay, "is an absurdity . . . an incongruity," characterized by that kind of "grimmest humour" which warns against "sentimentalizing" its "cosmic mockery."[12] *Heartbreak House* suggests that Shaw's reading of *Lear* is that if Shakespeare had not meant it that way, he should have.

Sir Cedric Hardwicke (who was in one of the first English casts of *Heartbreak House*) was probably echoing Shaw when he observed that Captain Shotover was meant to be "an up-to-date King Lear," yet although he intended recognizable similarities—his remark to Lillah McCarthy makes this clear—Shaw seems to have intended as well some meaningful differences. In both lie a measure of *Heartbreak House*'s significance, in what might be identified as its *Lear* dimension. Without offering any explanations for them, critics have long pointed to tantalizing hints of *Lear* in Shaw's play. As one notes, it is "apocalyptic. Captain Shotover is eighty-eight and mad. His two daughters have an aspect in which they are fiends. Boss Mangan, the business man driven to a frenzy by Heartbreak House, proposes [like Lear] to strip himself naked. 'Poor wretch!' Hector Hushabye exclaims at the end of the second act—and adds, as 'he lifts his fists in invocation to heaven': 'Fall. Fall and crush.' "[13] (This parallels, perhaps, Albany's similar gesture and invocation, "Fall and cease!" near the close of *Lear*.[14]) Even the air raid that brings the play to a violent conclusion seems a modern embodiment of the great storm in *Lear*. "These reverberations," J. I. M. Stewart observes, "are not insignificant. For *Heartbreak House* is the play in which Shaw confronts, for the first time in his imaginative writing, the small extent of his faith in man. What lies just beneath the play's surface is despair. It is thus in intention, or impulsion, radically different from almost all the rest of his work...."[15]

Albany's words in *Lear* sound the note of *Heartbreak House*:

> If that the heavens do not their visible spirits
> Send quickly down to tame these vile offences
> It will come,
> Humanity must perforce prey on itself,
> Like monsters of the deep.

Hector, Shaw's Albany, in words as reminiscent of Don Juan (*in Hell*) as of *Lear*, provides a twentieth-century echo:

> [*Fiercely*]. I tell you, one of two things must happen. Either out of that darkness some new creation will come to supplant us as we have supplanted the animals, or the heavens will fall in thunder and destroy us.

G.B.S.'s play, basically the characteristic later Shavian juxtaposition of theatrical and intellectual elements one can label *serious farce*, was intended, indeed, as apocalyptic farce. Contrary to the fate of most prophecy, the thunder from heaven came even before the play had been completed, and in fact offered Shaw, via a Zeppelin raid he observed from his country house, an appropriate ending at a time when an ending was eluding him. Although the bursting bombs have their counterpart in the last-act thudding of axes upon Chekhov's cherry trees and the ominous and premonitory breaking string is paralleled by the Beethoven-like drumming of distant aircraft engines, that the major characters in *Heartbreak House* are as much at home in a

Lear framework as in Chekhov's overheated drawing rooms suggests that the blending of concepts occurred early in the play's development, perhaps before the first words were written. Europe, a newly pessimistic Shaw realized even before the first shots were fired, was in its self-destructive selfishness (the only sense of purpose which European nations seemed to evidence) heading toward catastrophe.

Heartbreak House's outlook, nevertheless, is also radically different from *Lear* and in some ways almost its inversion. "There is nothing real in the world," says Ellie, "but my father and Shakespeare," and her favorite reading is *Othello*, whose recital of his exploits to Desdemona seems to have its parallel in Ellie Dunn's naive acceptance of Hector Hushabye's tall tales of heroism. The unconscious irony of her pointing to Shakespeare's epitome of Nature's Nobleman, as well as to that impractical, naive anachronism of an idealist, Mazzini Dunn, as all that are real in the world may mean something more. To Shaw, in the midst of a brutal, wasteful war, there was no longer room or reason for impractical nobility of Lear's (or Othello's) stamp, and the element of weary hope and faith that concludes *Lear* is twisted sardonically in *Heartbreak House*; Hesione Hushabye and Ellie Dunn hope that the air raid which had put such excitement into their aimless lives will be repeated. "I hope theyll come again tomorrow night," says Hesione, and Ellie eagerly adds (*radiant at the prospect*, Shaw notes), "Oh, I hope so."

This savoring of the violence which has brought new interest into jaded lives is grotesque and indicative not only of Shaw's war-bred despair but, through contrast with Lear's daughters and especially the scorned Cordelia, his reaction to it. To recall her, and her relationship with Lear, Shaw had earlier portrayed Shotover dozing on the shoulder of Ellie, to whom he had declared himself mystically joined. (In the 1949 *Shakes vs. Shav*, after Shakes asks, "Where is thy Hamlet? Couldst thou write King Lear?" and Shav replies, "Aye, with his daughters all complete. Couldst thou have written Heartbreak House? Behold my Lear," the dramatist's stage directions read, "*A transparency is suddenly lit up, shewing Captain Shotover seated, as in Millais' picture called North-West Passage, with a young woman of virginal beauty.*"[16] And Shotover and Ellie speak, aria-like, several passages from Shaw's play.) Ellie suggests Cordelia in other ways as well, for she is also "fresh, loving, dowerless, heartbroken, and strongminded," while Shaw's "old daughter-troubled man has his Goneril and Regan [in] Hesione and Ariadne [who] are modern embodiments of the wicked sisters' sexuality and worldliness."[17] At play's end the three daughters (for Ellie is "adopted") are defeated or dead in *Lear*, but in *Heartbreak House* they live and thrive in their open cynicism and their absorption in self-interest. At the same point in each play, mad old Shotover is strangely satisfied (as war apparently begins) that all is temporarily well, while Lear finds, contrastingly, his personal world crumbling still further as tranquility is apparently restored.

The paradox and the horror are, by comparison with *Lear*, "civilized" reactions. But Lear recovers his sanity long enough to cry out when Cordelia dies (largely the result of his own irresponsibility),

> Why should a dog, a horse, or rat have life,
> And thou no breath at all?

while no one finds it necessary to ask why a bomb should drop without warning onto the grounds of Heartbreak House, killing two people. (Only a few lines earlier an unexplained order to black out the lights had been the only clue that there is a war or that one is imminent.) On the grounds of their opportunistic morals the two who die might be denied pity, but Shaw rejects conventional poetic justice as he rejects questioning destiny's selectivity. Meaning lies less in who has died and more in the fact of death, as Hector emphasizes in scolding the incurably idealist Mazzini Dunn for his concern about one of the victims: "Are you immortal that you need pity him? Our turn next." The words recall us to the problem of finding meaning for existence in an irrational world, the dilemmas of both *Lear* and *Heartbreak House*.

As absurd and irrational as are some of the rambling lines of the octogenarian Shotover, he shares with the quixotic Hector the words of wisdom Shaw has written into his play. Lear, on the other hand, although he reaches a condition of understanding, is given little wisdom of thought or act. The aged Lear early in the play becomes a king more in memory than in fact, while Shaw's half-mad Shotover, at eighty-eight, is a sea captain only in memory. He is nevertheless, a critic notes, "a King Lear without the tragedy (though certainly with hints of pathos) and still, in spite of his calculated senile absent-mindedness, in full command of his kingdom and his daughters. He is a prophet thundering in navigational terms."[18] A "very foolish fond old man,/Fourscore and upward," Lear is what Shotover describes as the "drifting skipper"—the irresponsible captain who runs his ship onto the rocks because he has trusted his navigation to Providence rather than to himself. In search of a life free at last from responsibility, his mind weakened by his years, Lear relinquishes his kingdom and his power to his two selfish daughters who have flattered him with love they do not feel and promised him the ease and the continued glory they do not intend to furnish. Shaw's old man steadfastly remains the intellectual force and financial mainstay in the house of his daughter —legally still his own house. Though his mind sometimes drifts and wanders, his sense of purpose is too sharply focused to permit him to abdicate any of his failing (but formidable) powers.

Shotover understands his daughters, too, where Lear does not. The old skipper's heart is not easily broken. Six years, he insists, is the normal span of filial affection; thus he has learned not to "make distinctions between one fellowcreature and another." Yet his children, although as sharp-tongued and cynical as Lear's, reverse Goneril's and Regan's unkindness and are indulgent to a fault. Lear expects total and permanent affection, and is disillusioned when hypocrisy and deceit are what he receives instead. In short, while one realizes that heartbreak is "the end of happiness and the beginning of peace," the other, having raged helplessly against the storm, hopes, at best, to conclude his days in a state of happiness that is only freedom from anxiety. "Come, let's away to prison," he comforts the fellow captive, Cordelia:

We two alone will sing like birds i'th' cage.
. . . So we'll live,
And pray and sing, and tell old tales, and laugh
At gilded butterflies, and hear poor rogues
Talk of court news; and we'll talk with them too—
Who loses and who wins; who's in, who's out—
Take upon's the mystery of things,
As if we were God's spies. . . . (V, iii, 8–17)

Happiness, which Lear craves as the fulfillment of his old age, is the very thing Shotover most fears—the "accursed happiness . . . that comes as life goes, the happiness of yielding and dreaming instead of resisting and doing, the sweetness of the fruit that is going rotten." A sense of purpose—of using one's self up in finding and fulfilling that purpose—is the Shotover antidote to happiness. Thus he longs in his old age for the tests and trials of youth and is given by Shaw a grateful apostrophe to the sea storms that compelled him to savor his vigor. "I was ten times happier on the bridge in the typhoon, or frozen into Arctic ice for months in darkness, than you or they have ever been," he tells Ellie. "At your age I looked for hardship, danger, horror, and death, that I might feel the life in me more intensely. I did not let the fear of death govern my life; and my reward was, I had my life." (It is an ironic commentary upon the times that to do the same, Ellie and Hesione must summon back the bombs. It is all they have.) Shotover's nostalgic savoring of the typhoon is in obvious contrast to Lear's noble, yet pathetic, defiance of the storm:

Blow, winds and crack your cheeks!
. . . Rumble thy bellyful! Spit, fire; spout, rain!
. . . I tax you not, elements, with unkindness;
. . . You owe me no subscription. Then let fall
Your horrible pleasure. Here I stand your slave. . . .

Weary, helpless, and insignificant, Lear no more wants to be a slave to the elements than he had wanted to be a slave to responsibility. He had divided his kingdom only in order "to shake all cares and business" and enable him to "Unburthened crawl toward death." Shotover is aware of the hazards of so yielding to one's years. "Old men are dangerous," he warns; "it doesnt matter to them what is going to happen to the world."

"Age . . . has its blindness and decay," writes a modern director of a highly regarded *Lear*. "However true sight comes from an acuteness of living that can transform the world."[19] The insight can be used to contrast Lear and Shotover, but the larger meaning of such a contrast must be Shaw's commentary upon those bleak lines of Gloucester so equally applicable to Lear: "The lot of the man who sees life truly and thinks about it romantically is Despair." That Lear's weakness is the strength of Shotover, G.B.S. knew from his own transient wartime bout with Giant Despair; and the heart of his indictment of Shakespeare is the Bard's "putative despair. . . . Lacking hope, and knowledge, Shakespeare and his characters lace will."[20] As opposed to Lear's "despair made stage-sublime," Shotover is a Bunyanesque hero. It is easy to recognize his ancestry—and his antithesis to Lear—in Shaw's insistence that "All that you miss in Shakespeare you find in Bunyan, to whom the true heroic came quite obviously and naturally. The world was to him a more terrible place than it was to Shakespeare; but he saw through it a path at the end of which a man might look not only forward to the Celestial City, back on his life and say:—'Tho' with great difficulty I am got hither, yet now I do not repent me of all the trouble I have been at to arrive where I am. My sword I give to him that shall succeed me in my pilgrimage, and my courage and skill to him that can get them.' "[21] It would not be too much to suggest that, his encomiums for the play's music and poetry notwithstanding, Shaw privately thought of *Lear* what he had written of *Othello*: "Tested by the brain, it is ridiculous: tested by the ear, it is sublime."[22]

Other themes may be organic to both plays—the increasing inhumanity that increasing civilization seems paradoxically to bring (our cruelties merely becoming more sophisticated); the dominating drive of the female of the species; the inevitable humiliation and defeat of the idealist and the dreamer; the misleading appearances we mistake for reality (dramatized through symbolic unclothing in both plays). It is also possible, but not very fruitful, to find thematic reasons for seeing equivalents not only to Lear and his daughters, but to the Fool, to Cornwall, Edmund, Gloucester, and others in Shaw's play;[23] yet the crucial fact is the fact of clear and intended reverberation. Shaw's *Lear* is less despairing, although "the rack of this tough world" on which Lear is stretched is only technologically different from the world of *Heartbreak House*. Most of the inhabitants of Heartbreak House will endure. Learn navigation, and live, Shotover exhorts them. Leave it, and be damned. Until they begin learning, Shotover intends to remain on the bridge.

Sources

Source notes are supplied where the origin of the material is not clear or is insufficient in the text itself. In most cases information from easily accessible newspapers is not cited. Manuscript sources are identified in full in the first citation and abbreviated thereafter.

CHAPTER 1

[1] Shaw, "Beerbohm Tree," *Pen Portraits and Reviews* (London, 1932), pp. 271–272.

[2] Hesketh Pearson, *Beerbohm Tree: His Life and Laughter* (London, 1955), pp. 178–179.

[3] Margaret Bussé Halford, who played Clara Eynsford-Hill, quoting Mrs. Campbell at rehearsal, in Author's Note to Richard Huggett's play *The First Night of "Pygmalion"* (London, 1970), p. 12.

[4] Pearson, *Beerbohm Tree*, p. 179.

[5] Shaw to Mrs. Campbell, 11 April 1914, in *Bernard Shaw and Mrs. Patrick Campbell: A Correspondence* (hereafter referred to as *Correspondence*), ed. Alan Dent (New York, 1952), p. 180. All further references to this correspondence are from this source.

[6] Pearson, *Beerbohm Tree*, p. 180.

[7] Shaw to Mrs. Campbell, 11 April 1914; Mrs. Campbell to Shaw, 11 April 1914.

[8] Shaw to Charlotte Shaw, 12 April 1914, quoted in Martin Meisel, *Shaw and the Nineteenth Century Theatre* (New York, 1963), p. 177.

[9] Quoted in Huggett, *First Night,* p. 57.

[10] *Ibid.,* p. 59.

[11] Beatrice Webb, ms. diary entry for April 22, 1914 (London School of Economics).

[12] Mrs. Campbell to Shaw, 17 April 1914.

[13] Mrs. Campbell to Shaw, 29 April 1914.

[14] These and other financial records appear in Shaw's income ledgers at the Humanities Research Center, University of Texas, Austin.

[15] Janet Dunbar, quoting Charlotte, in *Mrs. G.B.S.* (London, 1963), p. 221.

[16] Shaw, *What I Wrote About the War* (London, 1931), p. 21.

[17] Barbara Tuchman, *The Guns of August* (New York, 1962), p. 77.

[18] Shaw, t.l.s. to Montague Bull, as June 1914 (Lafayette Butler Collection).

[19] Denis Mackail, *Barrie, the Story of J.M.B.* (New York, 1941), pp. 468–470; Lady Howard de Walden, *Pages from My Life* (London, 1965), pp. 97–98.

[20] *The Fabian Research Department: Report of its Work and Progress,* a 1914 pamphlet (Cambridge, Mass., Houghton Library, Harvard University).

[21] Sharp to Mrs. Webb, in Edward Hyams, *"The New Statesman." The History of the First Fifty Years* (London, 1963), p. 64.

[22] Aubrey Bagot in *Too True to Be Good* (1931).

[23] Mrs. Campbell to Shaw, 17 June 1914, 11 May 1914.

[24] Shaw, *Beerbohm Tree,* pp. 272–273.

[25] Shaw, a.p.c.s. to Sir Arthur Pinero, 21 July 1914 (British Museum).

[26] Pearson, *Beerbohm Tree,* p. 182.

[27] Quoted in *The Times* in translation from a translation in the Viennese press.

CHAPTER 2

[1] From Charlotte's Annuary (courtesy of Professor Dan H. Laurence).

[2] Shaw, *What I Really Wrote,* p. 197. Quotations from Shaw in this chapter not otherwise identified are from this source.

[3] Shaw, t.l.s. to James Muirhead, 16 January 1915.

[4] From a note dated August 1918 added to Beatrice Webb's ms. diary for August 1914.

[5] Quoted in the *New York Times* from a Viennese translation.

[6] Quoted in Allan Chappelow, ed., *Shaw the Villager* (London, 1961), pp. 180–183.

[7] Shaw, a.l.s. to Beatrice Webb, 26 August 1914 (London School of Economics).

[8] Bennett, letter to the editor, *NS,* 4 September 1914.

[9] Shaw, "Authors in war-time," *The Author,* 29 February 1940, p. 58.

[10] *Ibid.*

[11] Shaw to Dorothy Dix, 9 September 1914 (Lafayette Butler Collection).

[12] *Everyman,* November 1914, p. 26.

[13] Lucy Shaw to Ann Elder, 17 October 1914, quoted in Henry George Farmer, *Bernard Shaw's Sister and Her Friends* (London, 1959), p. 218.

[14] Quoted by Frank Swinnerton in a letter to the author, April 4, 1967.

[15] Roy Jenkins, *Asquith* (New York, 1965), pp. 344–345.

[16] *Nation* (New York), October 22, 1914, p. 504 (signed "F").

[17] Shaw to Sharp, 21 October 1914 (Austin, University of Texas).

[18] Shaw to Sutro, 15 October 1915, quoted in Hesketh Pearson, *George Bernard Shaw* (New York, 1963), p. 326.

[19] Shaw to Mrs. Campbell, 6 November 1914, (erroneously dated 6 October 1914).

[20] Shaw to Mrs. Campbell, 6 November 1914.

[21] Shaw to Mrs. Campbell, 13 November 1914.

CHAPTER 3

[1] Shaw to A. W. Pinero, a.p.c.s. 20 December 1930 (Austin, University of Texas).

[2] Julian Symons, *Horatio Bottomley* (London, 1955), p. 174.

[3] Cyril Scott, *My Years of Indiscretion* (London, 1924), p. 231.

[4] Shaw to Mrs. Campbell, 13 November 1914.

[5] *Ibid.*

[6] Shaw quoting Lynd in *Sixteen Self Sketches* (London, 1949), p. 118.

[7] "This Danger of War," BBC shortwave broadcast, 2 November 1937; first published in *The Listener,* 10 November 1937; reprinted in Dan H. Laurence, ed., *Platform and Pulpit* (London, 1961), p. 283.

[8] William Irvine, *The Universe of G.B.S.* (New York, 1949), p. 301.

[9] Quoted in Archibald Henderson, *Bernard Shaw: Playboy and Prophet* (New York, 1931), p. 633.

[10] Quoted in R. F. Rattray, *Bernard Shaw: A Chronicle* (London, 1931), p. 197.

[11] Bennett to Pinker, 15 November 1914, in *Letters of Arnold Bennett,* ed. James Hepburn (London, 1966), vol. 1, p. 215.

[12] Pinker to Bennett, 2 December 1914, in *Letters,* vol. 1, p. 217.

[13] "Keir Hardie," in *Pen Portraits and Reviews,* p. 113.

[14] *The Journals of George Sturt,* ed. George Mackerness (Cambridge, 1967), vol. 2, p. 714.

[15] *Punch,* November 25, 1914, p. 430.

[16] Hall Caine's letters to Shaw on the *King Albert's Book* imbroglio are in the British Museum (Add. Ms. 50531).

[17] T.l.s., December 12, 1914 (Austin, University of Texas).

[18] Shaw, *The Matter with Ireland,* ed. Dan H. Laurence (London, 1962), pp. 86–87.

[19] Shaw to Mabel Fitzgerald, 1 December 1914, in *The Memoirs of Desmond Fitzgerald* (London, 1968), pp. 185–187.

[20] Shaw to Mabel Fitzgerald, 12–13 December 1914, in *Memoirs*, pp. 194–196.

[21] Rebecca West, "Mr. Shaw's Diverted Genius," *The New Republic*, December 5, 1914, pp. 13–14.

[22] *Ibid.*

[23] As reported in the *Christian Commonwealth*.

[24] December 23, 1914.

[25] December 31, 1914.

[26] December 1914, in *Ellen Terry and Bernard Shaw: A Correspondence*, ed. Christopher St. John (London, 1931), p. 330.

[27] Winifred Loraine, *Robert Loraine* (New York, 1936), pp. 196–202.

[28] Shaw to Mrs. Campbell, 20 December, 1914.

[29] Loraine, *Robert Loraine*, p. 201.

CHAPTER 4

[1] Shaw to Mrs. Campbell, 13 January 1915.

[2] Beatrice Webb, *Diary*, 3 January 1915, p. 31.

[3] From a translation of a translation in the *Neue Freie Presse*.

[4] James Muirhead to Shaw, a.l.s. 23 January 1915 (British Museum Add. Ms. 50517).

[5] Loraine, *Robert Loraine*, pp. 202–210.

[6] Margaret Webster, *The Same Only Different* (New York, 1969), pp. 262–263.

[7] Max Eastman to Shaw, cablegram dated 21 January 1915 and 1 February 1915 (Austin, University of Texas).

[8] Shaw to Chesterton, June 1914, quoted in Vincent Brome, *Six Studies in Quarrelling* (London, 1958), p. 155.

[9] Shaw to Mabel Fitzgerald, 29 January 1915, in *Memoirs*, pp. 197–198.

[10] Shaw to Mrs. Campbell, 15 May 1915.

[11] From Shaw's holograph responses to the "Specials Agency" interviewer's questions; ms. (Lafayette Butler Collection). The interview appeared in the *New York American*, June 26, 1915, and other newspapers.

[12] Shaw, Introduction to American edition of Leonard Woolf's *International Government* (New York, 1915), p. xix.

[13] *Ibid.*

[14] Leonard Woolf, *Downhill All the Way* (London, 1967), p. 123.

[15] W. H. Howse in *The Times*, 10 November 1950, p. 106.

[16] Esmé Percy, "Charles Macdona and the Macdona Players," in Mander and Mitchenson, eds., *Theatrical Companion to Shaw* (London, 1954), pp. 296–297.

[17] Gilbert Keith Chesterton, pp. 389–392; and Vincent Brome, *Six Studies in Quarrelling*, pp. 155–156.

[18] "Preface on Bosses" (to *The Millionairess*).

[19] Dame Rebecca West to the author, 20 March 1967.

[20] *More Common Sense About the War*, typescript with ms. corrections and additions (British Museum Add. Ms. 50669A).

[21] *Yorkshire Post*, 18 August 1915.

[22] Shaw to Haldane, 3 August 1915, in Stephen E. Koss, *Lord Haldane: Scapegoat for Liberalism* (New York, 1969), p. 219.

[23] A. J. Beveridge, "British War Opinion," *Collier's*, June 12, 1915; reprinted in *What Is in Back of the War* (Indianapolis, 1915), pp. 382–394.

[24] Shaw to Ann Elder, a.l.s., undated (Lafayette Butler Collection).

[25] Draft Manifesto, 11 pp., dated 3 September 1915, with autograph notes on cover dated 4 November 1929 (Austin, University of Texas).

[26] Shaw to A. W. Pinero, t.l.s. 22 October 1915 (Austin, University of Texas).

[27] Sir Llewellyn Woodward, *Great Britain and the War of 1914–1918* (London, 1967), p. 137.

[28] Woodward, p. 139, quoting Haig's diary.

[29] Charles Hamilton Sorley, "All the Hills and Vales Along" (also known as "Route March"), in the posthumously collected *Marlborough and Other Poems* (London, 1916).

[30] Shaw to Mrs. Campbell, 19 December 1915.

[31] Arthur Marwick, *The Deluge* (Boston, 1965), p. 77.

[32] Shaw, *What I Really Wrote*, p. 155.

[33] Lord Derby to Shaw, t.l.s. 27 October 1916 (British Museum Add. Ms. 50517).

[34] Shaw, *What I Really Wrote*, p. 155.

[35] Shaw to Mrs. Campbell, 19 December 1915.

[36] H. M. Paull to Shaw, t.l.s. 20 October 1915 (Austin, University of Texas).

[37] Shaw to Henry Arthur Jones, a.l.s. 24 October 1915 (Austin, University of Texas). (First published in *Life and Letters of Henry Arthur Jones*, ed. Doris Jones.)

[38] *Life and Letters of Henry Arthur Jones*, ed. Jones, p. 312.

[39] Vincent Brome, *Six Studies in Quarrelling* (London, 1958), p. 46.

[40] Pinero to Shaw, a.l.s. 30 October 1915 (British Museum Add. Ms. 50547).

[41] Shaw to H. M. Paull, t.l.s. 28 October 1915 (Ithaca, N.Y., Cornell University).

[42] Israel Zangwill to H. M. Paull, carbon copy of t.l.s., 7 November 1915 (Austin, University of Texas).

[43] Hesketh Pearson, *George Bernard Shaw*, p. 322.

CHAPTER 5

[1] Ms. Cornell University Library, Ithaca, N.Y.

[2] Shaw, *What I Really Wrote About the War*, p. 356.

[3] Shaw to Mrs. Campbell, 19 December 1915.

[4] *The Autobiography of Bertrand Russell 1914–1944* (Boston, 1958), p. 53.

[5] Quoted in the *New York Times* from a Viennese translation. *Lytton Strachey. The Years of Achievement 1910–1932* (New York, 1968), p. 165.

[6] British Museum Add. Ms. 50685, folio 175.

[7] "The Illusions of War" [report of Shaw's speech], *Christian Commonwealth*, 3 November 1915.

[8] Preface to *O'Flaherty, V.C.* (1919).

[9] *Ibid.*

[10] *O'Flaherty, V.C.*

[11] St. John Ervine, *Bernard Shaw* (London, 1956), p. 471.

[12] Horace Plunkett to Shaw, a.l.s. 15 November 1915 (British Museum Add. Ms. 50547).

[13] Lucy Shaw to Ann Elder, 25 May 1916, in Farmer, *Shaw's Sister*, p. 231.

[14] Henderson, *George Bernard Shaw* (1956), p. 623.

[15] Gertrude Kingston to Shaw, t.l.s. 15 November 1915 (Austin, University of Texas).

[16] From rehearsal copies at the Humanities Research Center, University of Texas, Austin.

[17] Arnold Bennett, *Journals*, 15 November 1915.

[18] Desmond McCarthy, *Shaw* (London, 1951), p. 216.

[19] "Diplomacy After the War," [report of Shaw's speech], *Christian Commonwealth*, 1 December 1915.

[20] *Daily Herald*, 28 November 1915.

[21] The activities are described in Sydney Cockerell's ms. diary for 24 and 25 November 1915 (British Museum Add. Ms. 52652).

[22] Shaw to Frank Harris, March 1919, in Frank Harris, *Bernard Shaw* (New York, 1931), p. 339.

[23] "The Nation's Vitality" [report of Shaw's speech], *Christian Commonwealth*, 8 December 1915.

[24] Marwick, *The Deluge*, p. 82.

[25] Arthur Conan Doyle, *Memories and Adventures* (London, 1924), p. 251.

[26] G. S. Viereck to Shaw, t.l.s. 14 January 1929 (British Museum Add. Ms. 50551).

[27] Percy Burton to Shaw, t.l.s. 31 December 1914 (Austin, University of Texas).

CHAPTER 6

[1] C. B. Purdom, *Harley Granville Barker* (Cambridge, Mass., 1956), pp. 174–175.

[2] Shaw to Lillah McCarthy, 19 January 1916, in *Barker*, p. 175.

[3] Shaw to Lillah McCarthy, 23 January 1916, in *Barker*, p. 176.

[4] "Mr. Arnold Bennett Thinks Play-writing Easier than Novel Writing," *Nation*, 11 March 1916.

[5] "Skit for Lillah McCarthy and Gerald Du Maurier," ms. (Austin, University of Texas), published (ed. B. F. Dukore) in *ETJ*, 19 (October 1967), 343–348.

[6] Preface to *Heartbreak House* (1919).

[7] *Ibid.*

[8] Shaw to Arthur Bourchier, 6 January 1916; in E. J. West, ed. *Advice to a Young Critic and Other Letters* (New York, 1963), p. 195.

[9] Fenner Brockway, *Inside the Left* (London, 1947), pp. 189–190.

[10] *NS*, 12 February 1916.

[11] *Journals*, 27 February 1916.

[12] Especially Shaw to O'Bolger, t.l.s. 24 February 1916 (Cambridge, Mass., Harvard University).

[13] Shaw to Henderson, t.l.s. 8 March 1916 (Cambridge, Mass., Harvard University).

[14] Shaw to Mrs. Campbell, 14 May 1916.

[15] *Ibid.*

[16] Shaw to Bruno E. Kohn, t.l.s. 25 March 1916 (Lafayette Butler Collection); Mrs. Shaw to Mrs. R. D. Phillimore, a.l.s. 8 July 1916 (Austin, University of Texas).

[17] Professional income ledger through 1916–17 (Austin, University of Texas).

[18] Mrs. "Judy" Musters to Shaw, a.l.s. 15 April 1916 (Austin, University of Texas).

[19] Interview with Mrs. Gwenyth Grube, who was one of the schoolgirls.

[20] Quoted in *The Matter with Ireland*, p. 110n.

[21] James Camlin Beckett, *The Making of Modern Ireland* (New York, 1966), p. 441. Beckett also points to the importance of Shaw's letter of warning to the British authorities in the *Daily News*.

[22] Cockerell, ms. diary entry, 12 May 1916 (British Museum).

[23] Shaw to Mrs. Campbell, 14 May 1916.

[24] Shaw, *What I Really Wrote*, pp. 230–237.

[25] Lucy Shaw to Janey Drysdale, 6 June 1916, in Farmer, *Shaw's Sister*, p. 232.

[26] Quoted in Farmer, *Shaw's Sister*, p. 232n.

[27] Flight certificate signed 20 May 1916 by Bernard F. Hale, aviator, London Aerodrome, Hendon (Austin, University of Texas).

[28] Pearson, *Extraordinary People* (New York, 1952), pp. 221–222; *George Bernard Shaw*, pp. 329–330.

[29] Cockerell, ms. diary entry, 22 May 1916 (British Museum).

[30] "Mr. Bernard Shaw at Clapham," *South Western Star*, 26 May 1916.

[31] Reported in the *New York Times*, 7 June 1916.

CHAPTER 7

[1] Beatrice Webb, ms. diary entry, June 6, 1916 (London School of Economics).

[2] *Shaw: An Autobiography 1856–1898*, ed. Stanley Weintraub (New York, 1969), p. 11.

[3] Lena Ashwell, *Myself a Player* (London, 1936), pp. 13–21, 65–67.

[4] *Ibid.*, pp. 65–66; Shaw to Lord Alfred Douglas, t.l.s. 30 November 1944, Four Oaks Library (Mrs. Mary Hyde).

[5] Rattray, *Bernard Shaw: A Chronicle*, p. 201.

[6] Shaw to Mrs. Campbell, July 28, 1929.

[7] Shaw to Virginia Woolf, 10 May 1940, quoted in Leonard Woolf, *Beginning Again* (New York, 1964), p. 126.

[8] *Beginning Again*, p. 119.

[9] Leonard Woolf, a.l.s. to the author, 29 March 1969.

[10] H. G. Wells, *Experiment in Autobiography* (New York, 1934), pp. 579–580.

[11] From correspondence in the British Museum Shaw archives.

[12] Charlotte Shaw to T. E. Lawrence, 15 and 16 September 1927, quoted in Janet Dunbar, *Mrs. G.B.S.*, pp. 254–256; Shaw, letter to the editor, *The Irish Press*, Dublin, 15 March 1937, in *The Matter with Ireland*, pp. 134–135.

[13] Beatrice Webb, *Diary 1912–1924*, ed. Margaret Cole, pp. 62–63.

[14] Shaw, *A Discarded Defence of Roger Casement* and prefatory note, privately printed by Clement Shorter in 1922, reprinted in *The Matter with Ireland*, pp. 114–123.

[15] Shaw, *The Matter with Ireland*, p. 123.

[16] Both reprinted in *The Matter with Ireland*, pp. 125–131.

[17] Shaw to Lillah McCarthy, 30 July 1916, in Purdom, *Harley Granville Barker*, p. 184.

[18] Chappelow, *Shaw the Villager*, pp. 219–220.

[19] Shaw to Ellen Terry, 23 August 1916, letter 306 in *Ellen Terry and Bernard Shaw: a Correspondence*.

[20] Quoted in G. C. L. DuCann, *The Loves of Bernard Shaw* (New York, 1963), p. 215.

[21] Quoted as item 160 in the catalog of the Anderson Galleries sale #3485, 24 April 1930.

[22] Shaw to Mrs. Campbell, 4 September 1916.

[23] Alternate verse prologue to *Fanny's First Play*, in *Complete Plays with Prefaces* (New York, 1962), vol. 6, pp. 89–91.

[24] Autograph ms. dated 25 June 1916 (Austin, University of Texas).

[25] Shaw to Hugo Vallentin, t.l.s. 2 October 1917 (British Museum Add. Ms. 50562).

[26] Douglas H. Robinson, *The Zeppelin in Combat* (Sun Valley, Calif., 1966), pp. 7–11, 194–196.

[27] Charles Ricketts, *Self-Portrait*, ed. Cecil Lewis (London, 1939), entry for 1 October 1916, pp. 265–266.

[28] Shaw to the Webbs, t.l.s. 5 October 1916; in Henderson, *Man of the Century*, pp. 378–379.

[29] M. McDonagh, *In London during the Great War* (London, 1935), pp. 136–137.

[30] *Ibid.*, p. 138.

[31] Shaw to the Webbs, 10 October 1916.

[32] Arthur Nethercot, "Zeppelins over Heartbreak House," *Shaw Review*, 9 (May 1966), 49–50.

[33] Colin Wilson, *Bernard Shaw: a Reassessment* (New York, 1969), pp. 235–236.

[34] Shaw, "Bernard Shaw on 'Heartbreak House,'" *Illustrated Sunday Herald* (London, October 23, 1921).

[35] Lady Gregory, *Journals*, entry for 19 November 1916, p. 202.

CHAPTER 8

[1] "The Letter-Writing Mr. Shaw," *New York Times*, 30 September 1917, section 3, p. 8.

[2] Shaw to Granville-Barker, 28 February 1917, in Purdom, ed., *The Shaw-Barker Letters*, p. 194.

[3] "The Letter-Writing Mr. Shaw."

[4] The correspondence appears in Edward Hyams, *The New Statesman* 1913–1963, pp. 63–67.

[5] Shaw to Arnold Bennett, t.l.s. 9 November 1916 (Austin, University of Texas).

[6] Bennett to Shaw, t.l.s. carbon copy, 13 November 1916 (Austin, University of Texas).

[7] "Mr. Bernard Shaw's Lecture on Life," *Christian Commonwealth*, 1 November 1916.

[8] Shaw to Beatrice Webb, a.p.c.s. 29 October 1916 (London School of Economics).

[9] From correspondence in the British Museum Shaw archive.

[10] *Ibid.*

[11] Shaw to the Editor of *Puck*, 7 November 1916, from an unidentified newspaper clipping quoting *Puck*.

[12] Shaw, *What I Really Wrote*, pp. 182–183.

[13] 6 January 1917, pp. 270–276.

[14] Shaw, *What I Really Wrote*, p. 183.

[15] Lady Gregory, *Journals*, 19 November 1916, pp. 199–200.

[16] Purdom, *Harley Granville Barker*, p. 187.

[17] Preface to *The Apple Cart*.

[18] *Ibid.*

[19] *Ibid.*

[20] George Wellwarth, "Gattie's Glass of Water," *Shaw Review*, 11 (September 1968), pp. 99–103.

[21] Shaw to the Board of Trade, February 1917 (British Museum).

[22] Shaw to Arnold Bennett, t.l.s. 9 November 1916 (Austin, University of Texas).

[23] *New York Times*, 11 December 1916, p. 8.

[24] *New York Times*, 19 December 1916, p. 2.

[25] *New York Times*, 3 January 1917.

[26] Lady Scott, ms. diary, 24 December 1916 (uncorrected text in *Self-Portrait of an Artist* [London, 1949], p. 150) (Historical Manuscripts Commission, London).

[27] Lady Scott, ms. diary, 25 December 1916.

[28] Shaw, "The Emperor and the Little Girl," *New York Tribune Magazine*, October 22, 1916, pp. 1, 4.

[29] Shaw to Mrs. Campbell, 8 September 1913.

[30] R. J. Minney, *Recollections of George Bernard Shaw* (New York, 1969), pp. 111–112.

[31] Lady Scott in *Self-Portrait of an Artist*, diary entry for 19 September 1929.

[32] Florence Farr Emery to Shaw, a.l.s. 7 December 1916 (Austin, University of Texas).

CHAPTER 9

[1] British Museum Add. Ms. 50711A.

[2] Quoted in the *New York Times*, 22 January 1917.

[3] Shaw to Frank Harris, t.l.s. copy, 15 January 1917 (British Museum Add. Ms.).

[4] Quoted in Virginia Woolf, *Roger Fry. A Biography* (London, 1940), p. 208.

[5] "Shaw and Synge," *New Statesman*, January 23, 1917.

[6] Preface to *Augustus Does His Bit,* in *Heartbreak House, Great Catherine and Playlets of the War* (1919).

[7] Shaw's story of his trip to the front and reprints of the newspaper articles, "Joy Riding at the Front," which resulted from it (*Daily Chronicle*, 5, 7, and 8 March 1917) appear on pp. 248–279 of *What I Really Wrote*. Information in this chapter is based upon these pages unless otherwise noted.

[8] Philip Gibbs, *Now It Can Be Told* (New York, 1920), p. 30.

[9] "What the Soldier Thinks of Shaw," *Literary Digest*, 25 August 1917, p. 27–28, quoting Heywood Broun in the *New York Tribune*.

[10] *Ibid.*

[11] C. E. Montague, *Disenchantment* (New York, 1926), pp. 122–124.

[12] Charlotte Shaw to "Sissy" Cholmondely, 16 February 1917, in *Mrs. G.B.S.*, pp. 224–227.

[13] "What the Soldier Thinks of Shaw."

[14] H. M. Tomlinson, "Shaw at Armageddon," reprinted from the London *Daily News* in *Literary Digest*, 10 March 1917, pp. 623–624.

[15] Robert Blake, ed., *Private Papers of Douglas Haig* (London, 1952), entry for 1 February 1917, pp. 194–195.

[16] Charlotte Shaw to "Sissy" Cholmondely.

[17] Shaw in *C. E. Montague: A Memoir*, ed. Oliver Elton (London, 1929), pp. 163–164.

[18] Shaw to Henry Salt, t.l.s. 25 February 1919 (British Museum Add. Ms. 50562).

[19] Shaw, *What I Really Wrote*; Loraine, *Robert Loraine*, pp. 235–238.

[20] Shaw, *What I Really Wrote*; André Maurois, *The Life of Alexander Fleming* (New York, 1959), p. 93.

[21] Shaw to Barker, 28 February 1917, in *The Shaw-Barker Letters*, p. 195.

CHAPTER 10

[1] Frank Harris to Shaw, t.l.s. 1 February 1917 (Austin, University of Texas).

[2] *Morning Post*, 13 February 1917.

[3] *Morning Post*, 17 February 1917.

[4] *Morning Post*, 27 February 1917 (letters to the editor from M. T. E. Sandwith).

[5] Arthur Posonby, *The Crank* (London, n.d.), pp. 6–9.

[6] Beatrice Webb, *Diary 1912–1924*, 22 February 1917, p. 82.

[7] Bennett, *Journals*, 27 February 1917, p. 617.

[8] Masefield to Charles Ricketts, 23 March 1917, in Ricketts, *Diary*, p. 277.

[9] J. M. Hone, "Mr. Shaw in Ireland," *New Statesman*, March 17, 1917, p. 568.

[10] Robert Hogan and Michael J. O'Neill, eds., *Joseph Holloway's Abbey Theatre, A selection from his unpublished journal "Impressions of a Dublin Playgoer"* (Carbondale, Ill., 1967), entries for March 25 and May 9, pp. 191–193.

[11] "Brogue-Shock," *Nation*, 24 March 1917; reprinted in *The Matter with Ireland*, pp. 135–140.

[12] Letters to the editor, *Nation*, 18 April 1916.

[13] Shaw to Frank Harris, in Harris's *Bernard Shaw*, p. 352.

[14] Leonard Woolf's summary of the situation in an interview with the author, Monk's House, Rodmell, Sussex, July 1968.

[15] Marwick, *The Deluge*, p. 216.

[16] Shaw to General Dalme-Radcliffe, t.l.s. copy, 23 April 1917 (British Museum Add. Ms. 50518).

[17] Gorki to Shaw, cable, 2 May 1917 with Shaw's holograph instruction for reply (Austin, University of Texas).

[18] Farmer, *Shaw's Sister*, pp. 233–238.

[19] Shaw, *Sixteen Self Sketches* (London, 1949), pp. 95–96.

[20] Farmer, *Shaw's Sister*, p. 234.

[21] Charlotte Shaw to Lady Scott, a.l.s. 4 June 1917 (Historical Manuscripts Commission).

[22] Lady Scott, ms. diary, 8 June 1917.

[23] Lady Scott, ms. diary, 9 June 1917.

[24] Lady Scott, diary (*Self-Portrait of an Artist*), 10 June 1916, p. 156.

[25] Shaw to Mrs. Campbell, 15 June 1917; Mrs. Campbell to Shaw, 25 June 1917.

[26] Shaw to Graham Wallas, a.p.c.s. 11 July 1917 (London School of Economics).

[27] Mrs. Campbell to Shaw, 25 June 1917.

[28] Shaw to Lillah McCarthy, late July or early August 1918, in *Myself and My Friends*, pp. 202–203.

[29] Shaw to Lillah McCarthy, early August 1918, in *Myself and My Friends*, pp. 203–204.

[30] Lillah McCarthy, *Myself and My Friends*, pp. 207–208.

[31] Raymond H. Fredette, *The Sky on Fire* (New York, 1966), pp. 72, 75–81.

[32] "London and Its Defences," letter to the editor, *Nation*, 14 July 1917.

[33] Fredette, pp. 80–81.

[34] Shaw, *What I Really Wrote*, pp. 222–223.

[35] *Nation*, 7 July 1917, and 28 July 1917.

[36] Bennett, *Journals*, 27 July 1917.

[37] Bennett, *Journals*, 25 July 1917.

[38] *Ibid.*

[39] Northern Newspaper Syndicate to Shaw, 2 August 1917, with Shaw's notes for response (Lafayette Butler Collection).

[40] Shaw to Chesterton, 6 August 1917, in Ward, *Gilbert Keith Chesterton*, pp. 408–410.

[41] "War Thoughts of Bernard Shaw," *Literary Digest*, 4 August 1917.

CHAPTER 11

[1] Shaw to Ellen Terry, 7 January 1918, in *Correspondence*, pp. 331–332.

[2] Shaw to Beatrice Webb, a.l.s. 2 October 1917 (London School of Economics).

[3] Shaw, Introductory note to *How to Settle the Irish Question* (1917); in *The Matter with Ireland*, p. 143.

[4] Shaw to Haldane, 12 July 1917, in *The Matter with Ireland*, p. 142n.

[5] Blumenfeld to Shaw, 7 November 1917, in *The Matter with Ireland*, p. 141.

[6] Henderson, *Man of the Century*, p. 380.

[7] "The Children of the Dublin Slums," *The* [London] *Star*, 4 June 1918, reprinted in *The Matter with Ireland*, pp. 163–166.

[8] "The Letter-Writing Mr. Shaw," *New York Times*, 30 September 1917, p. 8.

[9] Ms. George Barr McCutcheon collection dated 12 October 1917 (Huntington Library).

[10] Shaw to Ervine, a.l.s. 10 October 1917 (Austin, University of Texas); Ervine in conversation with Lawrence Langner in *G.B.S. and the Lunatic* (New York, 1963), p. 29.

[11] "The Superman in the Britannic Alliance," *Christian Commonwealth*, 14 November 1917.

[12] Shaw, *What I Really Wrote*, p. 284.

[13] Lady Scott, ms. diary, 7 December 1917. (The version in the published *Self Portrait of an Artist* is inaccurate.)

[14] Lady Scott, ms. diary, 9 December 1917. (The version in the published *Self Portrait of an Artist* is inaccurate.)

[15] F. V. Conolly, "Bernard Shaw Sees Peace Now as Mere Breathing Spell Between Wars," *New York Tribune*, 10 March 1918 (thus much delayed in publication).

[16] Shaw to Ellen Terry, 7 January 1918, in *Correspondence*, p. 331.

[17] Shaw to A. M. Thompson, t.l.s. 22 December 1917 (British Museum Add. Ms. 50562).

CHAPTER 12

[1] Mrs. Campbell to Shaw, 7 January 1918.

[2] Barrie to Mrs. Campbell, 7 January 1918, in *Letters of J. M. Barrie*, ed. Viola Meynell (New York, 1942), p. 37.

[3] Shaw to Mrs. Campbell, 7 January 1918.

[4] Lady Gregory to Shaw, 8 February 1918, in *Modern Drama*, February 1968, pp. 343–344.

[5] Shaw, *Pen Portraits and Reviews*, p. 16.

[6] Lady Scott, ms. diary, 8 January and 10 January 1918 (Historical Manuscripts Commission).

[7] Shaw, "How Free is the Press?" *Nation*, 9 February 1918, in *Pen Portraits*, p. 37.

[8] Shaw, "What is to be Done with the Doctors?" *English Review*, January 1918.

[9] "Life Without Meat," *Daily Chronicle*, 1 March 1918.

[10] Shaw to Ricketts, 6 February 1918, in *Ricketts*, p. 288.

[11] Osbert Sitwell, *Laughter in the Next Room* (Boston, 1948), pp. 122–124.

[12] Forster to Russell, 2 February 1918, in *Autobiography of Bertrand Russell*, vol. 2, p. 108.

[13] Shaw to Dorothy Mackenzie, 18 March 1918, in *Autobiography of Bertrand Russell*, vol. 2, pp. 110–113.

[14] Shaw to Russell, 29 April 1918 in *Autobiography of Bertrand Russell*, vol. 2, pp. 113–114.

[15] "Shaw Speaks at Central Hall, Westminster," *The Times*, 4 May 1918, p. 8.

[16] "The Climate and Soil for Labour Culture," typescript (British Museum Add. Ms.).

[17] *Ricketts*, entry for 9 May 1918, pp. 294–295.

CHAPTER 13

[1] "Modern Religion," *The Religious Speeches of Bernard Shaw*, ed. W. S. Smith (University Park, Pa., 1963), pp. 38–49.

[2] Although parts of it have become obsolete because of newly discovered material, the best study of Shaw's sources for *Back to Methuselah* remains H. M. Geduld's doctoral thesis, a variorum edition of the play (Birkbeck College, University of London, 1961).

[3] Shaw to Loraine, 25 July 1918, in *Robert Loraine*, p. 242.

[4] Shaw to Siegfried Trebitsch, 20 July 1919 (Berg).

[5] Louis Crompton, *Shaw the Dramatist* (Lincoln, Neb., 1969), p. 175.

[6] Shaw to Langner, 3 May 1921, in *G.B.S. and the Lunatic*, p. 38.

[7] Shaw to Barker, 18 December 1918, in *Letters*, pp. 198–199.

[8] "Personalities and Politics," *The Times*, 25 February 1924, p. 13.

[9] J. W. Lambert, "Plays in Performance," *Drama*, Winter 1969, p. 25.

[10] "A Matter of History" (leading article) *The Times*, 14 February 1956, p. 9.

[11] Interview with Hayden Church, "Shaw Has Become a Prophet," *Evening Standard*, 8 February 1945.

[12] Crompton, p. 181.

[13] Preface to Oxford World Classics edition of *Back to Methuselah* (1944).

CHAPTER 14

[1] "Scratch Opera," *Nation*, 22 June 1918, pp. 308–310.

[2] Lady Scott, diary (*Self Portrait of an Artist*), 29 June 1918.

[3] Shaw to Wallas, a.l.s. 21 July 1918 (London School of Economics).

[4] Shaw to Loraine, 25 July 1918, in *Robert Loraine*, p. 242.

[5] Lady Scott, ms. diary, July 26, 1918.

[6] Shaw to Loraine, 4 August 1918, in *Robert Loraine*, pp. 242–243.

[7] Shaw to Loraine, 4 August 1918, but noted as written at a later time.

[8] Shaw to Lady Scott, a.l.s. August 1918 (Historical Manuscripts Commission).

[9] Shaw to Loraine, August 1918 in *Robert Loraine*, pp. 244–245.

[10] Shaw to Barker, 26 August 1918, in *Letters*, p. 197.

[11] Shaw to Lillah McCarthy, 12 August 1918, in *Myself and My Friends*, pp. 205–206.

[12] Shaw to Beatrice Webb, a.l.s. 17 August 1918 (London School of Economics).

[13] *Ibid.*

[14] C. E. M. Joad, *Shaw* (London, 1949), p. 35.

[15] Shaw to Beatrice Webb, a.l.s. 17 August 1918 (London School of Economics).

[16] Joad, pp. 35–36.

[17] *War Issues for Irishmen* (Dublin, 1918); reprinted in *The Matter with Ireland*.

[18] Shaw to Colonel Lynch, a.l.s. 23 September 1918 (Ithaca, N.Y., Cornell University).

[19] *Robert Loraine*, pp. 245–247; including Shaw to Loraine, late September 1918.

[20] Shaw to Harris, 27 September 1918, in *Harris*, p. 311.

[21] Lady Scott, *Self Portrait*, entry for 5 October 1918, p. 167.

[22] Holloway diaries, entry for 26 October 1918 in *Dublin Playgoer*, pp. 197–198.

[23] Shaw to Lillah McCarthy, 5 November 1918, in *Myself and My Friends*, pp. 225–226 (corrected from the original at University of Texas, Austin).

[24] Beatrice Webb, *Diary*, entry for 11 November 1918, p. 136.

[25] Leonard Woolf, *Downhill All the Way*, p. 9.

[26] Shaw, inscription to Frederick Evans dated 18 March 1919 on half-title page of *Peace Conference Hints* (New Haven, Conn., Yale University).

CHAPTER 15

[1] Shaw, *What I Really Wrote*, p. 296.

[2] Shaw to Pearson, 25 October 1918, in Pearson, *Modern Men and Mummers* (London, 1922), p. 22.

[3] T. S. Eliot, "London Letter," *Dial*, October, 1921, pp. 253–254.

[4] William Irvine, *Universe of G.B.S.*, p. 319.

[5] "What to Do With the Kaiser?" *Sunday Evening Telegram*, 6 July 1919.

[6] "Shaw Speaks at Royal Albert Hall," *The Times*, 15 November 1918, p. 8.

[7] Shaw to T. D. O'Bolger, 7 August 1919, quoted in Rattray, *Chronicle*, p. 106.

[8] Quoted in Mander and Mitchenson, *Theatrical Companion to Shaw*, p. 106.

[9] Shaw draft jacket copy for *What I Really Wrote* (British Museum Add. Ms.).

[10] "The War Indemnities," *Pearson's Magazine*, June, 1921.

[11] Irvine, *Universe*, p. 325.

[12] Quoted in Crompton, *Shaw the Dramatist*, p. 201.

[13] Paul Green, *Dramatic Heritage* (New York, 1953), p. 130.

[14] Cedric Hardwicke, *A Victorian in Orbit* (London, 1961), p. 94–95.

[15] Pearson, p. 363.

[16] *Shakes vs. Shav.* (1949).

[17] Hardwicke, p. 107.

APPENDIX

[1] First published by the author, in slightly different form, in *Ariel: A Review of International English Literature* (July 1970). Reprinted by permission of the publishers of *Ariel*.

[2] ". . . this masterpiece . . . an opera without music, or rather with its own verbal music . . ." (J. W. Lambert, *Drama*, Spring 1968, p. 21); ". . . one of the great plays of the century. . . . Shaw's best. . . ." (Walter Kerr, *The New York Times*, August 27, 1967, p. D9). These are no longer untypical comments.

[3] Paul Green in an interview with Shaw, *Dramatic Heritage* (New York, 1953), p. 127.

[4] Shaw to Lillah McCarthy, a.l.s. 10 August 1917 (courtesy the Academic Center Library, University of Texas, Austin).

[5] *George Bernard Shaw: His Life & Personality* (New York, 1963), pp. 362–363.

[6] Lillah McCarthy, *Myself and My Friends* (London, 1933), p. 207.

[7] "That Shakespeare's soul was damned (I really know no other way of ex-

pressing it) by a barren pessimism is undeniable; but even when it drove him to the blasphemous despair of Lear and the Nihilism of Macbeth, it did not break him. He was not crushed by it: he wielded it Titanically, and made it a sublime quality in his plays. He almost delighted in it: it never made him bitter: to the end there was mighty music in him, and outrageous gaiety." (Shaw, "Frank Harris's Shakespear," reprinted from *The Nation*, 24 December 1910, in *Pen Portraits and Reviews* [London, 1932])

[8] Preface to *Back to Methuselah* (London, 1921), p. lxxxvi.

[9] From Shaw's observations on his dramatic technique written at the request of Archibald Henderson and quoted in his *George Bernard Shaw* (New York, 1956), p. 741.

[10] *Heartbreak House* has several "storm trios" involving fools and sham madmen.

[11] *Shakespeare Our Contemporary* (New York, 1964).

[12] *The Wheel of Fire* (London, 1949).

[13] J. I. M. Stewart, *Eight Modern Writers* (New York and London, 1963), p. 171.

[14] Martin Meisel, *Shaw and the Nineteenth Century Theatre* (Princeton, N.J., 1963), pp. 316–317.

[15] Stewart, p. 171.

[16] Shaw might also have been remembering, although at 92 he did not recognize the fact, a painting he had written about some sixty years before, the pre-Raphaelite Ford Madox Brown's *Lear and Cordelia* (see *Music in London*, vol. 2, p. 15).

[17] Meisel, p. 317n.

[18] Audrey Williamson, *Bernard Shaw, Man and Writer* (New York, 1963), p. 172.

[19] Peter Brook, *The Empty Space* (New York, 1968), p. 93.

[20] Arthur M. Eastman, *A Short History of Shakespearean Criticism* (New York, 1968), pp. 172–173. "Between the vision of Shakespeare's characters and the vision of Shakespeare himself," says Eastman, "Shaw fails to discriminate." But Eastman fails to indicate the practical possibilities of such discrimination.

[21] *Saturday Review*, 29 May 1897.

[22] *Saturday Review*, 2 January 1897.

[23] Meisel sees "the wife-dominated Hector, the bamboo-wielding Utterword" as "reminiscent of Albany and Cornwall," and it is true, as he notes, that Hector even echoes Albany (p. 317). Richard Hornby sees, "Reminiscent of the extensive animal imagery in *Lear*, . . . references in Act III [of *Heartbreak House*] to *animals, horses, dogs, cat and mouse, jellyfish, flying fish, birds, rats* (twice) and *moths*" ("The Symbolic Action of *Heartbreak House*," *Drama Survey*, 7 [Winter 1968–1969], p. 19).

Index